Montana: A History of Two Centuries

MONTANA

A HISTORY OF TWO CENTURIES

By Michael P. Malone
and Richard B. Roeder

UNIVERSITY OF WASHINGTON PRESS
SEATTLE & LONDON

Library of Congress Cataloging in Publication Data

Malone, Michael P
   Montana: a history of two centuries.

   Bibliography: p.
   Includes index.
   1. Montana—History.   I. Roeder, Richard B.,
joint author. II. Title.
F731.M339   978.6   76-7791
ISBN 0-295-95520-1

MONTANA

A HISTORY OF TWO CENTURIES

By Michael P. Malone
and Richard B. Roeder

UNIVERSITY OF WASHINGTON PRESS
SEATTLE & LONDON

Library of Congress Cataloging in Publication Data

Malone, Michael P
  Montana: a history of two centuries.

  Bibliography: p.
  Includes index.
  1. Montana—History. I. Roeder, Richard B.,
joint author. II. Title.
F731.M339   978.6   76-7791
ISBN 0-295-95520-1

TO OUR PARENTS, *Dolores F. Malone Chard and the late John A. Malone, Herman H. Roeder, and Mary E. Roeder*

Preface

THIS book is meant to be a general, interpretive history of Montana for the mature reader. It arises from our teaching and researching of this subject over the past decade at Montana State University, Bozeman. We have attempted here to reassess Montana's history, to look searchingly into past interpretations, and to offer new ones where they seemed appropriate. Without de-emphasizing the frontier period, we have worked also to make this the first book to study the state's general development since the 1920s. Since this is a concise and interpretive history, it must be selective in its coverage. Seekers after "Wild West" lore will find nothing here about such Montana favorites as Calamity Jane, Liver-eating Johnson, or Kid Curry. We have focused instead upon those historical trends and personalities that proved vital to the shaping of present-day Montana. The state is a complex and fascinating place, with a complex and fascinating history.

Many friends, colleagues, and fellow Montanans have graciously helped us in preparing this volume. They include: Edward Barry, E. J. Bell, Jr., Harry Billings, Doc Bowler, Charles Bradley, Dorothy Bradley, Robert E. Burke, Merrill Burlingame, Brian Cockhill, Gail Cramer, H. Duane Hampton, Richard McConnen, John Montagne, Pierce Mullen, John Munsell, Rex Myers, Vivian Paladin, Robert Peterson, Richard Ruetten, Ken Ryan, Jeffrey Safford, Ted Schwinden, Richard Stroup, Thomas Wessel, Tom Wigal, and Lester Zeihen. Harriett Meloy and Lory Morrow of the Montana Historical Society and Minnie Paugh and Ilah Shriver of the Montana State University Archives gave us invaluable aid in gathering photographs and other materials. Stan James, Dianne Ostermiller, and Ellen Sanford assisted in the physical preparation. We are grateful also to the Department of History and Philosophy and to Dr. Roy Huffman and the Endowment and Research Foundation at Montana State University for travel and research assistance.

Finally, a special thanks to Robert Dunbar, who provided advice and assistance at many key points in the preparation of this work, and to Robert Taylor for his talents and efforts as a cartographer. We owe a special debt of gratitude to Gail Malone for her tireless help and encouragement from beginning to end of this project, and to Julidta Tarver, our very capable editor at the University of Washington Press. Naturally, we alone are responsible for the judgments here expressed and for the accuracy of what is said.

Bozeman, Montana
Summer 1976

Contents

Illustrations

MAPS

PHOTOGRAPHS

following page 82

Martin Maginnis
S. T. Hauser
Benjamin Potts
Twenty-fifth Infantry, Fort Shaw (photograph by Eugene LeMunyon)
Nelson Miles (photograph by L. A. Huffman)
Delegation of Flathead Indians to Washington, D.C.

following page 210

Herding cattle in eastern Montana
Sheep grazing in western Montana
James J. Hill
Railroad construction
Convertors, M.O.P. Smelter, Butte
Butte
Miners' drilling contest
Marcus Daly
W. A. Clark
F. Augustus Heinze
Ella L. Knowles
Railway advertisement
Homestead shack, Choteau County
Locator's promotion
Water wagon for threshing machine, near Scobey
Digging a well, Pleasant Valley
Tafts Holdup Saloon, Red Lodge
Joseph M. Dixon
Jeannette Rankin
Al Smith's presidential campaign tour, Billings
President Roosevelt and party at Fort Peck Dam

following page 274

Results of drought
Results of soil drifting, Coalridge
Cornelius F. Kelley
John D. Ryan
Berkeley Pit, Butte
Downtown Billings
Charles M. Russell
A. B. Guthrie, Jr.
Capitol Building, Helena
Main Hall, University of Montana, Missoula

Montana: A History of Two Centuries

CHAPTER I

Montana in Prehistory

A BOUT two hundred years ago, around the time of the American Revolution, the first white men came upon what is now Montana. Who these men were is open to conjecture. They might conceivably have been the Verendrye brothers, who crossed the plains westward until they saw "shining mountains" loom ahead of them in 1743. Or, more likely, they may have been anonymous French or Spanish adventurers trading for furs up the Missouri River. The first to record their discovery were the Americans Lewis and Clark in 1804, nearly thirty years after the birth of the United States. Whoever they were, the first whites surely marveled at the breadth of the land, its starkness, vitality, and overwhelming beauty. They must have paused in wonder, too, at the varieties of native peoples who had recently migrated here themselves. It was a vast and intriguing land then, two hundred years ago. It still is today.

THE ENVIRONMENT

Montana is a place of broad dimensions and sharp contrasts. In its sheer immensity, the state overwhelms its visitor. The "Treasure State" contains 147,138 square miles. It averages 535 miles from east to west and 275 miles from north to south. Yet, although considerably larger in size than such a nation as Italy, Montana recorded only slightly over seven hundred thousand inhabitants in the 1970 Census, fewer than metropolitan Seattle or Denver. It is a classic "acreage state," with lots of land and few people. In many other ways, too, Montana is a collection of contrasts. Its altitude, averaging 3,400 feet above sea level, ranges from a high of 12,850 feet at Granite Peak to a low of 1,800 feet where the Kootenai River flows into northern Idaho near Troy. Temperatures vary here from the very hottest, occasionally over 110 degrees in the far eastern sector, to a record cold of nearly −70 degrees near Helena in 1954.

The state's topography presents the most striking contrasts of all, from the alpine peaks of Glacier National Park to the rolling plains near the Dakota border. One sees on all sides, mainly in the far west, the evidence of a sometimes turbulent geologic past. Culminating about sixty million years ago, the mountains of western Montana were formed by incredibly massive shifts of the earth and the upward spurting of liquid rock and lava. Ancient seas and lakes rose and fell, covering at various times all of today's Montana, leaving behind fascinating geologic formations and sedimentary deposits of limestone, phosphates, and many other compounds. Great swamps formed east of the mountains and were later buried to become coal and oil fields.

During Pleistocene times, beginning two million years ago, declining temperatures periodically caused enormous glaciers to form across Canada. Four times, at least, these great ice sheets moved into the northern third of Montana, reaching as far south as Great Falls and Glendive. They retreated again and again with spells of warm weather, the last time roughly twenty thousand years ago. Building up huge lakes in their paths, the glaciers ground through the landscape and resculptured it. In the mountainous areas localized glaciers hollowed out and widened the valleys and created cirque lakes. The glaciers transformed the waterways of the area, most notably the Missouri River, which flowed to the Arctic north of Hudson Bay until the ice sheets blocked and shifted it eastward and eventually southward to the Gulf of Mexico.

What emerged, of course, was the land as we know it today. Perhaps the most striking feature of Montana is its geographically split personality—its western one-third, which is ruggedly and handsomely mountainous, as opposed to its eastern two-thirds, which breaks into clefted and undulating plains. These two geographical provinces were joined into one community, not by any geographical logic, but simply by the accidental occurences of history. Admittedly, eastern and western Montana do have much in common. Both are remote and rugged; both have a cold and, generally speaking, a semiarid climate. On the other hand, they reveal many differences, both in environment and in human history.

When speaking of "western" Montana, one may mean either the western one-third which is mountainous, or that smaller, far northwestern sector which lies west of the continental divide. Western Montana embraces the major American share of the Northern Rocky Mountains, a broad series of crosscutting and interlaced chains generally running northwest to southeast in direction. The main spine of the Rockies extends through today's Glacier National Park in a broken pattern southeastward into Yellowstone National Park in Wyoming. To the east and especially to the west of this main divide lie other ranges, for example, the Cabinet, Mission, Swan, Garnet, Ruby,

Map 1. Physiographic diagram (source, *Montana in Maps: 1974*)

and Tobacco Root mountains to the west, and the Big and Little Belt, Snowy, Judith, Absaroka, Beartooth, and Big Horn mountains to the east. Especially prominent are the massive shoulders of the Bitterroot Range, whose summits form the boundary with Idaho. The continental divide follows the primary chains southward from Glacier Park to Butte, where it bows westward to the Bitterroot crests like an inverted question mark, then turns southeastward again into Yellowstone Park, enclosing the Beaverhead Basin of southwestern Montana in the Atlantic drainage.

Two major tributaries of the mighty Columbia River drain northwestern Montana. Flowing out of Canada, the Kootenai River crosses the state's extreme northwestern corner and passes into the Idaho panhandle. Draining the larger portion of the west is the Clark Fork, which gathers its headwaters near Butte-Anaconda, then flows northwesterly through Hellgate Canyon to the key site of Missoula. In this general area, the Clark Fork gathers three important tributaries, the Bitterroot from the south and the Big Blackfoot and Flathead rivers from the north. It flows on, now a major river, through tortuous country into Idaho and Pend d'Oreille Lake.

In far southwestern Montana lies the bulge in the continental divide that is drained by the three streams which join at Three Forks to form the east-flowing Missouri: the Jefferson, Madison, and Gallatin rivers. This, like the westward inclined lands to the north, is also a region of fertile valleys and broken mountain chains. Western Montana's high mountain valleys, such as the Flathead, Bitterroot, Deer Lodge, and Gallatin, are truly some of the most beautiful locations in the United States.

In west-central Montana, the mountains give way to the Great Plains. At some points, especially in the north, the steep mountains break abruptly onto the plains. More generally, however, the Rockies slope into clefted foothills, steep valleys, plateaus, and mesas. The Shields River Valley and the Crazy Mountains north of Livingston are good examples of this terrain. So is the beautiful country around Great Falls, which Charlie Russell portrayed with such uncanny accuracy. Occasional isolated mountain ranges punctuate the hill country of central Montana; and in some choice locales, like the lush Judith Basin, they form fertile and lovely valleys between them. "These Thousand Hills," as author A. B. Guthrie, Jr., called them, form a sort of twilight zone between mountains and prairies.

Moving farther beyond the Rocky Mountain shadows, one enters the true Great Plains. Here, the landscape broadens its contour and extends eastward into eroded flatlands, whose windblown grasses give an oceanic appearance. Through these dry plains flow the fabled Missouri River and its tributaries. The upper Missouri and its principal branches, the Yellowstone and the Milk, cut meandering valleys through the Great Plains where much of today's population and best croplands are located. Since the

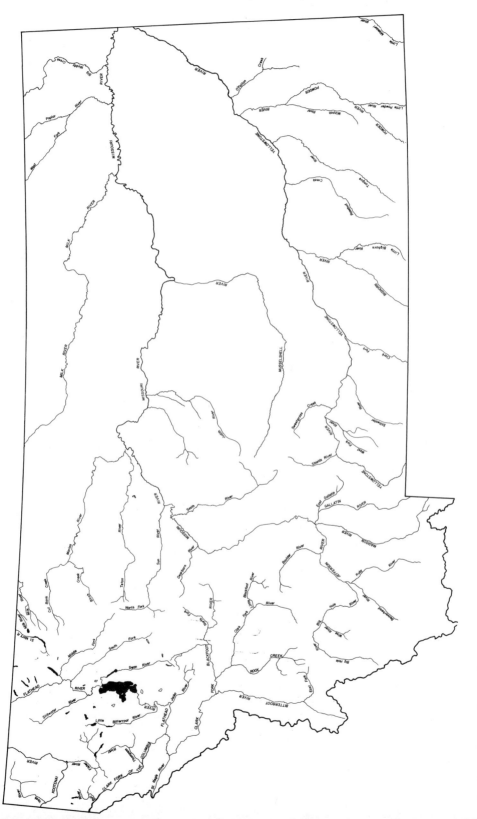

Map 2. Major water features (source, *Montana in Maps: 1974*)

Rockies trap most of the moisture from Pacific air masses, eastern Montana is drier than the west. Here, in fact, water means everything. Civilization clings to the vital waterways.

The mighty Missouri heads at Three Forks in southwestern Montana. It flows northward, breaking suddenly out of the mountains south of its Great Falls. Then, below the falls, it bends eastward toward Dakota, enroute to its rendezvous with the Mississippi. Major northern tributaries of the Missouri include the Sun, Teton-Marias, and Milk rivers. From the south come the Judith, the Musselshell, and, just beyond the Dakota line, the Yellowstone. The Yellowstone, which drains southeastern Montana, is a major river in its own right. It falls spectacularly out of Yellowstone National Park and then, flowing to the northeast, receives its major tributaries from the south: the Clarks Fork (of the Yellowstone), the Big Horn, Tongue, and Powder rivers. Out here, beyond the Rockies, lies the "Old West" of cowboy and Indian legend.

EARLY IMMIGRANTS

Man first appeared, not in the New World, but in the Old. Authorities have argued for many years about how and when prehistoric man migrated to North America, but they overwhelmingly agree as to the route. Climatic changes many thousands of years ago caused the formation of glaciers, with the obvious result of falling sea levels. This, in turn, caused a large land bridge to appear across the Bering Strait, connecting Asian Siberia to Alaska. Beyond doubt, Asiatic peoples began crossing this corridor into North America over ten thousand years ago; the earliest crossings may well have predated 30,000 B.C.

The immigrant peoples headed eastward through the interior of Alaska, then southward, mainly down the eastern slopes of the Rocky Mountains. Along this route, sometimes called the "Great North Trail," they pushed ever to the south, many of them passing through east-central Montana, until large numbers occupied South America. From the study of evidence these peoples left behind, archaeologists tell us that the first such prehistoric men to inhabit the Montana region were big game hunters, who pursued the now extinct bison and mammoth, primarily with a spear thrower called the *atlatl*. They occupied the Montana plains and mountain foothills from approximately 10,000–4,000 B.C., but they evidently seldom entered the Rockies, where glacial activity still continued.

Beginning around 5,000–4,000 B.C., a major change in climate turned the Great Plains into deserts and caused a gradual disappearance of the game herds and the hunters who pursued them. Eventually, after about a thousand years, a new cultural horizon emerged, lasting from roughly 4,000 B.C., or earlier, into the early Christian era. These were the plains archaic people, or "foragers." While they hunted some smaller animals, the foragers relied for the most part upon the plants and roots of the arid lands about them. The plains archaic people evidently entered Montana mainly from the southwest, in other words from the truly desert regions of Utah and southern Idaho. Unlike the earlier big game hunters, they occupied the valleys of western Montana.

Finally, starting slightly before or after the birth of Christ, the last of the cultural horizons of prehistoric man appeared in this area, that of the late hunters. These were the direct ancestors of those peoples whom the Europeans mistakenly named "Indians." While their cousins on the eastern fringes of the Great Plains practiced agriculture, the late hunters farther west pursued the bison herds which we know as the buffalo. The buffalo were the mainstay of their lives, supplying them with food, clothing, lodging, and weapons. The hunters killed them in communal hunts and often drove them over cliffs. These "buffalo jumps" are still interesting reminders of their culture. So are the "tipi rings," rocks laid in circles, some of which were weights for skin lodges and some of which no doubt had a ceremonial significance.

They lived in a primitive state that was suddenly shattered when the Europeans began to penetrate into what is now the United States after 1600. The coming of the white men, with their advanced technology, disrupted the Indian civilizations: many were killed, and most lost their lands. Interestingly, the Indians of the Far West actually felt the impact of the European invasion long before they ever saw a white man. Like ripples that spread outward from a stone thrown into a pond, the shock waves of the white man's intrusion rolled rapidly across the continent. The shocks came both from the Spanish colonies to the south in Mexico and New Mexico, and from French and English frontiers far to the east.

The Europeans destroyed some of the tribes, but they traded and allied with others. These Indians, in turn, moved upon the tribes farther west. Armed with guns and iron weapons obtained from the whites, they drove out their more primitive neighbors, who were forced to retreat toward the setting sun. So it became a process of falling dominoes, as tribe after tribe, hit by better armed peoples from the east, fell upon weaker neighbors to the west. Throughout the seventeenth and eighteenth centuries, wave upon wave of Indians, pushed ahead of the advancing European frontier, moved westward, across the Mississippi, beyond the woodlands, out upon the Great Plains, until they butted against the great Rocky Mountain barrier. Finally, they entered today's Montana. According to anthropologist Carling Malouf, not one of the Montana tribes which the white men found east of the continental divide had lived here before 1600.

As this bowling pin effect continued through the 1600s and 1700s, two of the white men's most valuable possessions fell into Indian hands and passed from tribe to tribe ahead of the slowly advancing European settlements. These were horses and guns. Both of them, especially the former, would revolutionize the life style of the plains Indians. The horse originated in North America during prehistoric times, but after spreading to Eurasia it became extinct here. The Indians of the West first acquired horses from the Spanish colony in New Mexico, especially after a revolt of Pueblo Indians in 1680 made sizable herds available for the taking. The Indians took to the horse immediately, and the creatures passed from tribe to tribe northward, up both the east and west slopes of the Rockies.

By the late seventeenth century the Shoshoni Indians, who inhabited the desert-mountain regions south and west of Montana, had acquired horses from their southern neighbors, the Utes. The Shoshonis, mounted and wearing leather armor in imitation of the Spaniards, fell upon their enemies to the north and east. Terrorizing their foes, they swept over most of Montana and invaded the Canadian prairies. Two factors finally halted them. Other tribes soon got horses of their own and learned to breed them. And Indians migrating from east to west brought guns with them. These smooth-bore trade guns allowed the foot soldiers to kill the Shoshoni horsemen, just as they had earlier dismounted the knights of Europe. Thus the horse culture, moving out of the southwest, met the gun frontier advancing from the east, here on the Canadian-American plains.

The plains Indian culture was well established over most of Montana by the late eighteenth century. When most of us today imagine an "Indian," we usually call to mind these people who so captured the American fancy one hundred years ago. Actually, the plains people were not a "pure" Indian civilization at all, but a society formed from various Indian and even some European roots during comparatively recent times. Most of them arrived in Montana well after 1650. All of them relied upon the recently obtained horses, and all of them longed for guns, which were hard to get and hard to keep supplied with powder and shot.

Unlike their brethren of the eastern prairies, the western plains Indians did not farm or live in permanent villages. They were nomadic hunters, and their lives centered upon the buffalo, the hunt, and the horse. They lived in tipis, which could be readily taken down and moved along with their other baggage on *travois*, horse-drawn platforms riding on two dragging poles. Socially, they were organized in extended families, and above this level in bands, and ultimately in tribes varying in size from several hundred to ten thousand people.

Women generally looked after the children and the day-to-day tasks of the bands, while the men absorbed themselves in hunting, raiding, and war. In order to become a chief, the male Indian usually had to be a distinguished warrior. For the most part, chiefs held only limited powers; few tribes recognized any one great chief as the supreme authority. Like most prehistoric peoples, their religion lay in close communion with nature. They sought supernatural visions through various rituals and sometimes practiced self-torture in the process. The major ceremony of almost all Plains Indians in more recent times was the Sun Dance.

While the plains culture dominated the eastern portions of Montana, the plateau culture prevailed in the western mountains. The plateau Indians lived throughout the basins of the Columbia and Fraser rivers in the interior Pacific Northwest. The easternmost of these tribes occupied the Rockies in Montana. Generally speaking, the plateau Indians lived more settled lives than did their neighbors on the plains, and they depended much more heavily upon fish, berries, and roots for food. But those plateau Indians who lived farthest to the east, like the Flatheads of Montana, exhibited many traits of the plains culture too. They also treasured the horse and the buffalo. As historian Thomas R. Wessel puts it, they were "seasonal people," who ranged onto the prairies to hunt buffalo in the spring and summer and returned to their mountain valleys during the remainder of the year. They combined the fishing and village life of the Pacific Northwest with the nomadic, hunting life of the Great Plains.

THE MONTANA TRIBES

The only Indians, apparently, who lived in Montana before 1600 were those whom the white men found in the western mountains, the plateau Indians. The best known of these were the Flatheads, who, like many other plateau peoples, belonged to the Salishan language group. The Flatheads (the origin of whose name is disputed) were the easternmost of all the Salishan tribes. Prior to the invasions of eastern Indians after 1600, they lived in the Three Forks area and ranged as far eastward as the Big Horn Mountains. Beginning before 1700, the arrival first of Shoshonis from the south, and then of Blackfeet from the northeast, forced them to retreat westward into the mountains. Their homeland, by the time Lewis and Clark found them in 1805, centered in the beautiful Bitterroot Valley.

The Flatheads combined in roughly equal parts the cultures of the plains and the plateau peoples. They joined forces once or twice a year with their allies, the Nez Perce of Idaho, to hunt buffalo on the plains. Like the other mountain tribes, they lived in constant fear of, and war with, the fierce Blackfeet of north-central Montana. The white men would find the Flatheads "peaceful," friendly, and especially interested in Christianity. This friendliness stemmed, most likely, not from any special meekness on their part, but from their need for allies, even white allies, against the better armed and more numerous Blackfeet.

Closely related to the Flatheads were the Pend d'Oreille or Kalispel Indians, who were also of Salishan linguistic stock. The Lower Pend d'Oreille lived mainly along the Clark Fork River and around Pend d'Oreille Lake in Idaho. The Upper Pend d'Oreille were located generally to the south of beautiful Flathead Lake and for a time even occupied the Sun River Valley east of the continental divide. These Indians intermingled and allied with their Salishan cousins, the Flatheads and Spokans, but they absorbed less of the plains culture than did the Flatheads. Instead, like most plateau people, they depended mostly upon plants and fish for food. After the invasion of the eastern plains Indians, the Pend d'Oreilles joined the Flatheads in their westward retreat. They too welcomed the white men and their religion.

In the far northwest corner of Montana lived the Kutenai Indians. Their ancestry is uncertain, and their language is apparently unrelated to that of any other tribe. Although they were not Salishan, the Kutenai had by 1800 become friends of the Flatheads and Pend d'Oreilles, and today they occupy the same reservation. Like the Flatheads, they merged the ways of the plains and the plateau. Until the Shoshonis and Blackfeet drove them out, the plains Kutenai traveled the prairies above and below the Canadian boundary. The Upper and Lower Kutenai lived for the most part in the rugged Kootenai Valley of southeastern British Columbia, northwestern Montana, and the Idaho panhandle. Later, many Kutenais moved southward to the Flathead Lake area. The first British and American explorers found these people isolated in their remote mountain valleys. They had only limited contact with the whites until later in the nineteenth century, and they caused the Americans few problems.

Beyond the mountains lived the invaders from the east, the plains Indians who had by 1800 driven the Salish and the Kutenai from their buffalo lands. The most fierce and powerful of these were the Blackfeet. The Blackfeet belonged to the Algonquian language group. They were very numerous, probably totaling fifteen thousand people by 1780. Three separate tribes made up the Blackfeet Nation: the Blackfeet proper, or Siksika, to the far north, the Kainah or Bloods south of them, and the Piegans or "Poor Robes" on the far south. The earliest white explorers found them prior to 1650 on the central plains of Canada, already migrating westward under pressure from eastern neighbors like the Cree. The Piegans led the Blackfeet advance, and they collided with the Shoshonis on the Canadian-Montana plains. After acquiring the horse, the Blackfeet drove the Shoshonis south and west. By 1800 they had entered the Rocky Mountain foothills and pressed far southward into Montana.

At the time of Lewis and Clark, early in the nineteenth century, the Piegan Blackfeet controlled north-central Montana east of the mountains.

Their war parties had forced the Shoshonis clear out of the Three Forks area of southwestern Montana, and that region remained a no-man's land where Blackfeet competed with other tribes for valuable game. Only the Piegans were true Montana Blackfeet, for the Bloods and Siksikas remained largely to the north in Canada. The Piegans, immortalized in the paintings of Charlie Russell, were classic plains people and among the most fierce and feared of all American Indians. Among the males, status depended almost exclusively upon one's role as a warrior. Those not belonging to military societies must join the women in their menial chores. Urged on perhaps by the Canadians, the Blackfeet became mortal enemies of the American fur traders, and they kept the invaders at bay until disease struck them down during the late 1830s.

To the south and east of the Blackfeet, mainly in the Yellowstone Valley of south-central Montana, lived their hated enemies the Crows or Absarokas—the "Bird People." The Crows, a handsome people of Siouan linguistic background, were among the earliest Indians to enter Montana from the east. Along with their close relatives, the Hidatsa, they broke away from the main Sioux Nation at an early date. Most likely, they lived originally in the upper Mississippi Valley areas of Minnesota and Iowa. The domino effect of Indian migrations drove them onto the eastern edges of the plains, where they paused for a time and tilled the soil. Eventually, Sioux and Cheyenne pressure forced them across the plains and up the Yellowstone Valley.

The whites found them divided into River Crows and Mountain Crows. The River Crows lived north of the Yellowstone River, especially in the Musselshell and Judith basins, while the Mountain Crows hunted south of the Yellowstone, primarily in the Absaroka and Big Horn regions. Although they still maintained clan societies acquired in the East, which most of their plains neighbors had abandoned, all of the Crows had become nomadic plainsmen by 1800. The American invaders found the Crows to be quite friendly and "peaceful." Such labels were misleading, however, because the Crows were as warlike as most plains Indians. They welcomed the whites because, surrounded by hostile Blackfeet and Sioux, they badly needed allies, especially allies with guns. They were famous travelers and horse thieves, and they traded with other tribes from eastern Dakota to the Rockies.

Two smaller Indian groups lived beyond the Blackfeet in northeastern Montana: the Atsina and the Assiniboine. The Atsinas spoke an Algonquian language. They were very close relatives of the Arapaho, who had earlier moved southward into Wyoming and Colorado. Misunderstanding sign language, as they so often did, the French traders named them the "Gros Ventre," meaning "big bellies." This was doubly unfortunate, both because the Atsinas had ordinary stomachs and because the Hidatsas of Dakota also became known as "Gros Ventre," leading to much confusion. The Atsinas migrated out of the Minnesota region, up onto the Canadian plains in close proximity to the Blackfeet, and they eventually settled directly to the east of them between the Missouri and Saskatchewan rivers. They became close allies of the Piegans, so much so that whites often mistook them for Blackfeet. Like their Piegan allies the Atsinas were extremely warlike and hostile to the Americans.

The Assiniboine Indians lived on the Canadian-American plains, with their southernmost flank extending down into northeastern Montana. They were Siouan in linguistic ancestry and at one time belonged to the Yanktonai branch of the Sioux Nation. The Assiniboines lived first, evidently, in the Mississippi headwaters area. Pressured by the Chippewa, Cree, and even the Sioux, with whom they became bitter enemies after their break from the Yanktonai, the Assiniboines migrated northward and westward onto the plains. They were typically warlike plains Indians, and, like other tribes of the upper Missouri, they would be hard hit by the smallpox epidemic of the late 1830s.

VISITORS AND LATE ARRIVALS

The artificial boundary lines later drawn by white men meant nothing, of course, to migratory Indians. Their hunting lands had only vague boundaries, and they freely invaded one another's territory. So the place we call "Montana" was often visited by neighboring tribes from all points of the compass. Later, well after the white invasion, some of these visitors came here to stay.

From the west, plateau neighbors of the Flatheads and Pend d'Oreilles frequently crossed over the Bitterroot passes and ventured onto the plains to hunt buffalo. These tribes, particularly the Spokans and Nez Perces, had to exercise considerable caution on their journeys, for plains Indians like the Blackfeet guarded their hunting lands jealously. The handsome and intelligent Nez Perces usually entered Montana over the Lolo Pass, dropping down into the Bitterroot Valley. Often with their Flathead friends, they would head through Hellgate Canyon into Blackfeet country, or they would pass southeastward into the lands of the more friendly Crows. The Nez Perces would follow this latter route on their famous retreat of 1877, which so fascinated the American public and so terrified the residents of Montana.

Indians of Shoshonean stock flanked Montana on the southwest and south. They included the Shoshonis themselves, the Bannocks, and the primitive Sheepeaters. The Shoshonean peoples were desert and mountain dwellers from the Great Basin country of Utah, Nevada, and southern Idaho; their easternmost lands extended into west-central Wyoming. As seen previously, their early mastery of the horse permitted the Shoshonis to conquer much of today's Montana during the eighteenth century, but by 1800 the Blackfeet had driven them into the state's southwestern corner. Lewis and Clark found them along the Idaho-Montana line near Lemhi Pass, where, without guns, they had lost control of the plains.

Neither the Shoshonis nor the Bannocks became "legal" Montana residents during the nineteenth century, but they entered its southwestern extremities to hunt. Peculiarly, even though these Indians no longer resided here, Congress momentarily entertained the idea of giving the name "Shoshoni" to the territory that became Montana in 1864. Indeed, the prominent Montana pioneer Granville Stuart thought an ideal name for the new territory would be *To yabe–Shock up,* the Shoshoni expression for mountainous country. Stuart's brainstorm, not surprisingly, failed to arouse much enthusiasm.

Eastward from present-day Montana, the great Sioux or Dakota Nation held control of the vast plains area north of Nebraska's Platte River. Prior to the mid-seventeenth century, the Sioux lived along the western edges of the Great Lakes and in the upper Mississippi woodlands. Invasions by well armed enemies, like the Chippewa, crowded them westward until, by the later nineteenth century, they covered an area reaching from western Minnesota across the northern plains into the easternmost fringes of Montana and Wyoming. The westernmost Sioux tribes of the Yanktonai and Teton groups lapped into Montana, and today there are Sioux living with the Assiniboines on Montana's Fort Peck Reservation. Although the center of Sioux power lay well to the east of Montana, these numerous Indians would figure largely in the state's frontier history, most spectacularly with their defeat of Custer in Montana Territory during the centennial year of 1876.

The Northern Cheyenne Indians intermingled with the Sioux and came to be their friends and allies. The Cheyennes belong to the Algonquian language group. Like the Sioux, they were elbowed from their traditional homeland in the Minnesota region. The Cheyennes paused for a time along the lower Missouri River and practiced agriculture. Then mounting pressure from the east forced them to resume their westward march. They crossed the Dakota plains, and by the time of Lewis and Clark they had reached the Black Hills. In the process, they adapted well to the nomadic ways of the plains Indians. Their warriors became outstanding cavalry: the Cheyenne Dog Soldiers were among the most respected of Indian fighting men.

After reaching the Black Hills, the tribe divided, with the more numerous Southern Cheyennes heading down toward Colorado and Oklahoma, and the Northern Cheyennes proceeding to the northwest. By the 1820s–1830s, the Northern Cheyenne lived among the Sioux in the area where the borders of Montana, Wyoming, and South Dakota converge. These late-arriving Indians would, in future years, join the Sioux in the wars that led to Custer's defeat, and they would eventually receive a small reservation on the Tongue River in southeastern Montana.

The last of Montana's Indian residents to enter the state were bands of Chippewas, Crees, and Metis who began filtering across the Canadian and North Dakota borders later in the nineteenth century. Some of these scattered bands and families were refugees from the unsuccessful rebellion that Louis Riel led against the Canadian government in 1885. Others, like the band of Chief Little Shell, came in from North Dakota, abandoning the squalor of their reservations. The Montana Crees and Chippewas are only splinters of much larger Indian groups. Of Algonquian heritage, the numerous Crees came originally from the frozen forests and plains of Canada. The Chippewa (Ojibwa) were Athabaskan-speaking people from both north and south of the Great Lakes. A large proportion of these latecomers consisted of the fascinating Metis, or mixed bloods. Predominately Cree, the Metis were actually a group apart, a racial mixture of Cree, Assiniboine, Chippewa, and French stock who spoke a language all their own.

These refugee Indians presented a problem to state and federal officials, who did not know what to do with them. Known as "Landless Indians," they moved about from town to town and became familiar figures at Havre, Chinook, and even Butte. Their ghetto in Great Falls, "Hill 57," was a byword for Indian poverty. Finally, in 1916 the federal government carved a tiny reservation for the Chippewa-Cree (and Metis) from the large Fort Assiniboine Military Reserve south of Havre. The reservation is known as "Rocky Boy's," named for the famous Chippewa Chief Stone Child, whose title was changed by the whites to "Rocky Boy." Thus the last of Montana's seven Indian reservations took shape, only sixty years ago.

So these were the native peoples of what became Montana. Most of them, interestingly, were late arrivals. Some others, like the Cheyenne, Chippewa, and Cree, would not even reside within Montana's borders until later in the nineteenth century. They formed a highly diversified group, combining plateau-mountain peoples from the west, Great Basin Indians from the south, hardy plainsmen from the north and east. Prior to 1800, Montana was the eye of a cultural hurricane, where Indians migrating from all directions, bringing horses and guns with them, met to create new and unuual societies. These Indians would share a common fate in the years following 1800, as Americans and Canadians drove them from their lands, reduced them by war, disease, and alcohol, and shattered their native cultures. Their descendants live today on seven Montana reservations.

CHAPTER II

Exploration and the Rivalry of Empires

THE explorers of northern North America were rugged and colorful men. Their names, now immortalized upon the map of Canada and the United States, still call to mind the incredible adventures and hardships they lived: Lewis and Clark, Mackenzie and Thompson, Simon Fraser and John Colter. Yet the significance of these men lies not so much in their individual feats as in the rivalry of the empires they represented. Four imperial nations, France, England, Spain, and eventually the United States, competed for mastery of the interior of North America. Usually hunting for furs, sometimes searching for the long-imagined "Northwest Passage" through the continent, the agents of these nations raced and sometimes fought one another in the drive to plant their flags upon new ground. The explorers, in other words, not only mapped these vast regions: they also determined, to a large extent, who would possess them.

THE RIVALRY OF FRANCE AND BRITAIN

During the century that followed the discovery of the Americas by Columbus, three of the great nations of Europe began the work of colonizing this continent. Spain based its North American empire upon the fabulously rich gold and silver mines of Mexico. Early in the seventeenth century the Spanish frontier pushed northward into New Mexico, carrying the flag of that nation onto the soil of today's United States. Meanwhile, the explorers of France moved up the St. Lawrence River toward the Great Lakes, planting the seed of French Canada. And British imperialists, beginning with Sir Humphrey Gilbert and Sir Walter Raleigh, worked at establishing English settlements on the Atlantic seaboard.

The French and British empires in North America grew apace during the 150 years following 1600, and they collided in a series of wars that would eventually decide the mastery of the continent. Beginning at Jamestown in 1607 and the Plymouth Colony in 1620, the English settlements grew steadily until by the mid-eighteenth century they reached from New England in the north to the borders of Spanish Florida in the south, and from the Atlantic coast westward to the crests of the Appalachian Mountains. The English colonies prospered, swelled in population, and would soon grow restive at the restraints placed upon them by the mother country.

France, in the meantime, forged an empire to the north and west that was smaller in population but larger in area. The builders of New France thrust up the St. Lawrence River and centered their operations at Montreal and Quebec. The bountiful trade in furs formed the life blood of New France, and the unending quest for virgin fur areas drew the French frontiersmen irresistibly westward, into and beyond the Great Lakes region. They pressed beyond the Lakes to the upper Mississippi, southward into the Ohio Valley, and inevitably down the great Mississippi toward the Gulf of Mexico.

In one of the epic journeys of North American exploration, Robert Cavelier, Sieur de La Salle, traveled down the all-important Mississippi River to its mouth in 1682. LaSalle there and then claimed the entire drainage of the mighty river for King Louis XIV, and in his monarch's honor he named this vast and little known province "Louisiana." All of the Mississippi-Missouri Basin thus became French territory, including, of course, the major portion of today's Montana. The French sweep southward from the Great Lakes set them on an inevitable course toward collision with the English. During the decades following LaSalle's journey, French traders moved up the Ohio River toward the westward slopes of the Appalachians, into the shadow of the advancing English frontier. Eventually, a major war would determine who would have these inviting lands between the Mississippi and the Appalachian divide.

The Anglo-French rivalry, meanwhile, flared up in another area, far to the north of New France. In 1670 the English crown granted a charter to a syndicate of traders that was destined to become one of the great corporations in world history, the "Governor and Company of Adventurers of England Trading into Hudson's Bay." The Hudson's Bay Company was given exclusive control over the lands draining into Hudson Bay and exclusive rights to the fur-bearing animals they contained. The firm erected posts on the west shore of the bay and soon had the Indians of the interior bringing in furs for trade. Enormous profits resulted. The leaders of New France now faced English competition from another direction.

In order to keep command of the fur trade, the French had to cut into the Indian traffic that funneled furs from the interior into Hudson Bay. They must advance northward and westward from the Great Lakes into the heartland of present Canada. The French, in their movement west, were seeking more than just fur. They also longed to find the legendary "Northwest Passage," the mythical waterway through the continent which, promising a short trade route to Asia, had eluded the explorers of America since the time of Columbus.

The Northwest Passage assumed differing forms in the European imagination as geographic knowledge slowly expanded. It might be a simple waterway from sea to sea, joining the Pacific perhaps to Hudson Bay or the Great Lakes. Or it might well be the "River of the West," a great west-flowing river which must head near the upper Mississippi. Another possibility was the long-imagined "Western Sea," from which rivers supposedly radiated to both the Atlantic and Pacific oceans. Of course, any nation that might find and secure the passage could then monopolize the trade with the Orient, and this realization led many eager souls to dream of and search for it. One of the most ingenious of these was the Baron de Lahontan, who wrote a popular account in 1703 of his "Nouveaux Voyages" in the interior of North America. Lahontan claimed to have ascended the Mississippi and wintered on a great stream, the "River Long," which flowed from the far west and was inhabited by many fascinating natives. The "River Long," naturally, was a fabrication, but it helped sustain the myth of a Northwest Passage.

Thus several motives—the quest for a Northwest Passage, the urgent need to expand the fur trade, the patriotic urge to beat the British—drew the French westward. The leader of their advance was Pierre Gaultier de Varennes, Sieur de La Verendrye, a dedicated soldier who had been wounded nine times serving his country. Having gained a trade monopoly over the areas west of Lake Nipigon–Lake Superior, Verendrye pressed steadily into the wilderness until by 1734 he had reached Lake Winnipeg, the great natural crossroads of central Canada. The French were now entering upon the Great Plains, and they began to hear Indian accounts of a mighty River of the West that lay to the south of them.

Searching for this long-awaited stream, Verendrye and his sons ventured southwestward in 1738 until they reached the villages of the fair-skinned Mandan Indians on the Missouri River in present-day North Dakota. Setbacks forced the aging Sieur de La Verendrye to return. But in 1742 he sent his sons, Louis-Joseph and François, to revisit the Mandans and to probe on westward in search of a route to the Pacific. The Verendrye brothers crossed the Dakota plains and encountered numerous Indian tribes, which they called by such names as the "Horse People" or the "Bow People." The Bow People, possibly Cheyenne or Crow Indians, told them of mountains to the west, beyond which lay the sea. The Verendryes traveled westward with a war party until, in January 1743, there arose before them what they called the "Shining Mountains." They could go no farther, for the war party of Bow People now turned back.

The Verendrye brothers returned to the Missouri and eventually to Canada. The "Shining Mountains" that they saw "were for the most part well wooded with all kinds of timber, and appeared very high." These may have been the Black Hills. More likely, they were the Big Horn Range of Wyoming; and, if so, the brothers may well have been the first white men to enter Montana. Be this as it may, the journey of the Verendryes signified the farthest thrust by the French into the American West below the present Canadian boundary. They had found no Northwest Passage. Indeed, what they had found was the eastern fringes of the Rocky Mountains, whose massive presence meant that there could be no water passage to the Pacific.

So the dream of the Sieur de La Verendrye ended in failure. The old man died in 1749, and the French empire in North America outlived him by little more than a dozen years. The last and greatest struggle between the French and the British over mastery of North America erupted in 1754. This all-important contest, variously called the Seven Years' War, the French and Indian War, or the Great War for Empire, ended in the triumph of Great Britain and the loss by France of almost all her hard-won possessions in North America. In 1762 France saw the inevitability of defeat and ceded all of her territory west of the Mississippi to her ally, Spain. The war ended in 1763 with the signing of the Treaty of Paris, which surrendered almost all the rest of France's American possessions to Britain. So the French domain in North America vanished. Louisiana now belonged to Spain. Canada and its rich fur trade passed into the control of Great Britain.

These defeats did not, however, mean the end of French influence in North America. Far from it. Although French Canada came under British control, the French fur companies, based mainly at Montreal, continued their competition with the Hudson's Bay Company. British and Scottish merchants began moving in on Montreal, but French *coureurs de bois* ("wood runners," or trappers), river-boat men, and *voyageurs* (traveling agents and explorers) remained in the field. Between 1779 and 1787 these Montreal firms joined forces to create the loosely organized outfit which, reorganized several times, came to be known as the North West Company.

While the newborn United States was fighting to win its independence from England, the North West Company pushed out onto the plains of Canada and headed northwest toward the Arctic. The "Nor'Westers," as the firm's men were called, were determined to move rapidly into the interior in order to cut off the slow-moving and conservative Hudson's Bay

Company. Stung by their competition, the Hudson's Bay Company thrust inland, too. Agents of both companies were soon advancing up the Saskatchewan River system toward the Rockies, and they quickly realized that the great distances to be traveled across the Canadian plains made a port of supply on the Pacific coast especially desirable. The Nor'Westers desperately needed such a port, for their supply routes to Montreal were much more difficult than those of their rival to Hudson Bay. So North West Company leaders Peter Pond and Alexander Mackenzie set out to find one.

Alexander Mackenzie, one of the truly great explorers in world history, made two incredible attempts to find a navigable river, a Northwest Passage flowing to the western sea. In 1789 he followed the large stream that now bears his name until, to his understandable dismay, it led him northward to the Arctic Ocean. He tried again in 1793, and this time succeeded in making the first northern crossing of the continent. His route to the Pacific, however, passed through the tortuous mountains of British Columbia and was too difficult for transportation use. Meanwhile other agents of both the North West and and Hudson's Bay companies were continuing the march into the Canadian West. In 1792, for instance, Peter Fidler of the Hudson's Bay Company pressed clear into the Blackfeet lands southwest of present Calgary. Fidler's trek brought the British advance, at that early date, to within one hundred miles of today's Montana-Canadian boundary.

The point is that, by the time of George Washington's presidency in the 1790s, the British-Canadian frontier was reaching into the Rockies and probing toward the Pacific coast. When the American Robert Gray discovered the mouth of the Columbia, the great river of the northwest, in 1792, British-Canadian imperialists like Mackenzie reacted with predictable alarm, urging their government to move rapidly before the Americans could occupy the strategic waterway. British control of the Columbia meant British control of the entire Northwest. The shrewd Mackenzie pressed for negotiation of a Canadian-American boundary at the 45th parallel, a line that would have placed the Columbia—and almost all of Montana—within the realm of Canada. Had the British government not been distracted by war with France, it might have pursued Mackenzie's plans and won these borders for Canada. If it had, the following pages would tell a much different story.

Intelligent Americans like Thomas Jefferson, who became President in 1801, watched these British-Canadian maneuvers closely and suspiciously. Indeed, one of Jefferson's prime motives in sending out the Lewis and Clark Expedition would be to counter the Canadian westward thrust and to strengthen the American claim to the Columbia River Basin. Lewis and Clark would carry a copy of Mackenzie's *Voyages from Montreal* with them to the Pacific. By the turn of the nineteenth century, therefore, the imperial vision of both British Canada and the United States was focused upon the far Northwest.

SPAIN, LOUISIANA, AND THE MISSOURI RIVER

Spain was the first European power to found New World colonies. By the early 1600s, Spain's American empire blanketed Central and much of South America and extended northward along the Rio Grande to New Mexico. As seen previously, Spain added Louisiana to its holdings in 1762, when France broke up its American realm at the close of the French and Indian War. Spain held Louisiana for thirty-eight years, from 1762 until 1800. During that time, she did little to develop the vast, little known province, valuing it mainly as an enormous buffer to insulate Mexico from approach by her enemies. The Spanish, like the French, based their activities at strategic New Orleans, which controlled the mouth of the Mississippi, and to a lesser extent at the village of St. Louis, near the confluence of the Missouri with the Mississippi.

By the 1790s, though, several considerations began to draw Spanish attention toward upper Louisiana and the river that drained it, the muddy Missouri. The Spaniards knew that British Canadians were trading among the Indian tribes who lived north of the Platte River. They wished, naturally, to hold the loyalty of these natives, to open a fur trade among them, and to prevent any British inroads into Louisiana which might one day threaten Mexico. They also realized that the wide Missouri offered the best remaining hope of a river route to the Pacific, a Northwest Passage.

In 1792 a French trader in Spain's service named Jacques D'Eglise traveled up the river to the strategic villages of the Mandan Indians, which were situated on the great bend of the Missouri near present Bismarck, North Dakota. These villages, which the Verendryes had visited a half century earlier, were the key Indian trading center of the upper Missouri. Here D'Eglise found plenty of evidence of British inroads from Canada. He returned to St. Louis warning his employers of British penetration into their lands and announcing that the Missouri could be navigated far into its upper reaches. The Spanish authorities reacted to this news by establishing the so-called Missouri Company to take over the upriver trade and forge a route to the Pacific Ocean.

Made up of St. Louis fur men, mostly French and English, the Missouri Company found little success. Sioux, Omaha, and Arikara Indians, who occupied the Missouri below the Mandans, were determined to keep white merchandise out of the hands of their enemies upstream; and they made passage up the river very difficult. Even though Indian resistance cut off trade and traffic, the St. Louis men still managed to break through occasionally and to pick up accounts of what lay beyond, to the north and west. Between 1793 and 1797 various employees of the Missouri Company, such as D'Eglise, Jean Baptiste Truteau, James Mackay, and John Evans, worked the river between St. Louis and the Mandans.

The Indians told them of the upper river, and so did a few Canadians who had taken up residence among the natives. One of these was an intriguing fellow named Menard, a Frenchman who claimed that he had been living with the Mandans for over fourteen years. Menard and other informants spoke tantalizingly of the "Stony Mountains" rising in the faraway distances, of a great cataract on the upper river, of native peoples like the Atsinas, Assiniboines, Blackfeet, and Crows. The St. Louis traders heard for the first time of a great southern tributary of the upper Missouri called "La Roche Jaune," river of the Yellow Rock. Menard told Truteau that he had traveled this area among the Crows and "that this river is navigable with pirogues more than one hundred and fifty leagues above its mouth, without meeting any falls or rapids." Thus, as Bernard DeVoto aptly put it, "another noble river had at last come into the white man's awareness."

The Missouri Company failed and, so far as we know, the Spaniards and their employees never approached the headwaters of the long river. Yet they began to grasp, however vaguely, the outlines of northern Louisiana, an abundant land that stretched westward into a mighty range of mountains. Some geographers came to think of these mountains as a long, single chain, which could easily and quickly be crossed from the Missouri headwaters to the west-flowing Columbia. The dream of a Northwest Passage, now in modified form, still survived! As the eighteenth century closed, therefore, the Spaniards had reached northward to the bend of the Missouri; and here they met the British Canadians, who, even farther west, had pressed to within a hundred miles of what would become the northern border of Montana. Neither the Spaniards nor the British, though, would win the race to the upper Missouri. The newly arrived United States would get there first, and in doing so it would solve forever the puzzle of the Northwest Passage.

The United States and Louisiana

The United States of America had not even existed, as such, when Spain received Louisiana from France in 1762. This new nation, destined to bestride the continent, was born with its Declaration of Independence from Great Britain in 1776. Following a seven-year Revolutionary War, the United States confirmed its independence by signing the Treaty of Paris with Britain in 1783. Significantly, the Treaty of Paris allowed the United States generous boundaries, which reached northward to the Great Lakes and westward to the Mississippi. The new American republic now looked across the big river into Spanish Louisiana.

During the two decades following the 1783 treaty, increasing numbers of aggressive American pioneers crossed over the Appalachian Mountains and came down into the valleys of the west-flowing Ohio and Tennessee rivers. They were farmers, primarily, and they relied upon the Mississippi as their avenue to national and world markets. Navigation of the river inevitably became a pressing issue between the United States and Spain. The Spaniards at New Orleans could easily strangle the western commerce of the United States, either by closing the river to its vessels or by refusing them the "right of deposit" to use the city's docks for transferring cargoes to ocean-going ships. This issue, combined with American hunger for the Spanish lands in Florida and lower Louisiana, caused considerable tension between the two countries. The friction never led to war, though, in part because Spain lacked the strength to build up its holdings in Florida and Louisiana.

The situation took a sudden and momentous turn with the dawn of the nineteenth century. France, the founder of Louisiana, had been bargaining with the Spanish government for several years about regaining its lost colony. Louisiana held the promise of a reborn French empire in the New World, an empire based on sugar, cotton, and grains. In October 1800 Napoleon, now rising to domination of France, wrung from Spain the secret Treaty of San Ildefonso, which ceded Louisiana back to its original mother country. Rumors of this agreement soon reached America, and in the fall of 1802 Spanish officials in New Orleans received orders to make way for the French.

The rumors, and then the certainty of a French return to America, sent shock waves through the United States, especially through its western frontiers. Unlike Spain, Napoleonic France posed the threat of establishing real military might along the western borders and of closing off the Mississippi commerce forever. President Thomas Jefferson, perhaps the most imperially inclined of all early American leaders, clearly understood the French threat. Of New Orleans in French hands, he wrote the famous words: "There is on the globe one single spot, the possessor of which is our natural and habitual enemy."

Jefferson moved shrewdly and decisively to meet this critical situation. He sent special envoy James Monroe to assist the United States Minister to France, Robert Livingston, in negotiating a possible agreement. Assuming wrongly that Napoleon had also obtained the Floridas from Spain, the President ordered his representatives to offer up to ten million dollars for both these areas and New Orleans. If this failed, they were to bargain for river frontage or permanent access to the docks at New Orleans. And if all negotiations failed, Jefferson was prepared even to seek an alliance with Great Britain against France.

Good fortune intervened for the United States. Napoleon finally found himself, by the spring of 1803, unable to pursue his plans for a new French empire in the western hemisphere. He had hoped all along to base this empire both in Louisiana and in the sugar-producing island of Santo Domingo in the Caribbean Sea. But native uprisings had forced Napoleon to send large armies into Santo Domingo; the natives, assisted by a yellow fever epidemic, had killed over fifty thousand French troops. Even more importantly, Napoleon now faced a war with Great Britain. Since the British navy would probably continue to maintain its control of the Atlantic, France had little hope of defending Louisiana against the British, or against the Americans for that matter.

Simple logic forced Napoleon to sell Louisiana to the United States. On April 11, 1803, Foreign Minister Talleyrand dumbfounded Livingston by raising the issue of selling all of Louisiana. The negotiators spent the rest of the month working out the details, and on April 30 they signed the agreement by which the United States paid fifteen million dollars for the entire province. No one knew precisely what this enormous land transfer entailed. But, generally speaking, Louisiana was understood to be the western drainage of the Mississippi River. Its eastern boundary, of course, was the Mississippi itself; and its western limit was probably the continental divide, wherever that was. The northern border of Louisiana with Canada, and the southern border with the Spanish possessions, remained to be defined.

The overwhelming significance of the Louisiana Purchase can scarcely be overstated. In one stroke the United States gained the midsection of the continent, including that far corner of Louisiana which would one day become Montana. This purchase, more than any other single occurrence, transformed the United States into a real imperial power. Over the next forty-five years the Americans would extend their newly acquired dominion to the Pacific. Thomas Jefferson obviously recognized the significance of the Louisiana Purchase, and he moved quickly to find out what it contained.

THE JOURNEY OF LEWIS AND CLARK

Any intelligent American could readily see the need to explore Louisiana, but this necessity had special meaning to the President. Jefferson was a man of many scientific and philosophical interests. Indeed, he had entertained the idea of exploring the western reaches of the continent since the 1780s. In 1793, when Louisiana still belonged to Spain, Secretary of State Jefferson had strongly encouraged a French scientist named André Michaux to follow the Missouri River to its headwaters and to pass from there to the Pacific. Michaux's mission, however, failed to materialize.

Jefferson continued to plan the exploration of Louisiana after his inauguration to the presidency in 1801. In January 1803, even before the United States had gained possession of Louisiana, he secured twenty-five hundred dollars from Congress to finance an overland journey of discovery via the Missouri and Columbia rivers to the Pacific. To lead this expedition Jefferson appointed his private secretary Meriwether Lewis, a young Virginian and a long-time acquaintance. At Lewis' suggestion, William Clark, his old friend from their days together in the Army, was made co-captain. Clark, at age thirty-three, was four years older than Lewis, was also a Virginian, and was the youngest brother of Revolutionary War hero George Rogers Clark. Although Clark failed to receive the captain's commission that had been promised him and thus remained a second lieutenant during the expedition, Lewis and the men recognized him as an equal commander of the enterprise.

Much of the success of this amazing venture was due, not just to the impressive abilities of Lewis and Clark, but also to the manner in which they complemented one another. They almost always agreed, publicly and privately. Lewis was more reserved, more of an introvert, Clark more gregarious and more the typical frontiersman. While they fully shared the various tasks of leadership, Lewis specialized more in collecting scientific data and specimens and in navigating their route. Clark, an experienced engineer, generally handled the boats, drew maps, and negotiated with Indians. He would also prove himself an ingenious makeshift doctor.

The success of the Lewis and Clark Expedition also reflected clearly the astute planning of President Jefferson. In a detailed letter to Lewis of June 20, 1803, Jefferson laid out his instructions with precision. The explorers were to follow the Missouri to its head and to pass from there down a west-flowing river, the Columbia, to the Pacific. Jefferson hoped that the continental divide would prove to be only a slight barrier, easily portaged, perhaps in less than a day's time, and that a Northwest Passage might yet be improvised. The President further instructed the captains to plot precise maps, to make extensive observations about the climate, and to collect specimens of soils, minerals, and plant and animal life. Well aware of the British thrust into northern Louisiana, Jefferson ordered Lewis to assess the fur potential carefully and to watch for signs of Canadian intrusion. The Indians must be informed that they now had a new master and that their interests lay in trading with the Americans. Jefferson clearly aimed, finally, not only to thwart British influence in upper Louisiana, but also to beat the Canadian explorers into the Pacific Northwest, an area he was anxious to gain for the United States.

The captains spent the winter of 1803–4 preparing for a spring departure. They gathered their personnel and encamped on the east bank of the Mississippi, opposite the mouth of the Missouri. The permanent exploring party consisted of the two captains, twenty-six regulars in the Army, Clark's Negro slave York, two French rivermen, and the highly valuable French interpreter George Drouillard, whose name usually appears in the Lewis and Clark journals as "Drewyer." Lewis and Clark divided their command into three squads, under Sergeants Charles Floyd, John Ordway, and Nathaniel Pryor. Throughout the winter Clark spent much of his time drilling the men and preparing the fifty-foot keelboat and the two smaller vessels (pirogues) which would carry their cargo up the Missouri. Lewis, meanwhile, concentrated on gathering information from French rivermen in St. Louis. An auxiliary crew of sixteen men would help them upstream as far as the Mandan Villages. In mid-May of 1804, they departed, heading up the endless Missouri enroute to the western sea.

Their destination for the first season of travel was the Mandan Villages, the already well known Indian crossroads which lay sixteen hundred miles upriver. They averaged ten miles per day by rowing, poling, or hauling the keelboat against the current. Late in October they reached the villages. The party settled down here for the winter, in a cluster of crude dwellings they named "Fort Mandan."

During the long Great Plains winter, the men occupied their time hunting and fraternizing with the Indians. The captains worked constantly at gathering intelligence from the natives. These Mandan and Minnetaree villages were a major trading area, and from these and other Indians Lewis and Clark obtained information that would prove vital to them. They learned that the upper Missouri flowed northward out of the Rockies before bending eastward and that these mountains consisted of many interlocking chains, not just one. They heard too of the Great Falls, which lay just below the river's exit from the mountains, and of the primary tributaries of the Missouri, especially the large northern fork that the Indians called "the river which scolds at all others."

A number of British and French Canadians frequented these villages, and Lewis and Clark eyed them suspiciously. Nevertheless, they hired a Frenchman named Toussaint Charbonneau to accompany them westward as an interpreter. Charbonneau proved to be more a liability than an asset. His Indian wife Sacajawea, on the other hand, later helped out as a guide and as an intermediary with her Shoshoni relatives. Later legends would distort and exaggerate the role of Sacajawea, portraying her as the indispensable heroine who saved the expedition.

Early in April 1805 the explorers broke camp. Corporal Warfington and the auxiliary crew returned to St. Louis with the keelboat and the specimens collected so far. Lewis and Clark headed upstream in the two pirogues and six canoes. They reached the mouth of the Yellowstone on April 25 and recognized its obvious strategic importance, recommending this location as the site of a future fort. The expedition entered present northeastern Montana in blustery weather. Clark thought it "a verry extraodernary climate, to behold the trees Green & flowers spred on the plain, & Snow an inch deep." They marveled at the enormous herds of buffalo, elk, and antelope, and they began to encounter the feared grizzly bears. The landmarks seemed to bear out what the Indians had told them. The large northern tributary appeared, and they named it the Milk. Two sizable southern forks they named the Musselshell and the Judith. Isolated mountain chains began to loom on the far horizons.

Then came the great lapse in their Indian information. On June 2 they saw ahead of them "the entrance of a very considerable river" flowing in from the northwest. They were painfully surprised, for they had assumed the Milk to be "the river which scolds at all others." This stream, which they eventually named "Maria's River," puzzled them even further because, swollen with late spring runoff, it appeared large enough to be the main stem of the Missouri itself. They spent several days examining each river and attempting to determine which was the Missouri proper.

It was a crucial decision, for a wrong choice here could mean a disastrous winter trapped in the mountains and the possible failure of the entire expedition. Even though the men unanimously believed the northwest fork to be the main Missouri channel, the captains shrewdly chose the southern fork instead, primarily because its rocky bed and its flow from the southwest indicated it to be a mountain stream. Their decision proved correct, as they learned on June 13, when Lewis suddenly saw "spray arrise above the plain like a collumn of smoke." That had to be the Great Falls, and this had to be, therefore, the Missouri. Their all-important decision at the Marias River had been impressively intelligent and right.

The beautiful falls, which Lewis described as "the grandest sight I ever beheld," were a welcome landmark, but they were also a formidable barrier to progress upriver. The explorers had to portage their canoes and cargo eighteen miles around the series of cataracts, leaving the remainder of their equipment in caches below the falls. It took a month of backbreaking labor, hauling their loads on carts made by cutting wheels from cottonwood logs, to move around the Great Falls. Afflicted by gumbo mud, prickly pear cactus, "Musquetores," and grizzly bears, the men nonetheless kept up their spirits. They celebrated Montana's first Fourth of July by drinking the last of the "grog."

Now the expedition entered the Rockies. The captains fretted about the massive mountain ranges to the west as they headed southward up the Missouri. Haste became imperative. They must find Sacajawea's people, the Shoshonis, in order to acquire horses to carry them over the mountains before snowstorms stopped them. Clark finally reached the long awaited Three Forks, headwaters of the Missouri, on July 25, 1805, in a state of fatigue, and Lewis arrived with the main party two days later. The explorers recognized this as "an essential point in the geography of this western part of the Continent" and named the three rivers which join to form the mighty Missouri after the three principal heads of state. The large west fork they named the Jefferson River, the middle branch the Madison, after Secretary of State James Madison, and the smaller east fork the Gallatin, after Treasury Secretary Albert Gallatin.

As August warned of summer's passing, the party headed southwest up the Jefferson River, pulling their canoes against the strong current and clambering over the slippery rocks. Lewis pressed ahead of the main group, trying desperately to make contact with the elusive Shoshonis. He and his companions crossed the continental divide on August 12 and came down upon the Lemhi, a fork of the west-flowing Salmon River. Lewis finally managed a meeting with the Shoshonis; and, after Clark had brought the major portion of the party up to camp, it was found, incredibly, that the Shoshoni chief Cameahwait was none other than the brother of Sacajawea. By trading with the isolated Shoshonis, Lewis and Clark obtained the horses they so vitally needed. But they learned, alas, that the wild Salmon River country was impassable and that they must skirt far to the north in order to cross the last, great Rocky Mountain ranges.

Guided by an old Indian whom they named "Toby," the party headed northward into Montana's Bitterroot Valley. They met the friendly Flathead Indians in Ross's Hole, an event immortalized in Charlie Russell's fine painting. From here, following Indian advice, they moved down the Bitterroot to the mouth of Lolo Creek, a spot they named "Traveler's Rest," and followed this creek westward, crossing over the Bitterroot summits. This autumn passage of the difficult Lolo Trail became an exhausting race against winter, made worse by the scarcity of game. It was the most desperate leg of the journey. By late September the famished explorers had dropped down into the meadowlands of the beautiful Clearwater River of Idaho. Friendly Nez Perce Indians helped them and kept their horses, and the Lewis and Clark party fashioned boats for travel to the sea. Floating down the Clearwater, the Snake, and finally the great Columbia River, they reached their destination in rain and fog on November 7, 1805. Clark wrote that evening: "Great joy in camp we are in *view* of the *Ocian*, this great Pacific Octean which we been so long anxious to see."

The travelers erected several cabins on the south bank of the Columbia, somewhat inland from the sea, and named the encampment Fort Clatsop after a local Indian tribe. It proved to be a long, wet, and dreary winter. Although British and American ships frequented these coasts, the explorers never made contact with any of them. So the captains occupied these long months plotting the return journey, and Clark prepared a brilliant map of the lands they had crossed. The men spent much of their time hunting and socializing with the natives, with the result that venereal disease became a problem. Lewis wrote on March 15, 1806:

> we were visited this afternoon by Delashelwilt a Chinnook Chief his wife and six women of his nation which the old baud his wife had brought for market. this was the same party that had communicated the venerial to so many of our party in November last, and of which they have finally recovered. I therefore gave the men a particular charge with rispect to them which they promised me to observe.

With the greening of spring, the Lewis and Clark Expedition headed back up the Columbia on March 23, 1806. Near the mouth of the Snake River, they traded for enough Indian horses to permit abandoning their canoes and traveling overland through the clefted hill country of present-day southeastern Washington. They moved up the Snake to the Clearwater River, where they found that the Nez Perces had dutifully kept their horses for them. Snow in the high Bitterroots delayed the recrossing of the Lolo Trail. Finally, with two Nez Perce guides leading the way, they headed over the rugged Bitterroots late in June, and on July 1 they reached Traveler's Rest once again.

Anxious to survey the areas north and south of the Missouri, the captains here divided their command. Lewis, along with a small party and the two Nez Perce scouts, headed down the Bitterroot River and northeastward toward the Great Falls. Clark took the larger segment of the party back up the Bitterroot, across the continental divide, and down the Jefferson drainage to the Three Forks of the Missouri. At the Three Forks, Clark divided his force. Sergeant Ordway and nine men headed down the Missouri, traveling in canoes they had stored the year before, to join Lewis at the Great Falls. Clark, with the remainder of the party and the horses, set out across the Gallatin Valley to explore the Yellowstone River, which lay to the east.

Clark's journey was relatively uneventful. Sacajawea knew this country and guided the party over strategic Bozeman Pass. On July 15 they reached the Yellowstone, the great southern fork of the upper Missouri. While the men were busily fashioning dugout canoes to descend the river, Crow Indians deftly stole half their horses. So Clark took most of his party downriver by boat, leaving Sergeant Pryor and two men to drive the remaining horses overland to the Mandan Villages. The float down the Yellowstone was peaceful and enjoyable, carrying them past the mouths of large southern tributaries, the Clark Fork, Big Horn, Tongue, and Powder. At the "remarkable rock" which he named "Pompey's Pillar" after

Sacajawea's son, Clark paused to carve his name and the date. His party reached the Missouri on August 3. A few days later, Clark was joined by an embarrassed Sergeant Pryor. The Crows, most renowned horse thieves of the plains, had stolen all the remaining horses, and Pryor had been forced to bring his men down the Yellowstone in makeshift skin boats.

Lewis and his group, meanwhile, faced greater challenges. The Nez Perces led them up the Big Blackfoot River, which they knew by the fine name Cokahlarishkit—"river of the road to buffalo." This trail took them over the divide via Lewis and Clark Pass and down the Sun River to Great Falls. Lewis reached the falls from Traveler's Rest in only one week. In the roundabout, reversed journey of the year before, it had taken fifty-eight days! Leaving Sergeant Gass and two men to assist the Ordway arm of Clark's party in moving their boats and equipment around the falls, Lewis headed north with Drouillard and the Fields brothers to explore Marias River.

The Marias impressed Lewis as a highly strategic river. It seemed to offer a navigable passage northward into the Canadian fur areas on the Saskatchewan, and its upper extremities might push the boundaries of Louisiana above the 50th parallel. But this enterprise very nearly resulted in disaster. The small party moved north and west up the Marias to its Cut Bank fork. Cloudy weather and a failure of their clock made it impossible to gauge their exact location, and, disappointed, they headed back toward the Missouri. In a rare lapse of judgement, Lewis agreed to make camp with a band of Blackfeet that they encountered, even though the Flatheads and Nez Perces had warned him about these Indians. During the night the Blackfeet tried to seize their guns, and in the ensuing melee two of the Indians were shot and killed. The Blackfeet fled, and, fearing their return, so did the Americans. Using Indian horses, they rushed southward at a hectic pace, covering over a hundred miles by daybreak. In a Hollywood-style stroke of luck, they reached the Missouri just in time to meet the Ordway-Gass party coming downstream from the Great Falls.

Now, with the current in their favor, traveling was easy. The Lewis group floated leisurely downriver and joined Clark's force below the mouth of the Yellowstone on August 12. The happiness of the reunion was marred by the fact that Lewis had been wounded by a gunshot in the thigh while hunting with one of his comrades. The explorers made good time returning to St. Louis. They reached that city on September 23, 1806, and the nation which had given up the expedition for lost accorded them a heroes' welcome.

The amazingly successful exploration of Lewis and Clark bears great significance in the course of national and regional history. Aside from the obvious importance of its observations, mapping, and gathering of scientific specimens, the Lewis and Clark Expedition left other lasting marks upon history as well. It began, except in the case of the Blackfeet, generally friendly American relations with the Indians of the Northwest. It countered the British-Canadian thrust into these regions and gave the United States a valuable claim to the Columbia Valley. And it ended, once and for all, the persistent hope for some sort of "Northwest Passage."

Most importantly, the expedition revealed to the world the immensity, beauty, and wealth of the far Northwest and advertised its potential to the nation. The journals and reports of the expedition spoke with special enthusiasm about one lucrative resource of this region—fur. The upper Missouri, they said categorically, "is richer in beaver and otter than any country on earth." These words would have an immediate and lasting impact upon the lands crossed by Lewis and Clark. The restless Americans were about to enter yet another new frontier.

CHAPTER III

The Era of the Fur Trade

THE fur trade formed the cutting edge of the European frontiers that moved inexorably across the northern reaches of this continent after 1600. Traders and trappers were usually the first whites into the western wilderness. Their craft drew them ever onward toward virgin environments and toward the unsophisticated Indians who would barter on the cheapest terms. The trade produced the first generation of American heroes from the Far West, and it lives on in folklore because of the amazing exploits of its best known characters, the "mountain men." The real historical significance of the fur frontier, however, lies not in the heroics of John Colter or Hugh Glass, but rather in its broader economic, social, and imperial aspects. The fur trade had an enormous impact, mostly negative, upon the Indians. It brought to a climax the rivalry between the Americans and the British for control of the far Northwest. Perhaps most strikingly, the fur trade began Montana's long and sad history of pillaging the environment. The fur men explored and "opened" this area, it is true, but in fact they stripped the surface wealth they were seeking and left little more than geographic knowledge behind them.

THE BRITISH IN MONTANA

The fur trade had been the mainstay of Canada ever since the beginnings of New France along the St. Lawrence River. For many years, as we have seen, the Canadian fur trade was dominated by the rivalry between the Hudson's Bay Company and the French fur interests based at Montreal. The Hudson's Bay Company, holding a monopoly charter over the vast lands draining into the bay, advanced westward cautiously, funneling a prosperous trade into its posts on the east-flowing rivers. Even after Canada fell under British rule in 1763, the French-Canadians were more expansive. Joined by enterprising Scots and Englishmen, they created the North West Company during the years prior to 1784, and they pressed steadily westward up the waterways beyond Lake Superior. The "Nor'Westers" were desperately anxious to beat the Hudson's Bay Company into the Canadian interior and to secure a Pacific seaport on the Columbia River before either their British or American rivals could get there. By the time of Lewis and Clark, both companies had posts on the central Canadian plains, and the North West Company had men as far west as British Columbia and as far south as the Mandan Villages on the Missouri River.

The first of the Nor'Westers to enter present-day Montana came only months after Lewis and Clark. During their stay at the Mandan Villages in the winter of 1804–5 the American explorers had encountered a number of Canadian traders, one of whom was François Antoine Larocque. "Mr. La Rocke," as Clark called him, wanted to accompany the Americans; but they, ever suspicious of the Canadians, refused. So Larocque, along with two assistants, set out on his own during the summer of 1805, southward from the Assiniboine River to scout the upper Missouri. Traveling usually with Indians, the Canadians crossed the Little Missouri River into southeastern Montana and headed up the Powder River, which was so named by the Indians, according to Larocque, because of "a fine sand which obscures and dirties the water." According to Larocque's sketchy journal, they ranged far enough southwest to see the Big Horn Mountains, crossed the Big Horn River, and then descended the Yellowstone on their return toward Canada. Larocque obtained a quantity of pelts and made good contacts with the Crow, Shoshoni, and Gros Ventre Indians. He promised to return for trade, but the North West Company failed to follow up his lead into the lands south of the Missouri.

Instead of penetrating the upper Missouri, which was obviously United States soil, the Nor'Westers moved westward up the Saskatchewan drainage into the Rocky Mountains, then headed southward into the mountain valleys that form the headwaters of the west-flowing Columbia, Kootenai, and Clark Fork rivers. This course brought them into what is now northwestern Montana. The leader of this thrust into the upper Columbia Basin was David Thompson, one of the truly great geographers of all time. The son of Welsh parents, Thompson migrated to Canada in 1784 and served the Hudson's Bay Company until 1797, when he moved over to the North West Company. The shrewd leaders of this firm quickly recognized his genius as a surveyor. Well aware of American interest in the Columbia Basin, they ordered Thompson to carry the fur trade into that region immediately.

In 1807 Thompson and his men penetrated the Canadian Rockies west of present Calgary. They erected trading posts—or "houses," as they often called them—on the upper Columbia and Kootenai rivers. The Canadians entered what is now far northwestern Montana in 1808. During the autumn of that year, Thompson sent his trusted lieutenant Finan McDonald with a crew of half-breeds down the Kootenai to open trade with the Indians of the same name. "Big Finan," a giant of a man, built a structure usually called "Kootenai Post" near present Libby, Montana, and spent the following year there. This post was relocated farther upstream three years later. Over the next few years Thompson and his men crisscrossed the drainages of the Kootenai, Clark Fork, and Flathead rivers, opening a friendly and profitable commerce with the Salish and Kutenai tribes. In November 1809 Thompson established the most important of his Montana posts, "Saleesh House," on the Clark Fork near the present town of Thompson Falls.

These posts formed part of a network of North West Company houses that extended westward, beyond the Rockies into the lower Columbia Basin. As trade prospered, Thompson pursued his first love, travel and mapping. In mid-1811, he set out upon what he called his "Voyage of a Summer Moon": "down the Columbia River to explore this river in order to open out a passage for the interior trade with the Pacific Ocean." At the strategic confluence of the Columbia and Snake rivers, he fastened a note to a pole bearing the solemn declaration "that this country is claimed by Great Britain as part of its territories." Alas, he soon learned that employees of the American fur baron John Jacob Astor had beaten him to the mouth of the Columbia. The Anglo-American struggle for mastery of the Pacific Northwest was beginning to kindle.

Thompson was back at Saleesh House during the following winter. In the early months of 1812, he surveyed the upper Clark Fork. From atop the towering butte now called Mount Jumbo, he mapped the complex Missoula area. His journey continued up the Flathead River and along the shores of Flathead Lake, all of which he mapped with amazing accuracy. He left the area during that spring, never to return. But behind him, Thompson left an impressive record of exploration. More importantly, he left the North West Company in firm control of the fur trade of the upper Columbia.

During the decade following Thompson's departure, the North West Company extended its trapping activities in the Pacific Northwest. The War of 1812 disrupted the fur trade, but it also helped the British force Astor's American traders from the lower Columbia. Saleesh House, under the direction of James McMillan and Ross Cox, was renamed "Flathead Post" and remained the company's key base in the western Montana area. The fur trade in these high mountain valleys was profitable and secure. Friendly Indians, some of them trained as trappers by Iroquois imported from the east, reliably brought in the pelts year after year.

Indeed, the Nor'Westers faced less danger from Indians or Americans than from their long-time rival, the Hudson's Bay Company. Stung by the success of the Nor'Westers, the venerable old corporation moved west with new vigor. In 1810, for instance, agents of the Hudson's Bay Company built a post with the unlikely name "Howes House" north of Flathead Lake. Competition between the two Canadian rivals became ever more fierce, until by 1816 it erupted in violence and death in the Red River Valley of Canada. Both sides realized that the dispute must end. In 1821 the two firms merged under the name of the Hudson's Bay Company. The British crown granted this newly consolidated corporation a twenty-one-year monopoly over the Pacific Northwest trade, and the company formed its Columbia Department to manage and expand the old North West Company operations there.

Having absorbed the North West Company, the Hudson's Bay Company now proceeded rapidly to solidify its control of the Columbia Valley. The governments of the United States and Great Britain had agreed by now to a "joint occupation" of this vast, little known region. "Joint occupation" meant, in effect, that whichever nation could first occupy the Pacific Northwest would eventually, no doubt, own it. The Hudson's Bay Company built its headquarters, Fort Vancouver, on the lower Columbia in 1824–25 and placed it under the command of huge, amiable, and shrewd Dr. John McLoughlin. McLoughlin had new posts built on the upper Columbia and its tributaries, and he sent large "brigades" of men to trap out the interior before the Americans could establish themselves there. Americans entering the Northwest joked that the initials "H.B.C.," which seemed to appear everywhere, meant "Here Before Christ."

Present-day northwestern Montana, on the upper Clark Fork and Kootenai tributaries of the Columbia, lay on the far eastern fringe of the Hudson's Bay Company's Columbia Department. The H.B.C. seldom pressed its activities far east of the continental divide. It continued to concentrate its trade in these valleys at the posts established earlier by the Nor'Westers, Flathead Post (Saleesh House) on the Clark Fork and Kootenai Post on the Kootenai. In 1846–47, H.B.C. men Neil McArthur and Angus McDonald erected the last of the major British posts, variously known as "Fort Connen" or "Connah," on Post Creek in the Flathead Valley. Fort Connah became the center of H.B.C. operations in Montana during the twilight years of the fur trade and continued in business until 1871. Through these fixed posts, and through their generally decent trading practices, the British won and held the loyalty of the western Montana Indians. Americans only randomly entered the area. In 1833 the Hudson's Bay Company signed an agreement with its great United States rival, the American Fur Company, whereby each agreed to stay out of the other's territory.

The H.B.C. complemented its trading posts with the use of large trapping "brigades." The brigades proved to be highly profitable, bringing in large hauls of fur through intensive trapping. And by stripping the outer reaches of the Columbia drainage of fur-bearing animals, they hoped to keep the aggressive Americans at a distance. The North West Company sent out the first brigade under Donald McKenzie in 1818, and the Hudson's Bay Company continued the practice in a big way. Alexander Ross led the first of the major H.B.C. trapping brigades, made up of fifty-five men, out of Saleesh House in early 1824. Ross's party followed a long twisting arc to the south and west into the Salmon River country of Idaho and returned to Saleesh House late in the year with an impressive haul of five thousand beaver skins.

Pleased by Ross's success, Dr. McLoughlin placed more emphasis upon the brigade method. Command of the brigades was now given to Peter Skene Ogden, one of the most able of the British fur men and one of the major explorers of western America. Ogden amply possessed the qualities most necessary to succeed in the fur business—shrewdness, toughness, even viciousness. Legends of his violent disposition abound. In a fit of anger, he once forced one of his men to climb a tree and then set the tree afire, forcing the poor chap to climb down through the flames. For six years, beginning late in 1824, he led large trapping brigades through the Northern Rockies and intermountain regions. Ogden's various trapping expeditions, some of them very large, traveled northward to the Marias country, eastward to the Gallatin, and southward to the Great Salt Lake, the Nevada deserts, and far into California.

So the Canadian fur frontier came to dominate the Pacific Northwest. While established houses like Flathead Post and Fort Connah held the Indian trade, the profitable brigades harvested a bounty of pelts from the eastern and southern extremities of the Columbia watershed. The dream of Alexander Mackenzie and David Thompson—British control of the Columbia—seemed destined to come true. Within future Montana, the Americans found their British adversaries in general control of the northwestern mountains.

THE AMERICANS

Even as David Thompson pressed the Canadian fur trade into the Columbia Valley, American traders at St. Louis turned their attention toward the far reaches of the muddy Missouri River. The fur trade of the United States was centered in the bountiful lands surrounding the Great Lakes and the Mississippi headwaters; but now, after the return of Lewis and Clark, the upper Missouri, Northern Rockies, and Columbia Basin regions beckoned as inviting new frontiers. St. Louis, located near the juncture of the Missouri with the Mississippi, was the natural gateway to these virgin lands. As Lewis and Clark's glowing assessment of the fur potential of the Northwest became known, St. Louis buzzed with excitement.

The first of the St. Louis traders to pursue the upriver region was Manuel Lisa. A Louisiana Spaniard by birth, Lisa was brave, tough, cunning, and, according to his many enemies, unscrupulous. Backed by two partners from Illinois, he led a sizable expedition out of St. Louis and up the Missouri in the spring of 1807. Lisa had with him a keelboat full of trade goods and a number of seasoned frontiersmen, including George Drouillard of the Lewis and Clark Expedition. At the mouth of the Platte River, his party met another Lewis and Clark veteran, John Colter, who had spent the previous year trapping on the Yellowstone. Colter agreed to hire on with Lisa and to return once again to the wilderness. No doubt following the advice of Colter and Drouillard, Lisa avoided the hostile Blackfeet of the upper Missouri and went up the Yellowstone instead. His party reached the strategic confluence of the Yellowstone and Big Horn rivers in November 1807. Here they built a trading post, the first permanent structure erected by white men in Montana. Lisa named it Fort Remon after his son, but it was usually known as "Lisa's Fort," or "Fort Manuel."

During the following winter, Lisa's men made ample contact with the Crows. These Indians, perennial foes of the Blackfeet and Sioux, needed American aid, and they generally cooperated with the fur traders. It was also during this first winter that the incredible John Colter, with a thirty-pound pack on his back, made his fabulous winter journey hundreds of miles in search of Indian allies and, perhaps, Spanish settlements to the south. His odyssey took him southwestward clear beyond Jackson Hole and the Grand Tetons and back, possibly through today's Yellowstone National Park. Colter's description of the natural wonders in that area earned him only the reputation of a great liar and the designation of such a peculiar place as "Colter's Hell."

Lisa returned to St. Louis in 1808, full of enthusiasm for the fur trade upriver. He now gathered some of the foremost merchants of that city into a partnership that would trap the upstream lands on a major scale. These men included, among others, Pierre Menard and William Morrison, who were Lisa's partners of the year before, Andrew Henry, William Clark, Reuben Lewis (Meriwether's brother), and Auguste and Pierre Chouteau, members of one of St. Louis' oldest and most powerful families. The firm they organized early in 1809 was capitalized at forty thousand dollars and named the "St. Louis Missouri Fur Company." Better known as the Missouri Fur Company, it would carry the first major thrust by the Americans into the northern plains and Rockies.

Manuel Lisa, always aggressive, dominated the organization. In June 1809 he took a party numbering at least 150 men, many of them French frontiersmen, up the long river. They traded profitably among the Crows during the next year, and in March 1810 Andrew Henry and Pierre Menard led a force of 32 men westward to the Three Forks of the Missouri. Here the partners planned to establish their central base and to open trade with the powerful Blackfeet, lords of the best fur lands in the region. Henry's men built a trading post on the point of land between the converging Jefferson and Madison rivers and found excellent trapping. Angry at this invasion, though, the Blackfeet and their Gros Ventre allies quickly reacted with violence. Eight of Henry's party lost their lives to the Indians. Among them was the valuable George Drouillard, who died in ambush only two miles from the Three Forks Post. Such losses were intolerable, and by the close of 1810 Henry had abandoned the Three Forks venture.

The Missouri Fur Company faced other problems, too. A fire destroyed nearly twenty thousand dollars' worth of furs and robes, and the approach of war between the United States and Great Britain threatened to disrupt European fur markets and to allow the Canadians to move south and cut off American traffic on the upper Missouri. So in 1811 Lisa and his partners vacated the post on the Big Horn and abandoned the upriver trade. Over the next few years, during and after the War of 1812, the Missouri Fur Company confined its activities to the lower course of the Big Muddy. The firm languished during this period, and most of the original partners left it.

Finally, in 1819, Lisa reorganized the old Missouri Fur Company and drew in such new and energetic partners as Joshua Pilcher, Andrew Drips, and Robert Jones. By now the United States and Britain had agreed to extend the 49th parallel boundary westward to the crest of the Rockies, and thus the northern plains and Rockies seemed more secure from Canadian inroads. Before he could re-establish his company on the upper Missouri, Lisa suddenly fell ill of some unknown disease and died in 1820. His untimely death removed the strongest of the early upriver traders, and Joshua Pilcher took his place. Once again, the Missouri Fur Company headed upstream.

With a large army of trappers, Pilcher established another post at the juncture of the Yellowstone and Big Horn rivers in 1821. The post took the name Fort Benton in honor of the influential Missouri senator and protector of the fur business, Thomas Hart Benton. During the following year Robert Jones and Michael Immel brought a group of 150 men up to Fort Benton. With roughly 300 men in the area, the Missouri Fur Company enjoyed real success. The company sent twenty-five thousand dollars' worth of furs down to market that autumn. But once again, the lure of the Blackfeet lands proved irresistible—and fatal. In the spring of 1823 Jones and Immel led a sizable force over to the Three Forks. They trapped successfully on the Jefferson, and in mid-May they managed to meet with a band of

Blackfeet. The Indians seemed friendly and welcomed the idea of an American post in their territory. One of them carried a letter bearing the inscription "God Save the King" that certified him as a friend of the whites.

But friends they were not. The Blackfeet secretly raised a large war party and stealthily pursued the Americans back into the Crow territory on the Yellowstone. As the Jones-Immel party was climbing down through the rimrocks along the river, near present-day Billings, the Indians ambushed them. Jones, Immel, and five of their men died in the attack. Fifteen thousand dollars' worth of furs were lost. The Americans naturally figured that the British had instigated the whole business, for the Indians carried guns acquired in Canada and took the stolen pelts there for sale. Again, the Blackfeet had driven out the American intruders with severe losses. Pilcher and his associates gave up the effort to establish an upriver trade and confined their activities to the lower Missouri. The Missouri Fur Company lingered on for only a few more years; by 1830 it had folded. So ended the first American efforts to win the fur business of the high plains and Rockies.

Even as Pilcher was developing his operation on the faraway Yellowstone, another organization began to take shape in St. Louis. In March 1822 an advertisement appeared there in the *Missouri Republican:* "To enterprising young men. The subscriber wishes to engage one hundred young men to ascend the Missouri River to its source, there to be employed for one, two or three years." The "subscribers" were General William H. Ashley, a prominent Missouri businessman, politician, and militia leader, and Andrew Henry, formerly Lisa's partner and also a well known Missouri investor. The outfit they were assembling, later to become known as the Rocky Mountain Fur Company, would play a key role in the exploration of the West. Among the young men responding to their notice were several, like Jim Bridger and Thomas Fitzpatrick, who soon rose to prominence in the Rocky Mountain fur business.

Ashley and Henry hoped to trade with the Blackfeet from a fixed post at either the Three Forks or the Great Falls, but the treacherous river and troublesome Indians enroute forced a change of plans. They built a post at the mouth of the Yellowstone instead, and Henry located his men there during the winter of 1822–23. In the spring Henry led his force up to the Great Falls and, predictably, the Blackfeet hit them at once. The Piegans struck Henry's party, killing four men and wounding several others. When Henry returned to the mouth of the Yellowstone, he learned that Ashley had suffered severe losses from attacks by Arikara Indians downstream. Their plans badly disrupted, the partners salvaged something when Henry moved over to the mouth of the Big Horn and set up yet another post among the Crows.

The combined dangers of the Blackfeet and the uncertainties of travel on the Big Muddy led Ashley and Henry to abandon their plans of commerce on the upper Missouri. They decided, instead, to divert their activities southward into the mountains drained by the Green, Snake, Wind, and Bear rivers of present Wyoming, Idaho, and Utah. The partners also abandoned the traditional method of relying upon fixed posts and trading with the unpredictable Indians. Rather, they would turn their employees loose in the wilderness as "free trappers" or "mountain men," who would work on their own and sell their furs to the St. Louis–based partners at an annual trading fair in the mountains called the "rendezvous."

Beginning in 1824, Ashley and his successors staged the rendezvous each year in the early summer, usually along the upper Green, Snake, or Bear rivers. The St. Louis merchants' caravan carried trade goods, guns, and ammunition, and flat casks of alcohol overland to the rendezvous site. There, the mountain men, and many Indians, too, congregated to sell the pelts from their spring and fall hunts. Several days, even weeks, of drinking, debauchery, mayhem, and sometimes murder ensued. Then the free trappers and their Indian cohorts returned to the wilderness for the fall hunt and a winter of cold and boredom. The mountain men, like Jedediah Smith, Kit Carson, and Hugh Glass, explored much of the Far West. Their exploits, usually exaggerated in the retelling, captured the nation's imagination. Glass's encounter with a grizzly bear and Jed Smith's desert crossings into California were, indeed, facts that were stranger than fiction. The mountain men introduced the Indians to the wilder side of the white civilization; and sometimes the whites degenerated into savagery, like the fictional hero of A. B. Guthrie, Jr.'s, fine novel *The Big Sky*.

The yearly rendezvous was one of the great spectacles in the history of the West, but for the mountain men the system returned little profit. Not surprisingly, the wealth passed into the hands of the investors who sent the trade caravans out from St. Louis. Ashley did so well at this that he was able to retire, a wealthy man, in 1826. He sold out to three of his men, Jed Smith, David Jackson, and William Sublette. They, in turn, sold to another group of partners, Thomas Fitzpatrick, Baptiste Gervais, Jim Bridger, Milton Sublette, and Henry Fraeb, in 1830. This latter group first officially used the name Rocky Mountain Fur Company, but that title is often applied to the firm from the time of its inception in 1822.

Although the Rocky Mountain Fur Company centered its activities to the south of Montana, its partners and trappers often entered the state's present borders. In the fall hunt of 1830, for instance, Sublette, Fitzpatrick, and Bridger led a party of more than two hundred men on a northward sweep. They descended the Big Horn River, crossed over to the Great Falls, and then followed the Missouri and Jefferson rivers on their southbound return. The size of their party kept the Blackfeet at a distance, and the result was a rich harvest of furs. A similar expedition in 1831, however, met frustration when the Crows, true to form, ran off its horses. The company's rendezvous system thrived from the mid-1820s until the mid-1830s. It faced some competition from various American rivals and from the Hudson's Bay Company. By the early 1830s, though, it found itself face to face with a rival that it could not match.

MONOPOLY: THE AMERICAN FUR COMPANY

The American Fur Company, incorporated in New York in 1808, grew eventually to dominate the fur trade of the entire United States. This firm was completely the creature of its powerful founder, John Jacob Astor. A German immigrant, Astor accumulated one of the great early American fortunes, first as a New York fur merchant and later as master of the fur business from the trapping stage to the marketing of finished products. In creating the American Fur Company, he aimed to take over the Great Lakes trade from the Canadians, who were flagrantly stripping this United States territory of its fur-bearing animals. He succeeded, during the years after the War of 1812, in capturing control of that vital area. Astor organized the Northern Department of the American Fur Company to manage the business of the Great Lakes–Upper Mississippi region. In the meantime, his effort to move into the Pacific Northwest, through the famous post at Astoria, had been defeated by the British North West Company.

By 1820 Astor had become the colossus of the fur business. The dwindling animal population of the old Northwest and the irresistible lure of new, untrammeled wilderness farther west drew him inevitably toward St. Louis and the Missouri. Fearing Astor's domination, the St. Louis merchants had kept him out of the old Missouri Fur Company. But they could not keep him out forever. In 1822, the very year that Ashley and Henry headed up the river, Astor formed the Western Department of his American Fur Company, centered at St. Louis under the tough-minded direction of his close associate Ramsay Crooks.

Astor and Crooks contracted with local St. Louis businessmen to handle the work of the Western Department. The firm of Bernard Pratte and Company proved itself the most efficient, and in 1827 it took over the entire management of Astor's western operation. One of Pratte's associates was Pierre Chouteau, Jr., an exceptionally shrewd, third-generation member of St. Louis's best established family. Chouteau would soon rise to command the entire western operation of the American Fur Company.

Directed by such able men as Crooks and Chouteau, the American Fur Company pushed inexorably up the Big Muddy. Of the several small firms that lay across its path, the most formidable was the Columbia Fur Company. A number of hard-nosed ex-Nor'Westers, who had left Canada after the absorption of that firm by the Hudson's Bay Company, ran the Columbia operation. They were making impressive profits and extending their system of posts far up the Missouri. When the Columbia Fur Company proved too tough a nut to crack, the American Fur Company simply bought it out. In 1827, through an agreement worked out by Crooks, it became the "Upper Missouri Outfit" of Astor's Western Department.

The path to the far upriver region now lay open to the American Fur Company. The company had a solid base of operations at St. Louis, and now the Upper Missouri Outfit provided the striking arm. Kenneth McKenzie, a tough and ruthless red-faced Scot and a veteran of the Columbia organization, ran the Upper Missouri Outfit. In 1828, he sent a workforce under James Kipp to erect a large trading fort at that most strategic of locations, the mouth of the Yellowstone. They named this post, located almost exactly on the later Montana–North Dakota border, Fort Floyd; but its name soon became Fort Union. Well situated and elaborate in construction, Fort Union became headquarters for Astor's Upper Missouri Outfit and was for years one of the major forts of the American West.

From St. Louis and now from Fort Union, the American Fur Company set out to monopolize the fur trade of the northern plains and Rockies. Beginning in 1829, the company sent its own trading caravans to the rendezvous, and by paying better prices for pelts, it put the squeeze on the Rocky Mountain Fur Company. The American Fur Company further harassed its competitor by sending parties of its own trappers to follow the Rocky Mountain men, thus finding their best beaver streams. This practice, not surprisingly, led sometimes to violence, as in 1832 when Bridger and Fitzpatrick lured one of McKenzie's best men, William Henry Vanderburgh, into a Blackfeet ambush that cost Vanderburgh his life.

For awhile, the Rocky Mountain partners and other independent "opposition" outfits fought back against the encroachments of the American Fur Company. The rendezvous became scenes of vigorous bidding for pelts, and the free trappers did well. The 1832 rendezvous at Pierre's Hole was the greatest gathering of them all. Two former Rocky Mountain men, William Sublette and Robert Campbell, even retaliated by building a post named Fort William in the shadow of Fort Union itself. Sublette and Campbell had the backing of William H. Ashley, and they posed a real threat to the company. But McKenzie drove them to the wall by underselling them and also, probably, by turning the Indians against them. Sublette and Campbell soon ended up selling out to the company.

The simple fact was that no "opposition" outfit, the Rocky Mountain partners or anyone else, could match the awesome resources of the American Fur Company. The company had the financial power to get the best men and the most potent weapons. Two such weapons proved especially critical—steamboats and a distillery. The steamboats, as Pierre Chouteau, Jr., foresaw, were the key, for they could haul much larger cargoes upriver much faster than the small, man-powered keelboats. Specially built for navigating the treacherous upper Missouri, the first of these light-draft steamboats, the *Yellowstone,* reached Fort Union on the high waters of June 1832. Thereafter, the boats traveled regularly to Fort Union and became the lifeline of the Upper Missouri Outfit. The Indians, overwhelmed by the white man's magic, gazed in awe at the "fireboats-that-walk-on-the-water."

The distillery also had a sizable impact on the trade. Liquor had long been the most valuable of the fur man's trade goods, and also the most lethal in its effects on the Indians. Most traders ignored an 1832 federal law specifically forbidding the transport of liquor into "Indian Country." Instead of trying to smuggle large quantities past government inspectors, McKenzie had a small distillery secretly brought up to Fort Union in 1833. With imported corn, his men began producing plenty of rotgut right on the spot. This ready supply of liquor gave McKenzie a formidable advantage over the competition, but it would soon be his undoing.

Under such pressure as this, the Rocky Mountain Fur Company buckled and folded. The partners tried desperately to bargain with the American Fur Company for a division of the trade, but to no avail. In 1834 the Rocky Mountain owners sold out to their giant rival. Most of their holdings and many of their men passed into the employ of the company. The American Fur Company continued the rendezvous for only a few more years; the last of the colorful meetings, in 1840, drew only 120 men. The day of the mountain men was coming to an end.

Even as Astor's giant company crushed its smaller American rivals, it turned its attention toward the prize that had eluded all of its predecessors—the Blackfeet lands of the far upper Missouri. Kenneth McKenzie was able to make friendly contact with these hostile Indians through one of his employees, a man named Jacob Berger. Berger, a former Hudson's Bay man, knew many of the Blackfeet, and he understood their language. Along with a group of terrified companions, Berger traveled from Fort Union to the Marias River on a peace mission in 1830. He parleyed with the Piegans and convinced a group of them to accompany him back to Fort Union for a conference with McKenzie. There, the Blackfeet seemed enthusiastic to have a post erected on their lands, and they agreed to a full-scale trade with the Americans. During the following year, McKenzie played upon their desire for guns, liquor, and trade items and won compliance from them, even including a treaty of peace with their old enemies the Assiniboines, who traded regularly at Fort Union.

The Upper Missouri Outfit now had its foot in the door. In the summer of 1831, McKenzie sent James Kipp upriver with twenty-five men to open the Blackfeet trade. Near the mouth of the Marias they erected a structure which they named Fort Piegan. The Blackfeet responded with surprising enthusiasm, reportedly bringing in twenty-four hundred beaver pelts in the first ten days of business. According at least to American suspicions, the British were so alarmed at American success on the Marias that they incited the Blood tribe of Blackfeet to strike at Kipp's post. They did, but Kipp deflated their attack by feeding them whiskey until they gave it up. Kipp returned to Fort Union with an impressive cargo of furs in the spring of 1832. Since none of his men would agree to stay behind in Blackfeet lands, Fort Piegan was abandoned, and the angry Indians burned it.

Later that summer, however, another of McKenzie's men, David D. Mitchell, returned and built a new post a few miles upstream from Fort Piegan. Mitchell and his men worked in an atmosphere of incredible tension, for thousands of suspicious and unfriendly Blackfeet gathered to watch them. This spot they named Fort McKenzie, and for years it served as the depot where the great wealth of Blackfeet furs were brought to market. In the autumn of 1832 McKenzie's men built a similar post among the Crows. They located it at the traditional spot, near the mouth of the Big Horn, and named it Fort Cass. Forts Cass and McKenzie both served as subposts to Fort Union. Combined, they cemented the hold of the American Fur Company upon the entire upper Missouri region.

So, by the mid-1830s, the American Fur Company reigned supreme. It had destroyed its American competition, contained the Hudson's Bay Company generally west of the continental divide, and gained a firm control of the Blackfeet trade. J. J. Astor, aging but still astute, foresaw the decline of the fur trade, as silk garments and textiles were beginning to supplant furs. In 1834 he abandoned the business and sold his Western Department to its long-time managers, Pratte, Chouteau and Company. When Pratte retired in 1838, Chouteau took over, and the firm became Pierre Chouteau, Jr., and Company. Actually, these changes meant little. The same individuals, mainly Chouteau, generally ran things; and most people still called the organization, even after 1834, the American Fur Company.

Kenneth McKenzie, the tough ruler of Fort Union and the Upper Missouri Outfit, soon left the scene, too. When the government learned of the distillery at Fort Union, McKenzie's superiors made him the scapegoat for its presence. The episode cost McKenzie his job, and it nearly cost the company its trading license. Alexander Culbertson took McKenzie's place at Fort Union. A tall, strong, and forceful man, Culbertson dominated the upper Missouri trade after 1840. His handsome Blackfeet wife Natawista Ixsana aided him in his dealings with the Indians.

Under Culbertson, the company maintained its smooth control of the region, but problems still arose. A major calamity occurred at Fort McKenzie in 1843 when two company men of especially vicious character, F. A. Chardon and Alexander Harvey, sought revenge against the Blackfeet for murdering Chardon's Negro slave. Using a concealed cannon, they slaughtered twenty-one unsuspecting Indians and wounded others. Then they murdered the wounded and scalped all of the corpses. Too frightened to remain, Chardon and his men soon abandoned Fort McKenzie, and the enraged Indians burned it.

For awhile, this appalling incident disrupted the Blackfeet trade, but Chouteau finally convinced Culbertson to try again. In 1845 Culbertson took a party of men up from Fort Union, past the site of Fort McKenzie, and built a new post called Fort Lewis. The Blackfeet, who trusted Culbertson, soon resumed trade with the company. Since they disliked the location of Fort Lewis, Culbertson erected an elaborate new post the following year, downstream at a more accessible spot on the Missouri. This post, first called Fort Lewis, was later renamed to honor the company's best friend in Congress, Senator Thomas Hart Benton. Built of adobe brick, Fort Benton arose to become a major trading center. Its 250-foot walls enclosed an interior courtyard and several buildings. The fort served as the company's base of operations on the upper Missouri during the twilight years of the fur trade. It later became head of steamboat navigation on the river and a key transportation center during the mining rushes.

The American Fur Company, under Chouteau and then under later owners, continued its operations from these and other posts for many years. Various "opposition" companies entered the field to compete with it, but they had scant success. Culbertson ran the upriver trade from Fort Benton until his retirement in the later 1850s, when Andrew Dawson, another enterprising Scot, took his place. Dawson ably oversaw the operation until his retirement in 1864. By then buffalo hides were replacing beaver pelts in importance.

The fur trade had faded appreciably even before the 1860s mining rushes. It left behind a mixed, but generally negative legacy. The fur frontier, in a positive sense, caused intensive exploration and widened the horizon of geographical knowledge. As an instrument of empire, the fur trade had far-reaching results. It solidified the American grip upon most of Montana and almost, but not quite, gained the Columbia Valley for Great Britain. In 1846 the British government agreed to cede all lands below the 49th parallel to the United States. In general, though, the fur trade had a negative impact upon the region and its native peoples. It skimmed off a valuable resource, fur-bearing animals, without heed; and the consequent profits passed only to a few, faraway individuals.

Surely the most tragic aspect of the fur trade was its impact upon the Indians, who were generally introduced to the seamy side of Anglo-American civilization. The traders and trappers plied the Indians with liquor and armed them with guns against their native enemies. They taught the natives to rely upon whites for "iron and firewater," and quickly the Indians' independence broke down. Then there came the inevitable curse of disease. In 1837 a terrible smallpox epidemic, carried by the fur traders' vessels, swept up the Missouri. It struck the settled Mandans with such fury that they became extinct. The Assiniboines contracted it at Fort Union and died by the hundreds. Charles Larpenteur did a good business at the fort selling liquor to Indians who wanted one last drunk before death found them. The Crows fared better. They heard of the epidemic and stayed away from Fort Cass. Having been partially immunized in an earlier epidemic, the Gros Ventres escaped the worst ravages this time.

The Blackfeet suffered terribly. A keelboat brought the disease to Fort McKenzie. Culbertson tried to warn the Indians away, but his warnings only aroused their suspicions. They came, then left—ominously, they failed to return. Culbertson went out in the fall to find them. At the Three Forks he discovered a major camp where only two people remained alive, amidst the stench of dead bodies: "Hundreds of decaying forms of human beings, horses, and dogs," he reported, "lay scattered everywhere among the lodges." Half or maybe more of the Blackfeet died of smallpox, and their military supremacy was broken forever. It was a tragedy beyond description.

THE INDIANS AND THE MISSIONARIES

The fur trade did bring to the Indians one glimpse of a generally more admirable side of the white man's civilization, religion. Many of the Canadian fur men who came to western Montana after 1808 were French Roman Catholics. They brought with them a number of Iroquois Indians from the East. The Iroquois were experienced trappers, and the Canadians wanted them to teach their skills to the local tribes. According to one disgusted Nor'Wester, however, the Iroquois "preferred to feast and dance in the tents of the Flatheads than hunt for beaver."

Naturally, the Iroquois told the Flatheads about the mysteries of Christianity. The most influential of them was Ignace La Mousse, better known as "Big Ignace." Ignace told the Flatheads, as Father Gregory Mengarini later learned, "of certain white men clothed in black whose practice it was to instruct people, bring them to know God and all good things, and enable them to live after death." The Flatheads, who got along well with the whites anyhow, reacted enthusiastically. They determined to find a "Black

Robe" who would bring them religion and the "white man's Book of Heaven."

The Flatheads were remarkably persistent in their "quest" for Christianity. Along with their Nez Perce friends, they sent four different parties, in 1831, 1835, 1837, and 1839, on long and dangerous journeys through enemy territory to St. Louis in search of a missionary. The first group aroused the interest of Protestants, but their missionaries ended up in the Oregon Country, not the eastern Rockies. Big Ignace led the next two journeys, and on the latter expedition he was killed by Indian foes. Finally, the fourth effort brought results. Bishop Rosati of St. Louis received the Indians, who were led this time by Ignace's son, and he promised to send them a priest.

The priest he sent was a Jesuit named Pierre-Jean DeSmet, one of the truly remarkable missionaries in American history. A Belgian by birth, Father DeSmet, even though often in poor health, would prove himself one of the frontier's greatest travelers and one of the most patient and understanding friends the Indians ever had. Along with young Ignace, he accompanied an American Fur Company caravan to the 1840 rendezvous. There, a large Flathead–Nez Perce party welcomed him, and DeSmet traveled with them into the Three Forks area. Much impressed by their zeal for religion, he took leave of them in the Gallatin Valley and promised soon to return.

Father DeSmet spent the following winter raising funds for his project, and in the spring of 1841 he set out once again for the Rockies. Along with him came two other priests, Gregory Mengarini and Nicholas Point, and three lay brothers. They met the Flatheads at Fort Hall on the Oregon Trail and accompanied them to their favorite domicile, the Bitterroot Valley. There, in September 1841, they began construction of the St. Mary's Mission, which Montanans have recognized ever since as one of the birthplaces of their history. While comrades worked at the building, Father DeSmet made one of those epic treks for which he was legendary, clear to the Columbia River and back, bringing seed wheat, potatoes, and oats for planting. This marked the real beginning of agriculture in Montana, and it enthralled the Indians, who watched the ripening plants in wonder.

For a few years the St. Mary's Mission seemed a remarkable success. Father DeSmet returned east in 1842 and went on to Europe, raising support for his endeavors. Meanwhile, other Jesuits came out to St. Mary's, and some continued west to build more missions beyond the mountains. DeSmet returned to St. Mary's in the spring of 1845. With him came the very capable Italian Jesuit, Father Anthony Ravalli, a dedicated priest and a man of many skills. Largely through his efforts, the fathers put together crude flour and sawmills, and in 1846 they built a new and larger church.

All went well until the Indians returned from their summer hunt in 1846. Then they seemed, all at once, indifferent to Christianity and openly hostile to the priests. There were probably several reasons for this turnabout. Father DeSmet, whom the Indians liked, departed again for the East; this left Father Mengarini, not a favorite of the Flatheads, in charge. Another problem arose when white trappers settled around the mission and began exerting a worldly influence upon the natives. Probably the main reason for the Flatheads' "apostacy" arose from Father DeSmet's effort in 1846 to take religion to the Blackfeet. To the Flatheads, no doubt, this meant near treason, the sharing of sacred "medicine" with their mortal enemies.

Whatever the cause, relations became so bad that in 1850 the priests closed their Bitterroot mission. They sold their properties to Major John Owen, who converted them into a trading post which became a notable gathering place of early Montana. The Jesuits' setback among the Flatheads, however, proved to be only temporary. For a few years, they focused their activities among the Indians to the west. Then in 1854 the Jesuits returned under the leadership of Father Adrian Hoecken and located a new mission in the fine country south of Flathead Lake. This was the famous St. Ignatius Mission. A cluster of buildings sprang up nearby, and the Indians responded with amazing enthusiasm to this renewed missionary effort. Over a thousand Kutenais, Pend d'Oreilles, and Flatheads came to the Easter services at St. Ignatius in 1855, and hundreds were baptized.

Years later, in 1866, Fathers Ravalli and Joseph Giorda came back to the Bitterroot and reopened St. Mary's Mission. Father Ravalli, whose name was given to the county embracing this area, remained among the Flatheads until 1884, beloved by Indians and whites alike. The mission closed in 1891, when the Flatheads sadly left their beloved valley for the reservation to the north. At St. Ignatius, Father Hoecken and his colleagues continued their work among the growing Indian population moving onto the reservation south of Flathead Lake. Sisters of Providence came from Canada to open a school there in 1864. The Catholics remained, helping their native wards adjust to the new, closed world of the reservation.

The Catholics made the major missionary efforts in frontier Montana. Although the Methodists did some work among the Crows and the Fort Peck tribes, Protestant ministers, generally speaking, came with and stayed among the whites. The Catholics eventually expanded their activities throughout Montana. They established the St. Peter's and Holy Family missions among the Blackfeet, St. Paul's for the Indians at Fort Belknap, St. Xavier's on the Crow Reservation, and a mission-school on the Northern Cheyenne Reservation. As in Oregon, California, and Arizona, missionaries played a significant role in the "opening" of Montana.

CHAPTER IV

The Mining Frontier

Montana's foundation, like that of several other western states, stands upon a golden cornerstone. The glitter of gold first attracted significant numbers of white men to this area, and their coming laid the basis of a community. The initial gold rush to Montana was part of a population movement which crisscrossed much of the Mountain West; and, as happened in other areas, it lost its momentum in only a few years. As the first, easy diggings played out, some miners turned to more elaborate methods of extracting the gold. Others prospected for new deposits. The discovery of new gold fields, the opening of transportation routes, and the application of new mining technology all made for a constant shifting of population. New boom towns appeared and old ones died. In Montana, as in Colorado, Nevada, and Idaho, gold soon gave way to silver, a metal much more difficult and expensive to extract. Eventually, silver mining, too, would fade. By the mid-1890s copper would prove to be Montana's premier metal, its production centered at Butte; and gold and silver would become, increasingly, mere byproducts of the copper industry.

GOLD: THE PLACER BOOM

The question of who first discovered gold in Montana has always been, and will always be, a matter of conjecture. Some credit Father DeSmet or John Owen on the Bitterroot; others argue, plausibly, that fur trappers, such as John Silverthorne or François Finlay, made the first find. The first discovery definitely to be recorded occurred in the spring of 1858, when James and Granville Stuart, along with Reece Anderson, found traces at Gold Creek east of present Drummond. By the summer of 1862 the Stuart brothers and other men were at work here. A small settlement called American Fork sprang up at Gold Creek, but neither the diggings nor the town ever amounted to much.

By mid-1862 general conditions favored a major gold rush to the Montana area. Earlier centers of gold mining opportunity, namely California, Nevada, and Colorado, were now in decline, and prospectors were combing the western slopes of the Rockies in present-day Idaho. Not surprisingly, some groups of Idaho-bound miners filtered into the southwestern portion of today's Montana as they attempted to find short cuts through the Bitterroot barrier. John White, a member of one such Colorado-based party, touched off Montana's first major placer rush in the summer of 1862 when he uncovered sizable deposits of placer gold on Grasshopper Creek, a tributary of the Beaverhead (upper Jefferson) River. Here, at the "Grasshopper Diggings," sprang up Montana's first boom town, a typically hell-for-leather burg named Bannack City.

Bannack's population, by the fall of 1862, stood at roughly four to five hundred. As usual on mining frontiers, the early arrivals grabbed up the best paying gold claims, and the latecomers had to turn elsewhere. Prospectors fanned out through the upper Missouri drainage and, as a result, new discoveries came in rapid-fire succession. A cluster of claims appeared, for instance, on Horse Prairie Creek, fifteen miles west of Bannack; other activity took place on the Prickly Pear, far to the north. These smaller placers, though, paled in comparison to the deposits found in May 1863 at Alder Gulch, seventy miles east of Bannack.

The opening of Alder Gulch would prompt the greatest placer rush of Montana's history. A prospecting party under the leadership of James Stuart left Bannack in the spring of 1863 to look over the Yellowstone Valley. Several members of the group, including Bill Fairweather, Henry Edgar, and Barney Hughes, failed to make a rendezvous with the main Stuart party, which ended up colliding with hostile Indians and traveling a circuitous sixteen hundred miles back to Bannack via the Oregon Trail. The smaller Fairweather-Edgar group, after running into Crow Indians, headed despondently back through the Gallatin and Madison valleys enroute to Bannack. On the evening of May 26, 1863, after making camp atop the Madison-Jefferson divide, Fairweather and Edgar decided to prospect for some tobacco money. Their first pan turned up $2.40; and they knew at once that Alder Gulch, as they christened it, held great potential. Always looking out for prospectors who acted suspiciously, hundreds of Bannack miners followed the discovers of Alder Gulch on their return. Within the next year and a half, ten thousand or more people crowded into the steep, rugged contours of this area. Mining districts named Fairweather, Summit, Highland, Pine Grove, and Junction blanketed the gulch. Several towns appeared, the best known being Virginia and Nevada Cities; but population was so scattered that some contemporaries called the area "Fourteen-mile City."

Alder Gulch–Virginia City grew to become one of the great gold camps of the American West and the hub of early Montana. In its first five years the gulch produced an estimated thirty to forty million dollars' worth of gold. More importantly, the diggings attracted into the area several thousand prospectors who, arriving too late to cash in at Virginia City, ranged out in all directions looking for new bonanzas. Traveling usually in groups of from five to fifty men, they understood the miners' craft, and they could easily recognize gold-bearing terrain. Many were veterans of the rushes to California, Colorado, Nevada, or Idaho.

Thus the years following the Alder Gulch strike of 1863 witnessed one new discovery after another. The most important of these was Last Chance Gulch, which happened to lie at the geographic center of the Montana mining region. A group of Virginia City prospecters destined for the Kootenai country first found color here in the spring of 1864 but then moved on to the north, where they met no success. This party, later known as the "Four Georgians," came back to what they now named, appropriately, Last Chance Gulch; and on July 14, 1864, they uncovered significant placer deposits. When two of them returned to Virginia City for supplies, the usual horde of miners followed them back. A town named Helena arose in Last Chance Gulch. Well situated on major transportation routes, well supplied with foodstuffs from the nearby Prickly Pear Valley, and ringed by other mining towns, such as Montana City and Jefferson City, Helena would survive and grow. Next to Alder Gulch, the Last Chance gold deposits proved to be the most extensive in Montana: within four years, the gulch produced an estimated nineteen million dollars.

That same summer of 1864 saw the opening of Confederate Gulch, the third of the most important Montana placer districts. The rush to these diggings, located east of Helena in the Big Belt Mountains, reached boom proportions in 1865. Confederate Gulch miners found gold deposits, like Montana Bar and Diamond Bar, which in terms of yield per acre were richer than any others in the territory. At the crest of the boom Confederate Gulch and its vicinity housed some ten thousand people. Diamond City, the most spectacular of Montana's boom-and-bust gold towns, dominated the area and served as the seat of Meagher County. Although accurate records do not exist, the Confederate Gulch diggings produced roughly ten million to thirty million dollars in gold.

Many other gold camps sprouted up throughout west-central Montana during the middle and late 1860s. Too numerous to mention, they were smaller than those described above but similar in atmosphere and ethnic composition. They lay scattered over a huge, tangled area, from Emigrant on the upper Yellowstone westward to Cedar Creek on the Clark Fork.

Most, of course, played out quickly and then died. Only in favored places like Butte did gold mining lead into big-time industrial mining.

The movement of miners to Montana, sudden as it was, seemed less a stampede than the rushes of "Forty-niners" to California or of "Fifty-niners" to Colorado. The sheer remoteness of the place limited the size of the miners' invasion, and so did the fact that Americans were fighting a Civil War. Nevertheless, even by 1866, enough miners had come to catapult Montana into second place among United States gold producers. Only California ranked higher. According to federal estimates, Montana's population peaked at roughly 28,000 in 1866 and then declined to 21,000–24,000 later in the decade. The 1870 Census, Montana's first, listed the population as a mere 20,595.

The mining profession has always tended to draw together a diverse, cosmopolitan population, and Montana was no exception. Many came from the Midwest and from "border states" like Missouri, but more drifted in directly from mining states and territories like California, Idaho, and Nevada. Because they moved about constantly, frontier prospectors and miners cared little about their neighbors' background or status. Even proper names had small meaning among casual acquaintances, and nicknames predominated. A typical roster of Montana miners might include: Wild Goose Bill, Cayuse George, Nubbins, Roachy, Canary Bird, Old Badger, Frenchy, Dirty Ike, Jewsharp Jack, Whiskey Bill, and Black Jack. Such nicknames still abound in Montana's premier mining camp, Butte.

Most of the prospectors simply looked for placer gold. Erosion and other natural forces had created placer, or surface, gold deposits by disintegrating large veins of ore. In the slow process of geological time, flowing water and glacial ice carried away the particulate gold and deposited it in the beds of ancient or still active streams, where it lay as dust, flakes, or nuggets. Placer gold, scattered about in its natural state, usually required no special processing. Such deposits were "poor man's diggings": men of little wealth or special skill could work them easily. For this reason, new-found placers always attracted a sudden population of young men, motivated by little else than a get-rich-quick impulse. Placer towns, naturally enough, were jerry-built, ephemeral, and hectic places. When production began to decline or news arrived of new strikes elsewhere, the unattached population simply evaporated.

Placer miners, in Montana as elsewhere, stampeded easily. "There is no animal on earth," wrote pioneer Robert Vaughan, "that will stampede quicker, keep on going with the same stubbornness and determination, as a fortune hunter; they are worse than Texas cattle." A classic case of such lemminglike behavior occurred at Helena in the winter of 1866. When

John McClellan, a prospector of exceptional reputation, left town for the Sun River country, hundreds of men immediately followed him, even though no one knew for sure the purpose of his trip. Many of them left in such a hurry that they made no preparations for winter travel. As a result of this misadventure, so many prospectors returned to Helena with frostbite that the residents of the town came to their aid by establishing a hospital.

In its simplest form, placer mining involved little more than scratching the surface. Using simple picks and shovels and usually working in small groups, miners dug up the gold-bearing dirt and then used water to flush the waste material. Small-scale washing could be done with a flat-bottomed washpan, in which the sourdough dissolved and sloshed away the dirt while its gold content fell to the bottom of the pan. Panning was simple and cheap, but it allowed the miner to work only small amounts of gold-bearing soils. So the frontiersmen most often used the pan to prospect and then used other methods to work larger quantities of promising ground. In some places, like Alder Gulch, they had first to remove a heavy overburden in order to get at the gold. This meant digging shafts and tunnels and using hoists to carry the gravel to the surface for washing. It was dangerous work, and some died in cave-ins.

In order to wash larger quantities of dirt, miners often worked in groups and used more elaborate methods. The simplest of these was the rocker, or cradle. Workmen simply filled the upper end of the rocker with soil, then rocked the device while pouring in water. As the material dissolved and floated out of the rocker, gold particles lodged in cleats along the bottom. Where ample water and manpower existed, the "tom" or the "sluice" often supplanted the rocker. The tom, a long wooden trough with perforated sheet metal at the lower end, allowed six or more men to wash large amounts of dirt. Sometimes one hundred, even one thousand feet in length, the sluice employed the same principle of using water and gravity to trap the gold. Oftentimes, twenty or more men worked together on sluices in Montana; sometimes they added mercury to gather the gold by amalgamation.

With each of these steps beyond the simple washpan, miners could afford to work lower and lower grades of ore. In some places, like Confederate Gulch, they turned to the ultimate form of placering, hydraulic mining. Hydraulicking, first developed in the "Mother Lode" country of California, involved the use of high pressure hoses called "little giants" to blast away whole stream banks and beds. The water separated earth from rocks and carried it through long series of sluices. Some hydraulic outfits worked up to one hundred cubic yards of gravel per day. By the late 1860s, as Montana's placers were fading out, hydraulic mining became more and more popular. The 1870 Census found sixty-four such operations employing 434 men in Montana, nearly half of them in Deer Lodge County. Hydraulic mining, like the floating dredges later used to tear up the Ruby River, involved high costs, both in capital and in environmental damage. Expensive ditches and flumes for transporting water to dry gold beds required large investments, and local capitalists like Samuel T. Hauser and Conrad Kohrs provided them. Of course, such operations played havoc with the environment, as they tore up the gulches, scattered rocks in all directions, and flushed huge amounts of silt into lower streams and rivers.

The surface mining of gold, whether by washpan, sluice, or hydraulic method, never lasted for long; it depended on isolated, eroded deposits, not the large and rich "mother lodes" lying imbedded in buried rock. These larger, "quartz" veins required heavy, expensive machinery for reduction and railroads for transportation service. Montana placering reached its peak as early as 1866, when the territory produced $18 million in precious metals. Although the booming Comstock Lode in Nevada then dropped Montana from second to third place among mining regions, annual yields of over $10 million continued for several more years. By the close of the boom decade, though, prospectors were leaving Montana in droves. The 1870 Census revealed only about six hundred placers, employing roughly three thousand men. Gold output continued to decline until 1883, when it amounted to only $1 million; then it began to climb again, this time mainly as a byproduct of industrial silver and copper mining.

THE TRANSPORTATION FRONTIER

As mining began to boom in Montana, transportation routes quickly emerged to link the gold towns and to connect them to the world outside. Before the gold bonanza, of course, trappers and explorers marked out and followed the favored trails of Indians and buffalo. One such route, even in the mid-1850s, ran from Fort Hall on the Oregon Trail northward into the Bitterroot, Beaverhead, and Deer Lodge valleys of southwestern Montana. This trail would later become the major freight and coach road into frontier Montana.

Montana's first really improved route of traffic, the Mullan Road, began to take shape in the late 1850s. In 1853 Governor Isaac I. Stevens, enroute to his post in newly created Washington Territory, led a sizable expedition westward to lay out the course of a possible transcontinental railroad between Minnesota and the Northwest Coast. One of Stevens' most valuable men was a young West Point graduate named Lieutenant John Mullan. While exploring the mountain mazes of the Northern Rockies, Mullan became enthusiastic about the idea of building a road to link Fort Benton on the upper Missouri with the Columbia River above its northward bend near Walla Walla, Washington. Mullan convinced Stevens of the feasibility of his plan, and after gaining election to Congress, Stevens pushed through a bill providing for construction of such a road in 1857.

Mullan, who was designated to build the road, arrived in Washington Territory from the East in the spring of 1858. Local Indian disorders delayed his plans for a year. Then, beginning early in 1859, the first season of construction extended the route across the hill country of eastern Washington, up the Coeur d'Alene River of Idaho, and over Sohon Pass to the St. Regis River in western Montana. During the following year, Mullan continued his road up the Clark Fork and Little Blackfoot rivers and over Mullan Pass to the vicinity of future Helena. The roadbuilders continued in a northeasterly direction, roughly paralleling the Missouri River, and reached Fort Benton on August 1, 1860. Crossing through such rugged, mountainous country, the Mullan Road never became a major thoroughfare. On large sections of its mountain crossings, it was really no more than a pack trail, too rough for consistent wagon use. Nevertheless, the road proved significant to early Montana. It connected the local gold fields, however tenuously, to Idaho and the Columbia River, and it provided a link between Fort Benton and the gold camps lying to the south and west.

During the peak years of the fur trade, steamboats from St. Louis halted at Fort Union, near the mouth of the Yellowstone. But Pierre Chouteau, Jr., and his associates, anxious to secure government contracts for carrying Indian goods and military supplies to the upper Missouri, saw the advantages of attempting to get the boats clear to Fort Benton on the flood waters of early summer. In 1859 Chouteau dispatched the *Chippewa*, a steamboat especially designed for the shallower upstream channel, to carry Indian annuity cargoes to Fort Benton. A fuel shortage forced the *Chippewa* to unload its cargo fifteen miles short of its objective. During the following year, at Mullan's suggestion, the government contracted with Choteau to transport Major George Blake and three hundred soldiers to Fort Benton. Two boats, the *Chippewa* and the *Key West*, arrived at the fort with the troops aboard early in July. Anxious to prove the utility of his road, Mullan then escorted the soldiers over it in a journey of less than two months.

The gold boom which began in 1862 suddenly turned sleepy Fort Benton into a busy river port. Except for 1863, when drought and low water stopped the steamboats downstream at Cow Island, the number of boats docking at Fort Benton increased each year, disgorging passengers, mining equipment, and supplies and loading up stocks of gold bullion, hides, and wool. The traffic reached a peak in 1867, when thirty-nine boats tied up at the Benton docks. Booming little Fort Benton, thirty-five hundred miles from the Gulf of Mexico, was America's most remote port. Major freighting outfits, such as the Montana and Idaho Transportation Line, J. J. Roe and Company, J. T. Murphy, and King and Gillette, shuttled back and forth between Benton and the mining camps. After 1867, dockings at Fort Benton fell off each year until they reached a low of six in 1874. Both the decline of placer mining and the completion of the transcontinental railroad through northern Utah in 1869, which increasingly robbed the port of its traffic, contributed to this result.

After 1875, however, Fort Benton sprang back to life again, this time primarily as a base of supply for the isolated settlements on the Canadian prairies. Fort McLeod, Fort Whoop-Up, and other Canadian outposts could be reached more easily via the Missouri River and the "Whoop-Up Trail," which ran north from Benton, than they could by way of Winnipeg. For a time, this trade meant big business as Fort Benton's aggressive "merchant princes," T. C. Power, I. G. Baker, the Conrad brothers, and W. S. Wetzel, transshipped goods from the river northward over the long Whoop-Up route. They prospered for a time, hauling merchandise and sometimes illegal whiskey for the Indians northward and returning with loads of hides, coal, and produce. The sordid trade on the Whoop-Up Trail fell off in the 1880s, as the Royal Canadian Mounted Police brought law and order to the scene; by then the arrival of railroads was bringing Fort Benton's river commerce to an end.

For residents of Minnesota, Wisconsin, and the upper Midwest, the natural route to the gold mines of the far Northwest lay straight across the broad plains of the Dakotas and Montana. Unfortunately, hostile Sioux Indians made travel across this otherwise easy country very hazardous. So promoters of a "Northern Overland Route," primarily Minnesotans, pushed for and got from Congress a special appropriation in 1862 to provide military protection for wagon trains through the Dakota country. The Minnesota-Montana Road, as it was often called, closely followed the route of the 1853 Stevens expedition through northern Dakota and Montana; it connected to the Mullan Road at Fort Benton. Between 1862 and 1867 eight wagon trains left Minnesota for Idaho and Montana. Four of them were led by the famed wagon master and Montana pioneer James Liberty Fisk, a tough Yankee frontiersman and a capable organizer and propagandist. Significantly, the "Fisk Expeditions" provided the first real transportation link between Montana and the upper Midwest, and they brought an important Yankee-Republican element into early-day Montana.

The famed Oregon Trail, which passed through southern Wyoming and Idaho, was of course the main route of immigration into the Far West, and many Montana-bound pioneers detoured northward from the trail to reach their objective. From a strictly geographical viewpoint, John Bozeman and John Jacobs laid out the most sensible cutoff from the Oregon Trail into Montana in 1863. Their route, the Bozeman Road, left the Oregon Trail near present Casper, Wyoming, flanked northward along the east slopes of the massive Big Horn Mountains, and then headed westward along the Yellowstone River, over Bozeman Pass and across the Gallatin Valley to the gold-bearing areas.

Wagon trains could cross the Bozeman Road with relative ease, but the trail passed through the best buffalo lands of the powerful Sioux Indians. The Sioux turned back the first train that Bozeman and Jacobs tried to lead over the road in 1863, but Bozeman succeeded in bringing a caravan through in 1864. In that same year, friends of Bozeman laid out the town bearing his name in the shadow of Bozeman Pass, and for a few years wagon trains continued to cross the road. The Sioux, however, made such travel extremely dangerous and finally, as we shall see, the federal government abandoned its efforts to keep the road open. Meanwhile, the old mountain man and guide Jim Bridger laid out an alternate route called the "Bridger Cut-off," which passed to the west of the Big Horns through the Wind River Canyon and down to the Yellowstone. Bridger's route had the advantages of bypassing the Sioux menace, but shortages of forage and steep grades made it unpopular.

Montanans resented the government's failure to keep the Bozeman Road open, but in truth the road had lost much of its usefulness by 1869. Completion of the Union Pacific Railroad through southern Wyoming to northern Utah in that year meant that Montana immigrants could travel by rail to the vicinity of Ogden, Utah, and then head directly north into southwestern Montana. Even before the rails reached Utah, the route later known as the Corinne–Virginia City Road or the Salt Lake Trail connected the Mormon settlements to the Montana gold camps. Mormon merchants did a thriving business over this road, and when the Union Pacific reached Corinne, thirty-two miles west of Ogden, that town became the major freighting depot for Montana. Merchants at Walla Walla, Washington, and Portland, Oregon, tried desperately to compete with Utah for the Montana trade by compaigning for improvement of the Mullan Road, but they never had a chance.

Simple geography made the Corinne–Virginia City Road Montana's primary transportation artery, and the road's connection with the Union Pacific allowed Montanans to ship freight and to travel on a regular, predictable basis. The road headed northward through Utah and eastern Idaho over arid plains and plateaus, and it crossed the continental divide into Montana via Monida Pass. Along the Red Rock–Beaverhead River, the road forked, with a branch leading to Bannack and on to the Deer Lodge Valley, while the main stem led to Virginia City and Helena, where it connected with the Mullan Road. An alternate fork led from Alder Gulch to the Gallatin Valley.

Keeping this and other roads in decent shape proved to be nearly impossible. Since the territory had few tax dollars to spend, the legislature resorted to the practice of granting franchises for toll roads, bridges, and ferries. Predictably, this system led to few improvements, poor services, and the gouging of travelers. Freighters, in turn, blamed their extremely high rates on high tolls and the poor condition of roads. Finally, the United States Congress received so many complaints about local roads that it expressly amended the Montana Organic Act so that the legislature could no longer grant such special charters.

At its peak, Montana wagon freighting was a really big-time business, which employed hundreds of men and thousands of draft animals. The Diamond R Freighting Company, founded at Virginia City in 1864 and later based at Helena, came to dominate the local carrying trade. Managed efficiently by the influential C. A. Broadwater and his partners, Matthew Carroll, E. G. Maclay, and George Steel, the Diamond R outfit owned 300 wagons, 350 mules, and 500 yoke of oxen and extended its service throughout the territory. The freighting business involved high overhead, with heavy investments in stock, stables, wagons, and warehouses, but it also returned handsome profits, making fortunes for some of Montana's leading capitalists, such as Broadwater, T. C. Power, and I. G. Baker. By wintering thousands of mules and oxen on the open range, these freighters helped to establish the fact that Montana's grasslands were well suited for livestock production.

Freighting on the Corinne–Virginia City Road or on the Whoop-Up Trail followed general western patterns. In April and May, as the weather moderated and the fields began to green, long lines of mule-trains and bull-trains began to roll out. Mule-skinners usually rode the left wheel mule and controlled the lead animal with a jerkline. Bull-whackers walked alongside the slower, plodding teams of oxen and expertly cracked their whips over the animals while shouting directions of "Gee" and "Haw." Respected for their skills, the mule-skinners and bullwhackers were also legendary as hard drinkers and masters of profanity.

Most often in Montana, a hitch of eight mules or oxen drew three coupled wagons holding a cargo of about twelve thousand pounds, but really big loads employed as many as twelve teams of oxen. Travel on local roads peaked in mid-summer, when low water ended steamboating on the Missouri and released equipment from Fort Benton for the southern run. Generally, it took teams about three weeks to deliver goods from Corinne to Helena. With time out for resting the draft animals, each unit could make three round trips per season. Freighters who gambled on attempting four trips ran the risks of getting mired down in spring mud or being trapped by late spring or early winter snowstorms. The freighters hauled surprisingly large quantities and varieties of goods. In the early 1870s shipments from Corinne averaged between six and seven million pounds annually and included everything from tools, machinery, dry goods, and coal oil to whiskey, fresh fruit, and carefully packed eggs.

Freight rates varied widely, depending upon such factors as the season, local demand, and the availability of men, animals, and equipment. In June 1873, for instance, the Diamond R charged for hauling one hundred pounds from Corinne: $3.75 to Missoula, $4.12 to Deer Lodge, and $5.00 to Bozeman. Sometimes the freighters hauled cargoes of wool, hides, furs, or ores to Utah on their return trips. But often they returned with empty wagons, and this simply meant higher charges on goods brought north to Montana.

Soon after the discovery of gold at Alder Gulch, stage lines began to serve the larger towns, offering regular service to Corinne and to Salt Lake City. As early as autumn of 1863, the A. J. Oliver and the Peabody and Caldwell outfits operated lines between Virginia City and Bannack. During the winter of 1863–64 Oliver opened regular service between Virginia City and Salt Lake. Ben Holladay, the transportation baron of the West, drove out this competition by gaining a government subsidy to carry the mail to Montana; and he, in turn, sold out to Wells, Fargo and Company in 1866. Traveling day and night, the Wells Fargo stages took four and a half or more days to cover the 550 miles between Helena and Corinne. The company charged $145 for this trip, and, even at that, it needed the mail contract to make a profit. Not surprisingly, the stage operators often seemed more interested in the mail than they did in the passengers.

In Montana as elsewhere in the West, handsome Concord coaches served as the standard carriers. Stage companies maintained "swing stations" every ten to thirteen miles for changing horses, and "home stations" every forty to fifty miles where drivers began and ended their runs. Passengers suffered the rigors of cramped quarters, jolting rides, extreme heat and cold, asphyxiating dust, and swarms of insects. But, since the coaches offered the only commercial method of travel, people learned to endure the hardships. Daily stagecoaches from Helena to Fort Benton and Salt Lake did a good business, and the regular mail service that the coaches made possible turned local post offices into community social centers. The arrival of the telegraph in 1866 allowed, of course, even closer contact between Montana and "The States."

Yet, even with these improvements in transportation, Montanans were terribly isolated. Elaborate as it was, wagon freighting often proved very unreliable. Heavy snows during the winter of 1863–64 caused a flour famine in Virginia City which ended in a "Bread Riot." Even in the summer of 1871, scarcity of flour at Deer Lodge drove the price up to fifteen dollars per sack. So long as the territory relied upon roads and waterways for transportation, the local economy would stagnate and the local population would suffer real inconveniences. Montanans of the 1860s and 1870s well understood this fact, and they waited eagerly for the rail connections that would truly join them to the outer world.

THE VIGILANTES

Frontier miners, usually moving ahead of federal authority, had to improvise when it came to law and law enforcement. Since most of them were transients, they had little civic pride or interest, with the predictable result of inefficient, often corrupt government. Once a gold camp had sprouted up, a miners' meeting usually convened to organize a "mining district" and provide basic laws. The Montana gold towns naturally relied upon the precedents of earlier mining frontiers, especially California, when they established their governments and laws. The elected officers of most mining districts included a president, who presided over miners' meetings, a judge who met with the democratic miners' court, a sheriff, and a "recorder," who kept the records of mining claims. Local laws dealt heavily with mining claims—their size, the number that an individual could acquire, the volume of water each could use, and the amount of work necessary to secure claim titles.

Very often, particularly in Montana, this casual, democratic form of government proved woefully inadequate. Mining camps, after all, attracted large numbers of cutthroats, thieves, and fast-buck artists. Sometimes, as in the rush to British Columbia, well-organized government kept lawlessness to a minimum; but more often, as in California, Colorado, and Montana, crime became rampant. When neither federal nor local law provided order, vigilanteism and lynch law raised its head.

The 1862–63 gold rushes to Bannack and Virginia City brought a large, turbulent population to a remote area where the federal government exercised almost no authority. From mid-1862 until the end of 1863, anyone who traveled this area literally risked life and limb. Most of the disorder arose from a violent crew of road agents who followed the gold rush over the Bitterroots from the mining camps around Lewiston, Idaho. Their leader was one of the most amazing of western outlaws, Henry Plummer. Still a young man in 1862, the handsome Plummer combined in one unstable personality qualities of charm and intelligence, but also of psychotic viciousness. His career of murder and lawlessness took him from California and Nevada to Idaho and eventually Montana. Amazingly enough, the engaging Plummer got himself elected sheriff of Bannack, and later his authority extended to newborn Virginia City in 1863. His henchmen, who identified one another by a special knot of the tie and cut of the beard and by the password "I am innocent," received intelligence from Sheriff Plummer and preyed upon gold shipments, stagecoaches, and individual travelers. In its brief career, the Plummer Gang probably murdered over one hundred people.

One brutal killing followed another, but the Bannack–Virginia City populace was slow to react. People neither knew nor trusted one another, and besides, the miners wanted only to work their claims, accumulate some cash, and then leave. Even open and revolting murder went unpunished. In January 1863, for example, two "roughs" named Charles Reeves and William Moore shot up an Indian camp, killing several natives and a white man. A jury voted to banish the murderers for their crime, but a subsequent miners' meeting rescinded even this light sentence.

During the hectic summer of 1863, three of Plummer's cronies, Buck Stinson, Haze Lyons, and Charley Forbes, killed the Chief Deputy Sheriff, D. R. Dillingham, because he had informed on them as outlaws. A Virginia City miners' court acquitted Forbes but convicted Stinson and Lyons and sentenced them to death by hanging. The crowd which made up the miners' court, however, weakened under the influence of weeping women and the outlaws' pleading lawyer. After many of the miners had gone back to work, those remaining voted to reverse the verdict, and both Stinson and Lyons immediately fled.

The beginning of the end for the Plummer Gang came late in 1863 after Plummer's cohort George Ives brutally murdered one Nicholas Thiebalt. When Ives faced trial on December 19, a courageous young attorney named Wilbur Fisk Sanders served as prosecutor. After convincing the jury to return a verdict of guilty, Sanders moved, again successfully, that the hanging sentence be carried out at once, before the crowd could be swayed to leniency. Armed guards surrounded Ives and faced off the crowd, which included many of the condemned man's friends. The hanging took place in less than an hour.

The execution of Ives led directly to formation of a vigilance committee. By now many of the law-abiding majority of citizens, among them a large number of Masons, had become acquainted. And by now, winter weather filled the streets with miners no longer able to work their claims. On December 23, 1863, men from Bannack, Virginia City, and Nevada City met secretly and organized a vigilance committee based on the California model. They drew up an oath, regulations, and bylaws, and appointed an executive committee and captains to head up local committees. The key officers included Paris S. Pfouts, president; James Williams, executive officer; Wilbur Sanders, official prosecutor; and John S. Lott, treasurer. As a warning signal and symbol of recognition, they used the numbers "3-7-77" (sometimes 3-11-77), the exact meaning of which is still a subject of debate.

Ably led by tough and fearless James Williams, the Montana Vigilantes destroyed the Plummer Gang in a surprisingly short time. Their first two victims were G. W. Brown, secretary of the gang, and Erastus "Red" Yeager. Yeager, who seemed to have a death wish, revealed the identities of gang leaders and then resigned himself contentedly to his own hanging. His confession allowed a rapid crackdown on the criminals. Between January 4 and February 3, 1864, the vigilantes tracked down and hanged twenty-four men. Vigilantes from Bannack and Virginia City arrested Plummer and his lieutenants Buck Stinson and Ned Ray on January 10 and hanged them immediately. While Stinson and Ray swore and resisted, Plummer wept and pleaded for his life, to no avail. All three were strung up at once, and the hanging party departed, "leaving the corpses," as one contemporary wrote, "stiffening in the icy blast."

On January 14, five key members of the gang were seized and summarily hanged in Virginia City. Among them was Boone Helm, reputedly the most violent man in the area. Standing with the noose about his neck, Helm looked casually at the still lurching corpse of one of his pals and remarked: "Kick away, old fellow; I'll be in Hell with you in a minute." Then, just before the rope broke his neck, Helm shouted: "Every man for his principles—hurrah for Jeff Davis! Let her rip!" Some of the road agents fled the territory. Others went to outlying areas like Hell Gate (Missoula) and the Deer Lodge and Gallatin valleys, but the vigilantes tracked many of them down and hanged them on the spot. In only a month and a half, the vigilantes had ended the road agent menace.

Ever since the 1860s Montanans have dwelt upon these dramatic happenings and honored the vigilantes as men larger than life. State highway patrolmen wear the emblem "3-7-77" on their shoulder patches, and Helena named one of its athletic fields "Vigilante Stadium." Actually, however, we know precious little about the secret operations of the vigilantes. Two prominent Montanans, both of them participants in these events, wrote highly influential accounts of what happened, but both men wrote to justify the vigilantes. Thomas J. Dimsdale's *The Vigilantes of Montana,* published serially in the Virginia City *Montana Post* in 1865, and then as Montana's first book in 1866, argued that "swift and terrible retribution is the only preventative of crime, while society is organizing in the far West," and that the "positively awful expense and delay" of established law and order could not be tolerated. Nathaniel P. Langford's *Vigilante Days and Ways,* published later, in 1890, followed a similar tack. More recently, some scholars have questioned the actions of the vigilantes and have raised doubts about the relability of Dimsdale and Langford. J. W. Smurr, for instance, faults the vigilantes for bypassing the miners' courts and argues plausibly that both Dimsdale and Langford wrote to counter widespread local criticism of vigilante deeds.

Certainly, the incredible lawlessness at Bannack–Virginia City called for some action, and most of the convictions of January 4–February 3, 1864, seem to have been necessary and appropriate. But the dangers always inherent in secret trials and mob action sometimes led to excesses, for instance, the execution of Joe Pizanthia at Bannack in January, 1864. Pizanthia, locally known as "The Greaser," came to Montana with a bad reputation, but the vigilantes had no proof of his being a local road agent. When a vigilante group approached his cabin, Pizanthia shot two of them as they entered his door. The enraged crowd outside then blasted the cabin with a howitzer, dragged out the badly wounded Pizanthia, hanged him, riddled his corpse with gunfire, and then burned it on a funeral pyre made from his cabin. In another case, which caught the fancy of Mark Twain, the vigilantes apprehended a local hell-raiser named "Captain" J. A. Slade; even though Slade had no apparent connection with the road agents, they hanged him dramatically and quickly, before his attractive wife could arrive on the scene and change people's minds.

Perhaps the greatest problem with vigilanteism was that of ending it once regular courts began to function. When he opened Montana Territory's first official court, at Virginia City in December 1864, Judge Hezekiah L. Hosmer acknowledged the necessity of past vigilante actions but added a note of caution:

> Let us give to every man, how aggravated soever his crime, the full benefit of the freeman's right—an impartial trial by jury. Vigilantes and courts—and all good men can cooperate in fulfilling the grand purpose of the criminal law; that of bringing offenders to justice, without violating any of its provisions; but the very first element in such a warfare against crime, must be the general recognition of courts of law, as the great conservator of peace and safety.

Not everyone heeded the good judge's advice. Alder Gulch vigilantes hanged James Brady in June 1864, then learned afterward that his murder "victim" was recovering nicely from his wounds. In Helena, where the "Hanging Tree" became a local landmark, a number of controversial hangings, like those of James Daniels and John Keene, aroused considerable controversy. On another occasion, a respected and law-abiding young man, enroute from Bannack to Salt Lake City, overtook and rode along with a stranger who, unbeknownst to him, was a horse thief. Vigilantes, who were trailing the thief, caught up with them and promptly hanged both men. Such incidents led to mounting public anger at unauthorized vigilante groups. In March 1867 miners from the Highland District of Alder Gulch posted a notice in the local paper that they would retaliate on a five-to-one basis against any further vigilante executions. Clearly vigilanteism was becoming a menace. It soon faded into memory and folklore.

THE URBAN FRONTIER

The mining frontier of the Far West differed sharply from the normal pattern of America's westward movement. Ordinarily, as in the westward advances of trappers, stockmen, and farmers, towns and cities arose only after the hinterland had been occupied and only in order to serve a rural population. But on the mining frontier, this process reversed itself. Instant "cities" sprang up along forlorn gulches, often in extremely remote locations, and then the surrounding countryside attracted farmers and ranchers to feed the towns. This was, indeed, an "urban frontier." As historian William J. Trimble aptly put it, these ugly and isolated towns seemed to be "ganglia of civilization, comparable to Roman Colonies."

To the boom-and-bust mining towns came not only miners, but also merchants, freighters, saloon-keepers, gamblers, and prostitutes. Mobile young men made up most of the population; one encountered few children, old people, or "respectable" women on the streets of the mining town. Precisely because of their scarcity, in fact, women enjoyed special status here and throughout the Mountain West. For this and other reasons, they would win their political rights here earlier than in the previously settled parts of the nation.

Mining towns were cosmopolitan places. The miners, generally poor and unpretentious, tolerated most ethnic groups, with the glaring exception of Indians, Negroes, and Chinese. In contrast to Colorado, Arizona, or the Black Hills, Montana's gold rush centered in an area of only slight Indian population, and it did not lead to a major war with the local natives. Nonetheless, Indian "scares" were common in Montana, and Indians who came in contact with the miners were often mistreated. Black Americans, freed from slavery in the same year as the discovery of Alder Gulch, did not come in large numbers to early Montana; but enough of them showed up in Virginia City to establish a "Pioneer Social Club" there in January 1867. Despite their limited numbers, the Negroes sometimes became the focus of heated public debate. Towns like Helena and White Sulphur Springs passed Jim Crow laws which openly discriminated against them.

The largest, and most sorely afflicted, minority in the gold camps were the Chinese. According to the 1870 Census, 2,070 Chinese resided in Montana; at Butte and Alder Gulch, they made up over one-third of the total population at one time. They drifted with the mining frontier from California to the interior, and their exotic customs and willingness to work for much less than "normal" pay usually led to harsh reactions. In all the Montana mining towns the Chinese suffered job discrimination. Whites tolerated them only so long as they did menial work, operated restaurants and laundries, and mined "worked over" placers that the whites had abandoned.

At one point the Montana Legislature even prohibited Chinese ownership of mining claims. United States Commissioner of Mining Statistics Rossiter Raymond correctly labeled this a foolish move, for the territory benefited when Chinese miners worked marginal diggings that the whites had left as useless. Pointing to the "amoral and filthy habits" of the Chinese and their "extreme carelessness as to fires," the white populace of Virginia City forced them to live in restricted areas. Much of this white resentment stemmed not only from race prejudice but also from the fact that the arrival of the Chinese usually signaled the decline of a mining area. Few of the Chinese remained in Montana. Most returned to their homeland or to the Pacific Coast.

Life in the mining camps was hard and unromantic. Men worked from sunrise to sunset six days a week in the warm season, and then usually faced unemployment and boredom when the long winters made placering impossible. During the busy half of the year, the miners left their claims only on Sundays. Most of them, though, enjoyed the Sabbath not as a day of rest but as an opportunity to transact business, attend court, and socialize in town. Sunday in the mining camps was always the busiest day of the week.

A surprisingly small percentage of the Montana miners actually owned their own claims. Most of them worked for wages, and wages in the remote gold camps were excellent. Men skilled as blacksmiths, carpenters, and butchers often gave up their hopes of quick riches at placering and returned to their original crafts for wages which ran up to fourteen dollars per day. Naturally, these high rates of pay did little more than meet the incredibly high cost of living in such faraway places. When improved transportation brought down living costs, pay scales fell to the more normal level of three to seven dollars per day.

As usual, the road to riches on the mining frontier lay not in manual labor but in investment. Shrewd and enterprising young capitalists like William A. Clark and Samuel T. Hauser grasped instinctively the wisdom of the old frontier adage: "It is good to be shifty in a new country." Some did well speculating in townsites and real estate, but the instability of gold camps made this a risky business. The buying and selling of claims was more lucrative, more hectic, and very often less honest. Since claim-holders often "salted" their property with false indications of gold, buyers had to beware. Any prospector could salt his claim by loading shotgun shells with gold particles and firing them into a stream bank, producing the appearance of rich, gold-bearing sands. Another slick scheme was the "freeze-out." Local operators would convince outside investors to buy into a mine, then take out only worthless ore until the outsiders sold out at a loss to their "partners" on the scene. The freeze-out became such common practice at Alder Gulch that eastern capital began to avoid the area.

The miners suffered many hardships. Few of them, for instance, enjoyed an adequate year-around diet. The mining camps usually had ample supplies of beef and wild game, salt pork and beans. Within a year or two, the bigger towns attracted enough farmers to supply them with potatoes and vegetables, but only at high prices and unpredictable intervals. Fruit and eggs, often imported from great distances, were rare, highly treasured, and costly. So were breadstuffs. When flour supplies ran out or became very scarce, prices soared so high that whole towns went on straight meat diets for long periods of time.

Isolated, eating poorly, and dwelling in unsanitary conditions, the urban pioneers lived in constant dread of accident, illness, and disease. Epidemics of typhoid, diphtheria, smallpox, and scarlet fever claimed many victims, especially children; and for much of the population, dysentery became an unpleasant fact of life. Doctors, especially competent ones, were few and far between, and dentists often simply traveled from town to town. Under such conditions many a young man returned to the States broken in body and spirit. The tough realities of mining camp life contributed to the mobility of the population: anything new seemed better than one's surroundings.

Some of the restless miners left their claims during the long and idle months of winter, but most stayed and kept an eye on their property. For those who remained, escape from sheer boredom presented a real challenge. Some, as on all frontiers, turned to drinking and dissipation. The ever-present saloon offered escape and male companionship, sometimes games and gambling. Nearly as ubiquitous as the saloons, "hurdy-gurdy" houses flourished as places where men could buy both a drink and a dance with a woman. Naturally, a thin line separated the hurdy-gurdies from the houses of ill repute that served every mining camp of any size. Most often, as the mining camp grew to maturity, women, ministers, and business leaders crusaded to close down the red light districts. Their efforts seldom succeeded for any length of time, but the reformers had better luck in doing away with the "opium dens" that the Chinese, as well as many whites, frequented.

Contrary to Hollywood mythology, though, the mining towns witnessed little, if any, more drinking, gambling, whoring, and violence than most other places in the nation. The majority of residents, anxious to improve their positions in life, behaved with propriety. Homespun music and dancing, especially to a fiddle, seemed the miners' favorite diversion. Picnics and weddings drew large crowds, and everyone celebrated the major holidays, the most festive ones being July Fourth, Christmas–New Year's, and

St. Patrick's Day. Aside from hunting and fishing, the most popular sports included sledding, skiing, and ice skating, as well as foot and horse races, rock drilling contests and baseball. Boxing matches drew big crowds and large wagers. In January 1865 a tremendous Virginia City crowd watched one of the longest fights in history when Con Orem and Hugh O'Neil struggled to a 185-round draw.

Considering the handicaps of their situation, the mining towns displayed a hearty appetite for cultural refinement. The theater often provided evening entertainment. Shortly after the first strikes at Alder Gulch, Jimmy Martin staged melodramas and comedies in Virginia City. In 1867 Martin persuaded Denver's famous Jack Langrishe to come to Montana; and during the next three fall and winter seasons, Langrishe and his troupe performed regularly at Virginia City's People's Theater and at Helena's Wood Street Theater. The audiences tremendously enjoyed ornate melodramas and farces, but, interestingly, they liked Shakespeare best of all.

The majority of mining town residents spent far more time with books, magazines, and newspapers than they did with drink and "loose" women. Books and magazines passed from hand to hand until they literally fell apart, and when newspapers arrived, weeks late from the States, homesick miners read them over and over again. The famous Stonewall Building at Virginia City symbolized public tastes in the mining West. Although the Gem Saloon occupied the lower floor, the second story housed a reading room where subscribing members enjoyed all forms of reading matter, as well as chess, checkers, and dominos. Similarly, the Helena Library Association, organized in 1868, enjoyed wide support.

Obviously, the forces of stability and civilization came early to the "wild and woolly" mining frontier. Fraternal groups, most notably the Masons, not only provided benevolences for their members but also worked for law and order, community improvement, and cultural and charitable activities. As always, main street merchants campaigned tirelessly to improve their towns; and newspaper editors, anxious to increase circulation by boosting the community, beat the drum incessantly for civic improvement. The *Montana Post* of Virginia City, Montana's first newspaper, was edited by schoolteacher Thomas J. Dimsdale and spoke constantly for the "law and order" virtues of vigilanteism and the Republican party.

As on most frontiers, the church and the school provided the two primary forces of civilization. Roman Catholic priests, already active among the western Montana Indians, moved immediately into the nearby mining camps. Father Joseph Giorda came to Virginia City in the fall of 1863 and had a chapel ready in time to celebrate Christmas. Among Protestants, the Methodists and Episcopalians arrived first. The Methodists, always on the vanguard of the frontier, were conducting services at Bannack by early

1864; and the Episcopal Church of Montana took root in 1867, when Bishop Daniel Tuttle and Reverend E. N. Goddard came to Virginia City. The Baptists and Presbyterians, two other Protestant denominations usually active on the frontier, got off to a slow start in Montana, in large part because their churches were so bitterly divided by the Civil War. Churches failed really to thrive in most gold camps until women and civic leaders arrived in large enough numbers to lend them strength.

Considering how few children there were in the mining camps, schools appeared at remarkably early dates. Subscription schools, where parents had to pay directly for their children's education, appeared first; Kate Dunlap ran one of these at Nevada City, and Lucia Darling operated another at Bannack. Soon after the 1864 creation of Montana Territory, the first legislature took the normal step of providing for public education by authorizing the county commissioners to levy property taxes for schools. Virginia City became the first community to set up a public school district. Education began there early in 1866, and the schoolhouse opened its doors during that summer. Governor Sidney Edgerton appointed English-born schoolteacher and author-editor Thomas J. Dimsdale as Montana's first Superintendent of Public Instruction, but Dimsdale died of illness in 1866. The legislature soon made this office elective. After gaining election to the post in 1868, Superintendent Thomas Campbell filed his first report, showing 704 children enrolled in twenty-five schools throughout the territory.

In contrast to their success at founding schools and libraries, the mining towns faced other social challenges more difficult to master. Gumbo mud and blowing dust often made traffic even on main streets almost impossible. In boom towns of uncertain longevity, the citizens seldom chose to tax themselves in order to build decent water and sanitation facilities. Since they relied on unpredictable property taxes for revenue, local governments were usually anemic and hence unable to take much positive action. Fire, especially, posed a constant, frightening threat. Six major fires, for example, gutted Helena between February 1869 and January 1874. The last of these destroyed one of the town's most prized possessions, the library and archives of the ten-year-old Montana Historical Society.

To put it simply, the transient population of early Montana took little pride in their towns and little interest in developing the territory as a whole. Most of them had no special intention of staying here, but only desired to "make a pile" and head back for the States. The mining towns, they well knew, would soon disappear: why worry about improving them? So the miners, at least most of them, moved on—to the Black Hills gold rush, to a life of farming in the West, or, as in most cases, back home to the East. And their towns became ghosts. Only Butte and Helena lived on to become major Montana communities.

CHAPTER V

Montana Territory

Eᴀᴄʜ of the United States of America, except for the original thirteen, Texas, and California, was first organized as a "territory" before achieving admittance to the Union as a full-fledged state. Originating with the famous Ordinances of 1785 and 1787, the territorial system provided the expanding United States with a method of governing frontier areas until they gained sufficient population and economic maturity to qualify for equality with the older states of the Union. Territories represented a sort of compromise between colonies and states. They had limited powers of legislative self-government, but their executive and judicial officers were appointed by the federal government. Not surprisingly, residents of these frontier territories usually demanded quick admission to statehood, so that they could gain full control of their local governments. Until they had such control, federal supervision over their local affairs caused constant frustration. In Montana, this time of frustration lasted for twenty-five years, from the creation of Montana Territory in 1864 until the admission of the territory to statehood in 1889.

Tʜᴇ Bɪʀᴛʜ ᴏꜰ "Mᴏɴᴛᴀɴᴀ"

The mining boom of the 1860s brought the first large white population, and thus the first demands for government, to the vast empty region that became Montana. Prior to this time, the large eastern and small western sectors of future Montana had simply been attached to huge frontier territories whose centers of population lay hundreds, even thousands of miles away. The eastern two-thirds of Montana, which is the far northwestern corner of the Mississippi-Missouri Basin, had been joined to a number of different territories. It formed the far extremity of Indian Territory until 1805; then was part of Louisiana Territory until 1812, Missouri Territory until 1821, a general Great Plains "Indian Country" until 1854, and Nebraska Territory until 1861, when it became the eastern sector of newly created Dakota Territory.

The northwest corner of Montana lies, of course, on the outskirts of a different geographic province, the Columbia Basin. The United States and Great Britain held this area, known then as the "Oregon Country," under a joint occupancy agreement until 1846, when they agreed to extend the 49th parallel boundary to the Pacific as the dividing line between the United States and Canada. Then, the western portion of future Montana became the easternmost outskirts of Oregon Territory from 1848 until 1853 and of Washington Territory from 1853 until 1861.

It was, quite by accident, the advance of the mining frontier that caused the eastern and western halves of today's Montana to be joined together in one political unit. In 1861–62, as miners began flocking into the newly opened gold fields of present-day north-central Idaho, the demand arose for creation of a new territory in the Northern Rockies. Congress responded in March of 1863 by creating Idaho Territory. Carved out of Washington, Dakota, and Nebraska territories, Idaho embraced an enormous area, including all of present Idaho and Montana and most of Wyoming. Its capital lay on the far western border at Lewiston. Significantly, the creation of Idaho brought the two halves of Montana within a common boundary for the first time.

Idaho Territory was a geographic impossibility from the day of its birth. The massive ranges of the Rocky Mountains divided it in half, and a thousand miles separated Lewiston in the west from the far eastern extremities. Even in 1863, at the time of the territory's inception, Idaho's population was shifting rapidly eastward, across the continental divide to the mining camps on the upper Missouri. With good reason, the Bannack–Virginia City miners felt that Lewiston, hundreds of miles away over endless, snow-clogged mountain passes, could never govern them properly. The outrages of the Plummer Gang tended to prove their point. They began agitating for the creation of a new territory, to be split away from Idaho along the crests of the Rockies.

Fortunately for their cause, the newly appointed chief justice of Idaho arrived at Bannack in September 1863. Judge Sidney Edgerton, a former Ohio congressman, unable to proceed to Lewiston because of the approach of winter, soon learned that the governor of Idaho had snubbed him by assigning him to the faraway judicial district lying east of the divide, even though he was, after all, the territorial chief justice. Both Edgerton and his nephew, vigilante leader Wilbur Fisk Sanders, took up the crusade to divide Idaho Territory. As Edgerton knew the President and many congressmen personally, the area miners chose to send him to Washington,

D.C., to press their case for a new territory. Carrying two thousand dollars in gold with him, Edgerton headed eastward in January 1864. Meanwhile, the Idaho Legislature at Lewiston agreed to the split and obligingly petitioned Congress to carve a new territory named Jefferson out of Idaho, with the dividing line along the continental divide and the 113th meridian. This would have located Idaho's new eastern border just west of the Deer Lodge Valley.

Arriving in Washington, Edgerton consulted with President Lincoln and found him agreeable to the idea of a new territory in the Rockies. More importantly, Edgerton discovered that his friend and fellow Ohioan, Congressman James M. Ashley, had already begun work on a bill to form the new territory. Since Ashley chaired the House Committee on Territories, he had the power to make his wishes felt. Ashley's political muscle and reports of the area's wealth of gold, which Edgerton reported very influential "in such a mercenary age as ours," pushed the bill speedily through Congress.

While the bill lay in committee, Edgerton and his allies broke with the Idaho Legislature by maneuvering the new territory's northwestern boundary three degrees to the west. This meant that the Idaho-Montana border would, generally speaking, follow the Bitterroot summits northward to the Canadian boundary and that Montana would take a 130-mile-wide bite out of northern Idaho. In this manner, Idaho lost the handsome Flathead, upper Clark Fork, and middle Kootenai valleys to its new neighbor. The arrangement reduced the width of northern Idaho by three-fourths, leaving it an awkward "panhandle," cut off from the southern portion of the territory by the rugged Salmon River Mountains. Idaho petitioned Congress, with no success, to restore these "stolen" lands. The Lewiston area even advocated establishing yet another territory named Columbia, which would join together today's western Montana, northern Idaho, and eastern Washington; but this plan got nowhere. So, by circumstance and scheming, the new territory emerged with its jagged western border.

Congress, preoccupied with the Civil War, devoted little time to the matter of founding yet another western commonwealth. The one serious threat to passage of the bill arose when the Senate voted to force the new territory to give the vote to Negroes. Even though there were few blacks in the Northern Rockies, this explosive issue caused a deadlock with the House of Representatives. The two houses of Congress finally compromised by restricting the vote to citizens of the United States, thus leaving the newly freed Negroes without a guarantee of the ballot on the distant mining frontier.

In a lighter vein, both the House and the Senate debated the name that

Congressman Ashley had placed upon his creation. That name, "Montana," no doubt stemmed from the Latin or Spanish adjective meaning "mountainous." It first appeared as a place name in 1858, when one Josiah Hinman gave it to a small mining town near Pike's Peak. The town soon died, but the name "Montana" lived on. Governor Denver of Kansas Territory remembered Montana and suggested it to powerful Senator Stephen A. Douglas as a possible name for a future territory in the Rockies. Ashley may or may not have heard the name from Douglas; at any rate, he picked it up somewhere and became enamored of it. After trying, unsuccessfully, to give the name to what became Idaho in 1863, Ashley determined to apply it to Idaho's new neighbor.

When Republican Ashley's Montana Bill reached the floor of the House, the Democrats began harassing him about the name. The Democrats suggested dropping it and substituting the title "Jefferson," in order to honor the founder of the Democratic party, or even "Douglas," to commemorate the prominent Democratic senator from Illinois. Ashley and the Republicans, of course, would have none of that. Congressman Cox of Ohio suggested the Indian name "Shoshone," but this was scuttled when the Colorado delegate pointed out that Shoshone meant "Snake." Such a word had unfortunate implications during the Civil War, when pro-Confederates from the North were called "Copperheads." The debate reached the point of true absurdity when Representative Washburn suggested the name "Abyssinia," taunting the Republicans about their fondness for Negroes.

Although Ashley won his battle in the House, two weeks later the Senate raised another challenge to "Montana." Again, as happened in the House, several members felt the classical name Montana inappropriate and argued that an Indian word would be better. As no one could suggest one with any relevance to the place, they too settled upon Ashley's title, but only after this illuminating exchange:

> MR. HOWARD: I was equally puzzled when I saw the name in the bill. . . . I was obliged to turn to my old Latin dictionary. . . . It is a very classical word, pure Latin. It means a mountainous region, a mountainous country.
> MR. WADE: Then the name is well adapted to the Territory.
> MR. HOWARD: You will find that it is used by Livy and some of the other Latin historians, which is no small praise.
> MR. WADE: I do not care anything about the name. If there was none in Latin or in Indian I suppose we have a right to make a name; certainly just as good a right to make it as anybody else. It is a good name enough.

Montana it became, and Montana it has remained. Following approval by Congress, President Lincoln signed into law the bill creating Montana Territory on May 26, 1864.

THE POLITICAL SITUATION

The infant territory of Montana faced severe political and governmental problems during its first half-dozen years. Some difficulties stemmed from the territorial system itself. Others arose from the fact that the territory was born, after all, during a civil war. In drafting the 1864 Organic Act which established Montana Territory, Congress set up the system of government which had become standard for most western territories by this time. It placed law-making power in the hands of Montana citizens by allowing them to elect a bicameral legislature. The upper house of the legislature was a seven-member "council," and the lower house a thirteen-member "assembly." In addition, the Organic Act authorized the citizenry to elect one nonvoting "delegate" to the United States House of Representatives, who would speak for their interests.

The Organic Act, however, limited these powers of self-government by providing that the executive and judicial officers of the territory should be appointed by the President of the United States. The principal executive offices consisted of the powerful governor, who also served as Indian superintendent and commander of the militia, and the secretary, who kept official records and assumed command in the governor's absence. Significantly, the secretary held the exclusive power of authorizing the expenditure of federal funds in the territory. The judicial officers were the chief justice and the two associate justices, who combined to make up the territorial supreme court. In Montana, as in most places, this system fulfilled its basic purpose: it allowed a measure of self-government while keeping the area under tight federal control. But the system also led, notably in Montana, to wide-open struggles between the locally elected legislature and the federally appointed judges and executive officials.

Obviously, the Americans who followed the mining frontier to Montana brought their political beliefs with them. To a surprising extent, this simple fact meant that here, on this most remote frontier, the fierce political feuds of the Civil War echoed resoundingly. These first Montanans came from every section of the country. The first census taken in the territory, which was registered in 1870, revealed a population of 20,595. Of these, the largest bloc—7,371—came originally from the northern states. Another 2,272 were western born and 7,979 hailed from foreign lands. A total of 891 came from the states of the Confederacy, while another 2,060 were from Missouri and other "Border States." Since these population numbers were posted when the mining boom was in its decline, they do not necessarily indicate the makeup of the mining rush at its mid-1860s peak.

In their political affiliations, a solid majority of Montanans adhered to the Democratic party, while a strong minority were Republicans. Each party, in turn, consisted of a moderate and more extreme faction. The Republicans, of course, were the party of President Lincoln, the party of the Union. The more moderate wing of the Republican party included those who, agreeing with Lincoln, believed mainly in preserving the Union but did not wish to crush the South irreparably. They often called themselves "Unionists" and welcomed the support of northern Democrats. The more extreme Republicans, sometimes referred to as "Radical" or "Black" Republicans, demanded the crushing of the South and equality for Negroes. In Montana, the Radical Republicans wielded considerable power. They were led by Wilbur Fisk Sanders, of vigilante fame, and by Sidney Edgerton, whom Lincoln named to be the first governor of the territory.

The more powerful Democratic party showed a similar division between moderates and extremists. On the one hand there were many Union Democrats, who came mainly from the North and supported the Union, even while opposing the Republicans. On the other hand Montana attracted some Democrats from the South, and many others from states like Missouri which bordered the South. These individuals, along with "Copperhead" Democrats—that is, northerners who sympathized with the South—made up a strong and vocal minority in Montana. They hated the Radical Republicans, and especially they hated the idea of Black equality. The Confederate sympathizers never came near gaining a majority of the Montana vote, but they sometimes raised enough hell to give that impression.

During Montana's first years, which coincided with the close of the Civil War, the more extreme wings of each party thundered at one another and echoed the issues of the war. Radical Republicans, like editor Thomas Dimsdale of the Virginia City *Montana Post* and the Fisk brothers of the *Helena Herald,* blasted all Democrats as disloyal rebels. The venomous Dimsdale referred to "the arch traitor Jeff Davis" and concluded that Democrats "would vote for the Devil himself if his name were on the Democratic ticket." To Dimsdale the issues seemed simple: "There are but two parties now in this republic—patriots and traitors." N. P. Langford, another zealous Republican, wrote inaccurately to Washington, D.C., that he "was in a Territory more disloyal as a whole, than Tennessee or Kentucky ever were. Four fifths of our citizens were *openly declared* Secessionists." Pro-Southern Democrats replied in kind, branding their opponents as "Black Republicans" and "nigger lovers." Their leading newspaper, the *Rocky Mountain Gazette* of Helena, spoke often and heatedly of the race issue and used it as a club against the Republicans: "All the Irish have left them. The Germans (naturally Democratic and lovers of liberty) are leaving them. They now place their last hope on the irrepressible nigger." Racists from North and South were strong enough in early Montana to prohibit Negroes from testifying against whites in court and, in the following statute passed by the first legislature, to ban them from voting in school elections: "Every white male inhabitant over the age of twenty-one years, who shall have paid or be liable to pay any district tax, shall be a legal voter at any school meeting, and no other person shall be allowed to vote." Although some historians have exaggerated the role of Confederate sympathizers in early Montana, the fact remains that they were numerous and powerful enough to challenge the Unionists.

CIVIL WAR POLITICS

It was this volatile political situation that faced Montana's first governor, Sidney Edgerton, when he returned to the territory in mid-1864. Edgerton immediately chose Bannack to be the temporary capital and ordered a hurried census in order to hold elections in the autumn. Since the entire executive and judicial branches of their government were federally appointed, the Montana electorate would vote only for members of the two-house legislature and the man who was to be their delegate to Congress.

Montana's first political campaign centered on the race for delegate to Congress, the only official chosen by all voters in the territory. For this office the Republicans ran their most prestigious man, strong-willed Wilbur Fisk Sanders. Sanders enjoyed the advantages of his fame as a vigilante and the support of his uncle, Governor Edgerton. His Democratic adversary was Samuel McLean of Pennsylvania, a large, portly man who drank whiskey by the barrel. Backed by the only newspaper at that time in the territory, the *Montana Post*, Sanders and Edgerton ran a tough, free-swinging campaign. They attacked all Democrats as Copperheads and traitors and held themselves up as the only real guardians of the Union, but their intemperate strategy failed badly. In the election of October 24, 1864, Sanders lost to McLean, who carried the big Democratic counties of Madison and Jefferson. Otherwise, the Republicans held their own. The election produced an even political balance in the legislature: the Council went Unionist (Republican) by one vote, and the House went Democratic, also by one vote.

Clearly, if he wished to succeed, Governor Edgerton had to find a way to work with the Democratic majority in Montana. But for this rigid Ohio abolitionist, who had already antagonized the Democrats in the recent election, such compromise was impossible. When he addressed the opening session of the legislature, Edgerton rubbed more salt in the wound by referring to former Democratic President James Buchanan as an "imbecile" and by insisting that all legislators must swear to the "Iron Clad Oath," which Congress had drawn up for use in the defeated Confederate states. In taking the oath, one simply swore that he had never borne arms against the United States government. It needlessly offended the Democrats and forced one lawmaker, a Confederate veteran named J. H. Rogers, to resign his seat rather than perjure himself. The governor's actions guaranteed a continuation of political warfare, but the Democrats seemed willing enough to work with him in considering badly needed legislation. The first legislature passed a large volume of hastily written laws, dealing with such urgent matters as roads, public schools, irrigation, and mining.

Sidney Edgerton faced many frustrating problems in his new position, a number of them caused by federal negligence. Amidst the chaos of the closing months of the Civil War and the aftermath of Lincoln's assassination, faraway places like Montana were largely forgotten in Washington. Key federal positions in Montana remained unfilled for months. During its first sixteen months, Montana had no territorial secretary. Since only the secretary could sign federal warrants, this meant that no federal funds could be spent. Edgerton had simply covered many territorial expenses with his own funds, assuming that he would soon be reimbursed.

When a secretary, Thomas F. Meagher, finally arrived in late September 1865, Edgerton hurriedly turned over his duties to him as acting governor and left for the East. The governor departed in order to look after both his own personal affairs in Ohio and Montana's concerns in Washington. Unfortunately for himself, Edgerton neglected to obtain a leave of absence before he left. When he later sought to obtain a leave, federal authorities refused it and forced Edgerton to resign as governor of Montana early in 1866. Apparently the governor lost his job for two reasons: (1) such unexcused absences by territorial officials had become an open farce, and (2) the new President, Andrew Johnson, hated Radical Republicans like Sidney Edgerton. Thus, after a brief and hectic term, Montana's first chief executive left the scene, never to return.

Edgerton's absence led to one of the most chaotic periods in Montana's political history. At the center of the chaos and controversy stood the territorial secretary and acting governor, Thomas Francis Meagher. This colorful character, whose equestrian statue now stands before the state capitol, was a brash adventurer who came here with an international reputation and an appetite for even greater glories. Descended from a wealthy Irish family, young Meagher became a leading figure in the Irish independence movement, a noted orator, and an ally of the famous Daniel O'Connell. He narrowly escaped execution by the British because of his revolutionary activities and was banished instead to the penal colony of Tasmania. After escaping from Tasmania, Meagher came eventually to New York, and he soon rose to prominence there as a leader among the thousands of Irish immigrants in that city. During the Civil War, he became famous as the organizer and commanding general of the Irish Brigade. This hard charging outfit saw fierce action at such battles as Malvern Hill and Antietam. It was practically annihilated in the suicidal charge at Fredericksburg and was later disbanded. Meagher's fame and military record led President Andrew Johnson to appoint him secretary of Montana Territory in 1865.

As acting governor in Edgerton's absence, Meagher faced an angry situation in Montana. At first, both political parties saw him as a friend. He was a Union Democrat, and local Democrats welcomed him as one of their own. But he was also a Union general who had fought the rebels, and he had received his job from a Unionist administration. Meagher sided at first with the Republicans. He informed his immediate superior, the United States secretary of state, that the Montana Democrats consisted largely of "turbulent men," pro-Confederates who could not be trusted. Only a few weeks later, though, Meagher suddenly turned about and allied himself to the Democrats. He notified Washington that he had earlier been mistaken and "that these very Southerners and Southern sympathizers are now as heartily to be relied upon by the Administration . . . as any other men in the Territory."

Most likely, the acting governor shifted his loyalty to the Democrats because they were the majority and were heavily Irish. He could build a political future as their leader. However, he also had a falling out with the local Republican hierarchy, who included such Radicals as Wilbur Sanders and Judge L. E. Munson. Meagher told his superiors in Washington of "the bitter personal animosity of the ultra Republicans who calculated on my being a miserable and mischievous tool in their hands." As for the Republicans, they never forgave Meagher for deserting them. They sent wild complaints to Washington, charging that the acting governor has "been in fact drunk nearly everyday since he has been in the territory" and "that the executive office is a place of rendezvous for the vilest prostitutes and *they* state the fact publickly [sic] and *boast* of their profitable *intercourse* with him" (italics in original letter).

At this time, 1865–66, arose two crucial issues that sharply divided the Democrats from the Republicans, and on each of them Meagher shifted from the Republican to the Democratic position. The most pressing problem involved the legislature. The first territorial legislature had adjourned without passing a redistricting bill that would establish districts for the next legislative election. Knowing that the Democrats held a voting majority, the Republicans opposed holding another legislative session at this time. They argued that, since the legislature had not redistricted the territory, the acting governor lacked the authority to order a special session or to call for another election. The Democrats, on the other hand, insisted that the territory badly needed new laws and that Meagher did indeed have the authority to convene the legislature. After first accepting the Republican argument, Meagher suddenly changed his mind and agreed with the Democrats that a new legislature was both necessary and proper. He called the lawmakers to assemble in Virginia City on March 5, 1866.

The other emotional issue confronting Meagher concerned statehood. The majority Democrats desired quick admission as a state, for they knew that they could gain control of a state government. For exactly that reason, the Republicans opposed it. Montana obviously lacked sufficient population to justify statehood; but, after all, Congress had bent the rules to make thinly populated Nevada a state only two years earlier. Here again, Meagher reversed himself and shifted from the Republican to the Democratic viewpoint. Since a territory had to apply for statehood by submitting a state constitution for approval of Congress, Meagher summoned a constitutional convention to meet in Helena on March 26, 1866.

Both of these acts led to pandemonium. The second territorial legislature met during March and April of 1866 and conducted a great deal of business. Following a September 1866 election, the legislators met in a third session during the winter of 1866–67. All of this infuriated the Republicans, who felt that these sessions had been illegally called by the "Acting One." When a majority of the Territorial Supreme Court, made up of Republican Justices Lyman E. Munson and H. C. Hosmer, declared all acts of the second legislature null and void, both Meagher and the legislators simply ignored their ruling. In fact, the legislature struck back at Munson by rearranging the territorial judicial districts. They created a "sagebrush" district in vacant eastern Montana and then assigned Munson to this district, with the provision that he must live there.

In sheer rage and frustration, the Montana Republicans responded by sending Wilbur Fisk Sanders to Washington, in order to convince the leaders of Congress that Meager's legislative sessions should be declared illegal. In a highly unusual move, late in February 1867, the Radical Republican leadership in Congress pushed through a measure declaring the second and third Montana legislatures "null and void." This harsh and unfair move by Congress caused howls of protest from Montana, where badly needed laws were abruptly wiped from the books.

Meanwhile, the constitutional convention that Meagher had summoned met in Helena on April 9, 1866. This gathering never really got off the ground, partly because the legislature overshadowed it. Attendance by the delegates was spotty, and the entire convention lasted only six days. The delegates kept no formal records, but they did produce a state constitution, reportedly drawn largely from those of New York and California. Incredibly, the Constitution of 1866 was promptly lost, never to be seen again. According to legend, one of the delegates, Thomas Tutt, lost it while enroute to a printer in St. Louis. More likely, the document probably burned in a fire that years later destroyed the records of the convention secretary, H. N. Maguire. It made no difference, in any case, because Montana had no real hope for statehood in 1866. The territory lacked the requisite population, and the Republican Congress had no desire to create yet another Democratic state.

Thus confusion reigned through mid-1866. Finally, in early October a new governor arrived to succeed Sidney Edgerton. This was Green Clay Smith, who impressed Montanans by his adept handling of the third legislative assembly during that autumn. But, at the request of the legislature, Smith soon asked for and received permission to return to the nation's capital, in order to pursue Montana's neglected interests there. This once again made Secretary Thomas F. Meagher the acting governor and, as before, the result was chaos.

During the spring of 1867, attacks by Sioux Indians along the Bozeman Road touched off a classic frontier panic in Montana. Especially in the well settled Gallatin Valley, the fear spread that the Sioux would sweep westward along Bozeman's route and terrorize the Montana settlements. Although groundless, public fear heightened when John Bozeman himself was killed, reportedly by Indians, along the Yellowstone River in April. Besieged by pleas for military protection, Acting Governor Meagher asked for and finally received federal authority to raise a militia force to guard the Gallatin and surrounding areas.

Affairs quickly got out of hand, as they often did in such situations. Meagher raised an army of over six hundred volunteers, heavily staffed with high ranking officers. The army encamped in the Gallatin Valley and along the upper Yellowstone, but encountered very few Indians. By the time the "army" was finally disbanded, to the great anger of some of the troops, who wished to remain on the federal payroll, it had run up bills totaling $1,100,000! Realizing that local merchants had drastically overcharged the militia, the federal government refused to pay the full amount of the bills and eventually settled with local creditors for $513,000. It proved to be a senseless and very expensive "war."

Amidst this confusion, Thomas Francis Meagher's career came to its sudden, and still unexplained end. On July 1, 1867, while in Fort Benton awaiting the arrival of his wife and an arms shipment by steamboat, Meagher mysteriously disappeared from the docked boat on which he was staying. He apparently fell from the vessel during the night and drowned, but his body was never recovered. Whether accident, suicide, or even murder was involved, no one knows to this day. General Meagher remains a hero to the Irish of his homeland, and the thousands of Irish who came to the mining towns of Montana celebrated his memory with the impressive statue that now stands before the state capitol. Meagher's role in Montana's history, however, was less than constructive. In truth, he was overwhelmed and destroyed by the bitter partisanship of Montana Territory.

Just prior to Meagher's death, Governor Green Clay Smith returned to Montana in June 1867. Smith was a Union Democrat from Kentucky and a man of marked ability. He served with distinction in both the Mexican and Civil wars, and in 1863 he resigned from the Army with the rank of brigadier general in order to take a seat in Congress. Smith rose rapidly in national politics.

Governor Smith was a sensible political moderate, who succeeded in restoring calm and in working with both parties. He wrapped up the bogus Indian campaign begun by Meagher and convened the legislature in special session in order to pick up the pieces left by the nullification of the two previous sessions. Addressing the legislators, Smith pointed out the desperate need for education and land laws and the urgent problem of reducing the territorial debt, which stood at fifty-five thousand dollars. The counties of Chouteau, Meagher, and Beaverhead had paid no property taxes at all, and until tax collection was enforced the debt would continue to soar.

The legislature responded well to the governor's program, and it seemed at long last that the territory might look forward to responsible government. But this was not to be. The death of Meagher again left Montana without a secretary, and the long delay in appointing another secretary left the territory without access to federal monies. In order to straighten things out, Smith left for Washington in the summer of 1868; and, apparently deciding to give up politics altogether, he resigned his position and never returned. The abrupt departure of capable Green Clay Smith seemed a cruel blow to Montana, which once again faced governmental uncertainty.

For nearly a year, Montana remained without a federally appointed governor. James Tufts, who was finally designated secretary, served quietly during this period as acting governor. At last, in April 1869, President Grant appointed none other than James M. Ashley to govern Montana Territory. Ashley had just been defeated for re-election to Congress. Since he had engineered the creation of the territory, he might have seemed the ideal choice as governor. Actually, he proved to be very nearly the worst possible choice. For Ashley was a leading Radical Republican, an outspoken critic of slavery and the South, and was famed as the congressman who had filed the impeachment resolution against President Andrew Johnson. Ashley was rigid and moralistic, a tough, partisan campaigner. On one of his Ohio campaigns, he knocked out a heckler, and on another occasion, an angry member of the audience threw a live goose at him.

To the Democratic majority in Montana, the appointment of Ashley seemed a direct provocation. Democratic newspaper editors wailed in dismay at the news. "Angels and Ministers of grace defend us," groaned the *Montana Democrat*. Said the *Weekly Independent* of Helena: "The broken down political hack, James M. Ashley, has been appointed Governor of Montana. How long are the people to be scorned and insulted by being told . . . that there is not one among the thirty thousand freemen of Montana who is capable of discharging the functions of the Executive office?"

Ashley arrived with high hopes during that summer of 1869. He held a fatherly attitude toward Montana and seemed intent upon converting his territory to the ways of the Republican party. When the legislature convened late in the year, however, the governor faced overwhelming Democratic majorities in both houses. Unfortunately, Ashley demonstrated no skill whatsoever in dealing with the Democrats. He immediately locked horns with them by insisting that key territorial offices—treasurer, auditor, and superintendent of public instruction—must be appointed by the governor, not elected, as the legislature had provided by law. Ashley appointed Republicans to these positions, but they could not get the elected Democrats to vacate them.

Things got even worse when the Democrats demanded a share of the appointive offices of the territorial government. Ashley refused to give even one job to a Democrat. In retaliation, the Democrats in the legislature repealed the salary supplement they had provided the governor when Smith held the office; and, more importantly, they refused to approve any of the governor's appointments to territorial offices. "To the end of December, 1869," writes historian Clark Spence, "the council had rejected eleven nominations for the office of superintendent of public instruction, fifteen for auditor, and sixteen for treasurer."

This was government by deadlock, and a sorry situation indeed. It ended suddenly, late in 1869, when President Grant summarily fired Ashley. Evidently, Grant dismissed the governor because of a speech Ashley had made just before coming to Montana, in which he had described the Republican party as being "dumb in the presence of a dummy." Grant apparently recognized himself as the "dummy" in question and took the proper revenge. It was, said Ashley, "the hardest blow I ever received." Ashley's removal solved the immediate problem, but it left local affairs once again adrift and confused.

POLITICAL MATURITY: THE POTTS ERA

After six years, three governors, and two acting governors, Montana Territory seemed doomed to perennial misgovernment. Much of the trouble, admittedly, had arisen from local politics, but the major problem stemmed from federal mismanagement. Republican administrations in Washington paid little heed to local complaints and problems, and they insisted on sending unemployed Republican politicians to govern a strongly Democratic territory. There seemed little hope for improvement when, on July

e Three Forks of the Missouri. Pencil sketch by A. E. Mathews, 1868. (Courtesy of Montana Historical Society, elena)

row camp on Little Big Horn River. Photograph by Edward S. Curtis (Courtesy of Montana Historical Society, elena)

The Three Chiefs (Piegan). Photograph by Edward S. Curtis (Courtesy of Montana Historical Society, Helena)

Lewis and Clark Meeting Indians at Ross' Hole. Painting by Charles M. Russell (Courtesy of Montana Historical Society, Helena)

(*Top left*) Meriwether Lewis. Portrait by C. B. Fevret de Saint-Memin. (In the collection of the Corcoran Gallery of Art, Washington, D.C.; print provided by Historical Society of Montana Library); (*top right*) Manuel Lisa (Courtesy of Montana Historical Society, Helena); (*bottom*) Pierre Jean DeSmet, S.J. (Courtesy of Montana Historical Society, Helena)

Fight between Blackfeet and Gros Ventres. Painting by Carl Bodmer (Courtesy of Montana Historical Society, Helena)

Fort Union. Lithograph after Carl Bodmer's pencil sketch, 1833 (Courtesy of Montana Historical Society, Helena)

Hydraulic mining, Alder Gulch. Photograph by W. H. Jackson, Hayden Survey, 1869–71 (Courtesy of Montana Historical Society, Helena)

Virginia City. Sketch by A. E. Mathews (Courtesy of Montana Historical Society, Helena)

Bridge Street, Helena, 1865 (Courtesy of Montana Historical Society, Helena)

W. F. Sanders, 1869 (Courtesy of Montana Historical Society, Helena)

Martin Maginnis (Courtesy of Montana Historical
Society, Helena)

. T. Hauser (Courtesy of Montana Historical Society, Helena)

Benjamin Potts (Courtesy of Montana Historical Society, Helena)

wenty-fifth Infantry, Fort Shaw, 1890. Photograph by Eugene LeMunyon (Courtesy of Montana Historical Society, Ielena)

Colonel Nelson Miles, commander of the Fifth Infantry. Photograph by L. A. Huffman (Courtesy of Montana Historical Society, Helena)

Delegation of Flathead Indians to Washington, D.C., January 1883. Top, left to right: Hand Shot Off, Peter Ronan, Michael Revais; center: Antoine Moise, Chief Charlo, Grizzly Bear Far Away; bottom: Abel (Courtesy of Montana Historical Society, Helena)

13, 1870, President Grant appointed Benjamin F. Potts to be the new governor of Montana. Like Edgerton and Ashley, Potts was an Ohio Republican; and like Smith and Meagher, he had served as a brigadier general in the Union Army. Potts saw a great deal of action in the war; he served with Grant at Vicksburg and with Sherman on his march through Georgia, where Potts's regiment lost half its men.

Benjamin Potts provided Montanans with a pleasant surprise. Unlike Edgerton or Ashley, he was a moderate Republican, capable of compromising with the Democrats. He would record one of the longest and most successful careers in the history of American territorial government, presiding over Montana from 1870 until President Chester Arthur removed him from office in 1883. Potts was a large, powerfully built man of forceful personality. He adjusted so well to the Montana scene that after his removal as governor he remained on his ranch near Helena until his death in 1887. Beyond dispute, much of his success stemmed from the fact that by 1870 the violent political hatreds of the Civil War were beginning to abate. The more important factor, however, was Potts's reasonable spirit of conciliation.

Potts worked easily with the Democrats, so easily in fact that the more extreme, Radical Republicans turned against him. The Radicals became so angry with Potts that, in 1877, Wilbur Sanders and the Fisk brothers lobbied in Washington for his removal from office. They had reason to be upset, for Potts presided over a smoothly working arrangement between moderate Republicans and moderate Democrats, an arrangement in which party lines obviously counted for little. At the heart of this system was Potts's business and political alliance with Samuel T. Hauser, the shrewd Helena banker who was the most powerful capitalist and Democrat in Montana. As historian Kenneth N. Owens put it, Montana demonstrated a "no-party pattern of territorial politics," in which Potts, Hauser, and their allies "managed Montana's governmental affairs with a thoroughness their enemies could only admire." In other words, local businessmen and investors, often ignoring party loyalties, joined forces with leaders of government to gain control of the territory.

Governor Potts's first concerns were to stabilize the small bureaucracy and to bring the soaring territorial and county debts under control. It took him several years to settle, once and for all, the squabble over filling the executive offices which had begun under Ashley. When an 1870 investigation uncovered wrongdoing by the territorial secretary, whose name, appropriately, was Wiley Scribner, Potts forced him from office. The governor worried most about the alarmingly high territorial debt, which had surpassed one hundred thousand dollars, and about the staggering county debts, which had been amassed by county commissioners who often acted irresponsibly. Surely Potts's greatest achievement was his reform of territorial finances. Under his constant prodding, Montana and most of its counties began a general refunding of their debts at 10 percent interest in 1876. By the time Potts left office in 1883, the territory stood on a sound fiscal basis, and the millage tax had been reduced from 4½ to 2 mills.

As Montana Territory finally achieved stability under Benjamin Potts, it came to deal more realistically with its problems. The main political and economic questions in Montana were generally the same as those prevailing throughout the West at that time. Montanans argued about how best to cut down the size of the huge Indian reservations and open these lands for white "development," about attracting outside investors during the depression that began in 1873, about how to gain more independence from federal control while at the same time acquiring more federal military posts and other investments. Like all western territories, Montana longed for the arrival of railroads, which would surely bring growth and prosperity. And like other westerners, Montanans sharply debated the question of whether or not the territory should encourage the railroads by offering them subsidies or tax exemptions. Potts himself first opposed railroad subsidies, but he later moved cautiously to support them. Fortunately, though, Montana eventually chose not to run up large debts in order to finance railroads. The railroads came in good time, and Montana escaped the terrible indebtedness that rail subsidies forced upon some of her neighbors.

Another hot issue in Montana, as in other territories, involved the location of the capital. Every town always seemed to hunger for the capital, for it would bring jobs and prosperity, prestige and permanence. In effect, Bannack became the first capital, simply because Governor Edgerton ordered the legislature to assemble there. In 1865 the legislators moved the seat of government to the center of population, Virginia City. Even by that time, however, Virginia City was losing population to Helena, and a long struggle over location of the capital began between these two cities. The legislature ordered an election on the issue in 1867, which Virginia City won. As Helena continued to prosper, and Virginia City to decline, another election was held in 1869, this time amidst widespread accusations of fraud. Incredibly, after the ballots had been taken to the territorial secretary's office at Virginia City, an "accidental" fire destroyed them. Suspicions, naturally, abounded.

Helena, by now the hub of the territory, continued to press its case. The legislature ordered a third election on the issue for August of 1874, and this time the voters would choose only "For or Against Helena." Again, widespread irregularities occurred. The Gallatin County vote was thrown out, and the returns from Meagher County were certified as fraudulent. The whole matter finally ended up in a great legal hassle. After the United

States Supreme Court refused to consider the case on appeal, the Montana Supreme Court resolved it in Helena's favor. So Helena, centrally located, flanked by rich quartz mines, and lying on a projected rail route, finally became the capital city in 1875. Her victory, however, was not quite final. As we shall see, Helena would face an even stiffer challenge for the *state* capital honors from Anaconda.

Aside from such colorful squabbles as these, the quality of government and the tone of politics improved steadily during the 1870s and 1880s. More and more competent men began to appear in the elective and appointive offices, men like Cornelius Hedges, the long-time superintendent of public instruction who played such a key role in developing the territorial public school system. This trend toward better government was best reflected by the Territorial Supreme Court. Among the western territories, Montana gained recognition as having one of the most efficient court systems. This reputation arose mainly from the work of a few dedicated men: Hiram Knowles, the first Montana resident to receive a federal appointment in the territory; Decius Wade, who served as chief justice from 1871 until 1887, and Henry N. Blake, who rose to the bench in 1874. Decius Wade, the "Father of Montana Jurisprudence, dominated the territorial bench and later played a major role in codifying the laws of early Montana. Wade once estimated that he and Knowles both traveled over twenty-five thousand miles by coach during their years on the bench.

Montanans generally showed good judgment in their choices of delegates to represent them in Congress. Of the six men who served as Montana's congressional delegate, four were Democrats and usually faced the frustrations of dealing with Republican-controlled Congresses. Like all territorial delegates, they also faced the problem of having no vote. Nevertheless, the delegates performed vital functions: they voiced their constituents' concerns and looked after their interests in Washington, and they joined with other territorial delegates to speak for the West as a region.

The most able of the Montana delegates were William Clagett and Martin Maginnis. Clagett served only a brief term in 1871–72; but his ability, along with the fact that he was a Republican dealing with a Republican federal government, allowed him to accomplish a great deal for the territory. Democrat Martin Maginnis served ten years as delegate, from 1872 until 1882, and was surely the most effective and powerful of Montana's men in Washington. He worked smoothly with Potts and the Republicans, and he looked constantly after the interests of Samuel Hauser, C. A. Broadwater, and other local investors. Maginnis proved especially adept at removing lands from Indian reservations and at securing federal forts, agencies, and monies for the folks back home.

Under Governor Benjamin F. Potts, responsible government, along with the arrival of railroads and a new prosperity, placed Montana well on the road to statehood. Yet, Congress forced Montana to wait six long years after Potts's 1883 retirement before granting her admittance as a full-fledged state of the Union. During that period, Montana received five governors in quick succession. One of these, B. Platt Carpenter, reportedly lost his job because of absenteeism. Interestingly, two of them were local residents: powerful Democrat Samuel T. Hauser, who apparently resigned over a dispute with the United States land commissioner, and Benjamin White, a Republican businessman and founder of the city of Dillon.

Not surprisingly, the more Montana matured, the more she resented the "colonial" rule forced upon her as a territory, and the more her citizens demanded self-government and statehood. With the usual exaggeration, Delegate Martin Maginnis voiced a common complaint in 1884: "The present Territorial system . . . is the most infamous system of colonial government that was ever seen on the face of the globe." In that same year, the editor of *The Missoulian* wrote plaintively: "The President has nominated another carpetbagger for Associate Justice of the Supreme Court of Montana. Seventy-five thousand people in the Territory to make laws for themselves, and a Hoosier sent out from Indiana to tell us what we have done. How long, oh Lord; how long!"

In truth, the territorial system produced the same mixed record of success and failure in Montana that it did in most places. It succeeded in providing a measure of local self-government, balanced by federal supervision. Despite Maginnis' complaints, it made of early Montana neither a colony nor a martyr. The territorial system, most significantly, brought at least order and some form of government to the incredibly distant mining camps of the Northern Rockies, and it set these communities on a course of evolution toward political equality with the established "states."

To those who lived here, though, the disadvantages of territorial status far outweighed the benefits. Statehood, it was hoped, would bring an end, once and for all, to the federal meddling and bungling which had been upsetting them ever since 1864. Perhaps most important to Montanans of the 1880s, statehood meant recognition of their coming of age as a community. By the mid-1880s such recognition was clearly due. No longer did Montana simply echo the issues and concerns of the nation at large. The territory revealed, by then, a political culture of its own, a political culture arising out of the needs and demands of its major economic groupings—industrial miners, stockmen, merchants, lumbermen, farmers, and labor leaders. Statehood, in short, was no longer a mere pipe dream: it was a justified expectation.

CHAPTER VI

Indian Removal: 1851–90

EXCEPT perhaps for black slavery, the white conquest of the Indian forms the most sordid chapter of American history. Historians have focused much attention upon the defeat of the Indians, but they have stressed too much the blood and thunder involved, too little the broader aspects of the question. From the Indians' point of view, it was a genuinely tragic story, punctuated by war, disease, and fraud. But from the emotionless perspective of regional history, Indian removal marked a major turning point in the development of this area. The Indian's loss became the white man's gain. As the Indians lost the best of their lands, the vast reaches of Montana opened abruptly to white settlement and "development."

THE FIRST TREATIES

Montana Indians had been in contact with whites for nearly fifty years before the United States government began to deal formally with them. During the 1850s, on the eve of the mining rushes that were about to overwhelm them, these tribes signed their first treaties with the federal government. The treaty method of dealing with Indians seldom worked. It assumed that Indian tribes, like sovereign nations, were united under one supreme leader, or one group of leaders, who could speak for all the people. Such was seldom the case. More often, one or several compliant chiefs, oftentimes persuaded by liquor or bribes, signed away lands over which they lacked sole authority. In many cases a carnival atmosphere surrounded the treaty negotiations, and sometimes government agents practiced outright deception and fraud. Almost always, the Indians came out second best.

The first such agreement to affect the Montana area was the Fort Laramie Treaty of 1851. Government officials summoned Great Plains tribal leaders to assemble at Fort Laramie, on the Oregon Trail in present southeastern Wyoming, in order to negotiate a treaty of peace between warring Indians, and between the Indians and the advancing Americans. In return for the customary "annuities"—annual gifts of food, utensils, and other items—the chiefs signed a number of important agreements. The government promised to respect and protect their tribal lands, and the Indians consented to allow the construction of roads and forts on their territory. More importantly, the Fort Laramie Treaty mapped out the domain of each tribe and obligated each tribe to respect the lands of its neighbors.

In future Montana, the Blackfeet, who had no representatives at Fort Laramie, became the recognized proprietors, along with the Gros Ventres, of the north central area, east of the continental divide. Most of the upper and middle Yellowstone Valley was assigned to the Crows, and the Assiniboines received a sizable tract in northeastern Montana. The Fort Laramie Treaty had little immediate impact upon the native Montanans. It "kept the peace" for a dozen years, but only until white prospectors found a use for the lands involved. Understandably, the chiefs failed to foresee the treaty's major long-term significance. By assigning specific lands to particular tribes, it opened the way for future agreements in which each tribe would be cajoled or forced into giving up its own lands individually.

The Fort Laramie Treaty did not cover the mountain tribes living west of the plains. Only four years later, though, Governor Isaac I. Stevens of Washington Territory held a series of conferences with the plateau tribes of the Northwest. Stevens sought to place these tribes on large reservations and thereby to open choice areas for white settlement and transportation routes. In July 1855 Stevens convened a major council near present Missoula with the Flathead, Pend d'Oreille, and Kutenai tribes, led by their respective head chiefs Victor, Alexander, and Michel.

These tribes, traditionally friendly toward the whites, agreed to accept a common reservation; and, in return for lands thus ceded, the government promised to spend $120,000 over the next twenty years for improvements on the reservation. The one problem in Stevens' negotiations arose over the site of the reservation. The Pend d'Oreilles and Kutenais desired the Flathead Valley near St. Ignatius Mission, but Victor and the Flatheads wanted to remain in their beloved Bitterroot Valley. Finally, all sides agreed to the creation of the enormous Jocko Reservation, embracing over 1,280,000 acres to the south of Flathead Lake. In order to gain Flathead acceptance of the treaty, the negotiators inserted Article 11, which temporarily allowed Victor's people to remain in the Bitterroot above the mouth of Lolo Creek. The President would order a survey of the Bitterroot Valley and would ultimately decide whether the Flatheads should be given a reserve there, or whether they should remove to the Jocko. This clause would lead to confusion and sorrow, but for now the "Salish Council" opened much of western Montana to peaceful white intrusion.

Following this conference, the Stevens party moved eastward, and in mid-October of 1855 they opened a similar council with the Blackfeet near the mouth of the Judith River. Stevens wanted to confine the Blackfeet within a limited area and to convince them to make peace with Indians and whites alike. Here again, he proved his ability as a diplomat. In return for annuities, the Blackfeet accepted a general reservation with boundaries reaching from the crest of the continental divide to the mouth of the Milk River, and from the Canadian boundary southward to the upper Musselshell River. Furthermore, the Blackfeet promised to recognize the general area of southwestern Montana as a common hunting ground, where they would respect the rights of other tribes. They even agreed to limited white usage of their reservation lands. Stevens' Blackfeet Treaty of 1855 seemed a major triumph, a guarantee of peace for years to come.

THE WHITE INVASION

The gold rushes of 1862–63, of course, disrupted these fragile treaty arrangements. The Blackfeet felt the full impact of the mining invasion, for the prime gold fields lay along and below the southern limits of their reservation lands. When whites began entering the valuable hunting grounds of southwestern Montana, a number of "incidents," usually isolated killings or thefts of stock, naturally resulted.

The inhabitants of newly created Montana Territory demanded federal military protection. Like most frontiersmen, they panicked easily, and ordinarily they exaggerated the real Indian threat. They knew that military forts meant not only protection from the natives, but also juicy government contracts for local businessmen. Following the end of the Civil War in 1865, Washington began the task of garrisoning the Montana frontier. The Army located its first Montana posts in 1866, when it established Fort C. F. Smith ninety miles up the Big Horn River, and Camp Cooke near the confluence of the Judith and Missouri rivers. Neither of these isolated forts lasted long. In 1869 the small force from Camp Cooke moved over to old Fort Benton, where the troops spent most of their time policing whiskey peddlers and guarding government supplies.

In 1867 the Army established its two major bases on the Montana mining frontier, Forts Shaw and Ellis. Fort Shaw, regimental headquarters for the newly formed Military District of Montana, was located near strategic Sun River Crossing, where the Mullan Road forded that stream twenty miles above its juncture with the Missouri. Here, it guarded the northern fringes of the mining settlements from the Blackfeet and other intruders. Built mainly of adobe, Fort Shaw housed four companies of infantry. Fort Ellis, situated at the western portal of Bozeman Pass near the new town of Bozeman, was built in the aftermath of Governor Meagher's "Indian War" of 1867. It protected the southeastern flank of the Montana settlements against Sioux and other raiders from the Yellowstone Valley. Normally, between three and five companies were located at Fort Ellis; these included cavalry. In 1870 the military also based one company of infantry at Camp Baker (later named Fort Logan) in the Big Belt Mountains east of Helena.

Trouble between the proud Blackfeet and the whites was probably inevitable, but federal mismanagement made the situation worse than it need have been. Agent Gad Upson, assisted by Acting Governor Thomas F. Meagher and others, negotiated a Blackfeet treaty at Fort Benton in 1865 that might have avoided many problems. In return for the usual annuities, this treaty removed all lands lying below the Teton and Missouri rivers from the reservation, thus withdrawing the Blackfeet northward and away from the white settlements. The treaty, however, never became law. Believing that neither the whites nor the Indians would observe it, the secretary of the interior did not even bother to submit it to the Senate for approval.

So events took their natural course. Blackfeet and a few Sioux raiding parties ranged throughout the Montana settlements, stealing horses and livestock and occasionally killing whites. It was the Blackfeet, reportedly, who killed John Bozeman on the Yellowstone in 1867. Fort Benton lay in the heart of the troubled area. In mid-1869, following an Indian attack that killed two whites nearby, a couple of innocent young Blackfeet were wantonly gunned down on the street in Benton. One of the slain was the brother of the Piegan leader Mountain Chief, and the Indians retaliated over the next six months with raids that probably claimed well over two dozen lives. When the Piegans killed the well known trader Malcolm Clarke, who had a Blackfeet wife, white men in the Helena and Fort Benton areas reacted with near hysteria and shouted for military reprisal. Federal authorities demanded that the guilty Blackfeet be surrendered for punishment, but instead the Indians allowed them to flee into Canada.

Amidst a mounting chorus of demands for military action, General Phil Sheridan, in charge of the Army's Division of the Missouri, decided to act. The hard-boiled Sheridan, who believed in "total war" against Indians, ordered Major Eugene M. Baker at Fort Ellis to retaliate against Mountain Chief and his band. "Tell Baker," he telegraphed, "to strike them hard." He did. In bitter, sub-zero cold, Baker led four companies of the Second Cavalry north from Fort Ellis in January 1870 and picked up two infantry troops at Fort Shaw enroute. His scouts found an unsuspecting Blackfeet village on the Marias River, and at dawn on the terribly cold morning of January 23, reportedly while drunk, Baker attacked it.

In the ensuing massacre, 173 Indians, including 53 women and children, lost their lives. Worse yet, Baker had attacked the wrong village. This was not Mountain Chief's camp, but rather that of several other chiefs, including the friendly Heavy Runner. Heavy Runner rushed out, waving papers certifying his good character, only to be shot down by rifle fire. The carnage ended quickly. When Baker learned that some of the captive women and children had smallpox, he turned them loose to shift for themselves in the snow and cold. As a result of this vicious slaughter, the major faced considerable criticism from around the country. But many Montanans and many military men commended him. The major's superior, General Winfield Scott Hancock, concluded in his annual report that Baker and his command were "entitled to the special commendation of the military authorities and the hearty thanks of the nation."

The Baker Massacre largely ended Blackfeet resistance to the white invasion. During the next few years, the Indians of northern Montana began the hard adjustment to a new way of life. Beginning in 1868–69, the Interior Department established separate agencies and subagencies for these tribes. The Blackfeet agency was located first on the Teton River and later moved to the upper Marias. The Gros Ventres, Assiniboines, and River Crows received a subagency at Fort Browning on the Upper Milk River; in 1871, the subagency was transferred up the Milk to Fort Belknap. Other Assiniboines, along with Sioux bands who were pressing in from the east, were assigned to an agency at Fort Peck, near the confluence of the Milk and Missouri rivers, in 1873.

In 1873 an executive order of President Grant restructured the northern Montana reservation. Beginning in 1871, the federal government had discarded the old treaty system and had begun dealing with the Indians, instead, by executive agreements. This meant, in effect, that tribes could be dealt with more summarily and without long negotiations. The order of 1873 set aside, for the Blackfeet, Gros Ventre, Assiniboine, and Sioux tribes, all of northern Montana, from the continental divide to the Dakota border, with the southern boundary of the huge reserve running along the Missouri and Sun rivers. A year later, in 1874, the government moved the southern boundary of the Blackfeet territory northward from the Sun to the Marias River. This deprived the Blackfeet, to their dismay, of some of their best hunting lands.

By the mid-1870s, therefore, the Blackfeet and Gros Ventres, and also the more distant Assiniboines and Sioux, had been pushed completely north of the Missouri. This arrangement pleased the Montana settlements, for it opened the lush grasslands of the Judith Basin to penetration by stockmen. For the Indians, however, it meant the narrowing of horizons and a deepening dependence upon the federal government. An indifferent

Congress and an Indian Bureau riddled with corruption often failed to provide the food and annuities promised by law. Like so many others, these Indians faced a hard and depressing future.

Since neither the Flathead nor the Bitterroot valleys contained major gold deposits, the Indians of western Montana experienced less direct conflict than did the Blackfeet. But the Salish and Kutenai Indians on the Jocko Reserve well understood the meaning of neglect, as their buildings, herds, and crops suffered from negligence and scant funding. South of the reservation, the Flatheads still remained in the Bitterroot Valley. Despite the stipulations of Article 11 of the 1855 Stevens Treaty, the President had never ordered a survey of the valley, nor had he decided upon a permanent home for the Flatheads. Victor, head chief of the Flatheads, died and was succeeded by his son, Charlot. Understandably, Charlot and his people reasoned that, since their land had not been surveyed and assessed, the government had chosen to leave them there permanently. Once again, federal neglect led to problems.

Even though the Bitterroot Valley yielded little gold, its agricultural possibilities began to attract more and more white farmers. These settlers, naturally, raised the familiar cry that the Indians be removed. The Montana Legislature memorialized the federal government to this effect, and Congressional Delegate William Clagett pressed the case for relocating the Flatheads. Late in 1871 President Grant issued an executive order declaring that, a survey of the valley having been completed, he had decided that the Flatheads must move north to the Jocko. Still, the Flatheads sat tight, and in 1872 Congress entered the fray by ordering their removal and opening the Bitterroot lands for sale to white settlers.

In June 1872 the secretary of the interior sent Congressman James A. Garfield, a former Union general and future President, to negotiate the withdrawal of the Flatheads. Garfield found a tense situation in Montana. The Bitterroot settlers were organizing themselves into militia, demanding arms and ammunition from the governor, and pleading that a fort be erected to protect them. Accompanied by a party including Governor Potts and Delegate Clagett, Garfield traveled to the Bitterroot and conferred with Charlot and subchiefs Arlee and Adolph.

In return for government promises of buildings, annuities, and the provision that any Flathead might remain in the Bitterroot by becoming a land-holding United States citizen, Arlee and Adolph agreed to move to the Jocko Reservation. The proud Charlot, however, refused to join them. While Arlee led some of the Flatheads to the reservation, the majority remained with their head chief in the Bitterroot. Charlot became deeply embittered, and with good reason. He felt that the government had not honored the spirit of the 1855 treaty, and he deeply resented Garfield's dealing with Arlee as if he were the head chief. Most of all, the honorable and dignified chief reacted angrily when published accounts indicated that he had signed the agreement to move to the Jocko. As Garfield himself later admitted, Charlot never signed the 1872 removal pact; but the government nonetheless allowed reports to appear in print that he had.

Charlot and his dwindling band remained in the Bitterroot Valley for years, living in miserable poverty. The Flatheads remained peaceful, however, and even refused to help their old Nez Perce allies during their 1877 retreat. Meanwhile, the capable Jocko agent, Peter Ronan, coaxed Charlot's people to move. Finally, after Arlee had died, and after Charlot learned that Garfield had not literally forged his name on the 1872 agreement, the old chief relented. In 1891 Charlot and his people left their beloved valley and moved to the Jocko Reservation. The removal of the western Montana tribes was now complete. Peaceful and honorable to the end, Charlot and his followers received little in return.

Even though their domain lay east of the major mining areas, the Crows too felt the immediate impact of the white intrusion. Like the Flatheads, they got along reasonably well with the whites; and like the Flatheads, they lost most of their lands anyway. The 1851 Fort Laramie Treaty recognized the major portion of the Yellowstone Valley as Crow territory. A dozen years later, though, the Montana mining rushes began to cause complications. The Bozeman Road passed through the heart of Crow lands enroute to the mining camps on the upper Missouri. As prospecting parties increasingly entered the upper Yellowstone region, the inevitable thievery and violence resulted.

Anxious especially to move the Crows away from their advancing Sioux enemies on the east, the government negotiated a new treaty with them in 1868. Promising the usual improvements and annuities, the treaty lopped off the eastern extremities of the Crow domain. The new reservation was bounded on the north and west by the Yellowstone River, on the south by the Montana-Wyoming line, and on the east by the divide between the Big Horn and Rosebud rivers. The Indian Bureau established an agency for the Crows at the western end of the reservation near present-day Livingston.

Discoveries of gold on the upper Yellowstone led to irresistible pressure for opening the western end of the Crow Reserve. Sympathetic, as usual, to such demands, the government worked out a new agreement in 1873, whereby the Crows would give up their reservation entirely and take instead a much smaller one in the Judith Basin, north of the Yellowstone River. This plan, however, caused too many problems. Although the River Crows, who had long hunted in central Montana, liked the new location, the Mountain Crows balked at leaving their homeland. More to the point, cattlemen reacted angrily to the prospect of locking up the inviting Judith

Basin in a reservation. So, in 1875, President Grant rescinded his previous order and ended the plan to move the Crows.

Finally, the cattlemen won the Judith, and the miners got what they were after, the upper Yellowstone. The far western end of the Crow Reserve, which included the mining camps along the upper Yellowstone, was removed from the reservation. This cession included the site of the Crow Agency; so in 1875 the agency was relocated well to the east, on the Rosebud fork of the Stillwater River. Thus the Crows, crowded from the east by Sioux and Cheyennes, from the north by cattlemen, and from the west by miners, found themselves pressed into an ever shrinking remnant of their once great domain south of the Yellowstone River.

THE "SIOUX PROBLEM"

The Montana mining rushes provoked surprisingly little violence from those Indians who actually lived in the areas immediately affected. As earlier noted, though, some of the immigrants to early Montana traveled routes like the Bozeman and Minnesota-Montana roads, which followed short cuts across the northern Great Plains. This wide plains province, reaching from western Minnesota and Iowa into eastern Montana and Wyoming, was Sioux territory. Along with their Northern Cheyenne allies, the Sioux Nation had the strength, numbers, and determination to challenge the white thrust into their prized hunting lands.

Several factors drove the western Sioux and the Northern Cheyenne to war. Following a major uprising in Minnesota during the Civil War, the eastern Sioux retreated in large numbers onto the Dakota plains, spreading excitement among their brethren and accelerating the Sioux drift into eastern Montana and Wyoming. Then, the notorious slaughter of the Southern Cheyennes at Sand Creek, Colorado, in 1864, also spread waves of unrest among the tribes to the north. The Civil War added complications, too, by reducing military forces and creating uncertainty on the western frontiers. Most of all, the Sioux and Northern Cheyennes resented whites entering and disrupting their buffalo grounds.

From its opening in 1863–64, the Bozeman Road enraged these Indians and provoked them to violence. It crossed the prime hunting lands of the Powder, Tongue, and Big Horn rivers, lands which they—like their Crow enemies—considered properly their own. The last straw, from their point of view, came in 1866, when the government began fortifying the road in order to protect its travelers. In the summer of 1866, even as peace commissioners at Fort Laramie were busy trying to bargain the Bozeman Road area away from the Sioux, Colonel Henry B. Carrington arrived on the scene with infantry forces headed northward for the Powder River. Led by the most powerful of the Sioux chiefs, Red Cloud, the majority of the In-

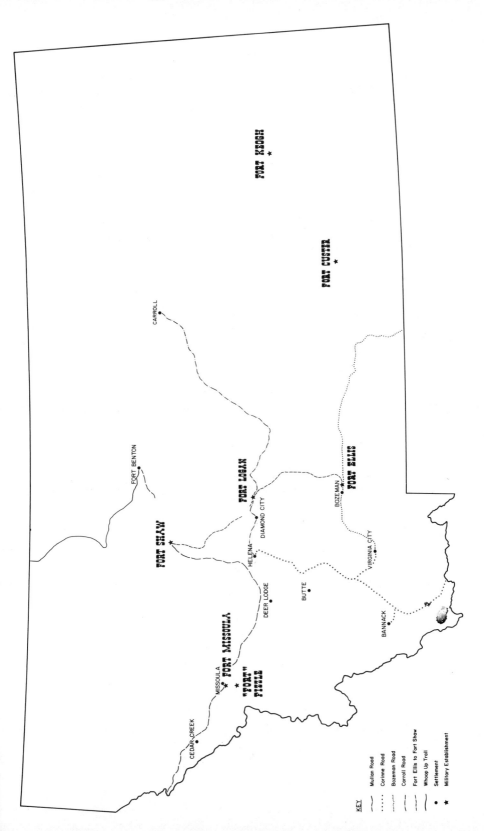

Map 3. Montana, 1876–77 (drawn by Robert L. Taylor)

dian leaders now angrily broke off the talks at Fort Laramie and left to protect their lands. Carrington, meanwhile, began construction of three small posts along the Bozeman Road: Fort Reno at the forks of the Powder and Fort Phil Kearny to the northwest in the Big Horn foothills, both in present Wyoming, and Fort C. F. Smith on the Big Horn River in southern Montana.

Carrington's troops quickly found themselves in an impossible situation. There were simply too few of them and too many Indians. Especially after the onset of cold weather, morale suffered. The men were poorly equipped; most of them had only outmoded Springfield muzzle-loading rifles. Red Cloud's warriors closed in upon them and placed the forts in a state of virtual siege. Fort Phil Kearny, Carrington's headquarters, faced the worst of it. Here, in December of 1866, a young captain named William J. Fetterman, who possessed more courage than sense, allowed a crafty young Sioux chief named Crazy Horse to decoy him into an ambush. In short order, Fetterman and his eighty men lay dead and mutilated.

The "Fetterman Massacre" shocked the nation. By the following summer, the Army had nine hundred men, better armed and supplied, on the Bozeman Road; and a new post, Fort Fetterman, was taking shape at its southern end. Still, the Sioux kept the soldiers on the defensive and allowed only a trickle of migration over the road. In late summer of 1867 the Indians mounted heavy attacks. Some of them carried repeating rifles obtained from white traders. Near Fort C. F. Smith, they hit a haying party, and in the famous "Hayfield Fight" they were beaten back by the newly arrived Springfield breach-loading rifles of the soldiers. In a similar action near Fort Phil Kearny, the "Wagon Box Fight," the Indians struck a woodcutting party, but again the quickly reloadable rifles drove them off.

The violent summer of 1867 cost the Indians dearly in lives, but it clearly underscored the government's dilemma: either Washington must vastly increase troop strength on the Bozeman Road, or it must abandon it. The government chose the latter alternative, in part because completion of the Union Pacific Railroad across southern Wyoming would now allow Montana-bound immigrants to bypass the Bozeman Road more easily and to use instead the Corinne–Virginia City Road from Utah. So once again federal peace commissioners journeyed to the council site at Fort Laramie and began bargaining with the warring chiefs.

In the resulting agreement, the Fort Laramie Treaty of 1868, the Sioux got basically what they wanted. To the angry dismay of white Montanans, the treaty closed the Bozeman Road and promised that the areas it crossed would remain unfortified. Red Cloud and the other chiefs who signed also made concessions. In line with the new federal policy of "concentration," which aimed to place most of the plains tribes on two large reserves, the commissioners persuaded the chiefs to accept a reservation. The reservation, centering on the Black Hills, consisted mainly of today's South Dakota west of the Missouri River. Significantly, the Powder–Tongue–Big Horn areas, where Red Cloud had just won his war, did not lie on the reservation. The treaty denoted these as unceded Indian lands, closed to general white entry and available for seasonal hunting, but not permanent occupation, by the Indians.

The Fort Laramie Treaty of 1868 seemed a model compromise: the Indians got the hated road closed, and the United States succeeded in concentrating them in a more restricted area. But in fact, this treaty, like so many others, turned out to be only a temporary truce, not a lasting peace. Red Cloud and most of the older and calmer chiefs went on the reservation. Many of the younger Sioux leaders, however, like the fiery Hunkpapa chief, Sitting Bull, and the Oglala Crazy Horse, refused to accept the decision of their elders. They kept their bands in the unceded lands crossed by the old Bozeman Road. Frequently, they ventured northward, into and beyond the Yellowstone Valley, giving Montana Territory a bad case of the jitters.

For a few years, the situation remained static. Few whites entered the areas south of the Yellowstone, and many Sioux and Cheyennes simply "commuted" between the neglected agencies in Dakota and the hunting lands lying to the west. Obviously, it was only a matter of time before trouble once again erupted. The problem this time involved the Northern Pacific Railroad, which by 1871 was heading across northern Dakota Territory toward the Yellowstone Valley. By a loose reading of the 1868 treaty, the Sioux and Cheyennes felt that the Yellowstone belonged in their unceded zone; many of the Indians, in fact, denied the legitimacy of that treaty altogether. As railroad surveying parties probed up the Yellowstone with Army protection, the Indians moved against them.

In August 1872 a large Sioux party struck one of these Army escorts under Major Eugene Baker (of Blackfeet infamy) near the mouth of Pryor Creek on the Yellowstone. Baker was too drunk at the time to lead his men, but they managed, in spite of heavy losses, to drive off the raiders. A larger military escort force came up the Yellowstone in 1873, and once again it ran into Indians. But then the Panic of 1873 closed down work on the Northern Pacific and left the railhead at Bismarck in north-central Dakota. That eased one problem for a time, but another one quickly arose in the Black Hills.

The Black Hills lay, beyond dispute, well within the 1868 reservation. Yet, as so many times before, rumors of gold drew in armies of white prospectors anyway. In 1874 Colonel George A. Custer led a large and leisurely surveying expedition through the Hills and reported the area rich not only in gold, but also in prime agricultural land. Predictably, this and other reports set off a rush of white intruders onto the reservation. Although the Indians killed some, and the Army halfheartedly threw out others, they continued to come by the thousands. By 1875 Montana boosters were beginning to worry that the Black Hills gold rush would empty their territory.

The Black Hills gold boom made a travesty of the 1868 Fort Laramie Treaty, and it brought the whole Sioux situation to a boil once again. As whites streamed onto the reservation, more and more Indians left the corruption-ridden agencies and headed west to join the nontreaty bands in the Yellowstone country. Peace commissioners tried, this time without success, to get the old Sioux chiefs like Red Cloud and Spotted Tail to sign away the Black Hills. Finally, at the close of 1875, the Grant Administration made its fateful decision. While passively allowing whites to enter the Black Hills, it would use military force instead to drive the Sioux and Cheyennes out of the unceded lands below the Yellowstone and back onto the ruptured reservation. Once again, the United States violated its treaty agreement, and this time, the last of the great Indian wars in American history resulted.

In early December 1875 the Indian Bureau sent messengers to the bands in southeastern Montana and northeastern Wyoming, ordering them to be back on the reservation by the end of January 1876. This ultimatum did not allow the tribes enough time to comply, but no matter, because the Indians planned to stand and fight in any case. Thus they became "hostiles," and the United States Army eagerly prepared to deal with them.

THE DEFEAT OF THE SIOUX: 1876–77

The Army made its first move against the "hostiles" in March 1876, when General George Crook, who had earlier proven his ability against the Apaches in Arizona, led an army of nine hundred men north from Fort Fetterman, Wyoming. Suffering terribly in subzero weather, Crook's command advanced to the Powder River, where some of his troops under Colonel J. J. Reynolds attacked and captured a large Sioux-Cheyenne village. Reynolds failed, however, either to hold or to destroy the camp, and the "Battle of Powder River" accomplished almost nothing. Largely because of the severe cold, Crook gave up his inconclusive effort and returned to Fort Fetterman.

Meanwhile, from his Chicago headquarters General Phil Sheridan, commander of the Military Division of the Missouri, planned a major spring–summer campaign to corral the Sioux and Cheyennes. Sheridan decided to send three large armies into the Powder–Tongue–Big Horn area, hoping that one or more of these forces would engage the hostiles and either defeat them or cause their surrender. General Sheridan's three-pronged offensive began soon after Crook's sad return from the Powder River. During April

1876 the "Montana Column," consisting of 450 infantry and cavalrymen from Forts Shaw and Ellis, began moving down the Yellowstone River under Colonel John Gibbon. Gibbon's assignment, essentially defensive, was to block any Indian movement north or west of the Yellowstone. The two larger armies came from Dakota and Wyoming. Under the command of General Alfred Terry, the "Dakota Column" left Fort Abraham Lincoln, near Bismarck, in mid-May. Moving across the Dakota plains and up the Yellowstone Valley, Terry led a large force consisting of the 700-man Seventh Cavalry under Colonel George A. Custer, 225 infantrymen, and a large contingent of scouts and teamsters.

Colonel Custer, a national hero because of his colorful career as a Civil War general and a dashing Indian fighter, had originally been assigned command of the entire Dakota Column. He had angered President Grant, however, by testifying before congressional committee about corruption in the Indian service, corruption that involved Grant's own brother. In retaliation, the President removed Custer from the command. Only at the last moment did he consent to allow the proud young officer to go along as the commander of the Seventh Cavalry. Some historians have speculated that Custer, a vain and egotistical yet capable man, may have been determined to win back the glorious reputation that Grant had seemingly tarnished.

As the Montana and Dakota columns moved toward a rendezvous on the lower Yellowstone, General George Crook once again led a large army northward from Fort Fetterman, Wyoming. His command included over 1,000 cavalry and infantry, an enormous wagon and mule caravan, and over 250 Crow and Shoshoni warriors, anxious to settle some old grudges with their Indian enemies. Of course, Crook, Terry, and Gibbon had only a general idea of where the Indians were and how many there might be. All through the spring of 1876, bands of Sioux and Northern Cheyennes fled the reservation and joined the hostile camps around the Rosebud and Little Big Horn rivers in southeastern Montana. By June their villages may have housed as many as 15,000 people, including possibly 3,000–4,000 warriors.

The three advancing columns had to act somewhat independently, since communications were slow and unreliable. The Army's greatest fear was that the Indians would scatter before one of the columns could hit them. Crook encountered the hostiles first. On June 17, as his men paused enroute down upper Rosebud Creek, a large Sioux-Cheyenne army under Crazy Horse attacked them. It was fortunate for Crook that he had paused before the canyon in front of him, for the shrewd Crazy Horse had hoped to trap him inside it. As it developed, the battle turned into a fierce, helter-skelter series of attacks and counterattacks, as the Indians showed an unusual ability to fight in well disciplined units. After six hours of fighting, the Indians withdrew. Crook, a capable general, had in truth been beaten by

Crazy Horse. The Battle of the Rosebud probably cost the general over twenty-five killed and fifty wounded. Cautiously, Crook moved back to Goose Creek on the upper Tongue River to await reinforcements. Meanwhile, Crazy Horse moved his people northwest to join their fellows.

The Rosebud Battle, in effect, removed Crook's column from the campaign. In the meantime, the Terry and Gibbon columns converged on the Yellowstone between the mouths of Rosebud Creek and the Tongue River. By scouting to the south, Terry figured that the Indians were located either on Rosebud Creek or, more likely, to the west of it on the Little Big Horn, a favorite camping spot. Terry and Gibbon knew nothing of Crook's whereabouts and feared that the hostiles might get away from them. Sensibly enough, they chose a strategy of attempting to entrap the Indians from both the north and south. They would send Custer's swift Seventh Cavalry on a sweep southward up the Rosebud and then across to and down the north-flowing Little Big Horn. Meanwhile, Terry and Gibbon would march the slower moving infantry-cavalry force southward up the Big Horn and then up its Little Big Horn tributary. Both armies, it was hoped, would reach the Indian village on June 26, 1876. Naturally, coordination would be difficult, and the Indians would probably flee if forewarned. So Terry gave Custer considerable discretion: he might change the strategy if the Indians seemed likely to escape.

Leading nearly seven hundred men of the Seventh Cavalry, along with some Crow and Arikara scouts, Custer rode up the Rosebud on June 22. On June 24, Custer made the first of his controversial decisions: instead of following Terry's order to advance to the head of the Rosebud before crossing over to the Little Big Horn, he pursued an Indian trail westward before reaching the upper Rosebud. Driving his men to exhaustion on a night march, Custer reached the divide between the two streams, and at dawn on June 25 his scouts saw the smoke of an enormous encampment in the distance. For whatever reason, whether to have all the glory for himself, or to hit the Indians before they could scatter—or, very possibly, both—the colonel decided not to wait until Terry's June 26 target date. He failed to realize the immensity of the Indian gathering, even though his terrified scouts warned him of it. No matter, for the Seventh, in his opinion, could whip any number!

By mid-day, Custer had his troops advancing down Reno Creek, southeast and out of sight from the Indian camp on the Little Big Horn. Planning to hit the encampment from two directions in order to stampede it, he divided his command into three units. He sent three troops under Captain Frederick Benteen to scout the hills west of the village, hoping that Benteen could contain any Indian retreat. Major Marcus Reno, Custer's second in command, was ordered to cross the Little Big Horn with three more troops and strike the camp at its southern end. With five troops, Custer would skirt the bluffs to the right of the village and then attack it at its center.

It did not work. There were too many Indians, and they refused to panic. When Major Reno hit the near end of the enormous village, the Indians rallied quickly under the able Chief Gall and rushed upon their attackers. Reno tried to form a defensive skirmish line. When this failed, he led his men in a disorganized and bloody retreat back across the river and dug in on the bluffs there. Benteen's returning force soon joined what was left of Reno's; and, with Benteen in effect taking over from the distraught Reno, their combined command held off the attacking Indians.

Unaware of these developments, Custer emerged from the bluffs to the east of the village and attempted to cross the river and attack it. But Gall's warriors, having left Reno's force behind, moved across the stream and attacked him instead. Custer began retreating back up the ridges to the north, but it was too late. More warriors joined Gall against him, and Crazy Horse led another attack flanking from the north. The Indians overwhelmed Custer's skirmish lines, and within a half-hour had wiped out his entire command. Amidst their wild victory celebration, the Indians kept Reno and Benteen under siege until the evening of the next day. Then they suddenly dispersed, aware that more soldiers were approaching. On the following day, June 27, Terry and Gibbon arrived at the battlefield. They buried the more than 260 dead and prepared the wounded for removal downriver to Dakota.

When news of the "Last Stand" on the Little Big Horn reached the American public early in July of 1876, it had a shocking effect. Accounts of the "massacre," often highly inaccurate, disrupted the patriotic celebration of the nation's centennial anniversary and sent Americans poring over maps of faraway Montana Territory. Custer became an even larger hero in death than he had been in life; generations of schoolchildren learned of his derring-do, but never of his impetuous recklessness. And every western saloon, it seemed, displayed a romantic Anheuser-Busch painting of the battle. Actually, despite all the attention it has received, the Battle of the Little Big Horn proved in no way decisive. The Indians won a major victory, but the victory only postponed for a short while their inevitable defeat.

Stung by public criticism, both Congress and the Army moved to bring the offending Indians to heel. Congress increased the maximum size of the Army and finally allowed General Sheridan the two forts on the Yellowstone he had long been demanding. These two large posts, Fort Keogh at the Tongue River juncture with the Yellowstone and Fort Custer at the confluence of the Big Horn and Little Big Horn rivers, would together house over a thousand men when completed in 1877.

During the weeks following the Custer Battle, Generals Terry and Crook received reinforcements and led their large, cumbersome armies in a slow and unrewarding pursuit of the hostiles. As summer turned to autumn, Terry broke up his command and sent most of it home, leaving only some infantry to guard the Yellowstone. Crook continued his quest of the bands scattered between the Yellowstone and the Black Hills. After destroying a Sioux village at Slim Buttes in Dakota, he too disbanded his forces, and they returned to their bases.

To the great anger of Montanans, the departure of Terry and Crook left only Colonel Nelson A. Miles, with his Fifth Infantry and eight companies from two other regiments, to police eastern Montana during the coming winter. This small army was based at the mouth of the Tongue River, the site of future Fort Keogh, and the town of Miles City arose to serve it. Colonel Miles was a shrewd, tough, and capable man and would gain fame as one of the greatest of all frontier commanders. He was also vain and ruthless, and he had the nice advantage of being married to the niece of General of the Army William Tecumseh Sherman. Although infantry troops were normally believed inferior to swift cavalry in fighting Indians, Miles drilled his men unceasingly and disciplined them for long winter marches. His tough foot soldiers proved themselves superior to cavalry, which required feed for horses and large supply trains.

Miles took the five hundred men of the Fifth Infantry into the field in October of 1876. After Sioux forces under Sitting Bull had disrupted wagon traffic between Glendive Creek and the Tongue River, Miles confronted the headstrong chief at Cedar Creek north of the Yellowstone. When negotiations between Miles and Sitting Bull failed, the soldiers, making good use of artillery, drove the Indians from their camps and scattered them in two days of fighting. This encounter cost the Sioux dearly in irreplaceable food, supplies, and horses, and some gave up afterward and went back to the reservation. Others under Sitting Bull fled.

The fight at Cedar Creek was only the beginning. Miles obtained winter clothing for his men, and they cut up wool blankets for long underwear. Shrewdly, the colonel acquired Indian spies and an efficient corps of scouts, the most valuable of whom was Luther "Yellowstone" Kelly. In the severe cold of November and December 1876, "Bear Coat," as the Indians called Miles, led his infantrymen north into the Missouri and Musselshell country. One of his battalions under Lieutenant Frank Baldwin hit Sitting Bull's camp on the Redwater River, and the losses suffered there soon convinced the chief to head for Canada.

General Crook, meanwhile, was rebuilding his forces in Wyoming. He brought a large army up the old Bozeman Road in November. Discovering the big Cheyenne village of Dull Knife and Little Wolf on the Red Fork of the Powder River, Crook sent out a powerful column under Colonel Ranald Mackenzie which attacked and decimated it. The Cheyennes fled with terrible suffering. Now Miles, too, closed upon the Indians south of the Yellowstone. Leading 350 of his men, who were by now calling themselves the "walk-a-heaps," he moved up the Tongue River in the last days of 1876. Early in January 1877 he expertly fought a stand-off battle with Crazy Horse at Wolf Mountain; both sides had to withdraw from the battleground, owing to weather and supply problems.

While Miles and Crook kept the pressure on the hostile bands, they also sent out emissaries to convince the chiefs that they should give up and return to the agencies. Hungry and demoralized, the Sioux and Northern Cheyenne bands straggled in and surrendered throughout the spring of 1877. Even the great Crazy Horse gave up early in May. Lame Deer's Sioux band still held out, though; so Miles struck it on Muddy Creek in May. In the ensuing violence, Lame Deer was killed, and Miles narrowly escaped death himself. The Army spent the summer of 1877 rounding up the remnants of this band, and by the following autumn the conquest of the Sioux and Northern Cheyennes was complete. Forts Keogh and Custer now stood guard over the Yellowstone country, and Montanans rejoiced at the removal of the Indian "menace." For this, the handsome, chest-pounding Miles claimed—and deserved—most of the credit.

THE NEZ PERCE RETREAT

Among the most impressive of American Indians were the Nez Perces of north central Idaho and northeastern Oregon. The Nez Perces had, over the years, exhibited a genuinely friendly attitude toward the whites; but the Idaho gold rush of the early 1860s soured relations. In 1863 the government negotiated with the Nez Perces a harsh treaty depriving them of much of their best land. While some Nez Perce bands accepted this treaty and moved onto a reservation, others refused to recognize it. Thus the tribe became divided into "treaty" and "nontreaty" factions.

For a dozen years the nontreaty bands, including that of Chief Joseph in the Wallowa Valley of Oregon, continued to live the old way, off the reservation. But by the mid-1870s increasing white penetration of these areas led to heightened demands for removal of the nontreaty Indians to the reservation. The demands finally came to a head early in 1877. In May of that year one-armed General Oliver O. Howard, commander of the Army's Department of the Columbia, conferred at Lapwai with Joseph and the other nontreaty chiefs. Howard ordered the chiefs to move onto the reservation within the impossible deadline of thirty days, and they sorrowfully agreed. In mid-June, as the bands gathered east of the Snake River, several bitter young braves struck out angrily and killed a handful of white settlers.

Fearing reprisals before they could explain what had happened, the Nez Perce chiefs fell back into the rough Salmon River country to await developments. Meanwhile, more whites lost their lives, and General Howard sent out a column to hit the Indians. When the soldiers mounted their attack, though, the Nez Perces beat them decisively in the Battle of White Bird Canyon. The chiefs, Joseph, White Bird, Looking Glass, and Toohoolhoolzote, then gathered on the large Clearwater River. Here, in the Battle of the Clearwater, they fought a pitched battle with Howard's troops and demonstrated impressive marksmanship and military ability. Leaving Howard's army behind on the Clearwater, the Nez Perces headed eastward over the Lolo Trail into Montana, hoping to join up with the Crows, or maybe even with Sitting Bull in Canada. They numbered roughly eight hundred people, and brought with them their prized horse herds and all their belongings.

The Nez Perce intrusion set off a near-panic in Montana. From his headquarters at Fort Shaw, Colonel John Gibbon hastily put together a force to intercept them. Meanwhile, local volunteers and troops from newly built Fort Missoula under Captain C. C. Rawn tried to block the Indians' passage down Lolo Creek by erecting a stockade, which was later appropriately named "Fort Fizzle." The Indians simply flanked the fort and headed southward up the Bitterroot Valley. They left the local settlers alone and crossed over the continental divide into the Big Hole Basin. Here, knowing that General Howard was far behind, they made camp and rested.

What they did not, and could not, know was that Colonel Gibbon was following them up the Bitterroot with a makeshift army of over two hundred men. At sunup on August 9 Gibbon attacked the sleeping village. His men peppered the lodges with rifle fire, resulting in the usual slaughter of women and children. They captured the camp but then lost it again when the Indians regrouped and outfought them. Nez Perce sharpshooters picked off Gibbon's men, especially the officers, with uncanny accuracy and drove them back into a coulee. The Indians held them under siege there until late the next day and then fled. The Nez Perces beat Gibbon decisively, killing thirty of his command. But they suffered terribly too, leaving eighty-nine dead, many of them women and children, at the site of the Big Hole Battle.

As Howard's army once again approached them, the crippled Nez Perces looped back momentarily into Idaho. When the slow-moving general drew near them at Camas Meadows, the braves ran off 150 of his pack mules.

Montanans stepped up their criticism of Howard and began to appreciate the Indians' nickname for him, "General Day after Tomorrow." In late August the refugees terrorized tourists on their way through newly created Yellowstone National Park. When they came out of the park area, moving northeast down the Clark Fork of the Yellowstone, they found units of the Seventh Cavalry under Colonel Samuel Sturgis in front of them. By feinting southward, they removed Sturgis from their path and then headed north across the Yellowstone River. Enroute, they shot up the settlements around today's Billings. Sturgis caught up with them at Canyon Creek, north of the Yellowstone, but the warriors smoothly held off his troops while their families escaped.

By now, mid-September of 1877, the Nez Perces were moving northward through central Montana, heading for Canada with General Howard, as usual, safely behind them. They might well have made it, but Howard now called for help from Colonel Miles at Fort Keogh. Wasting no time, Miles led an infantry-cavalry column on a diagonal march northward to intercept the Indians. The Nez Perces crossed the Missouri River at Cow Island. Here they found some troopers from Fort Benton guarding supplies recently unloaded from a steamboat. The Indians ran them off, helped themselves to what they needed, and moved on. Knowing that Howard was far behind, the exhausted refugees halted late in September on the northern slopes of the Bear Paw Mountains, only forty miles from Canada. Unfortunately, they had no way of knowing that Miles, who had by chance come upon a steamboat that ferried his command across the Missouri, was fast closing upon them.

Miles's cavalry, Sioux and Cheyenne auxiliaries riding with them, hit the Nez Perce camp on September 30. They captured most of the Indian horses, but again the Nez Perce marksmen made them pay dearly. The soldiers suffered sixty casualties in this charge, including many officers. Wisely, Miles now laid siege to the camp and used his artillery to pound it. In the meantime, he negotiated for their surrender. At one point, Miles deceitfully seized Joseph under a flag of truce, but the Nez Perces simply captured one of his officers and then exchanged him for their chief. As the Battle of the Bear Paws wore on, and Howard finally arrived with his army, the chiefs argued over whether or not to surrender. Joseph favored surrender; and finally, with Toohoolhoolzote and Looking Glass dead and with White Bird choosing to escape into Canada, he had his way. On October 5 Joseph surrendered his rifle to Miles and Howard. More than four hundred of his remaining people gave in with him, while some others fled across the border. Even though it now seems doubtful that Joseph really spoke the famous words, "From where the sun now stands I will fight no more forever," it was a dramatic and poignant moment.

So ended one of the most incredible Indian wars in history, a war in which the Indians far outperformed their white enemies. With the close of the fighting, a new hero passed into the realm of American legend. Chief Joseph emerged from the newspapers of 1877 and lived on in many later books and articles as a "Red Napoleon," a military genius who beat the best the United States Army had to offer. Actually, although Joseph was an exceptional man and a great leader, he shared command with the other Nez Perce chiefs and did not play a leading military role himself. The Nez Perces justly deserved the reputation they won as superb fighters, but in truth much of their success resulted from the bungling of the armies that pursued them.

After their surrender in the Bear Paws, the Nez Perces faced a miserable future. Although Miles and Howard had assured Joseph that his people might return to the Lapwai Reservation in Idaho, the government sent them instead to Kansas, and later to the Indian Territory of Oklahoma. Here they wasted away until finally Joseph, with the help of Miles and others, gained federal permission to return to the Pacific Northwest. In 1885 Joseph and the last of the Nez Perce refugees were located on reservations in Idaho and Washington territories.

In 1878, the year following Joseph's surrender, Montana saw its last real Indian "resistance." As a result of the wretched conditions on their southeastern Idaho reservation, a number of Indians, most of them Bannocks, fled the reserve and fought a series of skirmishes with pursuing armies. Twice the band of well known Bannock Chief Tendoy came into Montana during 1878, looking desperately for buffalo. Tendoy agreeably allowed military escorts to police his travels and caused no real problems. Later in 1878, though, larger and more aggressive Bannock parties crossed their old hunting trail through Yellowstone Park and emerged on the Clark Fork of the Yellowstone. By an amazing coincidence, Colonel Nelson Miles happened to be heading toward the Park with some of his men for a vacation. With little difficulty, Miles cut off the Bannocks and ended their flight from the reservation.

THE END OF THE BUFFALO DAYS

Although the Nez Perce and Bannock campaigns signaled the close of organized Indian resistance, friction still continued between red men and whites. Stockmen and miners, among others, still trespassed upon Indian lands, and this led to occasional violence and the inevitable demands for punishment. Sitting Bull and his band yet remained in Canada, and much of Montana lived in fear of their return. The heart of the problem, though, was the terrible situation on the reservations. The nomadic tribes had not really adjusted to reservation life, and the agencies seldom had enough foodstuffs, seed grains, or livestock to care for them. So the Indians naturally continued to hunt buffalo, as they had for generations.

Tragically, the seemingly limitless herds of buffalo vanished in an astonishingly short time as a result of the great hunts of the 1870s and early 1880s (see discussion in chap. VII). Despite warnings from the agencies, Washington failed to provide for the day when the Indians could no longer depend upon the buffalo for food. The results were truly ghastly. Beginning in the winters of 1880–81 and 1881–82, the tribes began to feel the full impact of the buffalo's disappearance, as their hunters returned almost empty handed. Now the Indians clustered desperately around the meager croplands and cattle herds at the agencies. The agencies, starved by Congress and sometimes drained by corruption, simply lacked the means to sustain them. In an atmosphere of nightmarish suffering, large numbers of Indians wasted away from malnutrition and starvation. According to John C. Ewers, "Between one-fourth and one-sixth of the Piegans in Montana must have perished from starvation in the years 1883–84." The Blackfeet recall a man named Almost-a-Dog, who cut a notch in a stick for each Indian who died: the notches eventually totaled 555. Mournfully, the Piegans buried their dead on a hill near Badger Creek still known as "Ghost Ridge."

Even as the Indians lost their capacity to make war, the rising white community in Montana Territory demanded greater military protection from them. Montanans worried especially about the Sioux under Sitting Bull who, eventually numbering over four thousand, remained north of the border in Canada. Fugitive Nez Perces and other Indians joined them. Sitting Bull's people generally behaved peacefully, but they perplexed both the Canadians and the Americans. As the buffalo herds began to thin out in Canada, Sioux bands roamed south of the border to hunt on the reservation lands in northern Montana. Eventually, indeed inevitably, the disappearance of the buffalo forced these Indians, like all the others, to give up the old ways. During 1879 and 1880, most of the chiefs moved back to the United States and went grudgingly on the reservations. In July 1881 Sitting Bull himself surrendered; and years later, he, like Crazy Horse earlier, died violently on the reservation.

Amidst the tension caused by Sitting Bull's wanderings, the Army built Fort Assiniboine in 1879 on the northwestern slopes of the Bear Paw Mountains. This million-dollar installation grew to become one of the major military bases in the West. As, one by one, earlier posts like Forts Shaw and Ellis were closed down, Fort Assiniboine's handsome brick buildings became the Army's central nucleus for all regional operations and headquarters for the District of Montana. One year later, in 1880, a smaller post named Fort Maginnis was erected in the Judith Basin, mainly in order to halt Indian thievery against stockmen. Fort Assiniboine, along with Forts

Keogh and Custer, and Fort Harrison, built near Helena in 1892, guarded the Montana frontier during its twilight years.

As the Indian wars faded into memory, the same problems that had caused them continued to plague the beleagured red men. The huge, seemingly near vacant reservations, especially the one above the Missouri River, attracted the interest of stockmen, farmers, miners, and rail promoters, all of whom demanded that the reserves be scaled down and that the lands thus freed be opened to more "beneficial" use by whites. Inevitably, the great reservations began to contract. During 1880–82 the Crows ceded away another 1,688,000 acres from the western end of their reservation, land long sought by mining promoters. The Crow Agency was moved eastward in 1884 to the Little Big Horn Valley. In 1887–88, more importantly, the government arranged the session of 17,500,000 acres from the enormous reservation lying north of the Missouri River. In return for long-term annuities, the Blackfeet accepted a smaller reserve in the upper Marias drainage. Similarly, the Gros Ventres and Assiniboines took a reservation on the Milk River, and the Fort Belknap Agency was moved there in 1889. And the Montana Sioux joined other Assiniboines on the Fort Peck Reservation in the state's northeastern corner.

In addition to these four reserves and the large Salish-Kutenai Reservation in the Flathead Valley, another was created for the Northern Cheyennes on the Tongue and Rosebud rivers in 1884. Following their defeats of 1876–77, they had been sent to live with their Southern Cheyenne kinsmen in the Indian Territory that became Oklahoma. Unable to adjust to the humid climate and the loss of their homeland, they suffered grievously and many died. So, during the "Cheyenne Autumn" of 1878, Chiefs Little Wolf and Dull Knife led their bands in a dramatic race back to Montana. Many of the Cheyennes lost their lives on this epic trek, but those who survived eventually joined the Two Moons Cheyennes on the Tongue River Reservation.

For the Northern Cheyennes, and for all Indians, reservation life proved difficult and degrading. Their nomadic, hunting civilization had been destroyed forever; and, like so many other races who have seen their cultural heritage shattered, they had great difficulty reorienting themselves. Increasingly during the 1880s thoughtful Americans began to conclude that the reservations offered no real solution to the Indians' plight. Idealistic reformers came up with what seemed a better answer: the "allotment" of reservation lands to individual Indians. If the natives received their own lands in severalty, so the argument went, they could learn to become efficient farmers, like any other Americans. In doing so, they would, it was hoped, give up the old tribal ways and adjust to the white civilization: eventually, they would be absorbed into American society and become full-fledged United States citizens.

This was the philosophy that produced the far-reaching Dawes Act of 1887. The Dawes Act granted plots of land to each member of a tribe— usually 160 acres or more to heads of families, with lesser amounts for dependents and unmarried persons. In order to protect the Indians from swindlers, the law denied them the right to dispose of this land within twenty-five years. It sought directly to break up the tribal units and provided that, when the Indians became legal landowners, they would also become United States citizens with all due rights. With the dawn of the twentieth century, the allotment process of the Dawes Act began to take effect on the Indian lands of Montana. The reservations were surveyed and the lands alloted to individuals. In some cases, as on the Flathead Reserve, the lands remaining after allotment were opened to white settlement. In other cases, as at Fort Belknap, they were not.

In the long run, the Dawes Act proved a failure. Under its provisions, in Montana and elsewhere, the Indians lost some of their best lands and got little in return. Most Indians could not make the transition from hunters to agriculturalists: their cultural background made it difficult if not impossible. Thus, as the twentieth century began, the Indian passed into the ranks of forgotten Americans. An "Indian," to the average American, meant the spirited warrior of the 1870s, not the impoverished native isolated on some faraway reservation. It would be many years before the United States would again take note of what had happened to its Indian population.

CHAPTER VII

Stockmen and the Open Range

Just as precious metals had first attracted a sizable population to western Montana in the 1860s, the more abundant resource of free grass first lured a permanent white populace onto the eastern plains during the 1870s. The natural vegetation of east-central Montana—blue gramma, needle-and-thread, buffalo grass, and western wheatgrass—had, after all, supported millions of buffalo for hundreds of years; and, since the range lay open, largely unsurveyed, and free for the taking, stockmen wasted little time in putting it to use. During the 1870s and 1880s, while the farmers' frontier paused well to the east of the semiarid Great Plains, the cattlemen's frontier entered east-central Montana from two different directions. An indigenous livestock industry, which had grown up in southwestern Montana during the mining rushes of the 1860s, began probing beyond the Rockies into the north-central part of the territory in the mid-1870s. By 1880 another invasion of stockmen, many of them driving longhorns north from Texas, was beginning to enter the Yellowstone drainage from the southeast. Like closing blades of a scissors, these two advancing waves of the stockmen's frontier met and commingled in central Montana during the 1880s. All across the eastern two-thirds of Montana, cattle and sheep outfits, some of them large, corporate ranches, sprouted like mushrooms, thriving on the free grass of the public domain. They prospered for a short while but soon began to fail, as the terrible effects of the "Hard Winter" of 1886–87 and wasteful overcrowding combined to speed the downfall of the open range economy. Eventually, as the unfenced open range system proved to be impractical, the pioneer stockmen abandoned it and turned to the closed range system of bought or leased land that still thrives today throughout Montana.

THE FIRST STOCKMEN

Cattlemen actually entered the Montana area even before the 1860s gold rushes. Jesuit missionaries and early traders, like John Owen in the Bitterroot, kept some domestic stock, but the first real trade in cattle resulted from commerce on the Oregon Trail. By the time travelers on the trail reached present southwestern Wyoming or southeastern Idaho, their livestock were usually famished. Recognizing an opportunity here, former fur trader Richard Grant and his sons, Johnny and James, began acquiring cattle through trade in 1850, driving them northward into the Beaverhead Basin of southwestern Montana for grazing. The Grants then herded the fattened cattle back to the Oregon Trail during the following spring, trading one fresh animal for two that were trail weary. Soon they had a sizable herd, and soon more pioneer stockmen began to join them in the high mountain valleys of southwestern Montana. In 1853, for instance, Neil McArthur and Louis Maillet brought cattle from the Oregon country, grazed them for a season in the Bitterroot-Missoula area, and then returned them to the Columbia Valley for sale.

So the first miners to enter southwestern Montana found cattlemen already on the scene. On his second trip to Montana, in the fall of 1863, James Liberty Fisk reported cattle grazing on the Morgan ranch in the Prickly Pear Valley and noted that the Grants had several thousand head in the Deer Lodge country. The mining rushes, along with new military forts and Indian agencies, now offered these stockmen lucrative markets. Not surprisingly, therefore, men like Conrad Kohrs and Philip Lovell gave up the uncertainties of prospecting and turned instead to buying, butchering, and selling beef.

Some of the prospectors-turned-cattlemen did very well. Conrad Kohrs moved naturally from selling meat to producing it. He bought the Johnny Grant ranch in the Deer Lodge Valley in 1865 and soon ranked among Montana's leading stockmen. Eyeing the isolated and hungry mining town markets, outside cattlemen now began entering Montana in significant numbers from all points of the compass. In the fall of 1864, for example, William C. Orr of the California-based Poindexter and Orr partnership drove a herd into the Beaverhead Valley for wintering. Within a few years Poindexter and Orr ran one of the territory's largest cattle-sheep operations. Dan Floweree brought a cattle herd from Missouri in 1865, and in 1866 Nelson Story drove the first Texas longhorns into Montana, locating in the Gallatin Valley.

These early outfits relied almost exclusively on the open, unfenced range. They simply allowed the animals to fend for themselves and used natural barriers like forests and rivers to limit their movement. Most ranchers cut only small amounts of hay, which they fed mainly to bulls and saddle horses. Usually, they drove their stock into the high country for summer grazing and saved the valley floors and foothills for winter pasture. Although a few drovers, like Nelson Story and Dan Floweree, brought in Texas longhorns, few of these lanky creatures arrived in Montana before 1880. The vast majority of early Montana cattle were shorthorns, mainly from the Pacific Coast states and Utah. The Montana livestock industry depended upon the territorial government for regulation and law enforcement from the very beginning. As early as 1865, the legislature enacted the first law requiring owners of stock to adopt and record distinctive brands as signs of ownership. Poindexter and Orr posted the first brand in Montana. In subsequent sessions the legislators passed many laws, regulating the use of summer and winter pasture, roundups, and the handling of estrays.

By the early 1870s rising meat production and the decline of gold mining were combining to glut the local market and drive down meat prices. In May 1874 the *New Northwest* of Deer Lodge estimated that Montana contained seventeen thousand cattle in excess of local needs, most of them four- and five-year-olds. Under the circumstances Montana cattlemen had to reach out for new markets by driving their stock to faraway railheads. The first long drives took place in 1868, when Montana drovers sold their animals to Union Pacific construction crews in southern Wyoming. Completion of the Union Pacific in 1869 brought rails into closer driving distance. By 1873–74 Montana herds began to appear regularly at Granger, Pine Bluffs and Cheyenne, Wyoming. Some Montana cattlemen, like Con Kohrs, joined the Wyoming Stock Growers' Association in order to secure brand inspection from that powerful organization.

Montana cattle drivers also headed northward into Canada. Robert Ford and other Montana herders drove stock up the Whoop-Up Trail and sold it for slaughter to the Royal Canadian Mounted Police and to Indian agencies. I. G. Baker, among others, secured handsome beef contracts to feed the crews building the Canadian Pacific Railroad. And even as early as 1872 stockmen like John McDougall moved animals onto the Canadian plains to form the nuclei of permanent herds there. Some ranchers drove their stock to Dakota Territory during the later 1870s, either to feed the mining camps in the Black Hills or to reach the Northern Pacific railhead at Bismarck. When the Northern Pacific resumed construction westward in 1879, drives in this direction became much more common.

The long drives to and from Montana fit the pattern that prevailed throughout much of the West during those years. In order to move a large herd of, say, twenty-five hundred cattle, an outfit needed as many as twenty men, several wagons, forty or more horses, and large amounts of equipment and provisions. Traveling at the common rate of ten miles per day, trail outfits often spent two months covering four hundred to six hundred miles. The drovers broke camp at daybreak, grazed the herds on the move throughout the day with only a brief noon break, and then usually stopped early for the evening. Through the night, pairs of mounted cowboys took turns circling the herd, often singing to pacify the animals. As cowboy John Barrows said, "It must never be thought that the cow has a good ear for music. If this were true, the herd would have been stampeded by his songs."

By the early 1870s overcrowded and overgrazed ranges and the rising competition of farmers and dairymen for use of the land began pressuring Montana stockmen eastward and northward, beyond the mountains into central Montana. The well grassed Sun River Valley served as the main portal for this northeastward movement of the Montana cattle industry. Possibly as early as the fall of 1869, Con Kohrs brought a thousand head onto the south bank of the Sun River. In 1871 another prominent rancher, Robert Ford, followed and established his famous outfit at the Sun River Crossing near Fort Shaw. Eastward momentum carried the pioneer ranchers on, beyond the Missouri into the sheltered confines of the Smith and upper Musselshell rivers.

William Gordon, among several others, had cattle in both these areas by 1872; and by 1875–76, the Moore brothers, Perry, Sanford, and John, had a sizable herd on the upper Musselshell. Over the next few years, the cattlemen braved Indian raids and pushed inexorably down the Musselshell Valley. Robert Coburn located his famous Circle C Ranch on Flatwillow Creek in 1877. Kohrs, in partnership with John Bielenberg, soon entered this area too. Most inviting of all to the stockmen was the luxuriant Judith Basin, lying north of the upper Musselshell. Once the Judith was freed of Indian claim, it filled rapidly with cattle. T. C. Power, the Fort Benton magnate, established his Judith Cattle Company there in the late seventies. In 1880 Granville Stuart located the famous DHS Ranch, a partnership between himself, Samuel Hauser, and A. J. Davis, at the northern end of the Judith Mountains near Fort Maginnis. Another well known pioneer, James Fergus, located nearby on Armell's Creek.

By the early eighties the entire central section of the territory, from the Sun River eastward to Fort Benton, the Judith Basin, and the lower Musselshell, supported large herds feeding on the public domain. For the most part, these ranchers north of the Yellowstone country were men like Granville Stuart, Con Kohrs, and James Fergus—older, well established Montana operators. Often in partnership with local bankers and merchants, they raised mostly shorthorn cattle and worked together easily in local stockgrowers' associations.

Interestingly, sheepmen and horse ranchers moved alongside cattlemen.

In contrast to some other places, like Wyoming, breeders of sheep and horses got along reasonably well with cattlemen in Montana; many operators, in fact, raised horses, sheep, and cattle together. Montana became famous by the 1880s for its fine horse herds. Among the territory's major horsemen were W. E. Larabie of Deer Lodge, J. S. Pemberston and C. E. Williams of Helena, and Nelson Story of Bozeman, who grazed a large herd on the upper Yellowstone.

Sheep appeared about as early as cattle in Montana. Jesuit priests raised them at St. Ignatius Mission in the 1850s. During the 1860s flocks of sheep accompanied herds of cattle onto the ranges of southwestern Montana. In 1869 John F. Bishop and Richard Reynolds began the territory's first major sheep operation when they brought fifteen hundred head from Oregon to the Beaverhead Valley. After wintering the animals there, they sold their fleeces to C. A. Broadwater, who hauled them to Utah for rail transport east in what may have been the first commercial wool shipment from Montana.

Until the mid-1870s the sheep industry amounted to little in Montana. The 1870 Census recorded only 2,024 sheep in the territory, and most of these were in the Beaverhead Valley. During the decade that followed, sheepmen increased rapidly in numbers and holdings, and they followed the same path of geographic expansion into central Montana as did the cattlemen. In 1874 the A. W. Kingsley outfit moved into the area south of the Great Falls, and Charles W. Cook took sheep into the Smith River Valley. William and John Smith led flocks into the upper Musselshell country in 1877. By early 1879 according to the *Rocky Mountain Husbandman*, fifteen thousand sheep were roaming the Smith River and sixty thousand were on the Musselshell.

During these pioneer years the sheep industry tended to attract more small investors than did cattle ranching. Like cattlemen, wool-growers relied upon the open range for forage, and sheep had the advantages of requiring only small original investments and of providing wool clips for extra profit. Well established Montana investors began to rise and take notice of the potential of the sheep industry, especially when John Healy, representing a major wool purchasing concern, opened a depot at Helena in 1878. Such successful miners as Thomas Cruse, whose Montana Sheep Company located the N Bar Ranch on Flatwillow Creek, or bankers like John T. Murphy of Helena, whose 79 Ranch ran both cattle and sheep, exemplified this trend. Anxious to broaden their range of investments, these local capitalists usually employed experienced stockmen to manage their flocks and paid them with half the annual number of newborn lambs. During the good years, they profited handsomely.

THE OPEN RANGE BOOM OF THE 1880s

A number of different factors combined to produce the great open range boom of the 1880s. The rising urban population of the United States and Europe increased the demand for beef, and newly developed railroad refrigerator cars made quick delivery possible. The resumption of rail building throughout the West in the late seventies brought access to world markets right to the doorstep of previously isolated stockmen. And most dramatically of all, the slaughter of the immense herds of buffalo, along with the resulting confinement of the Indians on smaller reservations, opened up huge, new expanses of free, publicly owned land for pasturage.

The destruction of the buffalo offers perhaps the most incredible example in all frontier history of devastating the environment. For years prior to 1871, Indians killed limited numbers of these animals, and white hunters also took some, but not many, in order to supply the small market for robes. In that year, though, tanners found a method of treating buffalo hides for use as salable leather. Now, hide hunters, often encouraged by the railroads and joined by thrill-seeking "sportsmen," began the great buffalo hunt that quickly ended in the animal's obliteration. Small parties, often consisting of one hunter, two skinners, and a cook, took to the field for months at a time. Unlike the sportsmen who hunted from horseback, the professional hunters normally set up a stand downwind from a herd, then used heavy-caliber Sharps rifles to slaughter as many as eighty of the dumb beasts at a time. The professional took only the hide, leaving the meat to rot on the prairie. On a spring trip in 1880, Granville Stuart found the plains littered with rotting carcasses all the way from present Forsyth to Miles City.

Perhaps thirteen million buffalo roamed the West before the great hunt commenced. The slaughter rose in intensity throughout the 1870s and climaxed on the northern range during 1881–82. By 1883 it was all over. A survey that year found fewer than two hundred of the shaggy animals in the entire West. When in 1884 the last trainload of hides pulled out of Dickinson, Dakota, the center of shipment for the northern trade, it carried only enough hides to fill part of one car. For years afterward, enterprising individuals made money by collecting buffalo bones for processing into fertilizer. The Indians, as noted earlier, suffered miserably as their staff of life so rapidly disappeared. Step by step, they saw their once-rich hunting lands lopped off the reservations, to the applause of Montana and its stockmen.

In 1880, on the very eve of the great invasion of outside cattle that would boom Montana's livestock industry, Granville Stuart toured much of eastern Montana and found mostly empty countryside. The census of that year recorded only 428,279 cattle and 279,277 sheep in the entire territory. Most of this stock, of course, grazed the ranges of southwestern and west-central Montana. In the far northern, eastern, and southeastern expanses of the territory, Indian removal was just beginning to open vast new areas to penetration by "foreign" stockmen.

The stockgrowers' invasion into eastern Montana after 1880 was part of a general movement of eastern and foreign capital into the lucrative livestock industry. From Texas to Canada, large, corporate ranches spread out over the empty western plains. Local promoters, anxious to lure outside capital, painted a rosy picture of the profits to be made in ranching. In 1881 two books appeared that brought much attention to eastern Montana range-lands: James Brisbin's *The Beef Bonanza; or How to Get Rich on the Plains,* and Robert Strahorn's *Montana and Yellowstone National Park.* Quoting experienced ranchers and selecting their evidence carefully, both authors assured their readers that small investments in Montana livestock would bring reliable profits of at least 15 percent per year. Outside "experts" sang much the same song. The *Breeders' Gazette* explained how a five-dollar steer could be run for a season or two and then sold for forty-five to sixty dollars. In 1882 the Cincinnati *Gazette* stated categorically: "In the region traversed by the Northern Pacific lie boundless, gateless and fenceless pastures of public domain, where cattle can be grown and fattened with little operating expense save that of a few cowboys, some corrals and a branding iron. There a poor man can grow rich while a rich man can double or even treble his capital."

The big outside investors came from all parts of the country and even from foreign shores. In the summer of 1882, the Nebraska-based Carpenter and Robertson outfit located three thousand head on the Rosebud, while the Niobrara Cattle Company, also from Nebraska, drove ten thousand cattle into the Powder River Valley. The Concord Cattle Company of New Hampshire established itself on the Tongue River. From Nevada came the Scott and Hanks outfit, which drove herds into the valley of the Little Powder. Texas, of course, provided many of the cattle and some of the largest concerns. The Hash Knife spread, possibly the first Texas enterprise north of the Black Hills, based itself at the head of the Little Missouri River. By late 1883 the Hash Knife had moved northward astride the Montana-Dakota border, where it was joined by other Texas outfits like the 777 and the Mill Iron ranches. Soon, more large Texas investors, like the XIT and the Matador Land and Cattle Company moved heavily into Montana.

The established Montana ranchers reacted to the "Texas invasion" with less than enthusiasm. Many of them had never seen a longhorn. John Barrows once recalled that, when he and other DHS cowboys came to Miles City in the early eighties, they happened upon some of the wiry Texas creatures and saw them as an interesting curiosity. Probably reflecting a common Montana opinion, Robert Coburn viewed the longhorns, "all horn and bushy tails," as inferior to the shorthorn stock that he and other "old-time" Montanans were running on the western and central ranges of the territory. With some justification, men like Coburn, who used graded bulls and took pride in the quality of their stock, feared that the imported, low-quality longhorns would both overcrowd the range and endanger their quality bred herds.

These fears point to an interesting and neglected fact about the open range boom: the division between the older Montana ranchers, who generally grazed quality shorthorns to the north and west of the Yellowstone, and the newcomers, many of them Texans, who entered the territory from the southeast and expanded into the far eastern and northern areas. The established cattlemen differed from the newcomers, especially the Texans, in many ways. While the former were usually "she stockmen," who used the ranges for breeding purposes, the recent arrivals tended more often to be "steer men," who brought cattle from Texas for maturing on the northern grasslands. Outfits like the XIT, the Mill Iron, and the Matador Land and Cattle Company drove yearlings and two-year-olds up north, double wintered them in Montana and Wyoming, then marketed them as four- and five-year-olds. These steer operators were generally more speculative than the older Montana ranchers: they ran bigger herds, overcrowded the range, and aimed for a quick profit.

The two groups differed in other, more subtle ways, too. Teddy Blue Abbott, who worked for Granville Stuart and married one of his daughters, noted how Montana-based owners showed more concern for their men and provided them with better food and shelter. The cowhands themselves contrasted sharply. As Walt Coburn observed, the Texans, in comparison with the Montana cowboys, "were a different breed of cowhand for the most part." They roped differently, handled their horses differently, even dressed differently. The Texans wore drab clothes and chaps, while the Montana hands often adorned themselves in fluffy angora chaps of bright colors.

Tension between the older "Montanans" and the newly arrived "Texans" flared most openly over the question of a "national cattle trail." Texans, and other operators who drove southern bred stock north for maturing, desperately petitioned the federal government to lay aside a broad corridor of land for their use in moving cattle from Texas to the far northern ranges. The established Montanans opposed the idea vigorously. Since they raised their own calves, they had no need of a national cattle trail, and they argued against it as a source of overcrowding the range and introducing longhorn-carried diseases like the dreaded Texas Fever. The Texans never got their national cattle trail, but long drives continued to pour into southeastern Montana until well into the 1890s.

Enthusiasm for the livestock business also spread overseas. Some of the foreigners who turned up on the Montana range were known by the locals as "remittance men"—rich and adventuresome youngsters who lived mainly off the funds sent to them by their families. Others, however, were serious cattlemen, like the famous French stockman Pierre Wibaux, who built up a large and prosperous operation in the Beaver Valley along the Montana-Dakota line. Englishmen and Scots predominated among foreign investors. By the later 1870s so much American meat was pouring into the British Isles that a delegation from the Royal Agricultural Commission conducted a full investigation of the western cattle industry. Its report, brimming with enthusiasm over the profit potential of the Plains grasslands, convinced many British capitalists to invest in livestock. Englishmen controlled, among many others, such prominent firms as the N-F Ranch on the lower Musselshell, the Montana Sheep and Cattle Company, Ltd., and the Chalk Buttes Ranche and Cattle Company, Ltd. Although the enormous Matador outfit was Texas-based, Scottish investors actually owned it.

Foreign capital continued to pour into western ranching until Congress passed an 1887 law prohibiting aliens from owning any real estate in the territories. By that time the inflow of such heavy investments had drastically altered the organization of the business. Before the boom of the eighties, most Montana cattle operations were partnerships or family affairs, but many of the new outfits were full-fledged corporations with access to plenty of capital and thus plenty of stock. Dozens of such corporate ranches held Montana charters by 1886; and many others, like the Texas-based XIT, 777, and Continental Land and Cattle spreads, were incorporated in other states or territories. By 1886, at the peak of the open range boom, roughly 664,000 cattle and 986,000 sheep grazed the range lands of Montana. A heavy percentage of these animals belonged to the new corporate ranches, whose managers packed them onto limited ranges with no provisions of winter hay, in the hope of quick profits from minimal investments.

Flocks of sheep intermingled with herds of cattle on the booming open range of the 1880s. In fact, throughout the eighties, the sheep population steadily outpaced cattle in growth. By 1890 Montana ranked as the nation's sixth largest sheep producer. Prior to the 1890s most of the sheep brought to Montana were Merinos from the Pacific Coast, Idaho, Utah, and Nevada. After the decline of wool prices during the Panic of 1893, though, Montana sheepmen would turn increasingly to mutton breeds such as Cotswolds and Rambouillets crossed with Lincolns and Cotswolds to produce better feeder lambs.

By the late seventies and early eighties sheepmen, like cattlemen, were pressing into the far northern, eastern, and southeastern reaches of the territory. The leading pioneer sheepman of northern Montana was Paris Gibson, founder of the city of Great Falls. In 1874 Gibson and his son Theodore moved sheep into the vicinity of the present town of Belt, and soon afterward a partnership including Governor Benjamin Potts located a band of ewes on the Dearborn River. More and more sheepmen pressed into the northern Judith and eastern Musselshell country; and, with the removal of the Indians, into the Yellowstone Valley. Even in the frenzied spring of 1876, John Burgess brought eighteen hundred head of California sheep down the Yellowstone to the site of Miles City—without losing his scalp. Many others followed; and the lower Yellowstone became, for sheepmen as for cattlemen, the center of the great 1880s boom. A. M. and A. D. Howard pioneered the Rosebud country by driving in eleven thousand sheep in 1884; and a number of large operators led flocks into the Tongue and Powder valleys south of Miles City, among them W. E. Harris and the Myers brothers. By the mid-eighties sheep ranches dotted southeastern Montana; an 1884 map of Custer County reveals that one operation in every five raised sheep.

Interestingly, some sheepmen trailed their flocks through Montana enroute to markets in the Midwest. For example, J. B. Long of Great Falls would buy wethers in Oregon and trail them through the mountains to north central Montana. Then, each spring he moved his flocks, sometimes totaling 160,000 head in number, eastward, with shearing stops at Malta and Glasgow. In the autumn he shipped the fattened animals by rail out of Culbertson. Most operations, however, were smaller, less migratory, and more centrally based at one ranch headquarters. Ordinarily, wool-growers invested prudently in lambing pens, some sort of winter shelter, and at least some hay for use in the most severe cold. Herders tended the animals in bands of about two thousand and corralled or posted them at night to protect them against predators. In June the managers hired nomadic shearers to handle the wool clip. The shearers were, by and large, a rough lot. According to Walt Coburn, some of the shearers who worked for his father drank a quart of whiskey a day, and many mixed marijuana with their cigarette tobacco.

The Ways of the Open Range

Most of the open range cattlemen, and some sheepmen too, relied entirely upon unfenced pasturage for their animals. There were exceptions, of course, especially among the experienced ranchers of the western valleys and the north central region. Even in eastern Montana, intelligent newcomers like Pierre Wibaux raised enough alfalfa to provide feed in severe winter weather. But for the most part, the newer outfits, especially the big corporate ranches, made few investments and took few precautions. In any given grazing area, each ranch laid claim to an "accustomed range," which neighbors ordinarily recognized as private property, even though the land was public domain. The accustomed range, however, meant nothing to wandering animals; so the local ranchers had to cooperate in segregating animals and determining ownership. This need gave birth to the central institution of the open range, the roundup.

Cattlemen staged two roundups each year, one in late spring–early summer and one in the fall. By the early eighties territorial and county laws laid out roundup rules with precision. The territory was divided into districts. In 1886 seventeen districts covered central and southeastern Montana, each bounded by the natural configurations of the land. The Musselshell Valley, for instance, encompassed two districts, one for the upper drainage and one for the Flatwillow country. In each district the scattered ranches joined forces for the roundup. The larger roundups were colorful affairs, employing up to sixty or seventy men and hundreds of horses, with each outfit contributing according to the size of its herd. A roundup captain oversaw the entire operation and held the unlimited authority to hire, fire, and command any cowboy from any ranch.

The purpose of the all-important spring roundup was to gather up the cattle that had scattered during the winter, segregate them by brands, and return them to their home ranges. While segregating the stock, the cowboys branded the new calves and tallied the increases of their herds. During the spring roundup, cowboys often had to ride as many as seventy or eighty miles each day. The initial job of gathering the cattle took about three weeks, and the work of branding and driving the herds to home ranges sometimes carried well into July. As the roundup proceeded, the owners sent representatives, or "reps," as the cowboys called them, to neighboring district roundups in order to watch for brands from their ranges. Since the "reps" operated under their own supervision and held responsibility for many different brands, they, like the roundup captains, were considered a notch above most of the hired hands.

The principal task of the fall roundups, which were much smaller in scale than those of the spring, was to select out the mature cattle that were ready for market and then trail them off to a railhead. In the process, of course, the cowhands branded calves that had been missed in the spring. After the fall roundup the owners laid off many of the hired hands, a select few being retained for winter work. Those who found employment spent their time breaking horses, patrolling range lines, and working at general maintenance. Those left unemployed frequently "rode the grub line," or, in other words, bummed food and shelter from one ranch to another.

Since the stockmen and their roundup associations did not own their range land, they faced many perplexing problems. Running bulls on the open range caused constant headaches. If any individual rancher ran inferior bulls, or if he ran them at the wrong time of the year, all his neighbors suffered. The handling of mavericks, calves that could not be identified with their mothers, also led to frustration and trouble. In some districts local custom dictated that the maverick belonged to the "owner" of the range on which it turned up; but, predictably, this arrangement led to the dishonest practice of "mavericking," or indiscriminately branding any stray calf that turned up on one's territory. Many open range ranchers increased their herds by such methods. The district associations tried to control the maverick situation by prohibiting the use of branding irons at any time except during the common roundup. Finally, the stockmen found an answer to the problem by declaring mavericks common property of the district associations and selling them to raise money for association expenses.

The roundup associations faced other, larger problems that could not be handled on the local level. To deal with these difficulties, they had to organize on a territory-wide basis and turn to the government for help. One such problem arose from wandering Indian hunting parties, who preyed on livestock in the absence of buffalo. Largely in order to deal with Indian thievery, northern Montana stockmen formed what may have been the territory's first really effective regional cattlemen's organization, the Shonkin Association, in July 1881. The Shonkin Association, which covered the Shonkin, Highwood, Belt, and Arrow Creek districts, joined with other groups during 1882–83 to break up Indian camps south of the Missouri and drive their inhabitants back to the north. In October 1883 the newly arrived ranchers in the east formed a large organization of their own, the Eastern Montana Livestock Association, at Miles City. This group also fretted about Indian raids and petitioned the government to provide the reservations more adequately so that their residents would not have to steal.

Since the early 1870s Montana ranchers had been trying, without success, to create one, large, territory-wide organization to pursue their interests. With powerful James Fergus providing the leadership, they held a series of meetings at Helena early in 1879 and put together a group called the Montana Stock Growers Association. But this outfit, confined mainly to western Montana, faltered until 1884, when it reorganized and began to reach out toward cooperation with the Eastern Montana Livestock Association. Finally, in April 1885, the older stockmen of the Helena group joined the Eastern Montana Livestock Association at Miles City to create a territory-wide Montana Stockgrowers Association. At last the Montana cattlemen had joined permanently together in one, big organization. The Montana Stockgrowers Association wielded great economic and political power from the day of its birth; but it never quite matched the strength of its

Wyoming counterpart, mainly because Wyoming ranchers had no large mining interests with whom to compete.

The Montana sheepmen, who faced problems similar to those of the cattlemen, also organized themselves. Although little is known about its antecedents, the Montana Wool Growers Association took shape at Fort Benton in January of 1883, with Paris Gibson as its president. The sheepmen had trouble keeping their association going and had to reorganize it in 1895, this time with T. C. Power as president, and again in 1906. Amidst these reshufflings, which lasted until 1921, the Montana Wool Growers Association spoke out constantly in the interests of its members, demanding, among other programs, a protective tariff on wool and the establishment of a board of sheep commissioners to help protect them against disease and theft.

The open range stockmen reached the peak of their power in 1885, the year in which they organized the Montana Stockgrowers Association. That was also the year of the famous "Cowboy Legislature," when the livestock interests had things their own way in Helena. The legislators bestowed many favors upon the stockmen that year, such as the law outlawing branding at any time except during the roundup season. Of special significance, the 1885 Legislature created two new functions of government: a territorial veterinary surgeon, with vested power to quarantine cattle, and the all-important Board of Stock Commissioners, which would conduct brand inspection at marketing points and supervise the range industry in general.

Even with such aid from the territorial government, the open range stockmen faced difficulties that could never be fully mastered. Natural or man-caused prairie fires might destroy them at any time, and predators such as wolves and coyotes took a heavy toll. Both the territorial government and the associations placed bounties on wolves, and ranchers used poison against them. Thievery presented the knottiest problem of all, for rustlers could steal stock easily on the unfenced range. By the eighties, rustling had reached epidemic proportions in southeastern Montana–western Dakota, and was even worse in the Judith-Musselshell areas. Taking refuge in the Missouri Breaks, a motley assortment of unemployed whiskey traders, wolf hunters, woodchoppers, and trappers brazenly stole livestock in both Montana and Canada, then took the animals across the border for sale.

Like the miners of the 1860s, the cattlemen of the 1880s turned to vigilanteism. In mid-1884 a group of central Montana stockmen banded together under the leadership of Granville Stuart. Their organization, which came to be known, appropriately, as "Stuart's Stranglers," killed at least fifteen men. They staged a major shoot-out at Bates Point on the Missouri in July with eleven reprobates who were led by one John Stringer (alias "Stringer Jack"). A number of the outlaws died in the battle that day, and others were later seized from a deputy marshal and hanged. Stuart also joined another group of vigilantes on the lower Yellowstone. This band, whose activities have been lastingly veiled in secrecy, ran a special train down the Northern Pacific tracks, stopping periodically to deal with rustlers. They continued their manhunt in Dakota, and some old-timers figure they killed more than sixty men. James Fergus justified the vigilante killings by reasoning that "we must either gather up what stock we have left and leave the country or gather up these desperadoes and put them where they will kill and steal no more; there is no alternative, and we choose the latter. It is now simply a state of war." Fergus had a point, and the vigilante killings proved highly effective as a deterrent to rustling. But, as in the case of the infamous Johnson County War in Wyoming, the stockmen were severely criticized for their arbitrary killings.

In the final analysis, the open range stockmen faced one basic insurmountable difficulty: they could not control rangeland which they did not own. Few of the big outfits of the eighties owned much of their "accustomed range." Usually, the owners homesteaded or purchased land along rivers or streams and then claimed contiguous rangeland as theirs by prior appropriation. Sometimes ranchers had their cowhands file homestead claims on the range and then bought them up to form workable landholdings. Walt Coburn recalled that his father located "all the Circle C cowpunchers on the choice bottomlands along the creeks with various springs and water resources within a twenty-five mile radius on all sides of the home ranch."

Montana ranchers found another way to pick up title to rangeland by manipulating the Desert Land Act of 1877. This misguided law, which allowed "farmers" to buy 640 acres of land for only $1.25 per acre, provided that they irrigated a portion of it, was meant to encourage reclamation and improvement of the arid lands of the West. In practice, however, farmers could seldom irrigate such large plots without government support. Instead, cattlemen often claimed a section of range under the act, made some token effort to irrigate the land, and used it for pasturage until the end of the three-year "prove-up" period. Then they would simply forfeit the land to the government, having used it for three years at almost no expense. In another maneuver, stockmen bought or leased sections of land, and then fenced them in such a way as to enclose public lands as well as their own.

But, so long as the federal government refused to lease public lands for grazing purposes, a system the Canadian government found to be practical, open range cattlemen could not gain firm control of their range unless they bought it or leased it from private landlords. So they "squatted" on their "accustomed range" and protected it as best they could. If an interloper tried to crowd his stock onto someone else's range, local ranchers could refuse to allow him the privileges of belonging to the area roundup district. In 1885, for instance, John H. Conrad, a Fort Benton area rancher, moved six thousand cattle onto rangeland east of the Musselshell River which was claimed by the Niobrara Cattle Company. A fall meeting of Miles City stockmen condemned Conrad for this violation of range law and warned him that they would not handle his stock or cooperate with him in any way. He got the message and withdrew his herd; but such methods were not always so successful, simply because the unfenced ranches, especially the large corporate ranches, crowded in and overstocked the grasslands.

As Granville Stuart wrote, "Cattle men found ways to control the other difficulties but the ranges were free to all and no man could say, with authority, when a range was overstocked." So the great open range boom mounted steadily through the mid-1880s, and the ranges became more and more dangerously overcrowded. At its 1886 meeting in Miles City, the Montana Stockgrowers Association discussed the problem of overstocking with intense anxiety; and during the fall of that year the Little Missouri Stock Growers' Association even announced that its members would not cooperate with any more new outfits. Stuart observed: "The range business was no longer a reasonably safe business; it was from this time on a 'gamble' with the trump cards in the hands of the elements."

The "Hard Winter" of 1886–87 and Its Aftermath

Montana cattlemen had seen hard winters before 1886–87, for instance in 1880–81. They came through those winters in reasonably good shape, mainly because the ranges were not overgrazed, feed was abundant, and most of the cattle were well acclimated to northern climates. And in those days, before the great open range boom, a fair percentage of ranchers put up winter hay. The year 1886, however, dawned upon plains cattle ranges that were recklessly overstocked and prone to disaster. The winter of 1885–86 was warm and "open," with little snow. A hot, dry summer followed, and autumn found the grass in poor condition. "Our ranges are already bare," wrote Governor Samuel T. Hauser to the secretary of the interior, "or so nearly so that our stock is in poor condition for the winter, and should it prove long and severe great loss must inevitably follow." Still, the range continued to fill. A market glut and falling beef prices in 1885–86 produced a carryover of many steers, which otherwise would have been marketed in the fall of 1886. At the same time, cattle and sheep poured into the territory in larger and larger numbers. Many of the trail cattle, especially those from the south, arrived late in the autumn, in poor condition to face the winter.

The snow and cold set in during November. Following a brief chinook in

January, a long and terribly severe cold spell caked the scant forage with ice. The cold, wind, and snow continued through February, frightfully punishing man and beast. Some ranches recorded temperatures of −63 degrees. As Joseph Kinsey Howard described it, "Starving cattle staggered through village streets, collapsed and died in dooryards. Five thousand head invaded the outskirts of the newborn city of Great Falls, bawling for food. They snatched up the saplings the proud city had just planted, gorged themselves upon garbage." When chinook winds in March finally lifted the cold, plains cattlemen looked in horror upon the results of their ill-planned misuse of the environment. The bloated carcasses of their once-great herds lay scattered across the landscape. For most of them it was a wrenching emotional experience. "A business that had been fascinating to me before," wrote Granville Stuart, "suddenly became distasteful. I wanted no more of it. I never wanted to own again an animal that I could not feed and shelter."

The losses were hideous, perhaps 362,000 head of cattle, 60 percent of the territory's entire beef population. Losses are actually impossible to determine, partly because many managers used the winter kill to cover up careless bookkeeping. One ingenious manager, in fact, blamed the hard winter for a total loss of 125 percent—50 percent steers and 75 percent cows! Clearly, west-central Montana ranchers fared much better than the reckless newcomers to the east. From loss rates of less than 40 percent in the valleys of the Sun, Teton, and Marias rivers, the curve reached upward to 90 percent kills on some lower Yellowstone ranches. The winter wiped out many of the speculative, corporate ranches. As creditors demanded liquidation of their assets, these outfits rounded up their remaining steers and shipped them east, furthering the decline in beef prices. A typical casualty was the Niobrara Cattle Company. In the fall of 1886 it listed assets of over $1 million. By the following spring it had only 9,000 head of cattle left and claimed assets of less than $250,000.

Recovery from the disaster came surprisingly soon. The winter of 1887–88 was mild, and the following spring brought a good calf crop. A combination of ample rainfall and understocking brought the range back quickly, and the losses of 1887 cut the supply of beef, thus raising prices. Those with financial reserves, intelligence, and stamina stayed on the range, and many of them prospered. Pierre Wibaux, for example, returned to France, secured further credit, and steadily expanded his eastern Montana herds until he ranked as one of the largest individual cattle owners in the United States.

The hard winter broke the back of the open range empire, but large, unfenced outfits persisted in some areas for years afterward. Cattle drives from the south and west continued to enter Montana throughout the late eighties and early nineties. At the same time further reductions in the huge

Indian reservations opened vast new grazing areas to stockmen, especially above the Missouri River. During its twilight years the open range became increasingly concentrated in northern Montana, and especially in that large triangle of land lying between the Missouri River on the north, the Yellowstone on the south, and the Musselshell on the west—the area that Miles City photographer L. A. Huffman called the "Big Open." Open range outfits thrived in the Milk River Valley and other choice northern Montana areas, especially now that the Great Northern Railroad served the region, until homesteaders began arriving after 1900. The North Montana Roundup Association, organized after the open range had declined elsewhere, remained a potent force until well into this century.

In general, however, the open range system declined rapidly after the winter of 1886–87. The boom atmosphere evaporated, and the trend toward reckless investment in livestock reversed itself. While some big outfits, like the XIT and Matador spreads, continued to rely mainly on open range, the tendency everywhere was toward smaller ranches whose operators either owned or leased most of their land. The hard winter taught everyone the value of winter feed, and hay acreages increased rapidly, from about fifty-six thousand acres in 1880 to more than seven hundred thousand in 1900. Even the larger outfits began to provide feed and shelter for calves and weak cows.

Yet another response to the lessons of 1886–87 was the drastic increase in sheep ranching, for sheep weathered the crisis much better than did cattle. Stockmen who had formerly specialized in cattle, like Robert Coburn, now turned heavily to sheep. In northern Montana, men like B. D. Phillips and Angus Dunbar ran their flocks over enormous acreages, freed by the recent contraction of the reservations. The year 1887 witnessed the birth of two exceptionally large Montana sheep operations. With the backing of New York capital, Lee Simonsen began a large enterprise in the Castle Mountains and the Stillwater country; and Charles M. Bair originated an immense sheep empire based at Lavina, Hardin, and Martinsdale. The sheep population expanded throughout the 1890s until by 1900 it stood at roughly six million head, making Montana the nation's number one wool-growing state. Soon thereafter, though, the arrival of homesteaders would deprive both sheepmen and cattlemen of their choicest grasslands and put an end forever to the open range.

Like the miners who came earlier, the open range stockmen laid one of the cornerstones of the Montana economy. The open range also gave to Montana, and to the nation and, indeed, the world, one of our favorite heroes—the cowboy. Ever since he first appeared in late nineteenth century pulp fiction and in Owen Wister's popular novel *The Virginian* (1902), the cowboy has captured the American imagination as the embodiment of free and unfettered manhood. Actually, the realities of the cowhand's way of life, hard and monotonous as they were, scarcely warrant such sentiments.

The typical cowboy was young, probably in his early twenties, and wiry. Although our folklore fails to say so, he was often either a Negro or a Mexican. Especially when on the trail or during roundups, he worked long days with little sleep, and he labored under trying conditions, facing searing heat and bitter cold, drenching rains or snows and choking dust, kicking horses and nervous cattle. For this, he received wages lower than what most workers received in settled areas, thirty to forty-five dollars per month, plus keep. The keep left something to be desired, for the camp cook fed him a steady diet of beef, bacon, beans, bread, and sometimes canned fruit. The cowboy relished canned tomatoes as a luxury and viewed canned milk as a miracle. A. B. Guthrie, Jr., recalls one cowboy's poetic reaction to seeing his first can of milk:

> No tits to pull.
> No hay to pitch.
> Just punch a hole
> In the son of a bitch.

The cowboy relieved the monotony of his life with practical jokes and wry humor. He cut loose on his infrequent trips to such cow towns as Miles City, Chinook, or Lewistown. Here he could find liquor and beer and such exotic foods as eggs, celery, and oysters. Saloons, the cowhand's social centers, offered not only drink but also entertainment and the companionship of prostitutes. In Miles City, the epitome of cow towns, the Cosmopolitan Theater or the Gray Mule Saloon provided popular shows of all kinds. In the process of squandering their pay and raising hell, the cowboys frequently got out of hand and perturbed the local residents. According to Nannie Alderson, an astute observer, the residents of Miles City viewed them as a wild and undesirable lot. "Nice people in Miles City," she recalled, "would as soon have thought of inviting a rattlesnake into their homes as a cowboy." Reflecting, perhaps, such attitudes, Teddy Blue Abbott, a literate cowboy, commented that cowhands feared only two things: a decent woman and being set afoot.

The cowboys had their better side, too. Most of them were honest, loyal, and courageous; most of them seemed less interested in making money than in seeking adventure before growing old. Perhaps this is why they have always loomed so large in our folklore. Unlike the colorless and overburdened farmers, they seemed to be the last of the really free frontiersmen—mounted, unrestrained, and adventuresome. As America became an increasingly urban and industrialized society, the cowboy, who was not tied down to an industrial job and who seemed so free from the rat race, became a lasting, romanticized reminder of the way of life we were leaving behind.

Historian Lewis Atherton reminds us that our preoccupation with the cowboy leads us to neglect the role of the ranch owners themselves, who after all made the system work, and the important role played by women on the stockgrowers' frontier. Theodore Roosevelt, a one time Dakota rancher, put it aptly: "There is an old and true saying that 'the frontier is hard on women and cattle.' " Isolated and lonely, ranch women lived in a male dominated world. They dwelled in crude shacks or cabins with leaky dirt roofs, and pests such as bedbugs, flies, mosquitoes, and snakes added considerably to their discomfort. Water often had to be hauled and sometimes boiled before drinking. Since doctors were few and far between, women worried constantly about injury and disease. Those near reservations lived in fear of theft or violence.

They made the best of a tough situation. Ranchers tried to provide their womenfolk with such amenities as books and musical instruments, and many of the successful ones located their families in town. The mail order catalogs kept them in touch with the larger world, and picnics, parties, and dances broke up the monotony. Hoping for a better future, ranch women tolerated their unenviable situation on the assumption that "civilization" would soon come to them. Perhaps Nannie Alderson best summed up their stoical outlook: "When you live so close to the bare bones of reality, there is little room for sentiment." In contrast to Hollywood myth, life on the open range was hard and demanding.

CHAPTER VIII

Railroads, Silver, and Statehood

To the remote territories of the Far West, railroads meant everything during the decades following the Civil War. Boosters of every region and town prayed and plotted for a railroad that would build to their doorstep and bring them instant prosperity and the guarantee of permanent growth. Ranchers and farmers needed railroad access in order to reach national and international markets, and mining developers had to have rails, both to import heavy machinery and to export their precious metals. Once the rails arrived here, a boom in silver mining began that lasted into the 1890s and made Montana one of the leading industrial mining areas of the world. So the coming of the railroads, along with the resulting growth of corporate mining and livestock production, led to the flush times of the 1880s and paved the way for Montana statehood in 1889.

NORTHERN PACIFIC AND UNION PACIFIC

The dream of a transcontinental railroad, spanning the continent and linking the Mississippi Valley to the Pacific Coast, arose long before the Civil War. Until the southern states left the Union in 1861, however, jealousies between North and South over the route to be followed made Congressional action impossible. Once the South had seceded, Congress moved quickly to authorize and encourage the building of rails to the Pacific. The first transcontinental was the Union Pacific–Central Pacific line, which reached from Omaha to Sacramento over the old Oregon-California Trail route and was completed in 1869. Both the Union and the Central Pacific received generous federal aid in the forms of large government loans and huge grants of land, which could be sold to defray the costs of construction.

Announcement of this first transcontinental railroad convinced the states and territories far removed from its tracks that they, too, should have lines to serve them. Obligingly, in July 1864, Congress issued a charter for construction of a Northern Pacific Railroad, which would link Lake Superior to the north Pacific Coast. Congress offered the Northern Pacific a very lucrative subsidy. While refusing the Northern Pacific the loans that had been granted the Union Pacific–Central Pacific, lawmakers compensated by giving the N.P. the largest land grant in the history of American railroads. In its final form, the Northern Pacific land grant provided twenty sections of land per mile of track built in the states of Oregon and Minnesota, and forty sections per mile in the territories lying between these two states. This enormous swath of land, which was granted in alternate, checkerboard sections along each side of the right-of-way, eventually amounted to a total of forty-four million acres. Of this total, seventeen million acres lay within the boundaries of Montana Territory. Thus the Northern Pacific became, with the exception of the federal government itself, the largest landowner in Montana.

Raising money for construction proved difficult in the years following the Civil War. Since the Northern Pacific route crossed a generally uninhabited region, the railroad had little hope of immediate profits. But the land grant offered a powerful lure. In 1870 the great Philadelphia banking house of Jay Cooke and Company, which had handled government loans during the Civil War, agreed to finance construction of the N.P. and floated a one-hundred-million-dollar bond issue to raise the funds. Cooke sold the bonds to over eight thousand investors, and he promoted the N.P. route with such gusto that it soon became known as "Jay Cooke's banana belt." Starting from Pacific Junction, Minnesota, in 1870, crews pressed the rails westward until they reached the Missouri River at Bismarck, Dakota Territory, in 1873.

The enormous expenses involved in such rapid construction proved too heavy a burden, even for so great a banker as Jay Cooke. He overextended himself so severely that his bank failed. Its collapse, in turn, touched off a major nationwide depression, the Panic of 1873, which had a deadening impact upon all western rail building. The Northern Pacific fell into bankruptcy and remained halted in central Dakota. The failure of Cooke and the N.P. deeply distressed the small communities of Montana, who were hard hit by the Panic of 1873 and desperately sought rail connections. Without the N.P., as the *Bozeman Times* put it in 1876, Montana seemed doomed to remain "a dull monotonous Territory, cut off from the world and civilization."

Meanwhile, other rail promoters turned their attention toward Montana. For most of a decade, Mormon merchants in Utah had held sway over the markets of southwestern Montana by way of the Corinne–Virginia City

Road. Now that the Union Pacific had crossed Utah north of the Great Salt Lake, they could hold their share of the Montana trade by forging a rail spur north from the Union Pacific over the Corinne route, beating the N.P. into the Montana mining region. In the summer of 1871, therefore, Mormon investors led by John W. Young, the son of Brigham Young, joined a group of eastern capitalists led by Joseph Richardson to create the Utah Northern Railroad Company, which would construct a narrow gauge line north through Idaho into Montana.

The little Utah Northern also felt the financial squeeze of the 1873 Panic, and to the anguish of Virginia City and other southwestern Montana towns, it crept northward at a snail's pace. By 1874, its tracks reached only seventy-seven miles beyond Ogden to Franklin, Idaho. Realizing Montana's frustration, U.N. executives asked the territorial legislature for construction aid in the forms of tax exemption and territorial bonds. This, in effect, would pledge Montana's credit to the railroad. Many local businessmen, led by Sam Hauser of Helena, strongly supported subsidies to hurry the arrival of the U.N., and the legislature very nearly agreed to grant them. But the subsidy never quite materialized. Montana communities divided, according to their locations, over whether the territory should aid the U.N. or the N.P. Critics of any form of subsidy argued that rivalry between the two railroads would soon bring both of them into Montana without any financial aid. Events proved them right.

Fearful of the resumption of N.P. construction westward, the U.N. executives could no longer wait for aid from the legislature. In 1878 Jay Gould and Sidney Dillon of the Union Pacific secured full control of the Utah Northern and reorganized it as the Utah *and* Northern. They intended, obviously, to make the road an adjunct line of the Union Pacific, a feeder that would draw Montana traffic away from the Northern Pacific. Building now advanced rapidly, and in 1880 the Utah & Northern reached the Montana line. They built 110 miles into southwestern Montana in 1880, passing through the townsite of Dillon, which was named for the U.&N.'s president. On the evening of December 26, 1881, a night too cold for outdoor festivities, the first U.&N. train entered Butte, the railroad's real destination. The Utah & Northern–Union Pacific, winning its race with the N.P., had become the first railroad to enter Montana and had captured the fabulously rich mining trade of Butte.

The Northern Pacific, now recovered from the woes of the Panic of 1873, entered eastern Montana soon after the U.&N. came in from the southwest. The key figure in reorganizing the N.P. was Frederick Billings, who was determined to forge the road rapidly to the port of Tacoma on Puget Sound. Under the guidance of Chief Engineer W. Milnor Roberts, the road advanced out of Bismarck in 1879. By 1881 construction crews labored along both the Yellowstone River in eastern Montana and the Clark Fork in the west. While work continued, a power struggle arose over control of the Northern Pacific.

A group of investors who were interested in Portland, Oregon, and in rail-steamship lines extending eastward from there along the Columbia River, feared the plans of Billings and his associates to make Tacoma and Puget Sound their main seaport. The leader of this Portland group was Henry Villard, president of the powerful Oregon Railway and Navigation Company. As a friend of former President Lincoln and the son-in-law of abolitionist William Lloyd Garrison, Villard had excellent political and financial connections. After failing to convince the N.P. directors to make Portland instead of Tacoma their major port facility, Villard decided to attempt a direct takeover of the Northern Pacific himself. In one of the most spectacular moves in Wall Street history, Villard organized in 1881 his so-called "Blind Pool," through which he secretly raised eight million dollars and purchased controlling stock in the Northern Pacific.

Villard's maneuver allowed him to take over the Northern Pacific and to replace Billings as its president. The German promoter, who was more a speculator than a railroad man, now set out to invest heavily, build the road quickly, and thus gain the land grant and develop Portland as the terminus of the Northern Pacific. Through 1882 and into 1883, large construction crews extended the line from both east and west. Crews moving eastward from Washington and Idaho laid rails along the Clark Fork in western Montana. At the same time, rail gangs moved up the Yellowstone, across the new townsites of Billings and Livingston, through the Bozeman Pass tunnel, down the Missouri system to Helena, and westward over the continental divide. The climactic driving of the last spike to complete the Northern Pacific took place in a gala celebration at Gold Creek, Montana, on September 8, 1883. Five excursion trains brought out the celebrities, including former President Grant, who joined in the festivities. The telegrapher's key matched the blows of Villard's sledge as it drove home the final spike.

Montana had ample reason to celebrate in the fall of 1883, for by then, two major railroads had linked her to the outside world. A golden age of economic growth seemed near at hand. But the popularity of railroads soon began to fade. Mainly due to Villard's frenzied campaign, the Northern Pacific faced huge debts and severe financial problems. Villard resigned from the presidency of the N.P. in 1884, and a more conservative management began cautiously building branch lines to open up the empty territories that the railroad crossed. In the eyes of Montana boosters, these branch lines took shape at a disappointingly slow pace.

Local critics also pointed angrily to the fact that their two railroads carefully avoided the direct competition that might lead to lower prices. In

1882–83 the directors of the Northern Pacific and of the Utah & Northern–Union Pacific worked out agreements whereby the Northern Pacific agreed to stay out of the rich mining center of Butte, and in return the Utah & Northern promised not to build northward from Butte to Helena. In order to exchange passengers and freight, the two railroads jointly constructed the Montana Union line from Butte to Garrison. This pooling arrangement meant, as Montanans well knew and resented, that rail rates would remain high. Such an agreement, however, could only last until competition arrived on the scene.

JIM HILL AND THE GREAT NORTHERN

The vast, wind-swept "high line" of northern Montana, still enclosed in reservations, meanwhile lay open and inviting to developers. The man who, more than any other, seized this opportunity was James J. Hill of Minnesota. Hill, whom Stewart Holbrook once characterized as "the barbed-wire, shaggy-headed, one-eyed old sonofabitch of Western railroading," was a stockily built man of great forcefulness and ability. A Canadian by birth, Hill first came to St. Paul in 1856. He learned the transportation business from the ground up. In close collaboration with Canadian investors, Hill began developing transport routes down the rich Red River Valley, which tilts northward along the Minnesota-Dakota border, draining across the Canadian line into Lake Winnipeg.

Hill's prospering freight activities naturally led him into the rail business, and he played an important role in the early stages of building the Canadian Pacific Railroad. His major entry into the rail business came in 1878, when he joined with a group of Canadian partners to buy control of the St. Paul & Pacific Railroad, an ailing line that reached from Minneapolis to the Red River and aimed northward toward Canada. The main value of the St. Paul and Pacific lay in its land grant, which promised future profits. In 1879 Hill and his partners incorporated the St. Paul & Pacific into the St. Paul, Minneapolis & Manitoba Railroad Company, known popularly as the "Manitoba." The Manitoba laid its rails quickly down the Red River and into Canada. With its handsome land grant, its control of a fine agricultural area, and its capable management, the railroad prospered.

The vision of Jim Hill extended well beyond the Dakota-Minnesota border. Hill held great hopes for the arid high plains country that reached endlessly across Dakota toward the Rocky Mountain foothills in central Montana. With the proper promotion, he felt that these prairies could become a rich grain-producing empire, dotted by thousands of family farms. So he pressed the Manitoba's tracks steadily westward across northern Dakota Territory until, by 1886, the railhead stood at Minot, to the east of the Montana line.

Within Montana Territory, Jim Hill saw highly desirable prizes for his railroad. The booming silver-copper mines of Butte remained under Union Pacific monopoly, and Hill now promised copper baron Marcus Daly efficient service at "such rates as will enable you to largely increase your business." Areas north of Butte also intrigued the "Empire Builder," as Hill became known. Paris Gibson, an old Minnesota friend of Hill's, was now a successful sheepman near Fort Benton; and the two men maintained a correspondence that kept Hill interested in this area. In 1884 Hill visited his Montana friend and readily agreed to help him in developing a townsite at the Great Falls of the Missouri and in exploiting the coal fields nearby. In order to establish a right-of-way from Great Falls to Helena and Butte, Hill cleverly financed another Montana friend, Helena capitalist C. A. Broadwater, when he incorporated the Montana Central Railroad in 1886. The expressed purpose of the Montana Central was to link Great Falls to Helena and Butte.

As Broadwater's crews laid out grades between Great Falls and Helena, Hill faced the tougher problem of gaining access for the Manitoba to build through the Indian reservations north of the Missouri River. In his first attempt to penetrate these Indian lands, Hill failed, both because President Cleveland feared that Indian rights would be violated and because Jay Gould of the Union Pacific had used his influence to block the access. Defeat, however, only spurred the tough-minded Hill to counterattack. He personally warned Gould to call off his opposition, with the threat that, otherwise, he would "nail every one of your crooks to the doors of the Capitol by their————ears." By early 1887 Congress had granted Hill his easement through the Indian lands of northern Montana, and the President had approved it.

What followed these maneuverings ranks as one of the epic chapters in the history of railroading. Beginning in April 1887, huge construction gangs began spanning the Manitoba Railroad westward from Minot. Hill and his chief contractor, D. C. Shepard, hired veteran contractors fresh from building the difficult Canadian Pacific. The grading crews numbered 8,000 men, and 650 more worked at bridge building and track laying. From early May until mid-October of 1887, they averaged 3¼ miles of track per day, reaching from Minot to the Manitoba's rail center of Havre, and from Havre southwest to Great Falls, a total of 550 miles. One month after the Manitoba reached Great Falls, the Montana Central was completed northward from Helena to join it. Indeed it had been, as Hill put it, "a long and hard summer's work." All of this, of course, had an immediately dynamic effect upon Montana. New rail cities like Great Falls and Havre sprang up nearly overnight. By 1889, when the Montana Central was completed to Butte, Hill could ship the ores of Montana mines directly to the Great

Lakes. As a result, the pooling agreement between the Union Pacific and the Northern Pacific broke open, and Montana freight rates fell sharply. The Northern Pacific cut its Helena–St. Paul rates by one-third in reaction to the Manitoba's competition.

With his rails now poised along the continental divide, Jim Hill still faced the difficult question of whether and how to complete his line to the Pacific. The Northern Pacific completed its Cascade Branch to Tacoma in 1887, thus gaining a better route to the sea; and this competition forced Hill to make a coastal connection of his own. The main problem was that, between the Northern Pacific's crossing of the Rockies to the south and the Canadian Pacific's route to the north, there was no feasible pass through the mountains, at least none that was generally known.

Hill desperately needed to find a passage through the mountains lying due west from Havre in northern Montana. Legend told of a "lost Marias pass" in this area, a pass discovered years earlier but then forgotten. In 1889 Hill's highly capable location engineer, John F. Stevens, set out to find the elusive passageway. In a terrible December blizzard, so intense that his Indian guide refused to accompany him, Stevens walked into the Marias Pass, at the southern edge of what is now Glacier National Park. Stevens' dramatic discovery of Marias Pass opened the way to the Pacific, over the easiest crossing of the Northern Rockies. Hill's successor Ralph Budd later noted the significance of the discovery:

> The actual location of it [Marias Pass] was at an altitude of five thousand two hundred feet on a 1 per cent grade Westbound and 1.8 per cent Eastbound, and without a summit tunnel. It fully confirmed Stevens' report. At one stroke the discovery of Marias Pass shortened the proposed line to the Coast by over one hundred miles, afforded better alignment, much easier grades, and much less rise and fall.

Now the path lay open to the sea. Shortly before the Stevens discovery, on September 16, 1889, Hill and his associates had consolidated their holdings into the Great Northern Railway Company. In 1890 the Great Northern formally took over the Manitoba, and with it the Montana Central, and became proprietor of 2,770 miles of track. The board of directors of the newly created Great Northern voted at once to "extend its lines westwardly from some suitable point in Montana to Puget Sound." The Great Northern built hurriedly westward from Havre over Marias Pass, down the Middle Fork of the Flathead River to new-born Columbia Falls and Kalispell, and then turned northwest to follow the Kootenai River into the Idaho panhandle. Hill's railroad passed through Spokane and crossed the Cascade Mountains to reach Everett, Washington, on Puget Sound in 1893. Great Northern trains soon steamed into the fine port city of Seattle, Jim Hill's real destination. With justification, Hill could boast to his stockholders that, without a transcontinental land grant, the Great Northern had built a solid line to the Pacific, "shorter than any existing transcontinental railway, and with lower grades and less curvature."

LATER DEVELOPMENTS: THE BURLINGTON AND THE MILWAUKEE

The very year of the Great Northern's completion saw the beginning of a severe nationwide depression, the Panic of 1893. This drastic downturn of the economy spelled disaster for many of the heavily indebted railroads. Among these was the Northern Pacific, which had never really recovered from the Villard building campaign. For James J. Hill, whose well managed Great Northern barely came through the panic without going under, the bankruptcy of the N.P. presented a glowing opportunity, a chance to gain control of his major rival. During 1895–96 Hill and a number of his Great Northern associates, including the powerful banker J. P. Morgan, bought controlling shares of the Northern Pacific and reorganized it under their own management. From this time on, the Northern Pacific and the Great Northern became popularly known as simply the "Hill Lines." Hill the "Empire Builder" was, practically speaking, the master of the northern transcontinentals.

Meanwhile, yet another major railroad extended its tracks into Montana. This was the Chicago, Burlington and Quincy Railroad, an older, established midwestern carrier with excellent connections to Chicago, Omaha, and Denver. The efficiently managed Burlington occupied a prosperous area in the Midwest. Pressed by tough competition from transcontinental railroads, however, it needed trackage to the Pacific in order to maintain itself. Beginning late in 1889, the Burlington extended its main line from Alliance, in western Nebraska, through the Black Hills of South Dakota and into northeastern Wyoming. Its rails reached the town of Sheridan, just south of the Wyoming-Montana line, in late 1892.

For some time the Burlington directors had considered building their own independent line to the West Coast. A less expensive alternative, though, was simply to extend their tracks northward to connect with the Northern Pacific—if, that is, the N.P. would allow use of its tracks to the west. The Northern Pacific came to terms with the Burlington after the latter road threatened otherwise to build its own line into the lucrative mining areas of Montana. According to their agreement, each railroad would allow traffic from the other over its tracks and into its territories. The Burlington thus gained access to the Northwest Coast, and the N.P. an opening into the Midwest. The Panic of 1893 stalled the Burlington momentarily, but in late 1894 it reached the N.P. tracks at Huntley, east of Billings. By opening its "Billings Gateway" to the West, the Burlington spared itself the expense of building to the sea. The Burlington also boosted the economy of the

Billings area, especially after the railroad later extended its tracks from Billings-Laurel southward to reach Denver.

Jim Hill had, for some time, held an interest in the Chicago, Burlington and Quincy. Unlike the Great Northern–Northern Pacific, the Burlington had a direct connection into Chicago, the rail center of America. It also held the promise of extending Hill's rail empire into the center of the nation. So the Hill-Morgan team set out to buy control of the Burlington. They met stiff competition from Hill's great rival, E. H. Harriman of the Union Pacific; but in 1901 they succeeded, and the Great Northern–Northern Pacific jointly purchased control of the Burlington.

Hill thus emerged victorious—the Emperor of the Northwest—but he still faced problems. After failing to gain the Burlington, E. H. Harriman retaliated by attempting to buy command of the Northern Pacific. Hill and Morgan succeeded in stopping him, but only at great expense. The solution to such reckless competition seemed to lie in formation of a holding company, which would weld the northwestern roads permanently together under safe ownership and management. So Hill and Morgan, with the cooperation of Harriman, formed the Northern Securities Company, a giant, monopolistic holding company that would formally merge the three Hill carriers. The Northern Securities Company, capitalized at four hundred million dollars, promised Hill and Morgan secure control of northwestern transportation. As J. P. Morgan said, it placed these railroads in a firm "with a capital large enough so that nobody could ever buy it."

In Montana and other northwestern states, creation of the Northern Securities Company aroused howls of protest that the rail merger meant monopoly and permanently high prices. Responding to these justifiable charges, the administration of President Theodore Roosevelt charged the Northern Securities Company with violating the Sherman Antitrust Act. In 1904, to the delight of the Northwest, the United States Supreme Court declared the new corporation an illegal monopoly and ordered it disbanded. In truth, the breakup of Northern Securities made little real difference, for the Hill-Morgan team still maintained control of each individual railroad concerned. As Hill put it: "Two certificates of stock are now issued instead of one. They are printed in different colors. That is the main difference." But a formal merger was postponed for sixty-five years. Then, in view of the mounting competition from trucks, airplanes, and pipelines, the federal government permitted creation of the Burlington Northern Railroad to place the three roads again under one corporate head.

So, even after the dissolution of Northern Securities, the Hill-Morgan roads still dominated regional transportation. Competition soon arrived, though, in the form of the Chicago, Milwaukee & St. Paul Railway Company. Like the Burlington, the "Milwaukee Road" was an established

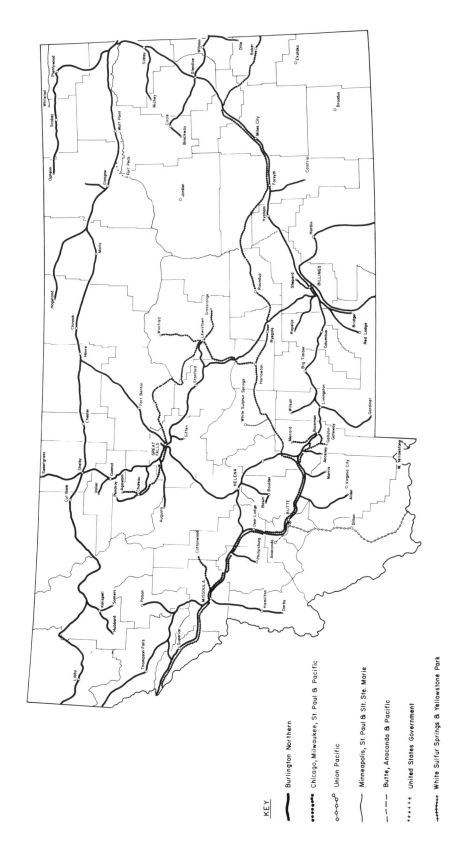

Map 4. Montana railroads (source, *Montana in Maps: 1974*)

midwestern carrier. Fearing that, unless it built to the Pacific, it could not compete with the powerful Hill and Harriman lines, the Milwaukee management decided in 1905 to build westward to Puget Sound. Now christened the Chicago, Milwaukee, St. Paul & Pacific, the railroad set to work in 1906 on a 1,385-mile westward extension of its tracks from Glenham, South Dakota. Large construction crews laid the tracks rapidly into eastern Montana, entering the Yellowstone Valley near Fallon. Their path then led westward toward one of the Milwaukee's prime objectives, the Musselshell Valley of central Montana, which lay between the domains of the Northern Pacific and the Great Northern.

This promising agricultural area was partially crossed by the Jawbone Railroad, so named because its owner, Richard Harlow, relied more upon fast talk than upon wage payments to keep his men at work. Harlow, who gave his name to the town of Harlowton, had mortgaged his road to Jim Hill; and this caused problems for the Milwaukee, which desperately needed control of Harlow's line. Despite the danger that Hill might someday gain control of the Jawbone, the Milwaukee leased it anyway and was later able to purchase it outright. The Milwaukee built southwesterly from Harlowton to Butte, and from there on through the Deer Lodge Valley, along the Clark Fork and into the Coeur d'Alene mining area of Idaho. By the time the last spike was driven, in May 1909 at Gold Creek, Montana, the Milwaukee reached through Spokane to touch the sea at Seattle.

The Milwaukee ran up huge debts in this great construction program, and it faced hard competition from the Hill carriers flanking it. At the instigation of John D. Ryan of the Anaconda Copper Mining Company, who was also a member of the board of directors of the Milwaukee, the railroad decided to electrify its tracks from Harlowton across the Rockies to Avery, Idaho. The railroad contracted with various small electric companies, which Ryan was just then busily organizing into the Montana Power Company, and by 1916 it had 438 miles of mountain rails electrified for cheap power. This was the first long-distance electrified rail span in America, and it paid off well, both for the Milwaukee and for Ryan's Montana Power Company. But the Milwaukee, hard fought by the Hill railroads and staggering under the massive debt of its western construction, failed to prosper. In 1925 it fell into receivership.

The driving of the Milwaukee's final spike in 1909 signaled the end of main line rail construction in Montana. In the course of thirty years, the railroads had literally transformed the state. They gave birth to important new cities like Great Falls, Billings, and Havre; and they breathed new life into towns already established, such as Butte, Miles City, Bozeman, and Missoula. The railroads spurred the development of Montana's major industries—mining, stockgrowing, and lumbering—and in 1909 they were just beginning to promote this area to farmers of the United States and Europe. As the nineteenth gave way to the twentieth century, Montanans, like other Americans, became more and more critical of the railroads, and they eventually came to rely more upon other forms of transportation. The fact would remain, however, that during the period 1879–1909, the railroads had, to a large extent, built the economy of Montana.

THE SILVER YEARS

Among the Montanans who longed for railroads, no one waited more eagerly than mining promoters. By the depressed 1870s, as we have seen, the easily mined deposits of placer gold had pretty well played out. Only with rail transportation could the much richer bodies of rock-imbedded quartz gold and silver be developed. These deposits required heavy stamping mills, smelters, and other machinery, as well as ore shipment capacity, which only rails could adequately supply. They also required large investments, skilled workers, and intricate new methods of extracting and treating complex ores. Montana miners learned first how to handle quartz gold. Then, mainly after the arrival of railroads, they tackled the more abundant but harder to mine veins of silver, whose riches contributed so much to the boom of the 1880s.

Naturally, the large veins of quartz gold, from which erosion had worn away the glittering placer deposits, usually lay in the same vicinities as the here-today, gone-tomorrow gold camps. So prospectors immediately set to work seeking them out, digging them up, and extracting the gold from the quartz. Evidently, the first mining of quartz gold took place at the Dakota Lode near Bannack. During the winter of 1862–63, William Arnold and J. F. Allen built a crude stamp mill from old freight-wagon parts and began working the Dakota ores. Over a dozen gold mills operated in the Bannack area by mid-1864, possibly two dozen by 1867. The cumbersome machinery for these mills came either by Missouri steamboats or by wagons across the plains.

During the placer rushes of the sixties, several locations produced significant quantities of quartz gold. One of these was the Summit District of Alder Gulch, the site of F. R. Steel's Mountain Sheep Vein, and the Oro Cache, Lucas, and other lodes. To the north, Silver Star on the Jefferson River became a center of quartz gold output, as did Radersburg. Helena itself became the early hub of quartz gold milling, and it drew most of this gold from its southern hinterland. Even as placer output around Helena began to decline, quartz lodes like the rich Whitlatch Vein and the deposits in Oro Fino and Grizzlie gulches poured their riches into the future capital city and gave it a new lease on life.

Most of Montana's early mills handled "free milling gold." This was rich, oxidized ore that lay near the surface and could easily be recovered by milling and amalgamation, without roasting or chemical treatment. Even so, development was painfully slow. The United States Mint reported in 1867 that the output of quartz as compared with placer gold in Montana was so small that it could not be estimated. In 1870 the census listed only 172 underground miners in Montana, all of them working in only four mines near Helena and eight others in Madison County.

Up until the early 1870s Montana miners paid little attention to the silver ores that were frequently intermingled with the gold. Silver, after all, was harder to treat and of less value than gold. Montana's first recorded silver discovery occurred in 1864 at Argenta, near Bannack. Silver mining progressed very slowly, in large part because local miners did not know how to work the many different amalgams of ore in which silver was found. As late as 1874 United States Commissioner of Mining Statistics Rossiter Raymond observed that Montana had "not been fruitful of inventions and improvements in mining. Its isolated and remote position has caused it rather to lag behind other mining regions of the country, even in the adoption of improvements already known."

Local silver promoters faced many other problems besides metallurgy. The most serious of these was transportation. Montana's isolation meant that machinery and construction materials had to be freighted in, with great difficulty and at high costs. The Missouri River provided the best freight route; but the steamboats could only reach Fort Benton a few months each year, and the freight had to be transhipped more than one hundred miles from the port to the mining areas. Still another difficulty arose from the lack of skilled labor. Since the placer miners were unskilled at deep mining and usually unwilling to work for any but the highest wages during the warm season, they formed a highly unreliable labor force. Above all, the promoters of industrial mining needed capital, capital to invest in the mines, in stamping mills, in smelters and concentrators. Since investment capital was scarce on the frontier, the mining promoters usually had to lure outside investors and convince them that the high risks of investing in unproven mines would pay off.

Among the first and most influential of Montana's silver promoters was Samuel T. Hauser of Helena, the territory's most powerful capitalist. Drawing upon his family and business connections in Missouri, Hauser helped organize the St. Louis and Montana Mining Company in 1866. This firm invested thirty-six thousand dollars in machinery and equipment and erected Montana's first silver smelter at Argenta in December 1866. To manage operations, the firm employed August Steitz and Philip Deideshei-mer, the famed inventor of the square-set timbering first used in Nevada's Comstock Lode. The St. Louis and Montana Company soon gave up its

Argenta operation and concentrated instead on investing at Flint Creek, west of Deer Lodge.

At Hauser's direction, Deidesheimer inspected the Flint Creek vicinity and recommended investments there. The St. Louis and Montana Company bought up several claims, including the Hope Lode; and in 1867 Deidesheimer completed construction of the James Stuart Mill, named for its superintendent, the brother of Granville Stuart. The Stuart Mill employed the pan amalgamation process and was the first mill of this type in Montana. To serve the local mill and mines, the town of Philipsburg, named after Deidesheimer, grew up at Flint Creek. By 1867 it had six hundred inhabitants. But the local veins proved disappointing, and in 1868 the Stuart Mill shut down. The St. Louis and Montana Company, which reorganized in 1872 as the Hope Mining Company, laid off all its employees except for the few it kept on at the Hope Mine. Philipsburg nearly became a ghost town during the seventies, but it would spring back to life again in the 1880s. Such were the uncertainties of silver mining.

The Panic of 1873 sharply curtailed the mining of quartz silver and gold in Montana. Outside sources of investment dried up, and the vital railroads lay stalled faraway. Nonetheless, even during these hard times, some Montana promoters persisted, and limited amounts of high grade ore found their way to Fort Benton and Corinne during the mid-seventies. From these points the Montana ores went clear to California, Germany, and Swansea, Wales, for smelting. In the meantime, Montana miners stockpiled lower grade ore until either railroads or local smelters made its treatment possible.

By 1875–76 the worst effects of the depression were wearing off, and the mining horizon began to brighten. Concentrators at Argenta made it possible to convert low grade ore into first class shipping product, and the rise of a silver industry in Utah brought final treatment facilities closer to home. Montana's silver output for 1875 nearly doubled that of 1874. More and more experienced silver miners, many of them foreign born, began filtering into Montana from that center of American silver mining, the Comstock Lode. As the great Comstock declined, these highly skilled workmen, especially the Cornishmen ("Cousin Jacks"), headed for the land of new opportunity and brought their desperately needed talents with them.

At precisely this time, the mid-1870s, the inconspicuous little town of Butte began its rise, eventually to become Montana's greatest silver and later copper producer. Butte began as a placer gold camp in 1864, but its shallow diggings and remoteness from a water supply supported only limited growth. The Butte–Silver Bow camps reached their peaks in 1867 and thereafter faded rapidly. Prospectors here found promising quartz lodes from the start, but Butte's gold was difficult to mill and remained largely neglected.

The man who first recognized that silver, not gold, held the key to Butte's future was William L. Farlin, a typically restless placer miner. Farlin first drifted into the camp in 1864. Over the next decade he moved about constantly, but he never forgot the silver leads that he had seen at Butte. Late in 1874 he returned, and in early 1875 he located a lead which he called the Travona. Recognizing that his ore would have to be treated on the spot in order to pay returns, Farlin began construction of the Dexter Mill. At about the same time, Helena merchant John How started work on his Centennial Mill. Both the Dexter and the Centennial began operations in 1876. When Farlin failed to make payments on his loans, Deer Lodge banker William A. Clark took over operations of his Travona-Dexter properties and built them into big-time producers.

By the centennial year of 1876, Butte's fame was spreading far and wide. Visiting the camp in July, R. N. Sutherlin of the *Rocky Mountain Husbandman* found this "quartz eldorado of the great North-West" to be a beehive of activity. New silver mines like the Lexington and the Nettie were beginning to produce, and in August an event of major importance occurred: the highly respected miner Marcus Daly arrived in town. Daly, a veteran of the Comstock, came to Butte in order to assess local silver properties for the Walker Brothers of Salt Lake City, prominent bankers and mining investors. Taking their agent's advice, the Walkers purchased the Alice Mine, and they hired Daly to manage it. These events held much significance. They heralded the arrival of big-time investors from the outside and brought one of the world's greatest miners into Montana.

Of course, the arrival of rails in western Montana during 1880–83 immediately boomed the already rising silver industry. Improved transportation brought many new ore deposits within range of smelters and reduction works. More importantly, it allowed the finished metals from these plants to enter the stream of national commerce on a large scale. In 1880, before the arrival of rails, Montana produced less than $3 million in silver, roughly 7 percent of total United States production. By 1883 the territory ranked as the nation's second largest supplier of silver, a position it maintained until the mid-1890s, except for 1887 when it ranked number one. Montana produced about one-fourth of the nation's silver in 1889, and from 1890 through 1893 its annual silver output averaged about $20 million. With the fantastic increase of deep silver mining came a rebirth of gold mining, for veins of gold, zinc, lead, and other metals intermingled with the silver. By the late eighties Montana shifted between second and fourth ranks among American gold producers.

Aside from Butte itself, which was very much *the* silver town in Montana, the industry centered also at the booming towns of Philipsburg and Helena. The key figure in the 1880s rebirth of Philipsburg was Charles D. McLure, who became superintendent of the Hope Mine in 1877. McLure played a major role in organizing both of Philipsburg's renowned silver firms: the Granite Mountain Mining Company and the Bi-Metallic Mill. For a time each of these outfits became fantastic producers. At its peak, Granite Mountain may indeed have been the world's greatest silver mine. One large, picturesque town sprawled across the Philipsburg-Granite-Clark area. By the early years of this century, the mines of the Philipsburg district had yielded an estimated $32 million, most of it silver from Granite Mountain.

Helena, already flanked by active gold and silver mines, enjoyed a major quartz boom when the Northern Pacific arrived there in 1882–83. Marysville, north of the city, became a major gold mining center. Here, in 1876, the legendary Thomas Cruse discovered his fabulous Drumlummon Mine, which he named after his native parish in Ireland. The Drumlummon, which eventually yielded nearly $16 million in gold and silver, was the greatest gold mine in Montana's history. In 1883 Cruse sold it to the Montana Company, Ltd., one of over thirty British corporations investing in Montana mining. As so often happened with great ore bodies, the Drumlummon became the object of a long-term legal hassle over ownership. The courtroom fight for the Drumlummon, waged between the Montana Company and the St. Louis Mining and Milling Company, began in 1889 and lasted over twenty-four years, costing the Montana Company over $400,000 in lawyer's fees.

To the south of Helena lay many rich silver lodes. The large deposits at Elkhorn, developed by Helena tycoon Anton M. Holter and later purchased by British capitalists, gave birth to one of today's favorite ghost towns. During the late 1870s energetic Sam Hauser shifted his focus from Philipsburg to this general vicinity and set to work consolidating claims and organizing eastern investors. In 1876 a syndicate of Montana and New York capitalists headed by William Wickes had formed yet another Montana Company and built an elaborate reduction-smelting works at the town of Wickes. The Wickes complex came under the control of Hauser's Helena Mining and Reduction Company, and it became the hub of operations throughout the region south of Helena. To the Wickes smelters came ores from as far away as the Coeur d'Alene district of Idaho. Aside from its own mines, the Comet and the Alta, the firm relied upon dozens of other small mining concerns to keep it supplied with ore from the surrounding area.

Although the heart of Montana's silver industry lay in a triangle joining Butte, Philipsburg, and Helena, silver towns sprouted randomly elsewhere. Two major silver centers, Lion Mountain and Glendale, grew up in the Big Hole country west of present Melrose. At Glendale, the prosperous Hecla Consolidated Mining Company paid dividends every year from 1881 until its demise in 1901. The silver boom also reached across the Missouri River into the Little Belt and Castle mountains of central Montana. Several interesting silver towns boomed in the Little Belts, including Barker, Hughesville, and especially Neihart. The remoteness of the area retarded its growth until the completion of a smelter at Great Falls in 1888 and the construction of the Great Northern's Belt Mountain branch opened it to the outside world. Southward in the Castle Mountains, promising silver-lead deposits began to attract population in the late 1880s. The town of Castle arose to serve the area, and the Cumberland Mine there thrived for a time. But rail service did not reach this area in time to aid its development, and the Castle Mountains boom, like that in the Little Belts, collapsed quickly in the mid-1890s.

By focusing exclusively upon the great operations, like Granite Mountain, we may easily lose sight of an important aspect of the silver boom: the fact that silver, unlike copper, attracted many small operators. Especially during the later seventies and early eighties, dozens of small outfits, some with fewer than ten employees, were able to survive in the business. Although outside capital was involved in Montana quartz mining from the very beginning, local residents, most of them men of limited means, clearly controlled the industry. Of the sixty-eight deep mines noted in the 1880 Census, not one was yet foreign owned; over 84 percent of the capital invested in local mines came from local sources. Even in 1890, at the peak of the silver boom, small-time operations remained the rule: two-thirds of Montana's seventy-five active mines produced less than $100,000 worth of ore annually, and only eight yielded more than $500,000 during the year.

Inevitably, as Montana's silver boom reached major proportions, the big investors increasingly came to dominate the scene. Some of these big-time silver men were local magnates, like Sam Hauser and the Butte silver-copper baron William A. Clark; but most were outsiders, locally faceless individuals who poured money into silver firms that promised a quick profit. The states providing the largest investments in Montana quartz mines included Minnesota, New York, Missouri, Utah, Colorado, and California. Throughout the eighties and early nineties, more and more foreign capital, especially British capital, poured into Montana mining investments. The large outside-owned mining corporations, like the British-controlled Montana Company, Ltd., or Butte's Colorado Smelting and Mining Company, led in local efforts to professionalize mining. They brought in college-trained foremen and superintendents from such prominent centers of mining and metallurgy education as Freiburg, Germany, and New York's

Columbia School of Mines. The English often refused to invest in American mines unless an experienced Cornish expert was placed in charge.

Silver mining was always a fragile and risky business. Since so much silver was sold for use as currency around the world, prices rose and fell sharply according to the monetary policies of various nations. The great western silver boom coincided with a worldwide increase in silver production and also with decisions by some nations to drop the silver standard as a base of their currencies. These two factors combined to cause sharp declines in silver prices. In desperation, United States producers turned to the government for help, demanding that Uncle Sam buy up the domestic output of silver for coinage into money. For a time the government cooperated, and through several laws bought most or all of the silver flowing from American mines. So long as the government's silver purchase program remained in effect, the western silver industry continued to flourish.

The Panic of 1893 literally devastated the silver industry of western America, for President Grover Cleveland became convinced, rightly or wrongly, that the silver purchase program was the prime cause of the depression. Accordingly, Cleveland called a special session of Congress in mid-1893 and prevailed upon the lawmakers to repeal the Sherman Silver Purchase Act and end the mandatory government purchases of silver. As silver prices plummeted, the effect upon such mining states as Montana, Colorado, Idaho, and Nevada was quick and disastrous. One mine after another shut down, some never to reopen. The Wickes plant closed in 1893, and the company dismantled it. In August 1893 the great mining-smelting operation at Granite ceased operations. The management tied down the plant's steam whistle as a shrill, frightening announcement that employment was ended. According to some contemporaries, as many as three thousand people left the Granite-Philipsburg area in twenty-four hours.

Montana's smaller, marginal silver mines closed, one after the other, throughout the mid-1890s. Some of the larger smelting outfits managed to hold on, even at the lower prices; and they, in turn, continued to keep the highest grade mines in operation. Very rich deposits, like the Nettie at Butte, and mines where silver intermingled with other metals, like the Drumlummon at Marysville, came through the Panic without shutting down. Most of them, however, failed, some permanently and some later to reopen when prices climbed again to profitable levels. For instance, a reorganized combination of the Granite Mountain and Bi-Metallic companies resumed mining in 1898, only to close down again in 1905 due to renewed price failures. At various times during this century, such as the mid-1930s, rising silver prices have breathed new life, momentarily, into Montana's sagging silver industry. But, in the broad perspective of the state's history, the age of silver ended abruptly during the mid-1890s. Once great silver camps, like Castle, Granite, and Elkhorn, became fascinating ghost towns, whose collapsing stamps and smelters remind us of past glories. After 1893 silver, like gold and other metals, came to be for the most part a mere byproduct of large-scale copper mining at Butte.

THE WINNING OF STATEHOOD

To frontier westerners, who felt neglected and left out of national political life, statehood signified a "place in the sun," a recognition of their coming of age as a community. Statehood meant more concrete benefits as well. Once a territory became a state, it gained full representation in Congress, full power to tax local corporations, large grants of land to support education, and other functions of state government. Most importantly, statehood meant that local citizens could, at long last, elect their own executive and judicial officers and thus end the long procession of federally appointed "carpetbaggers" whom Washington had sent to govern them.

Montana's first try for statehood, under Acting Governor Meagher in 1866, had been premature and impossible from the start. The territory simply lacked the necessary population and political maturity at that time. During the 1870s economic depression and sagging population temporarily cooled the fires of statehood sentiment. By the early 1880s, though, the arrival of rails and the booming quartz mining and livestock industries combined to send Montana's population soaring and breathe new fervor into hopes for statehood. From a mere 38,159 in 1880, the territory's population climbed to a respectable 132,159 in 1890. By the close of the boom decade of the eighties, Montana's treasury held an impressive surplus of over $130,000.

With good reason Montanans felt by 1883 that they had a solid case for admittance to the Union as a state. Completion of the Northern Pacific Railroad that year strengthened their argument. It also whetted their appetite for statehood; for only states, not territories, had legal authority to tax this great landholding railroad. Surely, if Montana drafted a proper state constitution and presented it to Congress, the lawmakers must respond favorably! This logic moved the 1883 Legislature to call a special election for delegates to a constitutional convention. Following a November 1883 election, forty-one delegates assembled at Helena on January 14, 1884, to convene Montana's second constitutional convention.

The men of the 1884 Constitutional Convention had been elected on a nonpartisan basis, and they now organized themselves in the same manner. Naturally, mine owners and stockmen had strong representation, and the Butte mining king William A. Clark was elected president of the gathering. The convention met for twenty-eight days and produced a charter that drew heavily from precedents found in existing state constitutions. In the general election of November 1884 the voters ratified the document by an easy margin, 15,506 to 4,266, a degree of approval demonstrating that the voters cared less about the constitution itself than about the fact that it was the key which would open the door of statehood.

Montanans suffered a cruel disappointment, however, when Congress failed to approve their request. The problem in Washington arose, not from any fault in Montana or its constitution, but from political considerations. As a result of the 1884 election, the two national political parties faced each other in delicately balanced competition. While the Democrats controlled the House of Representatives, and also the White House under Grover Cleveland, the Republicans held a majority in the Senate. Several western territories were now clamoring for statehood, and neither political party would allow a new state into the Union that had voted regularly for the opposition. Among the territories in question, the Republican majority in the Senate wished to confer statehood upon Republican Washington Territory and also to admit Republican Dakota Territory as not one, but two states. This would allow four Republican senators from the two Dakotas. The Democratic House of Representatives, naturally, opposed this plan and favored statehood instead for the Democratic territories of New Mexico and Montana.

Political considerations, as usual, prevailed. Various efforts at compromise failed; and from 1885 through 1888, the Republican Senate regularly blocked admittance of any new Democratic territories, while the Democratic House held back the Republican territories. The logjam finally broke when, in the election of 1888, the Republicans scored a clean sweep. They won control of both houses of Congress and elected Benjamin Harrison to the Presidency. Realizing that the Republicans had only to await the seating of the new Congress to have their way, the outgoing, "lame duck" Democratic majority in the House of Representatives gave up the fight. The Democrats agreed to allow statehood to Republican Washington, and also to a North and South Dakota, while denying it to Democratic New Mexico.

As for Democratic Montana, the Republicans were now willing to allow it admission, too. They knew that the railroads were bringing in more and more Republican immigrants from northern states and that Montana might soon show a Republican majority. Thus Congress now acted speedily, and on February 22, 1889, outgoing President Cleveland signed into law the so-called Omnibus Bill. The Omnibus Bill was an "enabling act" which, in effect, notified the Dakotas, Washington, and Montana that, if they drew up proper constitutions, they would be granted immediate statehood.

Passage of the Omnibus Bill brought jubilation to the Northwest, for the citizens there knew that statehood now lay within their immediate reach. The federal Alien Land Law, passed in 1887, added to their desire for haste. This law, which restricted foreign investment in the territories but not in the states, threatened to cut off needed overseas investors from entering the Montana mining industry. Following a special election in May, Montana's third constitutional convention opened its deliberations on July 4, 1889. This time, in contrast to 1884, the delegates were elected and organized on a partisan basis. The close political balance, thirty-nine Democrats versus thirty-six Republicans, indicated the rising power of the Republicans. As in 1884, the mine owners and the stockmen were well represented; and as before, W. A. Clark won election as presiding officer.

The Constitutional Convention of 1889 did its work in an orderly manner, with a minimum of discord. No one wanted a fight over the constitution that might cause its defeat and thus delay statehood. Using the 1884 Constitution as a starting point, the delegates in committee put together a document typical of its time. Fearful of arbitrary government, they sharply limited the authority of the governor and of the executive branch in general. On only one major issue, apportionment in the state senate, did the delegates divide bitterly. The less populous counties, which were for the most part those in eastern Montana, demanded that each county be allowed one, and only one, state senator.

Although such an arrangement was obviously antidemocratic, the small country delegates argued that only this protection in the senate would allow them any voice in government. Otherwise, the large mining counties could always outvote them in both houses of the legislature. The big counties fought back, but they realized that their smaller neighbors might well reject the whole constitution over this issue. So they gave in, and the rural counties won over-representation in the Montana Legislature. Except for this one case, the delegates generally held down controversial issues. For instance, they voted against woman's suffrage, mostly out of fear that they might offend male voters and thus jeopardize the constitution and delay statehood. Fearing also the emotional issue of permanent location of the state capital, they decided to leave that decision to the voters in a future election.

The mining interests, of course, had things considerably their way in the convention. With little debate or acrimony, they managed to imbed in the constitution the same sort of "net proceeds" tax that they had earlier inserted in the 1884 document. This measure exempted unmined ore from taxation, which meant that mine owners would pay taxes only on ore extracted and upon surface land, buildings, and machinery. Surprisingly, the nonmining delegates offered little protest to this tax break. They apparently agreed that mining must be encouraged, at all costs, in order to build up the state economy. One wonders whether anyone even winced when President W. A. Clark, a mining millionaire himself, offered the delegates this justification of mining-caused air pollution:

> I must say that the ladies are very fond of this smoky city, as it [Butte] is sometimes called, because there is just enough arsenic there to give them a beautiful complexion, and that is the reason the ladies of Butte are renowned whereever [sic] they go for their beautiful complexions. . . . I say it would be a great deal better for other cities in the territory if they had more smoke and less diphtheria and other diseases. It has been believed by all the physicians of Butte that the smoke that sometimes prevails there is a disinfectant, and destroys the microbes that constitute the germs of disease . . . it would be a great advantage for other cities, to have a little more smoke and business activity and less disease. . . .

After six weeks of work, the delegates produced a state constitution; and on October 1, 1889, the voters of Montana approved it overwhelmingly, by a vote of 24,676 in favor to a mere 2,274 opposed. Obviously, the populace cared little about the substance of the new constitution. They viewed it primarily as a means to the end of immediate statehood. Federal approval of the Montana constitution followed quickly, and on November 8, 1889, President Harrison formally proclaimed Montana the forty-first state of the Union. After twenty-five years of frustration as a territory, Montanans celebrated their coming of age as the "Treasure State."

Unfortunately, the happy consensus Montanans displayed on the statehood question did not extend to other issues. In the same October 1, 1889, election that so resoundingly approved the constitution, the voters divided evenly and heatedly along party lines. Democrat Joseph K. Toole beat Republican Thomas C. Power by fewer than a thousand votes to become Montana's first state governor. And by a less than two-thousand-vote margin, Republican Thomas Carter downed Martin Maginnis to become the lone congressman.

Incredible as it seems, fierce partisanship literally destroyed Montana's first state legislature. As a result of the extremely close 1889 election, the state senate divided evenly, with eight Democrats facing eight Republicans and the Republican lieutenant governor holding the tie-breaking vote. In the house of representatives, twenty-five Republicans faced twenty-five Democrats. But a crucial five seats were disputed here because of irregularities in Silver Bow County Precinct 34, where each party accused the other of manipulating the election returns. Due to legal confusion over how such disputes should be settled, both parties laid claim to these five house seats. Whoever gained them would control the house. More to the point, whichever party gained them would control the joint balloting of the legislature in choosing Montana's first two United States senators. So the stakes were high indeed.

To put it frankly, the Montana legislators allowed partisanship to overcome good sense and ended up disgracing themselves. Since neither the Republicans nor the Democrats would give up the five contested house seats, each party met in separate chambers in order to protect its five challenged members from Precinct 34. In effect, the state had two houses of representatives; and they continued to meet separately throughout the ninety-day session, November 23, 1889–February 20, 1890. Meanwhile, the state senate also deadlocked. Attempting to stop the Republicans from organizing the senate and then joining their colleagues from the house to elect the two U.S. senators, the senate Democrats refused at first even to take their seats. Then, under legal compulsion, they attended but refused to vote for organizing the senate. When the Republicans counted them as present but not voting in order to organize the upper chamber, the Democrats refused once again to attend. Incredibly, the senate president finally ordered arrest warrants for the missing Democrats, who promptly fled to avoid capture. Before he could escape, Senator W. S. Becker was caught at Glendive, taken to Helena, and released upon promise that he would remain. Becker then departed for Idaho, where Montana officers could not touch him.

As a result of this foolishness, the first Montana legislature accomplished almost nothing. Each of the two houses of representatives passed bills, but the deadlocked senate failed to enact them. The main bone of contention all along, of course, was choosing the U.S. senators. Acting upon advice from their friends in the U.S. Senate, both the Democratic and the Republican factions finally met separately, and each elected two U.S. senators. The Republicans chose Wilbur Fisk Sanders and T. C. Power, and the Democrats elected W. A. Clark and Martin Maginnis. Montana calmly sent *four* senators to Washington! This, naturally, left the final decision to the Senate itself. Since the Republicans controlled that body, they seated Sanders and Power and sent the two Democrats home.

These ludicrous events severely embarrassed the newborn state of Montana, and they made for a rough start on the road of self-government. The legislators raised real doubts about their own integrity, and badly needed laws had to await the convening of the second session. But if Montanans questioned the purity of politics in 1890, events of the next ten years would raise their doubts even farther.

CHAPTER IX

Copper and Politics: 1880–1910

THE small community of "Montanians" who lived here a hundred years ago, gripped as they were by the hard times following the Panic of 1873, had one overriding obsession: to lure in the big outside investors whose capital meant prosperity. By the late 1870s these investors began to arrive, pouring their money into livestock production and quartz silver mining. Events of the 1880s and 1890s, though, proved that copper, not silver, held the real key to Montana's mining future. The massive copper bodies of Butte brought some of the world's greatest capitalists onto the Montana scene, and they, in turn, brought "development" and a measure of prosperity with them. "Big Money Came to Butte," and the state enjoyed its benefits. Unfortunately, the "Treasure State" had also to pay a high price, for copper came to dominate its economy and to rule the roost politically, sometimes with grim results. Today the greenish copper dome standing atop the capitol building in Helena symbolizes the legacy of those days when copper was king.

THE RISE OF KING COPPER

Butte, as we have noted, began as a middling gold camp in the 1860s, nearly faded into oblivion, then came to life again with silver mining in the mid-1870s. Even as silver rose to dominate Montana mining, the ever deepening mines of Butte proved to be more rich in copper than in any of the other commingled metals. As new inventions such as the electric light and the telephone drove up the value of copper, Butte developers began attempting to mine and market the red metal. They hauled their ore to Utah and shipped it from there to such distant points as Newark, Baltimore, even Wales and Germany for processing. High freight rates, of course, ate up the profits. So, for the time being, Butte miners stockpiled ores and waited eagerly for the rails and machinery that would allow their treatment.

The man who waited most anxiously, and who read the future of Butte most clearly, was William Andrews Clark, the classic rags-to-riches success story of the Montana frontier. Born in Pennsylvania, Clark moved with his family as a youngster to Iowa and later followed the mining frontier to Colorado. From there he traveled with several companions to the boom town of Bannack, arriving in 1863 at the age of only twenty-four. Clark was small of frame, with somewhat pinched and delicate features and cold, penetrating eyes. Beneath this unimposing exterior, though, worked a keen mind, a financial genius, a hard and ruthless ambition. "Inordinately vain," wrote C. P. Connolly, "he loved the flattery and adulation of women. He was a Beau Brummel in the midst of the awkward inelegance of the West."

With an unfailing instinct for profit, Clark moved quickly from prospecting into a variety of business investments—hauling produce from Utah, carrying the mail from Walla Walla, merchandising in Helena. By 1872 he had moved to Deer Lodge where, with two partners, he opened a very profitable bank. The lusty mining town of Butte, only forty miles from Deer Lodge, attracted Clark irresistibly. He invested heavily in silver-copper properties, picking them up at low prices before the great boom set in, and he convinced a group of Coloradoans to join him in a large-scale smelting enterprise. Remarkably, even while joining together these multifarious holdings, he managed to work in mining and mineralogy studies at New York's Columbia School of Mines. Clark's mines, smelter, banks, and other investments made him, at a very young age, one of the leading capitalists in the Mountain West, and surely one of the most egotistical and ambitious as well. He longed, according to the memories of those who knew him then, to be Montana's richest man and its most prestigious statesman.

Clark's great rival-to-be, Marcus Daly, came to Butte in 1876, at the age of thirty-five. A stocky, likable, and gregarious Irishman, Daly had immigrated to America in the 1850s and followed the mining frontier to California. Working in the bowels of Nevada's great Comstock Lode, he learned the ins and outs of hardrock mining. Daly came to be known as a "miner's miner," an expert whose "nose for ore" and practical knowledge of geology and mining methods won him considerable prestige. The wealthy Walker brothers of Utah, as we have seen, hired Daly and sent him to Butte in 1876 to assess the Alice Mine there as a possible investment. Knowing that Daly represented outside capital, Butte's newspaper, *The Miner*, welcomed him handsomely as "the best miner who has ever been in Montana."

Daly remained in Butte to manage the Alice property for the Walkers, and he soon became convinced of the great hill's richness. Anxious to strike out on his own, he sold the interest he had acquired in the Alice and invested it in the Anaconda Mine, a silver operation lying on the southeastern side of the Butte Hill. The Anaconda had been developed by Michael Hickey, who named it after General Scott's famous attempt to wrap the Confederate army in a snakelike grip. Daly poured thirty thousand dollars into improving the mine; but, of course, he needed large-scale support to convert the Anaconda into a major producer. When the Walkers refused to join him in this venture, Daly turned to some powerful friends, the "Hearst-Haggin-Tevis syndicate" of San Francisco. These men—George Hearst, the father of William Randolph Hearst, James Ben Ali Haggin, whose middle name indicates his Turkish ancestry, and Lloyd Tevis—ranked among the West's most powerful capitalists. They knew and respected Daly, and they readily joined him in the Anaconda enterprise. The Hearst-Haggin-Tevis syndicate, now joined by Daly as an occasional fourth associate, would eventually extend its control over one hundred different mines, including America's greatest copper producer (Anaconda), greatest gold property (the Homestake in South Dakota), and greatest silver mine (the Ontario in Utah).

Now with almost limitless backing, Marcus Daly rapidly developed the Anaconda. The mine proved, like others in Butte, to be much richer in copper than in silver. At the three-hundred-foot level, late in 1882, Daly's men struck a copper glance of remarkable richness and purity. As they soon learned, the Anaconda contained the richest bodies of copper sulphide the world had ever seen. Daly had the foresight to anticipate the expanding market for copper, and his partners had enough confidence in him to pour millions into a copper venture that was entirely new to them. By early 1883 they had driven the Anaconda shaft to the six-hundred-foot level, where their copper vein widened to one hundred feet in breadth and 55 percent in purity. When Daly sent some of the ore for treatment to Swansea, the experienced Welsh copper men wrote back expressing amazement at its richness.

Daly feverishly bought up the properties adjoining the Anaconda. According to Butte legend, he first assured their owners that his mine was not proving out and then acquired the adjacent mines cheaply. Fully supported by his partners, he poured over fifteen million dollars into new mines and the highly expensive facilities to treat their ores. A twenty-stamp reduction mill arose at Butte to handle the silver, but the heart of the syndicate's copper investment took shape on Warm Springs Creek, twenty-six miles west of Butte. Here, where there was plenty of water, the partners erected in 1883–84 their massive copper reduction works and the Washoe Smelter, the greatest of its kind in the world. Here, too, arose the small city that Daly would have given the tongue-twisting name "Copperopolis," had not another Montana burg pre-empted that title.

It became instead the city of Anaconda, one of the classic "company towns" of the American West. Anaconda was Marcus Daly's bailiwick, his pride and joy. He chose the townsite personally and dominated its management. He built the showplace Montana Hotel there (now the Marcus Daly), famed for its beautiful Victorian bar and its enormous dining room, where Daly often dined alone in regal splendor. Except for escapes to his magnificent ranch in the Bitterroot, where he raised some of America's greatest race horses, Daly spent most of his time at Anaconda. By 1894 the little Butte, Anaconda & Pacific Railroad—which never quite made it to the sea—shuttled constantly back and forth, carrying the Butte ores to Anaconda for treatment.

Year by year Daly steadily expanded his operations. He invested heavily in Montana and Idaho timberlands to provide fuel and lumber for his mines and smelters. He bought up coal fields in Montana and Wyoming. Like Clark and the other mining barons, he imported thousands of manual laborers, engineers, and hardrock miners. Many of these, especially Daly's men, were Irish, either straight from the Emerald Isle or by way of Nevada, Colorado, Utah, or California. Increasingly in the mid-eighties, as the great silver mines of Nevada faded out, large numbers of Cornishmen began to arrive. These, the "Cousin Jacks," were the aristocrats of metal mining, and they often clashed with the "Micks." There were others, too: English, Germans, Finns, Chinese, and, by the 1890s, mounting numbers of Italians and eastern European Slavs. Butte-Anaconda, East Helena, and Great Falls became fascinating "melting pots," where diverse nationality groups mingled, played, and fought with one another. But the numerous Irish, with their strongly held Catholic and Democratic beliefs, usually prevailed, sometimes resenting, and making life uncomfortable for, those who came later, as in this bit of Butte verse:

> O Paddy dear and did you hear the
> news that's goin' round?
> They're firin' all the Irish that
> are workin' underground.
> Oh I've rustled at the Belmont, and
> I've rustled at the Con.
> And everywhere I've rustled they're
> puttin' Bohunks on.

These immigrant workers left a lasting imprint upon western Montana, especially upon the Butte-Anaconda area. Butte, in fact, rose to fame as one of the toughest, most picturesque towns in America. It had its Finntown and Chinatown, its Slavic and English districts, and such colorful suburbs as Meaderville, Dublin Gulch, and the remote neighborhood of "Seldom Seen." Beneath the somber gallows frames that towered over the mine-shafts, Butte had some of the most famous saloons, gambling dens, and whorehouses in the United States. Not surprisingly, Butte came to dominate the new state of Montana, and it held that dominance until the middle of this century. Writing in the 1940s, Joseph Kinsey Howard could still refer to the city as the "black heart of Montana."

The hardrock miners, especially the veterans from Nevada and California, brought labor union loyalties with them, and they soon made Butte into a "Gibraltar of Unionism," one of the strongest labor bastions in America. Labor first raised its head in Montana during 1878, after the Walker brothers and other employers had selectively cut wages from $3.50 to $3.00 per day. Led by Aaron C. Witter of Indiana, the real "father" of Montana unionism, local miners organized the Butte Workingmen's Union, with Witter as president and a constitution based on Nevada precedents. This organization became the Miners' Union of Butte City in 1881 and welcomed all laborers into its ranks.

Unionism registered few gains until the mid-eighties, when the booming copper industry formed a large and highly skilled proletariat. By 1885 Butte had become the greatest mining camp in the West, with the largest army of organized miners—eighteen hundred strong. In that year the union reorganized once again, this time as the now famous Butte Miners Union. This was strictly a miners' organization. Other workers formed their own unions and joined the B.M.U. in creating the Silver Bow Trades and Labor Assembly in 1886.

Led by Cornishmen like William Penrose and Irish like Peter Breen and Patrick Boland, the Butte Miners Union sometimes rocked with tension arising between the English and the Irish. But it made solid gains, winning the closed shop in the Butte mines by 1887. Much of the B.M.U.'s strength and success arose from its friendly relationship with management. Marcus Daly easily identified with his men, and they with him. Arguing that contented employees meant safer profits and bigger gains than could be had by exploiting labor, Daly stoutly resisted any efforts to cut wages or discourage unionism. Other local employers, like W. A. Clark, generally shared this fatherly attitude toward labor. Thus Montana workers benefited from the fact that, until the turn of the century, they worked mostly for locally managed operations. They earned comparatively high wages; and, in contrast to Idaho or Colorado, they usually refrained from strikes and violence.

The Butte Miners Union steadily expanded its authority into other Montana camps, such as Granite and Neihart, and it became the pace-setter of mining unionism for the entire Mountain West. Montana revealed the full measure of its union strength in May 1893, when delegates from throughout the West met in Butte and founded the Western Federation of Miners. The Western Federation was launched, with the B.M.U. as Local Number

One, in an effort to bring all western underground metal miners into one big organization. Although it gained a reputation for toughness and violence in states like Idaho, Colorado, and Utah, in its Montana birthplace the Western Federation of Miners enjoyed peace and political harmony with the mine owners. Unionism thus came early and peacefully to Montana, and peace would prevail as long as Marcus Daly remained in charge of Anaconda.

When the Anaconda Reduction Works began full production late in 1884, Montana moved rapidly into the forefront among copper producing states. At first, though, it seemed that the Anaconda partners stood little chance of breaking the powerful Michigan producers' hold upon the American copper market. Backed by Boston investors and led by the great Calumet and Hecla Company, these Lake Superior operators enjoyed heavy advantages over their western competitors. The Michigan copper was high grade ore, compared to the generally mid-grade Montana deposits. Furthermore, the Lake Superior mines enjoyed the advantages of being well established and lying in closer water and rail proximity to the major eastern markets.

But the Anaconda partners had certain, less obvious factors working in their favor. They had a modern and highly efficient plant, capable of mass producing the red metal at a low cost. They enjoyed ready and cheap access to such vital raw materials as coal and wood. And, of course, they had almost unlimited capital reserves to fund their copper operations. Calumet and Hecla thus ran into trouble when, beginning in 1883, it attempted to close down the Anaconda upstarts by driving down the price of copper. Prices fell from eighteen cents per pound in 1883 to ten cents in 1886; but to the amazement of many observers, Anaconda continued to expand production. Daly's highly efficient reduction, concentration, and smelting plants allowed him to maintain operations, even at ten cents per pound; and the copper price war forced only a momentary shutdown in Montana. The price war became even more complicated when a group of French speculators attempted to corner the world market. They failed at this, however, and so did Calumet and Hecla's effort to drive Anaconda from the field. In 1889 the war ended with a negotiated agreement to peg the price of copper at twelve cents per pound. By then Montana had surpassed Michigan, producing 43.3 percent of the nation's copper, compared to the latter state's 38.7 percent. The newborn "Treasure State" ruled supreme.

While Anaconda was establishing itself as the nation's leading copper producer, other large investors were also moving into Butte copper mining. Their operations, combined with those of Anaconda, made Butte-Anaconda the greatest mining center in the United States by the 1890s. For instance, the powerful Lewisohn brothers of New York joined Boston copper men to found the Boston and Montana and the Butte and Boston Consolidated Mining Companies. These Boston companies poured large investments into both Butte and Great Falls and gained control of some of Butte's greatest mines, such as the Leonard, Mountain View, East Colusa, Gambetta, and Michael Davitt properties. Also prominent among Butte mine owners were the colorful millionaire James Murray, the Heinze brothers of New York, and of course, William A. Clark. The tightfisted Clark owned a sizable share of Butte's silver and copper wealth, as well as the Centennial and Dexter Mills, the Butte Reduction Works, a hardware firm, electric and water utilities, and plenty of real estate.

Towering over all of these, of course, stood the giant Anaconda itself, the undisputed master of Montana mining. The Panic of 1893, which toppled so many silver producers, did much less damage to the copper market. In fact, the panic strengthened the local position of the copper industry by destroying the silver operators. The Anaconda underwent a highly significant series of reorganizations during the 1890s. In 1891, the year of George Hearst's death, the Anaconda owners incorporated for the first time, taking the name Anaconda Mining Company and issuing capital stock to the sum of twenty-five million dollars. The firm reorganized in mid-1895, this time as The Anaconda Copper Mining Company, with James Ben Ali Haggin as president and Marcus Daly as superintendent. "The Company," as Montanans called their home-state colossus, would retain this title until 1955, when it renamed itself simply The Anaconda Company.

Few Montanans probably understood the importance of this incorporation, for management remained in the hands of Haggin and Daly. But the incorporation and issuance of stocks meant that "outsiders" would now share in, and might possibly gain control of, the firm. During the last years of the nineteenth century, control of American industry was becoming increasingly concentrated in fewer and fewer hands. It is hardly surprising that the lucrative Anaconda got caught up in this monopolistic trend. In 1899 executives and directors of the superpowerful and much feared Standard Oil Company, led by Henry H. Rogers, William Rockefeller, and A. C. Burrage, purchased control of the Anaconda Copper Mining Company. These men had already gained domination of the petroleum industry through Standard Oil. Now they aimed to extend the same kind of control over the rapidly expanding copper market.

Determined to corner Montana copper, and ultimately world copper production, Rogers and his associates had first bought heavily into the stock of the Anaconda and the Boston and Montana and Butte and Boston companies. Then they merged the latter two firms together. When they purchased the Anaconda outright in 1899, the Rogers group created the Amalgamated Copper Company as a "holding company" to control the

Anaconda and the other firms that they planned to add to it. They floated seventy-five million dollars in Amalgamated stock to fund the venture. In one of the most notorious chapters of Wall Street history, they soon manipulated down the price of Amalgamated stock in such a way as to squeeze out and fleece many stockholders. Then they bought it back cheaply themselves.

What did all of this mean to the Treasure State? As Montanans soon learned to their sorrow, it meant plenty. It meant that the industry that dominated their economy had passed out of the benevolent control of Marcus Daly and J. B. Haggin and into the hands of a group of corporate executives who were already notorious for their ruthless dealings. Haggin now sold out his Anaconda interest for fifteen million dollars. As for Daly, he became vice president of the new Amalgamated holding company. But this meant little, for he was a dying man. The real power lay in the hands of Henry Rogers, the president of Amalgamated, and William Rockefeller, its secretary-treasurer. The significance of Standard Oil–Amalgamated's takeover of Anaconda would soon become appallingly clear. In order to understand that significance, though, we must first examine the political results of the rise of King Copper.

POLITICS: COPPER KINGS AND POPULISTS

The 1890s, Montana's formative decade of statehood, was perhaps the most turbulent period in the entire political history of the commonwealth. During these years two major political developments combined to scramble party lines and disrupt affairs of state: the famous "Clark-Daly Feud," and the less famous rise and fall of the Populist party. The legendary struggle between mining barons W. A. Clark and Marcus Daly apparently arose at an early date, over issues shrouded in folklore. One story has it that their mutual hatred began as early as 1876, when Clark's bank refused to accept a draft from Daly in his purchase of the Alice Mine. Another identifies their first disagreement with Clark's fleecing of Daly when he purchased water rights on Warm Springs Creek. Other accounts recall such petty issues as Clark's supposed reference to J. B. Haggin as a "nigger," or Clark's childish envy of Daly's mining reputation.

Whatever the original provocation, rivalry between two such powerful men may well have been inevitable. For a time Clark and Daly cooperated in their common financial interest, for example at the 1884 Constitutional Convention. They became known, along with Helena capitalists Samuel Hauser and C. A. Broadwater, as the "Big Four" of the ruling Democratic party. The factor that turned the Clark-Daly feud into an explosive issue was Clark's unquenchable thirst for the glories of public office. While Daly found ample satisfaction in business achievement and such gentlemanly pursuits as horse breeding, Clark, like many other millionaires of his time, desired a seat in the United States Senate as the crowning achievement of his career. His desperate efforts to gain that position would polarize and disgrace the politics of Montana.

Clark first tasted public acclaim as Montana's Centennial orator at the Philadelphia Exhibition in 1876, and he clearly relished the praise he received as a constitution maker in the 1880s. In the election of 1888, Montana's last as a territory, he went after federal office for the first time and secured the Democratic nomination as delegate to Congress. This nomination, in a territory famed for its Democratic leanings, should have assured his election. When the votes were tallied, however, Clark learned that he had lost by over five thousand votes to a less than renowned Republican named Thomas H. Carter. Clark had suffered a humiliating defeat, and he never forgot it. Clearly, as he and most other observers well knew, Marcus Daly had played a hand in upsetting him. Those counties that Anaconda "controlled"—Silver Bow, Deer Lodge, and Missoula—all went Republican, even though all were confirmed Democratic areas.

Daly may have acted out of spite in opposing Clark, but he also acted in self-interest. Along with the Northern Pacific Railroad and a group of Missoula capitalists, he had in 1882 created the Montana Improvement Company, a lumber firm that became a vital supplier of timber and fuel to the Anaconda. This outfit, like others in the West, ran afoul of federal laws that prohibited lumbering on public lands, laws often violated in the absence of accurate surveys. Federal lawsuits against the Montana Improvement Company resulting from these violations posed the direct threat of cutting off Anaconda's access to cheap timber. Reading national political trends accurately, Daly and his associates foresaw that Republican Benjamin Harrison would probably win the Presidency in 1888. If he did, Democrat Clark would stand little chance of getting these lawsuits withdrawn, but Republican Carter might prove effective. Thus Daly's backing of Carter made political sense. Although the Montana Improvement Company and its successors continued to face federal litigation for many years, Congressman—later Senator—Thomas Carter proved to be an unfailing friend of Marcus Daly.

While Daly acquired a friend in Carter, he also acquired a bitter enemy in Mr. Clark. With a fair measure of truth, Clark's newspaper, the Butte *Miner*, accused Daly and his friends of "influencing" their employees to vote Republican. In response to Clark's attacks, Daly employed an experienced and capable New York newspaperman, John H. Durston, to establish a paper that would present his viewpoint. Durston's paper, the Anaconda *Standard*, gained wide recognition as a well edited sheet. But the *Standard*, like the *Miner*, often seemed less concerned with reporting the news than with advancing the interests of its owner. Unfortunately for Montana, the press was becoming a weapon of the warring copper kings.

W. A. Clark unflinchingly continued his quest for high national office. The gaining of statehood in 1889 made available, of course, two seats in the United States Senate, sometimes referred to in those days as the "Million-aires' Club." In 1890, as we have seen, Clark was one of the two Democrats sent to the Senate by the fractured first legislature. Once again he tasted defeat as the Republican majority in the Senate accepted the two Republi-can senators from Montana and sent the Democrats home. The persistent Butte mining king got his next chance during the legislative session of 1893. Throughout the sixty-day session, rumors of vote-buying by the Clark and Daly forces abounded. On the last day of the legislature, Clark sat in the front row of the assembly, with a speech of acceptance ready to deliver. Amidst great excitement, however, he fell three votes short of victory. The legislature adjourned without choosing a United States Senator, and until the lawmakers met again in 1895, Montana had only one man in the Senate. So, in addition to corrupting politics, the mining barons also cost the state its proper representation in Washington.

These burning defeats proved nearly unbearable to the vainglorious Mr. Clark, but he finally gained his chance for revenge during the election of 1894. The 1889 Constitution had left the permanent location of the state capital up to a vote of the people. An 1892 election had then failed to produce a majority vote for any one city. So a runoff election in November of 1894 would finally determine the issue once and for all. The contenders were Helena, the "temporary capital," and Anaconda, which Daly mightily wished to make the center of state affairs. Clark stepped forth as the cham-pion of Helena, not just to spite his foe, but also because he had invest-ments there and the loyalty of Helena's people.

The contest turned into a wide open frontier Donnybrook. Pointing to the obvious danger of placing the seat of government in a "company town," the Clark-Helena forces dwelt upon the feudal hold that Anaconda sup-posedly had upon its workers. The proponents of Anaconda answered, less persuasively, by ridiculing Helena's social airs, its cultural pretensions, and its Black and Chinese elements. Helena, they intimated, was a sissy and un-American town! Both sides generated more heat than light. There were gala parades with imported bands, barrels of free booze, even free money on occasion. The Clark people cleverly struck off small copper collars, with the obvious message of what an Anaconda victory would mean. A well in-formed observer guessed that Daly spent over $2,500,000 and Clark at least $400,000 on this campaign. Since the state cast just over fifty-two thousand votes in the election, that meant roughly $56 invested for each vote!

In the end, the "company town" issue undoubtedly sealed Anaconda's fate, and Helena won by just under two thousand votes. Marcus Daly was brokenhearted and never really got over his defeat. For once in his life, W. A. Clark was a hero, an object of real public affection. Under the flickering shadows of a giant bonfire atop Mount Helena, the grateful citizens of that city met Clark's victory train on election night and pulled his carriage by hand through the streets. After Clark's victory speech, the saloons of the capital city roared with free drinks on his tab. Clark had won the heart of Helena forever. Behind the celebrating, though, lurked a dark truth: like a spreading cancer, mining money was eating into and consuming the political integrity of Montana.

While the Clark-Daly feud kept the political pot boiling, another important development also unfolded: the rise of the Populist party. The Populist, or People's Party was one of the most significant "third parties" in American history. Arising mainly in the Midwest during the 1890s, the party consisted primarily of hard-pressed farmers. Its famous Omaha Platform of 1892 reflected the radicalism that economic hardship had spawned throughout the agricultural regions of the country. Among other things, the platform demanded a graduated income tax, government ownership of railroads, telephones, and telegraph, postal savings banks, and more direct democracy to counter the power of great wealth. Most importantly, silver provided the key to the Populist program, which called for the "free and unlimited coinage of silver," at a ratio of 16 to 1 with gold. This provision would cause inflation, and thus raise farm prices and reduce the burden of their indebtedness.

Even though few farmers had yet entered Montana, the Populist party took immediate and deep root here. The reason, as the late Professor Thomas A. Clinch of Carroll College pointed out, was the silver issue. While much of Montana's small farm population did flock to the Populist banner, the majority of Treasure State Populists came from the mining areas, especially from the hard-pressed silver towns after 1893. Most Montana Populists were laboring men and mining investors, for whom "free silver" promised renewed government purchases of silver, full employment, and restored profits.

The Populist movement surfaced in Montana with a series of meetings during early 1892. Drawing their delegates mainly from the mining towns and the scattered agricultural communities, the Populists held their first nominating convention at Butte in June. Their platform echoed most of the concerns the party voiced nationwide, especially the preoccupation with silver. But they also had emphases of their own, arguing, for instance, that the Northern Pacific should be forced to forfeit its land grant. The Populists produced some able candidates for office, such as Will Kennedy of Boulder for governor and Caldwell Edwards of Bozeman for congressman. Interestingly, they nominated a woman, Ella Knowles, for attorney general. Their selection of the attractive Miss Knowles, the "Portia of the People's Party," revealed the rising power of feminism in Montana and the close ties between the Populist and feminist movements here.

Even though their major candidates failed to win, the Populists made a respectable showing in 1892. Ella Knowles led the Populist ticket, losing the attorney general's post to Republican Henri Haskell by only five thousand votes. Ironically, Miss Knowles soon took a job on Haskell's staff and later became his wife, prompting one wit to comment that "politics makes strange bedfellows." The Populists elected three members to the state house of representatives and ended up holding the balance of power there.

The unfolding Panic of 1893, with its disastrous impact upon the silver industry, added many new converts to the Populist ranks. In the 1894 election they sent three of their number to the state senate and thirteen to the house of representatives. In Montana, and in the nation at large, the Populists reached the peak of their strength in the election campaign of 1896. At the national level, the Populists joined the Democratic party in supporting the presidential candidacy of William Jennings Bryan, a Democrat wedded to the idea of free silver. Bryan's popularity in the silver state of Montana allowed him to carry its presidential vote by a four-to-one margin. According to Bryan's biographer, Marcus Daly was the largest single contributor to the nationwide Democratic-Populist cause, putting up fifty thousand dollars.

In Montana the Populists followed a similar policy of "fusion," or uniting with the Democrats. The "Popocrats" ran a strong state ticket, led by Populists Robert B. Smith for governor and A. E. Spriggs for lieutenant governor. In the November 1896 election the Democratic-Populist "fusion" ticket won sweeping victories. Smith easily won the governor's chair, and the combined Democrats-Populists took overwhelming control of the house of representatives. Charles S. Hartman, a "Silver Republican" whom the fusionists supported, captured the state's lone seat in Congress.

Like most political marriages of convenience, the Democratic-Populist fusion soon came unstuck, at both the national and local levels. In joining up with the Democrats, the Populists had in truth destroyed the integrity and organization of their party. By 1898 Democratic king-makers Clark and Daly had drifted away from the fusion idea, and Populists like Governor Smith were returning to the Democratic party. The Montana Populists, like their brethren throughout the West, saw their power melt away by the early years of this century. The Clark-Daly feud helped destroy their unity and speed their demise; and many of them eventually closed ranks behind the rising copper baron F. A. Heinze. By late 1906, according to legend, so few loyal Populists remained in Butte that they were able to hold their last county convention in Barney Shanahan's cab.

What did the Populists leave behind in Montana? A great deal. They left the two-party system, which was never particularly strong here, in a shambles. Populism is one of the major historic causes of the lack of party regularity that persists in Montana to this day. Although the Populists failed to put through their main program, free coinage of silver, they gave a great boost to many reforms in Montana: the eight-hour workday, mine safety reforms, democratic measures like the initiative and referendum, the direct election of senators, and political equality for women. Most importantly, in Montana and in other mining-agricultural states of the West, the Populists laid the groundwork for twentieth century progressives and reformers. Their political philosophy—based on grass roots democracy, distrust of the East, and enmity toward railroads and other large corporations—has passed from one generation of Montana liberals to another, and it still thrives today amidst such heated issues as coal development and environmentalism. The heirs of populism, like Burton K. Wheeler forty years ago and Lee Metcalf today, have always been in the forefront of Montana's political arena.

MR. CLARK GOES TO WASHINGTON

Following the "Capital Fight" of 1894, the Clark-Daly rivalry slackened until the legislative session of 1899 when, once again, the legislators took up the matter of choosing a United States senator. Now sixty years of age, William Andrews Clark was determined to be elected this time, apparently without regard for the moral or monetary cost. From the day on which the legislature convened, January 2, 1899, rumors of bribery abounded in Helena. Charles Clark, W. A.'s son, supposedly remarked, "We will send the old man to the Senate or the poorhouse." The Clark and Daly organizations lined up for a fight to the finish.

Reports that Clark's agents were bribing members of the legislature became so widespread that the lawmakers chose to create a joint committee to investigate them. On January 10, the day on which balloting for senator was scheduled to begin, this committee presented sworn testimony to the legislature in joint session which brought the whole bribery matter out into the cold light of day. The key testimony, read aloud to the legislators, was that of state Senator Fred Whiteside of Flathead County, a prominent contractor and a legislator who had earlier exposed wrongdoing in the construction of the state capitol building. Whiteside testified that Clark's henchmen, led by attorney John B. Wellcome, had given him thirty thousand dollars to purchase for Clark his vote, as well as the votes of several other legislators. In an atmosphere of indescribable tension, the clerk presented the money in evidence, and Whiteside stood up to speak. He said that this exposure had caused threats to his life, but "if this be the last act of my life, it is well worth the price to the people of this state." The fearless Whiteside blistered his colleagues: "Men of apparent respectability and good standing in this community are trafficking in the honor of members of this body as they would buy and sell cattle and sheep. . . . What new code of morals or of ethics has been discovered which makes of bribery a virtue, and condones the crime of a man because he is rich?"

Now the issue was out in the open. The Daly and Clark newspapers responded emotionally, Daly's Anaconda *Standard* flaying the "Clark Bribers," Clark's Butte *Miner* charging a Daly frame-up. On the first senate vote, Clark received a mere seven votes. Meanwhile, as the senate deliberations continued, a Lewis and Clark County grand jury looked into the evidence of bribery. Over the next eighteen days, the pollution of Montana politics continued in an atmosphere of frenzy. The community of Helena, unfailingly loyal to Clark, seemed to accept bribery as a necessity and to shun those who stood against it. Reporter C. P. Connolly called it "a city hysterical with guilt and greed." Said Connolly, "The morning salutation with everyone was 'What's the price of votes to-day?' "

Just before the final vote on the United State Senate seat, the Helena grand jury delivered its verdict: inconclusive evidence! Rumors abounded, never proven, that the grand jurors had been bribed to the tune of ten thousand dollars apiece. Incredibly, on the same day that the grand jury announced its decision, the Montana Senate voted to unseat Fred Whiteside, following a committee ruling that certain contested votes belonged instead to his opponent, John Geiger. As a result of this farcical decision, the brave Whiteside stood before the joint assembly of the legislature and bade them farewell with these words:

> I understand that the fiat has gone forth, that this is the last day I am to be a member of this body; and if I failed to express myself at this time, I feel that I would be false to myself, false to my home, and false to the friends that have stood so manfully by me.
>
> Let us clink glasses and drink to crime. The crime of bribery, as shown by the evidence here introduced, stands out in all its naked hideousness, and there are forty members seated here who, today, are ready to embrace it. And what is the motive? Answer me that question, you who sit with bloodless lips and shifting eyes—answer if you dare.
>
> There are some features of this senatorial contest which would be ridiculous if it were not for its serious import to the people of this State. It has reminded me of a horde of hungry, skinny, long-tailed rats around a big cheese. . . .
>
> I am not surprised that the gentlemen who have changed their votes to Clark recently, should make speeches of explanation, but I would suggest that their explanations would be much more clear and to the point if they would just get up and tell us the price and sit down.

It seemed that nothing, not even Whiteside's exposure, could stop the Clark bandwagon. On January 28, 1899, the Montana Legislature elected the mining king to the United States Senate. Eleven Republicans gave Democrat Clark their votes. Clark later admitted to an outlay of over $272,000 in this campaign, and he may have spent over $400,000. Usually crediting some "lucky" circumstance, many Montana legislators suddenly turned up with large sums of money after the election. Helena put on another gala celebration for its favorite "statesman." It reportedly cost the old man $30,000 for champagne alone.

Clark's victory, however, was not quite complete. The Daly-Whiteside forces now petitioned the Montana Supreme Court to disbar attorney John Wellcome on charges of bribery. According to published reports, the Clark forces attempted to "influence" two members of the supreme court and also the attorney general in a desperate effort to clear Wellcome's—and thus Clark's—reputation. These public officials, however, proved to be honest, and Wellcome was disbarred. He never implicated Clark in the charges against him.

The Wellcome disbarment marked a defeat for Clark, but the main battle took place in Washington, D.C. Through Senator Thomas Carter, the Daly organization petitioned the Senate to refuse Clark a seat in that body, on the grounds that he had obtained it by improper methods. From January into April of 1900, the Senate Committee on Privileges and Elections conducted a massive investigation of Clark's election, including the questioning of some embarrassed Montana legislators. The committee voted unanimously to recommend that the Senate refuse to seat W. A. Clark. Before the Senate could unseat him, though, Clark resigned on May 15, with a fighting speech in which he defended his incredible outpourings of cash as a heroic effort to save his home state from the clutches of Marcus Daly and the Anaconda. In truth, the committee's findings did reveal questionable dealings by Daly as well as by Clark.

Although Clark's humiliation seemed complete, he had one last card up his sleeve, a maneuver so preposterous that it seems today impossible to believe. Senator Clark's resignation left the governor of Montana, Robert B. Smith, with the responsibility of appointing a successor to his Senate seat. Governor Smith was an outspoken foe of Clark; but the lieutenant governor, A. E. Spriggs, was a friend. Apparently, Clark's associates lured Governor Smith out of the state on legal business. While he was gone, Spriggs, who had been attending a Populist gathering in South Dakota, returned and thus became the acting governor. Charlie Clark then presented his father's letter of resignation to Spriggs who, amazingly, appointed none other than W. A. Clark to the Senate seat that he had just vacated!

This, of course, could never be. Governor Smith angrily returned to

Montana and revoked Spriggs's appointment of Clark, "as being tainted with collusion and fraud." Eventually, this vacant Clark seat went to the distinguished Paris Gibson of Great Falls, who served from 1901 to 1905. In the meantime, though, as in 1893–95, Clark's intrigues momentarily lost Montana one of its seats in the United States Senate. More importantly, the whole episode obviously disgraced the state. Observers around the country watched it all with amazement and horror. The St. Paul *Dispatch* published a large cartoon showing William Jennings Bryan fainting over the Montana situation and pictured a thousand dollar bill with the note: "The kind of bill most frequently introduced in the Montana legislature." Montana, it seemed, had been thoroughly debauched by mining money. Yet, even after all of this, William A. Clark's political hopes were still alive.

As Clark's position in the Senate crumbled under his feet during 1899–1900, events in Montana quietly worked in his favor. Standard Oil's takeover of the Anaconda through formation of the Amalgamated Copper Company occurred at exactly this time, and in effect it gave Clark a new life. Now he could stand forth as Montana's loyal son, defying the soulless corporate monster to which Daly had handed his company and his men. Of equal importance to Clark was the rising power of the man who now became his ally against Anaconda-Amalgamated, F. A. Heinze.

Frederick Augustus Heinze, known formally as "F. Augustus" and informally as "Fritz," occupies a unique and enigmatic place in Montana's history. He was the son of a wealthy and cultured German immigrant family. After receiving a fine classical education in both Europe and America, he attended the prestigious Columbia School of Mines and received his engineering degree in 1889. That same year saw his arrival at Butte, where he went to work for the Boston and Montana Company. Heinze possessed a quick intelligence, and he rapidly learned the Butte ore bodies and the secrets of how to work them. At the same time he became a leading social figure in the gaudy night life of the city. Handsome, vigorous, yet well mannered and somewhat shy, Heinze became a leader of men and a great favorite of women. His talents included a fine oratorical ability, a shrewd sense of politics, and, so valuable to him in Butte, a glaring lack of moral scruples.

Heinze was only twenty years old when he arrived at Butte, but he moved up rapidly. After learning the opportunities at Butte firsthand and then working briefly for the *Engineering and Mining Journal* in New York, he decided to launch his own business. In partnership with his influential New York brothers, Otto and Arthur, in 1892–93 he opened the Montana Ore Purchasing Company, which erected a large, modern, and efficient smelter and began the custom treatment of ores. Heinze handled the ores of independent companies at reduced rates, and this naturally made him a favorite of the smaller-scale mine owners of Butte. In 1895 he purchased the rich Rarus Mine. Along with other, leased properties, the Rarus fed a steadily mounting flow of raw copper into his reduction works and smelter.

Young, brash, and shrewd, Heinze's star rose spectacularly over the Butte horizon. He also moved into Canadian mining with a smelter at Trail, British Columbia. Heinze's Canadian venture turned out to be a sort of dress rehearsal of later and larger events in Montana. He became a vocal champion of the isolated provinces against the Canadian Pacific Railroad and threatened to build a competing line of his own. In the end, though, he sold out to Canadian Pacific for "a splendid profit." By 1899–1900 the swashbuckling Heinze had become the most celebrated and controversial man in Montana mining. As we shall see, he had by then begun an incredible legal battle against the Boston and Montana Company with enormous repurcussions for the entire state.

The election campaign of 1900 ranks as one of the most significant in the history of Montana. In this wild and wide-open contest, W. A. Clark, recently "resigned" from the Senate, allied himself to F. A. Heinze. Both were Democrats, both opposed the newly created Amalgamated Copper Company, and both had something to gain. Clark desired the election of a legislature that would quietly send him back to Washington, this time without any charges of bribery. Heinze wanted control of the government of Butte–Silver Bow County, especially the election of friendly district judges who would aid him in his legal battles.

The two "copper kings," so different in personality, made a powerful team, Clark with his millions and his established political organization, Heinze with his ability to woo the voters. Clark's Butte *Miner* and Heinze's free-swinging newspaper, *The Reveille*, began firing broadsides at Standard Oil and pointing with alarm to its lengthening shadow over Montana. In order to win the crucial support of organized labor, Clark and Heinze granted their miners the long sought eight-hour workday, with no cut in pay, and they challenged Amalgamated to do the same. Amalgamated's directors refused. Clark and Heinze also encouraged the Clerk's Union to demand a general 6:00 P.M. closing time. While other firms agreed to this, the "Company Store"—Hennessy's—refused. Thus labor broke ranks without Daly at the head of Anaconda, and fell in line behind Clark and Heinze. Amidst the wildest of cheering, the triumphant copper barons rode together in a carriage to lead Butte's Miners Union Day parade in June 1900. With labor's backing, the Clark men won control of the Democratic party organization away from the Daly—now Amalgamated—forces.

Even with the strength of Standard Oil and Anaconda behind it, the new-born copper giant Amalgamated could not match the Clark-Heinze effort. As an orator and campaign organizer, Heinze flailed the Amalgamated "copper trust," its directors and political servants. He branded Rogers, Rockefeller, and their associates as the "kerosene crowd," who aimed to use ruthless, Standard Oil methods to crush Montana in their grip. As for Daly's friend, Republican Senator Thomas Carter, Heinze dismissed him as an Amalgamated stooge and nicknamed him "Polly," in reference to his parroting of the Company line. Meanwhile, Heinze's *Reveille*, edited by acid-penned P. A. O'Farrell, tore the hide off the "trust" with biting editorials and graphic cartoons. A typical *Reveille* cartoon depicted Standard Oil–Amalgamated as a giant gorilla hulking up a mountainside with the unconscious maiden Montana held in its grasp. In reaction to these attacks, the Amalgamated began buying up more Montana newspapers in an effort to win the battle of public opinion.

In the ensuing frenzied campaign, party lines became hopelessly scrambled. One wing of the Democratic party followed the lead of Heinze and Clark. So did a fragment of the Republicans and most members of the smaller Populist, Labor, and Social Democratic parties. Most of the Republicans, along with the "Independent" Democrats, followed Senator Carter in backing the Amalgamated. Humorously, the Anaconda *Standard* described the wide range of forces lined up against Amalgamated as the "Heinzeantitrustboltingdemocraticlaborpopulist ticket." The November 1900 vote count registered a major victory for the Clark-Heinze team. While Clark obtained a friendly Democratic legislature, Heinze cemented his control over the government of Silver Bow County.

The 1900 campaign marked a major turning point in the "War of the Copper Kings." It ended the Clark-Daly feud and began a bitter contest between F. A. Heinze and the Amalgamated Copper Company. Only a week after the election, the fifty-nine-year-old Marcus Daly died in his New York hotel room of a failing heart and other illnesses. He died knowing that his archenemy Clark would win the Senate seat which Daly had so long denied him. Daly's death meant that his beloved Anaconda, now completely under the control of Standard Oil–Amalgamated Copper, would no longer be subject to the policies of a loyal "Montanan." It was now a "foreign corporation."

William Andrews Clark savored his victory. The legislature, without Daly's influence at work, quietly sent Clark to serve his term in the United States Senate (1901–7). Almost immediately after the election, Clark broke his alliance with Heinze and became, in effect, an ally of the Amalgamated. Rumor had it that Henry Rogers had given the old man a simple ultimatum: either break with Heinze or face another challenge to his seating in the Senate. At any rate Clark evidently found the Senate a less desirable place than he had imagined. Catering to the voters back home went against his grain. He proved to be, not surprisingly, a staunch Senate conservative and a vigorous opponent of Theodore Roosevelt's conservation policies. In a characteristic attack upon the creation of federal national forests, he remarked: "Those who succeed us can well take care of themselves." When his term expired, Clark did not seek re-election. But for the rest of his long life he was "Senator Clark." It was, after all, a hard won title!

Montana saw less and less of W. A. Clark after 1900. He spent more and more time in Europe, Los Angeles, Washington, and New York, where he built an incredible mansion which cost many millions and contained 121 rooms, 31 baths, and 4 galleries to house his massive art collection. As always, his investments absorbed most of his attention. Clark's investments included cattle, lumber, sugar beets, real estate operations, utilities, banks, newspapers, and a Los Angeles–Salt Lake railroad, along which grew up the city of Las Vegas, Clark County, Nevada. Mines, though, remained the key to the Clark empire. He owned six, each of which produced ores worth several millions. His great United Verde Mine in Arizona yielded nearly one hundred million dollars in dividends. When the old man died at age eighty-six in 1925, he left behind one of the great American fortunes. But he left few monuments to his memory at "home." The William Andrews Clark Memorial Library was given to the University of California at Los Angeles, not the University of Montana, and a million dollars went to a new law school at the University of Virginia. The Columbia Gardens, his pretty trolley park at Butte, now lies defunct. Today, a plaque in his memory stands triumphantly on display in Montana's capitol rotunda. That seems peculiar, in light of what happened over seventy-six years ago.

THE TRIUMPH OF AMALGAMATED

Although stung by the Clark-Heinze attacks of 1900, the newly formed Amalgamated Copper Company pressed inexorably onward toward its goal of a complete takeover of Montana's copper industry. Once W. A. Clark entered the Senate and abandoned the fight, F. Augustus Heinze and his Montana Ore Purchasing Company stood nearly alone in opposing the Standard Oil–Amalgamated "copper trust." Heinze, however, proved to be a tough opponent.

Heinze entered the legal-political arena even before the 1898–99 formation of the Amalgamated holding company. In 1898 he launched an incredible five-year war against the company which raged on many fronts at the same time. The hottest disputes centered upon the rich Michael Davitt Mine. A property of the consolidated Boston and Montana–Butte and Boston Mining Companies, the Davitt bordered Heinze's Rarus Mine. In March 1898 a legal battle erupted in federal district court at Butte between the Boston firms and Heinze's Montana Ore Purchasing Company over ownership of the veins that merged along the boundaries of the Davitt and Rarus mines. At issue was the Apex Law, a great source of litigation in the mining West. The Apex Law provided that the owner of the claim where a vein of ore "apexed" (touched the surface) could pursue that vein wherever it led, even laterally under the borders of adjoining claims.

Federal District Judge Hiram Knowles directed the jury in this case to decide in favor of the Boston and Montana Company. Such was "Fritz's" popularity, however, that the jurors defied the judge in their verdict. This forced a retrial, which occurred at Helena in 1900. By that time the Amalgamated was in the process of absorbing the Boston and Montana–Butte and Boston firms; so Heinze now found himself in a larger battle than the one he had entered. At Heinze's instigation, the Helena papers blistered the Amalgamated, and this jury also found against the holding company. Arguing that Fritz's propaganda had influenced the verdict, Amalgamated won a second retrial, this one in a faraway circuit court at San Francisco.

Since a court injunction forbade mining of the disputed veins, Heinze found himself cut off from ores that he desperately needed to keep his smelters running at capacity. With his back to the wall, he began to fight ruthlessly. He and his brothers simply transferred the holdings of the Montana Ore Purchasing Company to another of their firms, the Johnstown Mining Company. Then, arguing that the Johnstown Company was not subject to the injunction, they began mining the rich veins in dispute. The loyal Heinze miners drove intricate crosscuts into the Davitt from the Rarus and then sealed off the veins with bulkheads that kept out the Amalgamated crews.

The distant roar of underground blasting alerted the Amalgamated to the situation. Soon their men were also pouring into the disputed Davitt veins from the adjoining Pennsylvania Mine. An "underground war" resulted, as Amalgamated and "Johnstown" miners skirmished with jets of high pressured water, smudge fires, slaked lime poured through vents, even dynamite. After two Amalgamated men lost their lives in a dynamite blast, it seemed that widespread violence would engulf the Butte Hill. The war in the Davitt, though, soon flickered out. The court ordered inspectors into the mine, who uncovered the extent of Heinze's looting—an estimated million dollars worth of ore. For this he was fined a ridiculous twenty thousand dollars. The Davitt Case remained in federal courts for years. It eventually reached the United States Supreme Court, which ruled entirely in favor of the Amalgamated. A hollow victory, indeed!

As "underground warfare" flared in the Michael Davitt, Heinze and his army of over three dozen lawyers engaged the Amalgamated on other fronts, too. In creating the Amalgamated holding company, Henry Rogers had aimed to absorb not only Anaconda but also the Boston and Montana–Butte and Boston companies. When in 1898 Rogers tried to arrange an Amalgamated takeover of these consolidated firms, he found to his discomfort that two of Heinze's cohorts had each bought one hundred shares of Boston and Montana stock. The Heinze men brought suit in court, arguing that the Boston and Montana could not legally be transferred to Amalgamated without the consent of the minority stockholders. Accepting their argument, the Montana Supreme Court halted Amalgamated's takeover of the Boston firms and disrupted Rogers' strategy until the 1899 Legislature dutifully passed House Bill 132, which allowed stock transfers with the approval of only two-thirds of the stockholders. In the meantime the court placed the Boston and Montana Company in receivership, which cost it dearly in legal fees and falling stock values.

In this case, and others too, Heinze's trump card was his "friendship" with the judges elected to the district courts in Silver Bow County. William Clancy, a bearded Populist and curbstone lawyer, won election to one of these judgeships in 1896. Judge Clancy soon became famous for his unkempt appearance and his peculiar courtroom behavior, which included dozing during legal arguments and casually spitting tobacco juice at well placed spittoons. He also gained fame for his unfailing support of Heinze, which was so obvious that rumors of bribery abounded—rumors which were never proved. During his 1900 alliance with Clark, Heinze won another friend when, with his support, Edward Harney won election to the second district bench in Butte. With his allies on the local courts, Fritz could easily drive the titans of Standard Oil to absurd lengths.

For instance, take the incredible case of the "Copper Trust Company." While plotting the complex claims of the Butte Hill, Arthur Heinze discovered a thin, triangulated sliver of unclaimed land that lay between three of Amalgamated's greatest mines, the Anaconda, the Neversweat, and the St. Lawrence. With a fine sense of humor, Fritz claimed this forty-square-yard trace of land, named it the "Copper Trust" claim, and went before Judge Clancy's court arguing that all three of these mines were really his since they "apexed" on his claim. The judge unflinchingly shut all three of them down early in 1900 and, pending a court ruling, put three thousand Amalgamated miners out of work. This time, however, Heinze had gone too far. When an angry mob began talking of lynching the judge, Clancy hurriedly reversed his decision, and the mines reopened.

Fritz posed a much greater threat in the celebrated case of the Minnie Healy Mine. He first acquired a lease on the Minnie Healy from Miles Finlen, a friend of Marcus Daly who had had no luck in developing it. With his uncanny "nose for ore," Heinze quickly uncovered rich veins within the mine. Since Heinze had acquired the Healy lease by an oral agreement,

Finlen took him to court in an attempt to regain what was now a very valuable property. Even before the case reached court, however, Amalgamated bought up Finlen's claim to the mine, desperately afraid that Heinze might use it for more raids into adjoining properties.

The Minnie Healy Case came before newly elected Judge Edward Harney in 1901, and the judge predictably upheld his friend Heinze's claim. Now, the Amalgamated resorted to sordid methods. Learning of Judge Harney's fondness for liquor and his relationship with a Butte stenographer named Ada Brackett, Charlie Clark and Amalgamated attorneys A. J. Shores and D'Gay Stivers attempted to blackmail and bribe him. They acquired copies of correspondence between Harney and Mrs. Brackett, the so-called "Dearie letters," which seemed to indicate that Heinze had influenced the judge. Then they confronted Harney with the threat of impeachment and offered him $250,000 to sign an affidavit admitting that he had accepted bribes from Heinze. Harney steadily refused to make any such admission, and he was never impeached. The judge, in turn, attempted to have lawyers Stivers and Shores disbarred, but they were acquitted.

The evidence arising from this episode caused the Montana Supreme Court to reverse Judge Harney's decision and to remand the case to the other Butte district judge—none other than William Clancy. While the issue lay in court, underground warfare erupted in the Healy, just as it had in the Davitt. In the very rich veins of the "firing line" sector of the Minnie Healy, Heinze's men skirmished with Amalgamated miners who entered from the adjacent Leonard Mine. Each side attempted to flood the other's shafts, and large-scale loss of life seemed imminent until averted by a truce. The Healy Case remained in Judge Clancy's court from 1901 through most of 1903, and tension in this and other cases mounted toward an explosive climax. On October 22, 1903, Clancy awarded Heinze full title to the multi-million-dollar Minnie Healy. This marked a stunning defeat for Amalgamated, which not only lost the mine but would also face new Apex litigation along the Healy's borders. Even more importantly, on that same day, the judge also ruled against Amalgamated in the case of the Parrot Mining Company.

The Parrot Mining Company was an Amalgamated subsidiary. In a familiar move, two of Heinze's lieutenants bought some Parrot stock and then went to court in 1903. They charged, in effect, that the Amalgamated holding company, by managing the Parrot in the interests of its other subsidiaries, was infringing upon the rights of the Parrot stockholders. This case struck at the very heart of Amalgamated, and, once again, Clancy ruled in Heinze's favor. The judge declared, in essence, that the Amalgamated could not operate legally in Montana. According to Clancy's decision, Amalgamated subsidiaries like the Parrot, which were organized before House Bill 132 made such stock transfers legal, could issue no dividends to the parent company or its stockholders.

The Parrot decision prompted Amalgamated to square off for a fight to the finish. Even though the Montana Supreme Court would later reverse Clancy's ruling, the trust now had occasion to turn the tables, once and for all, against F. A. Heinze. Only hours after Clancy's decisions, the Amalgamated suddenly shut down most of its Montana operations. In the mines, smelters, refineries, and lumber camps, the doors swung shut. Fifteen thousand men, the majority of Montana's wage earners, were out of work. It seemed a case of waiting for the other shoe to hit the floor: would Amalgamated, which had large surpluses of copper on hand, reopen before winter brought suffering to the thousands of unemployed? If so, on what conditions? The Company laid down its terms by demanding that Heinze's lieutenants, John MacGinnis and Daniel Lamm, sell their stocks in the Parrot. Quickly, the Butte Miners Union, along with Senator Clark and other interested parties, offered to purchase and hold the troublesome stocks. The Company now wanted more, however, than the stocks. It wanted to smash forever Heinze's hold on the courts.

Under the pressure of the Amalgamated lockout, Heinze's popularity among the Butte miners began to fade. On the afternoon of October 26, 1903, he appeared before a crowd of perhaps ten thousand men assembled at the Silver Bow County Courthouse. Many of the men were hostile, and some were armed. Heinze offered evasive proposals to turn over the Parrot stock, offers that he knew the Company would never accept. Dramatically, he lashed out at the Standard Oil–Amalgamated octopus, warning his listeners in graphic phrases of what might happen to them:

> My friends, the Amalgamated Copper Company, in its influence and functions, and the control it has over the commercial and economic affairs of this state, is the greatest menace that any community could possibly have within its boundaries. . . . Rockefeller and Rogers have filched the oil wells of America, and in doing so they trampled on every law, human and divine. . . . The same Rockefeller and the same Rogers are seeking to control the executive, the judiciary [!], and the legislature of Montana. . . .
>
> You are my friends, my associates, and I defy any man among you to point to a single instance where I did one of you wrong. These people are my enemies, fierce, bitter, implacable; but they are your enemies, too. If they crush me today, they will crush you to-morrow. They will cut your wages and raise the tariff in the company stores on every bite you eat, and every rag you wear. They will force you to dwell in Standard Oil houses while you live, and they will bury you in Standard Oil coffins when you die.

It was a brilliant and moving speech, and it rewon for Heinze the loyalty of Butte, if only for a moment. The miners and their families knew that much of what he said was true, that with Daly gone, they were now the pawns of a cold, merciless employer. The Amalgamated, though, rejected any compromise with Heinze. Instead, they demanded that Governor Joseph Toole call a special session of the legislature in order to pass a "change of venue" law. Such a law would allow parties to a lawsuit to demand trial in a different court if they thought the local judge might be prejudiced against them. Obviously, this would destroy Heinze's advantages in the Butte courts.

Governor Toole resisted, for he recognized naked coercion. But in the end, he had no choice. The legislature convened in special session on November 10, 1903, passed the so-called "Fair Trials Bill," and disbanded. Montana went back to work, but only on Amalgamated's terms. The giant trust had literally beaten Montana into submission and taught her the price of defying its wishes. Observers around the nation watched in awe this shakedown of a "sovereign state" by a corporation. As the *Idaho State Tribune* commented: "It took the Amalgamated Copper Company just three weeks to coerce Montana into falling on her knees with promises of anything that big corporation might want."

The battle for Butte, for its mineral riches and its political mastery, was over. F. Augustus Heinze, who had presented the only real obstacle against Amalgamated's drive to "consolidate" control of the hill, lost the war when he lost control of the courts. In the 1904 election the voters removed his friends from the Butte bench. Contrary to his promises that he would never sell out to Amalgamated, Heinze began secret negotiations with John D. Ryan, who in 1904 had become the Company's managing director in Montana. After fifteen months of maneuvering came the February 1906 announcement that the Heinzes had sold their Butte holdings to Amalgamated. The Company paid a whopping 12 million to remove Heinze from its path. This price, it must be noted, covered more than mines and smelters. It also ended about one hundred lawsuits that were tying up about $50 million worth of property. In order to manage the Heinze properties, Amalgamated formed a new subsidiary, the Butte Coalition Mining Company. The question must always remain: did Heinze fight Standard Oil on principle, or did he merely shake them down? The answer, perhaps, is—both.

Still a young man, Fritz Heinze took his newly gained fortune and departed for Wall Street, seeking new worlds to conquer. He bought into a major banking chain and began developing a firm he had founded earlier, the United Copper Company, as a Wall Street syndicate through which he would compete directly with the great Amalgamated. This was foolish, for the Butte copper king had now started something he could not finish. Within months, "mysterious" purchases and sales of United Copper stock, along with runs on his major New York bank, had driven Heinze and his brothers from Wall Street in ruin. It seems clear that Standard Oil and its allies stood behind all of this, aided no doubt by Heinze's own mistakes. The destruction of the Heinzes on Wall Street, along with other factors, triggered a brief but sharp depression known in United States history as the Panic of 1907.

F. A. Heinze never recovered from his Wall Street shellacking. He faced trial on charges of fraud arising out of the whole affair, but was acquitted. Heinze attempted with some success to rebuild his western mining empire, but in truth he had burned himself out. After a 1910 marriage to actress Bernice Henderson, which brought little happiness, he died in 1914 of cirrhosis of the liver. Only forty-five years old at the time of his death, F. Augustus Heinze had packed much, indeed, into a brief lifetime.

Heinze's defeat in 1903 and sellout in 1906 brought "peace" at last to Butte and allowed the Amalgamated to consolidate its grip on Montana mining. Under the tough-minded direction of John D. Ryan, who succeeded Henry Rogers as president of Amalgamated in 1909, the Company became, practically speaking, the proprietor of the Butte Hill. In 1910 Amalgamated bought W. A. Clark's Montana copper mines and smelter. And in that same year, the great holding company merged all of its subsidiaries into one—the Anaconda Copper Mining Company. One reason for this maneuver arose from Amalgamated's increasing troubles. Standard Oil faced antitrust prosecution and was being forced to break up much of its empire, including its copper holdings. Finally, in 1915, the Amalgamated Copper Company was totally liquidated. But only in name—for the Anaconda Copper Mining Company simply replaced it. Since 1915, the Anaconda has had no Standard Oil affiliation.

The newly independent Anaconda Copper Mining Company of 1915 bore little resemblance to the firm purchased by Standard Oil–Amalgamated Copper back in 1899. With assets totaling $118 million, and a copper production capacity of three hundred million pounds per year, it was the giant of the world's copper industry. Its Montana empire included thirty mine shafts on the Butte Hill, reduction works and smelters at Anaconda, Great Falls, and East Helena, a big lumber operation based at Bonner, scattered coal fields, a railroad, hardware stores, hotels, and, ominously, a growing chain of newspapers that by now included most of the state's major dailies.

The Anaconda had crushed and absorbed its opposition, and by 1910–15 it clearly dominated the Montana economy and political order. In contrast to the old days, when Marcus Daly seemed to manage the Company with Montana's interests in mind, local folks now found themselves locked in the grip of a corporation controlled from Wall Street and insensitive to their concerns. Montanans would often forget that it was Clark, after all, who first tampered with the legislature and turned journalism to his own purposes, that it was Heinze who first corrupted the courts. With good reason, however, they would remember the shutdown of 1903 and the awesome political power now in the hands of the Anaconda. To many observers, both inside and outside its borders, Montana seemed to be the classic example of a "one-company state," a commonwealth where one corporation ruled supreme.

CHAPTER X

The Homestead Boom: 1900–18

> Bob you wouldent know the town or the country either it's all
> grass side down now. Wher once you rode circle and I night
> wrangled, a gopher couldn't graze now. The boosters say its a bet-
> ter country than it ever was but it looks like hell to me I liked it
> better when it belonged to God it was sure his country when we
> knew it.
>
> —CHARLES M. RUSSELL

> If farming could be made a success on the rocky hillsides of New
> England, what shall we say of the farmers' chances on these rich,
> non-irrigated highlands that skirt our mountains for hundreds of
> miles? These lands are only waiting the coming of industrious, in-
> telligent farmers to take their places among the most productive
> agricultural sections of the country. Our people cannot all be
> cattle kings, sheep barons and bonanza miners; some of them
> must occupy more humble but not less honorable positions on the
> farm lands of our state.
>
> —PARIS GIBSON

THE farmers' frontier came late to the vast plains area of east-central Montana. This semiarid region, the far corner of the great Mississippi-Missouri
Basin, seemed hopelessly dry to frontier farmers in the nineteenth century.
In fact, many of their maps and schoolbooks designated these rolling
prairies, reaching from the 98th meridian to the Rocky Mountains, as the
"Great American Desert." So, during the second half of that century,
westward moving farmers passed by this forbidding area and headed on instead to the inviting valleys of the towering Rockies and the Pacific Coast. It
was only after 1900, with the advent of new land policies, new farming
machines and methods, and new promotional groups, that the farmers'
frontier—the last frontier—broke upon the immense emptiness of the

Montana plains. The sodbusters' invasion, so long in coming, would now transform the young state, setting off the greatest boom in all Montana's history.

AGRICULTURAL BEGINNINGS

Naturally, the first white farmers in what became Montana were fur traders and missionaries. Vegetable gardens, crop fields, and grazing livestock surrounded such fur posts as Forts Benton and Connah. In the Bitterroot Valley, Jesuit priests began farming successfully in the 1840s. They imported seeds and domestic stock from the Columbia Basin and used irrigation to raise impressive crops of potatoes and wheat. They even built a crude flour mill. By the 1860s a few other isolated farmers, like the O'Keefe brothers near present Missoula, were also tilling the soil. But it was only with the great gold rushes of the mid-sixties, and the far-removed and hungry mining towns which they produced, that large demands for foodstuffs arose in the area. Farmers appeared quickly in response to these demands.

The placer gold towns of southwestern Montana faced severe food problems. Located four hundred miles to the south of them, the Morman settlements in Utah eagerly welcomed the Montana trade. They charged very high prices, though, and sometimes winter and spring snowstorms blocked the roads. During the hard winter of 1864–65, for instance, flour shortages in Virginia City drove the price of a hundred-pound sack up to $150, and riots broke out as a result. The high price of food convinced many prospectors to give up mining and to take up farming instead. Many of them, after all, came from farm families, and they returned instinctively to the life of their forefathers.

The pioneer farmers found, often to their surprise, that the high mountain valleys surrounding the gold fields were both richly fertile and well watered. By selectively irrigating, and by carefully skirting the late spring and early autumn frosts, they produced fine harvests of grain, vegetables, and even fruits. Small farms soon dotted the Jefferson, Ruby, Madison, Bitterroot, Deer Lodge, Prickly Pear, and other valleys along the continental divide. The broad and beautiful Gallatin Valley came to surpass all others in productivity and already housed three flour mills by 1867. With good reason Bozeman, the principal community in the Gallatin, boasted that it had a much more secure future than the gold towns lying to the west and north.

Yet, agriculture in early Montana remained limited for many years, restricted economically to local mining markets and confined geographically to the southwestern valleys. By 1870 the placer gold towns were fading rapidly, and Montana farmers faced a troubled future. The 1870 Census found only 851 farms and 150,000 cultivated acres in the entire territory. During the next three decades the farmers' frontier crept eastward and northward, but only at a snail's pace. Prior to the mid-1880s the aridity of the land, the lack of rail connections, and the presence of enormous Indian reservations and huge open range livestock outfits all combined to hold back the farmers' advance. Even the arrival of railroads failed to touch off a rush to the Montana plains. During the 1890s scattered farmers irrigated bottomlands along the Yellowstone, Missouri, and Milk rivers, and a few even tried dry farming on the bench lands of northern and central Montana. But they were few and far between.

As the twentieth century dawned, therefore, the eastern two-thirds of Montana lay wide open, with a settlement or Indian village here and there, occasional herds of cattle and flocks of sheep, and nearly everywhere vast expanses of vacant public lands. The cutting edge of the farmers' frontier stood far to the east, in central North and South Dakota. The farmers' advance, which began along the Atlantic seaboard early in the seventeenth century, had paused at the 98th meridian, the "rainfall line" that divides the subhumid from the semiarid Great Plains. Those acquainted with this region—eastern Montana and the western Dakotas—well understood the central fact of its geography: lack of adequate rainfall meant that farmers here must rely either upon large-scale irrigation or upon moisture-conserving dry land farming.

In the minds of many Montana and Great Plains boosters of the 1890s and early 1900s, reclamation seemed the key to prosperity. They saw big rivers, like the Missouri, the Milk, and the Yellowstone, carrying their heavy spring runoffs to the sea, leaving parched but fertile uplands unwatered. Paying little heed to the enormous amounts of land as compared to the light annual stream flows, they argued passionately that, once the Missouri and its tributaries were dammed and diverted, they could turn the deserts to gardens that would "blossom like the rose." Addressing Montana's Constitutional Convention of 1889, John Wesley Powell, the famed director of the United States Geological Survey, made the incredible prediction that one-third of Montana's land mass could be irrigated: "It means that no drop of water falling within the area of the state shall flow beyond the boundaries of the state. It means that all the waters falling within the state will be utilized upon its lands for agriculture." Boosters of Montana reclamation, such as Governor Joseph K. Toole and Billings promoter I. D. O'Donnell, saw their fondest dreams come true when Congress passed the Newlands Reclamation Act in 1902. This important law committed the federal government to a long-range program of building large-scale irrigation projects throughout the arid West. A prosperous era of high dams, gleaming canals, and verdant crop lands seemed at hand.

The grand vision of the early-day reclamationists proved, over the years, to be mostly mirage. Between 1904 and 1906 construction began on several large and important federal reclamation developments: the Huntley Project east of Billings, the Lower Yellowstone Project along the Dakota border, the Milk River Project in northern Montana, and the Sun River Project west of Great Falls. These federal irrigation developments meant much to Montana. So would others built much later, like Canyon Ferry and Tiber dams in the 1950s. Significant as they were, though, the federal reclamation projects obviously left most of Montana's wide open spaces unwatered. Realizing this inescapable fact, agricultural promoters abandoned their hopes of turning the semiarid western Plains into an irrigated "garden." They turned instead to the promise of dry farming.

BEHIND THE BOOM

The great Montana land rush began late in the first decade of this century. Viewed in proper perspective, it marked the culmination, the final thrust of the three-century advance of the American agricultural frontier. A number of complex developments lay behind this agricultural invasion of the Northern Plains. Perhaps most basic was the nationwide—in fact, worldwide—industrial revolution, which by 1900 had provided farmers with steel moldboard plows, grain drills, twine binders, discs, harrows, steam-powered threshers, and other increasingly effective machinery. Three factors, especially, gave rise to the homestead boom in Montana: the "dry farming" system of agriculture, the availability of large tracts of land either free or at low prices, and the mammoth promotional campaign which cranked up around 1908.

"Dry farming," says historian Mary Wilma M. Hargreaves, "may be generally defined as agriculture without irrigation in regions of scanty precipitation." By the early twentieth century, experienced farmers in such semiarid regions as Utah and eastern Washington had worked out various methods of moisture-conserving tillage. They allowed their lands to lie in summerfallow during alternate years, and they learned to work the ground intensively in order to retain soil moisture. Many individuals contributed to the development of dry farming, but by 1900, Hardy Webster Campbell was easily the best known. Campbell, a South Dakota farmer, stoutly maintained that, through scientific agriculture, these dry Dakota-Montana prairies could produce just as abundantly as the well-watered crop lands far to the east. As he phrased it in 1909, "I believe of a truth that this region which is just now coming into its own is destined to be the last and best grain garden of the world."

The "Campbell System" of dry farming aimed almost exclusively at conserving water in the soil. Campbell worried little about expanding acreages or encouraging crop rotation or diversification. Instead, he preached deep plowing and intensive cultivation in order to retain the precious moisture in the earth. Campbell's famous subsurface packer tamped the subsoil while loosening the topsoil. In order to maintain a fine surface mulch that would hold down evaporation, his system then called for constant discing and harrowing, especially after each rain. Campbell's theory was music to the ears of Great Plains promoters. Regional railroads soon had him, and others like him, running experimental farms and lecturing to enthusiastic farm audiences.

Campbell's influence came late to Montana. Prior to 1905 only a few local promoters, such as Paris Gibson of Great Falls, had advocated dry farming. After that date, however, the movement expanded rapidly. The railroads, first in Dakota and then in Montana, pushed the Campbell program with much fanfare. The Montana Agricultural Experiment Station, located at Montana State College in Bozeman, reacted somewhat more cautiously. Experiment Station experts like F. B. Linfield and Alfred Atkinson never fully trusted Campbell's optimistic theories. Not only was he too enthusiastic about moisture conservation, Campbell also paid little heed to such worthy ideas as developing drought-resistant plants or combining crop farming with livestock production. Despite their reservations, though, the Experiment Station authorities generally agreed that dry farming could work and that it was well suited to much of east-central Montana. So, with mounting enthusiasm, they lent their full support to the movement.

Although Hardy Campbell hesitated to admit it, dry farming required large tracts of land, units big enough to allow for summerfallowing and for lesser crop yields per acre. The potential settler could either buy this land from realtors or railroads, or he could get it free from the government. Ever since passage of the famous Homestead Act in 1862, the federal government had offered free farms to all American citizens. The Homestead Act provided the farmer with a quarter-section of land, 160 acres, free except for an incidental filing fee. Then, following a five-year "prove-up" period, the homesteader acquired full legal title to his land.

The original Homestead Act meant little to faraway Montana, where the farmers came late and where, in most areas, 160 acres was far too little land for a family farm. Realizing slowly that Great Plains agriculture demanded larger acreages, Congress passed several supplementary laws in order to provide more land to the homesteaders. One of these was the Desert Land Act of 1877, under which one could obtain a full 640-acre section of land for only $1.25 per acre, if he proved up in three years and irrigated part of the plot. This ludicrous measure, which was pushed through Congress by organized stockmen, offered little hope to real farmers, who could seldom bear the costs of irrigation by themselves. As seen earlier, the Desert Land

Act was widely used in Montana, mainly by ranchers who violated the spirit of the law in order to gain grazing lands. Over three million acres of public lands in Montana passed into private hands under its auspices.

Settlement of the Montana-Dakota plains obviously demanded a land law more suited to local conditions. Finally, in 1909, Congress seemed to meet this need by enacting the Enlarged Homestead Act. This measure, which Montana Senator Joseph M. Dixon played a major hand in formulating, offered free a 320-acre half-section of land to settlers in portions of Arizona, Colorado, Montana, Nevada, Oregon, Utah, Washington, and Wyoming. In 1912 Congress supplemented this law with the Three-Year Homestead Act, which reduced the waiting period for complete ownership from five to merely three years and permitted the settler to be gone from his homestead five months of each year. The westward looking home-seeker, not realizing that even 320 acres was usually far too little land on the arid plains, responded eagerly to this doubling of the original homestead grants. An eventual total of nearly thirty-two million Montana acres would pass from public into private hands under these homestead acts.

Not all of the sodbusters obtained their lands free from the government. Many of those who had some capital bought choice plots from private speculators. Some purchased directly from the Northern Pacific Railroad, which in 1900 still held 13,450,816 acres of its enormous land grant in Montana. Over the next seventeen years the Northern Pacific sold off most of its grants at rates of up to $8.56 per acre. By 1917 only 2,751,637 acres of the railroad's Montana domain remained intact. Many others bought from realty companies, who often bloc purchased railroad or ranch lands for resale to farmers. Some of these realtors were out-of-state speculators, like W. H. Brown and Company of Chicago. Others, such as W. G. Conrad of Great Falls, were local talent. Eagerly, numerous stockmen with large holdings platted their range lands for sale to the farmers. Joseph Baker summarized the attitude of many ranchers when he said: "Dry farming is the coming salvation of the west . . . I plan to put the dry farming system into effect on my Highwood land which has heretofore been considered by men as nothing but poor grazing land."

The ready availability of free or cheap land and the new methods of dry farming made the Montana homestead boom possible. But what really launched it was the great promotional campaign which began after 1908. The promoters came from many places. There were chambers of commerce, bankers' groups, and newspaper editors from the towns and cities. There were real estate boomers, state agencies like the Bureau of Labor, Agriculture, and Industry, and experts from the state college. Especially, there were the railroads. Obviously, the railroads had a vital stake in building up the region that they served, and they had advertising resources that no one else could match. Prior to 1906 the Northern Pacific, the Great Northern, and the Burlington, all dominated by James J. Hill, had advertised the northwestern plains to farmers, but only in comparatively modest terms. It was the Milwaukee Road, which thrust into central Montana after 1906, that really kicked off the great promotional boom. The Milwaukee promoted its prime areas, especially the Musselshell Valley and the Judith Basin, in such glowing terms that an Iowa immigrant ventured the opinion that the Judith was the most heavily advertised area in North America.

The most capable and powerful of all the railroad promoters, of course, was Jim Hill—or "Yim" Hill, as he was known to his Scandinavian friends. Never one to be outdone, Hill had his own promotional campaign in full swing by 1909. That was the year that Billings hosted a well attended Dry Farming Congress. Each year, advocates of the Campbell System held such a gathering in a different city, and the Billings meeting was one of the liveliest. Promoters, not farmers, dominated these conventions. At Billings both Jim Hill and his son Louis, who was president of the Great Northern, went so far as to urge the group to drop the term "dry farming." They felt that the emphasis upon "dry" was unflattering to the area and that it was bad publicity. The Hills lost this round, though, due mainly to the stand taken by F. B. Linfield of the Montana Agricultural Experiment Station. In solemn terms, Linfield warned the delegates that they were being asked to trifle with the truth.

The railroad advertising campaign reached its climax in 1911. Along with the Milwaukee, the three Hill lines used nearly every conceivable method to publicize the fertility of the northern Great Plain and to lure in farmers. They offered prizes for crops and livestock, sponsored farm exhibits, ran agricultural display trains around the country, and spread advertising leaflets and brochures throughout the United States and Europe. They encouraged Europeans, especially Germans and Scandinavians, to migrate here and offered them easy trans-Atlantic rates. Most importantly, they offered the home-seekers cheap rail fare to their new homes, either in boxcars or in the more comfortable "Zulu" cars which provided sleeping facilities. For as little as $22.50, the homesteader could buy space in a freight car from St. Paul to eastern Montana. In the car he could bring his family, all his belongings, even seed grains and livestock.

Hill, largely controlling three of the five regional railroads, had an obvious financial interest in promoting immigration. But Jim Hill pursued other motives than mere economic gain. He was very much a Jeffersonian democrat, who believed in rural virtues and saw the family farm as the backbone of American society. He envisioned the fertile plains of Montana and the Dakotas as the future granary of the world, neatly partitioned into small family farms and populated by tens of thousands of hearty yeoman farmers and their offspring. With his railroads linking the Great Lakes to Puget Sound on the Pacific, the "Empire Builder" dreamed of opening new markets in China and the Far East for the high protein wheat that would pour from the abundant harvests of the Northern Plains.

So the energetic Hill outdid all the other boosters. He took personal interest in livestock breeding and in importing new drought-resistant grains. His agricultural expert, Professor Thomas Shaw of Minnesota Agricultural College, came after 1910 to surpass even Hardy Campbell as the region's leading advocate of dry farming. Although Shaw was more open minded than Campbell, more understanding of the need to diversify regional agriculture, he still shared in full Campbell's devotion to deep plowing and intensive cultivation.

Jim Hill looked upon the Northwest in a fatherly manner. "You are now our children," he told the 1909 Billings Dry Farming Congress, "but we are in the same boat with you, and we have got to prosper with you or we have got to to be poor with you." In his massive settlement campaign, he saw the fulfillment of a great national purpose. "Population without the prairie," he once observed, "is a mob, and the prairie without population is a desert." Mercifully, Hill would not live to see his dreams blighted by drought, depression, and the exodus from small farms; nor would he read the words of Montana historian Joseph Kinsey Howard, who singled him out, rather inaccurately, as nearly the sole architect of later disaster. He would never know of the wild denunciation written by North Dakota journalist-historian Bruce Nelson, who flayed Hill as the "unremitting wrecker of the empire of the northern plains."

THE LAND TAKING

Under the stimulus of this propaganda barrage, the farmers' frontier swept dramatically into east-central Montana during the first and second decades of this century. Prior to 1900 farmers had already occupied some lands around Great Falls and Billings and in a few other favored locations east of the mountains. During the next half-dozen years, they probed into the "golden triangle" region north of Great Falls and into central Montana areas like the Judith Basin. Then, beginning in 1908–9, the railroads suddenly started moving a tidal wave of farm families into northern and eastern Montana. The boom swept westward across the "High Line" area north of the Missouri and engulfed the broad valleys and rolling plains above and below the Yellowstone River. New boom towns seemed to spring up overnight: Plentywood, Scobey and Rudyard, Ryegate, Baker, and Hardin.

The rush surged upward dramatically in 1910. The Great Falls land offices, which served north-central Montana, processed between a thousand and fifteen hundred homestead filings monthly during that turbulent year.

In the first quarter of 1910, the Great Northern moved over a thousand emigrant cars into northern Montana. On one spring evening that railroad debarked 250 homesteaders at Havre alone. The flood tide of immigration leveled off somewhat during 1911–12, then rose significantly again during 1913–18. Statistics revealed the mounting impact of the farmers' frontier. Even by 1910 agriculture had already surpassed mining to become Montana's major source of income. The state's population climbed from 243,329 in 1900 to 376,053 in 1910. During the same period the aggregate number of farms and ranches increased from 13,370 to 26,214. By 1920, even after the boom had collapsed, the census found 548,889 Montanans and 57,677 farms and ranches in the state.

Nature, it seemed, conspired with man to lure in the homesteaders. The boom period of land taking, 1909–16, was a time of generally ample rainfall, averaging sixteen inches of precipitation per year. Equally important, the rains came at the right time of the year, in the late spring and early summer months. Newcomers assumed, naturally, that this was the normal, predictable situation. Bountiful harvests of wheat averaged over twenty-five bushels to the acre. In 1909 total wheat production in Montana came to slightly under eleven million bushels; but in the "miracle year" of 1915 it totaled over forty-two million bushels. During the wet years of 1915–16, many northern Montana farms harvested thirty-five to fifty bushels per acre. And grain prices were high, especially after 1914, when the First World War stimulated increasing demands for United States wheat. Montana's high quality, high-protein, hard spring and winter wheat held top rank on the booming international markets. It is small wonder that the farmers came, and that they foresaw a rosy future.

Who were these people, these homesteaders who changed forever the face and complexion of Montana society? Writing in the 1940s, not long after John Steinbeck's *The Grapes of Wrath* was published, Great Falls journalist Joseph Kinsey Howard described this type of pioneer as "the Joad of a quarter century ago, swarming into a hostile land: duped when he started, robbed when he arrived." Howard demonstrated here, not only a tendency to stereotype reality and to overdramatize, but also a romantic view of history. For Howard looked upon Montana's history from the cattleman's perspective and thus tended, like painter Charles M. Russell, to view these dirt farmers as rubes and hayseeds who were despoiling the good earth. Howard resurrected the slang term "honyocker" to describe the homesteaders. In its earlier usages, "honyocker" was apparently a corruption of the term "hunyak," a racial slur referring to Slavic immigrants. To some "native" Montanans, all of the newly arrived farmers were "honyockers," all of them stupid and undesirable. By continuing to use this degrading cowboy slang, Howard, and other historians after him, have tended to picture the homesteaders as clods, social misfits, and incompetents.

In truth, it is difficult to generalize about the homesteaders: they were a very cosmopolitan and diverse group. Although many were foreigners, especially Germans and Scandinavians, most were native Americans. The 1920 Census indicated that only 17.1 percent of all Montanans were foreign born. Beyond dispute many of them lacked farming experience, and this simple fact undoubtedly caused hundreds to fail. In a sample of fifty-eight farmers in a "typical township" of Montana's north-central "triangle" region, agricultural expert M. L. Wilson found in 1922 only twenty-three who listed their former occupation as "farmer." Among the others, Wilson found two physicians, two school teachers, three "Maiden Ladies," six musicians, two wrestlers, and one "World Rover."

Wilson's sample was a bit misleading because it failed to note how many of these farmers, regardless of their former occupations, came originally from farm families and thus did have farming experience. But his research clearly indicated the broad variety of people caught up in the net of railroad promotion. "The one trait they had in common," notes Marie Peterson McDonald, "was youth. They were men and women in the prime of life, in their twenties and early thirties." In fact, they were neither the "Joads of their day"—1930s-style farm refugees—nor were they, by and large, "dumb honyockers." Some, indeed, were highly sophisticated businessmen. Thomas D. Campbell, for instance, acquired the backing of J. P. Morgan to lease 150,000 acres in the Big Horn Basin. At one time, he operated the world's greatest wheat farm, with five hundred plows, six hundred drills, seventy-two binders, and thirty-two combines and threshing machines. Campbell later taught farmers in Russia the dry farming methods he had worked out in Montana.

Montana's homesteaders were really an American and western European potpourri. They were the last wave, and a fairly representative wave, of the agricultural frontier. They found in Montana, as they had earlier found on the central Great Plains, a hard way of life. Most came by rail, but others arrived in Studebaker wagons and lurching Model T Fords. At the depot, they often ran into the infamous "locators." These were classic frontier salesmen who, for a fee of usually from twenty-five to fifty dollars, would find them a choice homestead plot, or perhaps a lucrative piece of railroad land. Some of the locators were honest, of course, but others were not. As a result, many pioneer families ended up located on desolate lands.

Sometimes the newcomers erected the sodhouse dwellings, made from slabs of turf, which were so common on the plains to the east. More often in Montana, though, they built two-, three-, or four-room shacks out of rough-cut lumber. The homestead shanties usually had tarpaper, at best, for an outer covering and often had nothing more than old newspaper sheets for interior "insulation." With only a pot-bellied stove for heat, these crude shacks could be frigid in the winter and terribly hot in the summer. Faced with constant wind and dust, long and bitterly cold winters, with spells of subzero weather when both children and valuable farm animals had to be huddled indoors, farm wives aged prematurely. As Ole Rolvaag revealed so beautifully in his novel *Giants in the Earth*, homestead life punished women severely, driving some of them to insanity and early death.

Water was the most precious commodity. In this arid and rocky land, well drilling proved difficult, expensive, and unpredictable. Some trapped rain water in cisterns, while others used tank wagons to haul water over long distances. A favorite story of those years concerned the farmer who told his friend that he had to haul his water seven miles. When asked why he did not drill a well, he replied that the distance was the same in either direction. The water problem led to the constant threat of sickness, especially typhoid, cholera, and the "Colorado quick-step" diarrhea. In fact, childhood diseases terrorized frontier families more than any other threat. The little children's gravestones in weed-grown cemeteries of homestead ghost towns tell a heart-rending tale of the horrors of scarlet fever, pneumonia, smallpox, and other dreaded killers.

However hard the environment, however long the winters and dry the summers, most of the homesteaders sank roots and built for the future. For, no matter how forbidding the land, still it was *their* land. Like American farmers of the previous three centuries, they valued a farm of their own above all other earthly possessions. Even though life on the farm was hard and monotonous, it also had many rewards: the closeness of family and neighborly ties, the excitement of weekend visits to town, and long-awaited events like buying the family's first automobile or piano. Especially, there was the unique joy of breaking the soil, and the fine sense of accomplishment when the land bore its harvest. In his memoir, *The Generous Years*, Chet Huntley recalled the exhilaration of spring and the feeling of communion with nature that it aroused in himself and others:

> I sat in the warm sunshine on tops of the hills overlooking the ranch house, the barns, the fields and the lake bed. I lay down and put my head on the grass. I could hear it! I could hear spring! The ground was a moving, writhing, stirring mass of movement and growth. Millions of tiny shoots were probing at the warm earth, drinking its moisture, absorbing its goodness and sending their growth to the sunlight. The earth, the sky, the air, the universe were throbbing with life . . . and it was good!

So they came, and they came to stay. Their determination to remain upon the land, to turn the land to their own wills, made them the last, the most important, and ultimately the most tragically afflicted of all the Montana pioneers.

THE AGE OF OPTIMISM

Not surprisingly, this era of land taking was a time of heady optimism and high hopes for the future. Both the homesteaders themselves and the residents of the small towns that grew up to serve them shared in the belief that they were building the model community here on the high plains and the floors of the mountain valleys. In those days, before the great "bust" of agriculture which followed World War I, time and human affairs seemed to be moving entirely in Montana's direction. The Montana settlers were true heirs of Thomas Jefferson, and of many farming generations before them, in their belief that the farm family and the small town formed the sturdy bulwark of America.

Well aware that they stood on the last frontier of American agriculture, the Montana homesteaders saw themselves in the role of taming the final wilderness and advancing the cause of civilization. In their eyes, growth was certain: growth was progress, and progress was good. The editor of *The Montana Churchman* expressed this sentiment in 1907: "That time [cowboy days] has gone forever. Already in her westward march Civilization has planted her feet firmly on this territory. Ten years from now 'the West' will be as the womb of the earth, teeming with people, seething with industry, alive with manifold activities—the center of population and civilization!"

The settlers saw in this "inland" or "midland empire" not only the last West but the best West. By taking advantage of modern technology and the lessons learned on earlier frontiers, they would remove much of the drudgery of farm life, provide their children with the finest of youthful environments, and combine the best of both rural and urban America. Their straitlaced and upright farms and towns, they felt, would soon overbalance the sinful and debased mining and cattle towns and would thus put an end to the corrupted political system of an earlier day. The open range grazing era, and the wide open spaces themselves, would give way to a more healthy social system. *The Gallatin Farmer and Stockman* phrased it nicely: "The rancher of the future will know the color of the smoke from his neighbor's chimney. The covert of the deer will be the retreat of the domestic animal and the lair of the wild beast the play house of the children. There will be no wilderness anymore."

Greatest of all homestead era boomers were the newspaper editors and city fathers of the farming communities. These towns sprang up literally by the hundreds during the three decades following 1890. Their names still punctuate the map of the state: Shelby and Chester, Geraldine and Joliet,

Gildford and Bloomfield. From either a physical or a cultural viewpoint, the homestead towns bore little resemblance to the cow towns like Lewistown or Miles City, which had served well enough the basic economic and social needs of cowboys and cattlemen. The cow towns made little pretense of refinement. Their stockyards and rail sidings were flanked by a scattering of cabins, tents, saloons, and brothels. Who cared about the town's appearance?

The farmers' towns, on the other hand, looked like what they tried to be—transplanted midwestern villages. Economic life centered on the grain elevators and the banks and sundry stores along main street. Off main street, white frame houses stood behind picket fences along dusty streets. In these towns, women and community leaders teamed up to keep life on the straight and narrow. This was the heartland of the Montana prohibition movement, which succeeded, at least in a legal sense, in "drying up" the state in 1916. It was the Middle America of its day. Each of these towns, it seemed, looked forward to a rosy future of unlimited growth. Each, as Robert G. Athearn has noted, planned to become a "great railroad center." None of them really ever did, and the traveler of today finds dozens of them abandoned or nearly abandoned. Of those that continue to support the population of rural Montana, the majority are either static or declining in population. These towns, and others like them throughout the nation, are today fighting against desperate odds to hold their population and to save a way of life which is being steadily eroded by modern economic trends.

The boom psychology of those years had perhaps its greatest and most negative impact in the form of the county splitting movement. Surely, it was inevitable that, with the great land rush, the huge counties of eastern Montana would be broken up. The vast distances involved and the needs of citizens to be near their county seats demanded it. As late as 1910, the northern-eastern 60 percent of Montana still remained enclosed in only nine huge counties—Teton, Chouteau, Valley, Cascade, Fergus, Dawson, Yellowstone, Rosebud, and Custer. During the fifteen years that followed 1910, twenty-eight new counties appeared, as the older counties divided, then divided again.

These counties did not usually divide along sensible geographic lines: the most intensive breakups took place in the south-central and the northeastern regions. But, then, county splitting was not primarily a rational process. Fast-talking promoters and political con-men dominated the movement. The best known of these was Dan McKay. Usually riding into town atop "the biggest horse in the Milk River Valley," McKay had the political knack of rallying public opinion behind his cause in a hurry. He had a personal hand in breaking up a dozen counties. McKay and other county splitters simply went from town to town, whipping up enthusiasm about the advantages of smaller counties and about the blessings that a county courthouse and its payroll might bring to any village, no matter how remote. Then, for a small fee, the county splitters would organize the signing of petitions and arrange the elections necessary to break up the units of government.

The county splitting frenzy peaked during the boom decade of 1910–20. At the height of the land rush, in 1915, the Montana Legislature enacted the Leighton Act. Passed in an irresponsible moment, the Leighton Act gave the counties an almost completely free hand to subdivide as each saw fit. They did, and by the time the multiplying process finally ended, the number of Montana counties had doubled to the present total of fifty-six. The new county governments, their courthouses and employees, obviously cost plenty of money. During the flush times, property taxes automatically increased to pay the bills. Soon the boom turned to bust, though, and property owners increasingly failed to meet their taxes. The counties ended up seizing lands for tax delinquencies, thus devouring their own property owners. Today, the problems arising from reckless county splitting are still very much with us. Many of these rural counties have either lost or barely gained population since 1920, and consequently they find themselves hard pressed to support their own local governments.

AGRICULTURE AND THE FIRST WORLD WAR

Few Montanans of those robust, optimistic years foresaw what hardships the future might hold. The state entered the year 1917 on a tidal wave of prosperity. Over the past eight years, ample moisture and high food prices had nurtured a remarkably persistent farm prosperity; and since 1915 lucrative new markets for American foodstuffs had opened in war-torn Europe. Then, in the spring of 1917, the United States entered the First World War. Entry into the Great War had an immediate, decisive effect upon agriculture, as the demand for food and the prices of commodities soared. In order to assure maximum farm output, Congress enacted the Lever Food and Fuel Control Act, which, among other provisions, empowered the President to peg the price of wheat at not less than $2.00 per bushel.

President Woodrow Wilson placed the Lever Act program of conserving food and assuring all-out farm production under a new federal agency called the Food Administration. Under the capable direction of Herbert Hoover, the Food Administration bombarded the nations' farmers with the message that, as patriots, they must produce to the utmost: "Food Will Win the War!" In addition, each state had its own Food Administrator. Alfred Atkinson of Montana State College held this post in the Treasure State. In countless speeches and newspaper advertisements, he told his fellow citizens: "The government of the United States, as well as its war associates, is

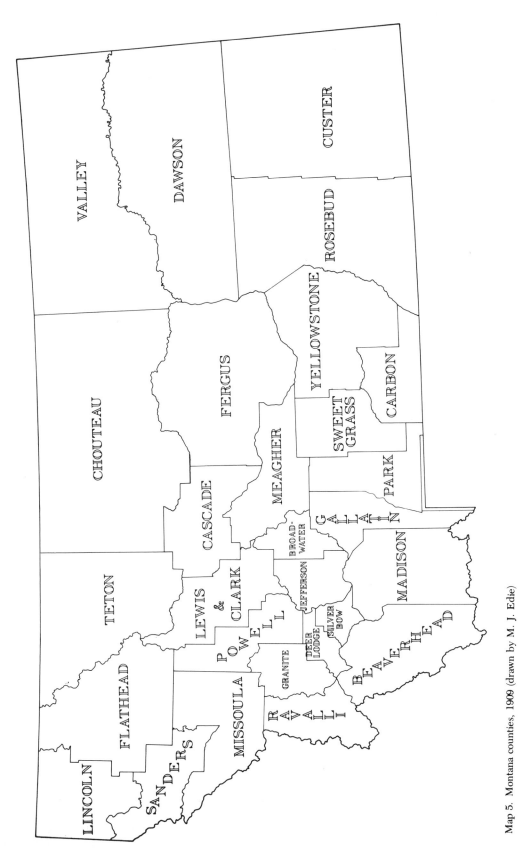

Map 5. Montana counties, 1909 (drawn by M. J. Edie)

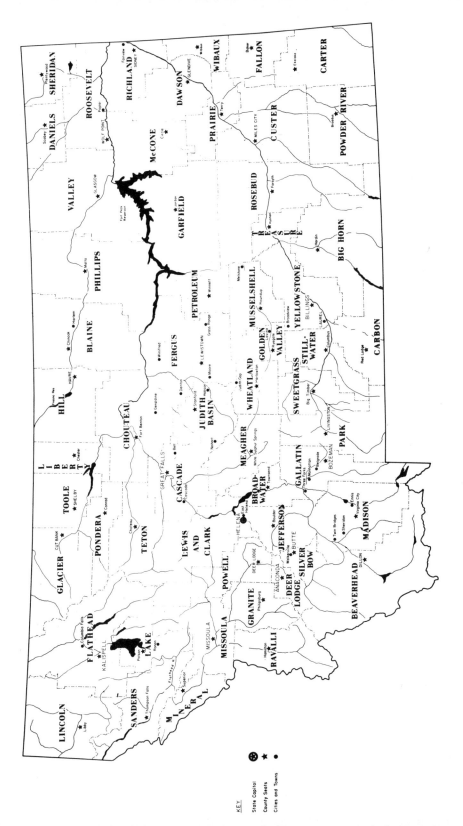

Map 6. Montana counties, 1976 (adapted from *Montana in Maps: 1974*)

KEY

⊛ State Capital

★ County Seats

• Cities and Towns

in great need of wheat. Every available pound is needed if the German flood is to be stemmed."

Farmers responded to this patriotic appeal, but they responded even more to the rising price of grain. By authority of the Lever Act, the Wilson Administration, through the Food Administration, set the price of wheat at roughly $2.20 per bushel for the duration of the conflict. Grain farmers criticized this move, since they felt that wheat prices without controls might have climbed up to $4.00 per bushel. But the controls still guaranteed them good profits, as they well knew. Uncle Sam encouraged farmers to expand production in other ways as well. The newly created Federal Reserve System extended easy credit to national banks, which in turn offered loans to farmers on appealing terms. A rising chorus of federal officials, bankers, patriotic orators, and, of course, land speculators urged the farmer to expand his operations. With readily available credit, he could mortgage his land, buildings, and machinery and buy more land, buildings, and machinery. And with wheat going for $2.00 + per bushel, he could even plow up some of his pastureland and plant it in grain. Surely the war would last at least until 1920, and by then his profits would make repayment of the loans easy. "Food Will Win the War!"

So, by a curious twist of fate, the peak of the Montana homestead rush coincided with America's entry into the Great War. High wartime prices and the patriotic urge to produce for victory added one final boost to the great Montana boom. Now, in 1917–18, the last great plow-up took place. Betting on continuing prosperity, the homesteaders went further into debt and turned their plows toward the pasture lands that yet remained uncultivated. Why leave these scrublands in their natural grass condition? If they would yield any crop at all, it seemed sensible to plow them up. The land rush, therefore, reached its climax in the enthusiastic spring and summer of 1917. Even at that optimistic moment, though, the first signs of drought were beginning to appear on the plains of eastern Montana.

CHAPTER XI

The Progressive Era and World War I

A MERICAN historians usually refer to the years between the turn of the century and World War I, 1900–16, as the "Progressive Era." During this period many thoughtful Americans, increasingly concerned about mounting social problems, took up the cause of reform. These progressive reformers faced a wide range of social ills, many of them rising out of the industrial revolution: business abuses, exploitation of women and children, the traffic in alcohol, and political corruption among others. The "progressives" did not, by any means, seek radical answers to the problems facing them, nor did they always agree, for there were many kinds of progressives. Most, however, were moderate, middle class Americans who felt that the "system" could be made to function properly with only a few alterations. Generally speaking, they believed that what America needed was direct democracy. With great optimism and moralism, they reasoned that, if the mass of citizens gained political power, they would set things right.

Progressivism had its impact upon every level of society and government and upon every region of the country. It took root in both major political parties and produced two Presidents: Republican Theodore Roosevelt and Democrat Woodrow Wilson. Although some historians have argued that progressivism had little effect upon remote Montana, the facts prove otherwise. In truth, progressivism took deep root in the Treasure State, producing a number of lasting reforms and four political leaders who reached nationwide prominence—Joseph Dixon, Thomas J. Walsh, Jeannette Rankin, and Burton K. Wheeler. In Montana, as in the nation at large, these years also produced a powerful radical movement on the far left. Throughout the country, and especially in Montana, the First World War brought the political passions of an entire generation to a boil, deflating the movement for progressive reform and destroying the radicals.

PROGRESSIVE REFORM IN MONTANA

In Montana, as in Oregon and other states of the Northwest, progressive reformers began making their influence felt during the first decade of this century. The Montana progressives included many different groups with many different concerns, but they all aimed generally at improving public life, public health, and public morality through direct action. In 1907 Randall J. Condon, secretary of the Helena Civic Club, summarized the goals not only of his organization but of progressives in general: "Better schools; better churches; better public buildings; better playgrounds; better public service; better support of disinterested public officials; unsightly bill-boards abolished; cleaner streets and alleys; a better enforcement of all laws and city ordinances."

Montana progressives shared, for the most part, the same aims as reformers throughout the country. At the local level, cities like Billings, Butte, Helena, Missoula, and Great Falls produced civic clubs and citizens' leagues which concentrated upon beautifying the towns and cleaning up government through such innovations as city managers and city commissions. At the state level, Montana progressives aimed to curb the power of large corporations, especially the Amalgamated Copper Company. They pushed an impressive number and variety of reforms through the legislature. These included laws that expanded popular participation in government, such as the initiative and referendum, direct primaries, and the direct election of senators; laws that protected workers, such as mine safety measures and workmen's compensation; and laws that protected the public, such as railroad regulation, pure food and drug legislation, milk and meat inspection, and creation of a state board of health.

Political reforms were the key to the entire progressive program. Once the mass of educated voters gained real political power, they could then put into effect all the other necessary reforms. Montana had a heritage of practicing direct democracy, of placing political power directly in the people's hands. As early as 1889, it became one of the first states to use the Australian ballot, thus assuring its citizens the right to cast their votes secretly. The most important political reforms on the progressive agenda were the initiative and the referendum. These laws allowed the voters to legislate directly and thus to bypass state legislatures that frequently seemed under the firm control of large corporations. The initiative permits the electorate to enact laws by a direct vote, while the referendum allows the voters to repeal unpopular laws passed by the legislature.

Political crusaders fought for ten years to win the initiative and referendum in Montana. Beginning in the mid-1890s, the Populists pressed hard for these direct legislation measures, and they gained firm support from the

Montana Federation of Labor and later from progressive leaders such as Livingston lawyer E. C. Day, Judge Theodore Brantly, and journalists William Greene Eggleston and Will Kennedy. The long struggle for the initiative and referendum finally ended with victory in November 1906, when the voters approved a constitutional amendment which wrote them into enduring law. These direct legislation laws have, of course, been used many times over the past seventy years.

Another instrument of direct democracy favored by the progressives was the direct primary system of nominating candidates for public office. Like progressives in other states, reformers in Montana watched in anger how such political "bosses" as William A. Clark and Marcus Daly manipulated politics by gaining control of the party nominating conventions. Enactment of a direct primary law could curb such abuses through allowing the voters to nominate party candidates by secret ballot in special primary elections. Beginning with the Populists in the 1890s, the campaign for the direct primary paralleled the fight for the initiative and referendum. Newspapermen like Miles Romney of the Hamilton *Western News* and W. K. Harber of the Fort Benton *River Press* and lawyers like Thomas J. Walsh of Helena led the attack, and by 1903 public opinion clearly favored such a system. The 1905 Legislature enacted a local option system of direct primary nominations; but this experiment proved unworkable and was repealed in 1907. Finally, by use of the initiative method, the citizens of Montana approved a statewide direct primary law in the election of 1912. It remains in effect to this day.

Yet another formula for putting political power directly in the hands of the people was the crusade for the direct election of United States senators. The United States Constitution, of course, placed responsibility for selecting senators in the state legislatures. Since legislatures could often be "influenced" or even bribed outright, this system had become scandalous and, in the minds of reformers, had filled the United States Senate with millionaires and flunkies for big business. The answer to the problem seemed obvious to those who believed in direct democracy: a constitutional amendment that would allow the people to choose their senators by popular ballot.

Montanans reacted to this issue with special enthusiasm. After all, W. A. Clark's notorious bribery of the 1899 Montana Legislature offered an especially sordid example of how badly the system worked. After 1893 almost every session of the Montana legislature memorialized Congress to pass a constitutional amendment providing for direct election of senators. By the early 1900s both political parties in Montana favored the system in their platforms. When Congress failed to act, the 1911 Montana Legislature followed the examples of Oregon and other states and passed the Everett

Bill. Through a complex system of permitting the public to vote for U.S. senators and then forcing the legislators to ratify their choice, the Everett Bill, in effect, allowed Montanans to choose their own senators. This complicated system became unnecessary in 1913, when the Seventeenth Amendment to the Constitution went into effect, making direct election of senators the law of the land.

In addition to these basic political reforms, Montana progressives also pushed many humanitarian measures through the legislature. They worried especially about children and their welfare. In 1903 the Montana lawmakers created a new state agency, the Bureau of Child and Animal Protection. Under the capable direction of Otto Schoenfeld, this bureau accomplished a great deal. For instance, even though Montana had very little problem with child labor, Schoenfeld's bureau, supported by the Montana Federation of Labor, the Montana State Federation of Women's Clubs, and the Women's Christian Temperance Union, mounted a major campaign to outlaw child labor. They won a major victory in the 1904 election, when the voters approved a constitutional amendment setting sixteen as the minimum age for employment in the mines. Other victories followed. The legislature created a compulsory school attendance law, and in 1907 it extended the minimum employment age of sixteen to other industries. Also in 1907 the lawmakers created a juvenile court system in order to assure, as the law put it, that a "delinquent child shall be treated, not as a criminal, but as misdirected and misguided, and needing aid, encouragement, help and assistance."

Like their counterparts around the country, progressive-minded Montanans saw the nation's number one problem in the emergence of the new supercorporations, or "trusts" as they were called then. Editor Miles Romney voiced a common progressive sentiment in 1906, when he declared that "the greatest living issue that confronts the nation today" was whether "the corporations shall control the people or the people shall control the corporations." Naturally, this issue hit close to home, especially after the Amalgamated Copper Company's 1903 shutdown and shakedown of the state government. Following the November 1903 special legislative session that the Company forced upon the state, six hundred angry Montana citizens assembled at Helena to form an Anti-Trust Party. This organization, however, was dominated by copper king F. A. Heinze and accomplished very little. In fact, as Governor Toole pointed out in his 1907 state of the state message, there was precious little that the states could do to regulate great corporations like Standard Oil or Amalgamated Copper. Only the federal government, by using the antitrust laws, could tackle them.

One class of corporation that states could and did regulate was the railroad. Montanans leveled many complaints against the railroads that served them: that they failed to pay their fair share of taxes, that accidents were far too frequent, that service was poor and rates too high, that the railroads "bought" politicians by giving them free passes. In contrast to the radical Populists, who favored a government takeover of the railroads, the more cautious progressives took up the idea of regulating them through a state railroad commission. Led by lawyer Thomas Walsh and other experts, the Montana progressives triumphed in 1907, when the legislature created a Montana Railroad Commission. Later, in 1913, this agency became the Montana Public Service Commission, with authority over other public carriers and also electrical utilities.

PROGRESSIVISM AT HIGH TIDE: 1912–16

The reform movement in Montana climaxed during and immediately after the hard-fought election campaign of 1912. At the national level, a three-way fight for the presidency dominated the 1912 campaign. Woodrow Wilson, a progressive Democrat, faced William Howard Taft, a conservative Republican, while former President Theodore Roosevelt broke with the Republican party and led its more reform-minded wing into the ranks of the newly organized Progressive or "Bull Moose" Party. Since the Republicans were bitterly divided, the Democrats predictably won the race, with Wilson taking the White House, Roosevelt finishing second, and Taft an embarrassed third. The result proved the nationwide popularity of progressive reform. Events in Montana closely paralleled national trends. Here also, the Republican party broke in two, with the progressives following Senator Joseph Dixon into the Bull Moose Party. In Montana attention focused on the Senate race. While the conservative Republicans ran Henry C. Smith, the real contest was waged between the state's two leading progressives, Democrat Thomas J. Walsh and the Bull Moose Progressive, Joseph Dixon, then the incumbent.

Joseph M. Dixon, an intelligent, handsome, and high-principled businessman-politician, was the leading figure of the Montana progressive movement. Born and raised in a North Carolina Quaker community, he came to Missoula in 1891. Dixon took up the practice of law, made a number of profitable business investments, and moved instinctively into Republican party politics. After serving briefly as Missoula county attorney and as a state representative, he won election as Montana's lone congressman and served two terms, 1903–7. Joe Dixon's ability and ambition led him naturally toward the United States Senate. Even though he clashed openly with powerful Senator Thomas Carter, the leader of the conservative Republicans, Dixon managed to gain his party's support for the Senate. In 1907 the legislature sent him to Washington as the successor to retiring Senator W. A. Clark.

Once in the Senate, Dixon began to sound more and more like a hard-nosed progressive, attacking the railroads and the Company and speaking out for such reforms as the direct primary. Always a great admirer of Teddy Roosevelt, Dixon served as chairman of the Progressive party convention at Chicago in 1912 and agreed to act as Roosevelt's national campaign manager. Back in Montana, Dixon's friends Sam Goza and Frank J. Edwards led in organizing a state Bull Moose organization, aimed mainly at putting Roosevelt in the White House and Dixon back in the Senate. The Montana Bull Moosers fought the Company head-on. Their stationery carried the letterhead: "Put the Amalgamated out of Montana Politics."

Dixon's Democratic opponent for the Senate was Thomas J. Walsh of Helena, who was also a progressive but closer to the middle of the road. Born into an Irish immigrant family, Walsh grew up in Wisconsin, taught for a time in country schools, and then took a degree from the University of Wisconsin Law School. He practiced law briefly in South Dakota, but greater opportunities led him on to Helena in 1890. Here he built a great legal reputation, especially in handling the cases of injured workmen, and both he and his wife became active in Democratic and progressive circles. Prior to his Senate race of 1912, Walsh made two tries for national public office and failed both times. He lost a 1906 congressional race and was denied election to the Senate in 1911, when the Company opposed him in the legislature.

At the height of his powers in 1912, Thomas Walsh stood on the threshold of a magnificent public career. Recognized by everyone as a great legal mind, Walsh commanded more respect than affection from the people. He was small of stature and mustachioed, cold and dour in personality. Pictures from those days show him glaring icily at the camera, even while surrounded by cheering crowds and grinning politicians. No one, though, ever doubted Walsh's ability or his integrity. As a newspaperman once said, asking him for special favors "would be like asking the statue of Civic Virtue for a chew of tobacco."

Due mainly to the split in the Republican ranks and the Company's determination to defeat Dixon, the Democrats swept the 1912 election. While Walsh easily captured Dixon's Senate seat, the Democrats also won the governor's chair for Sam V. Stewart, both the eastern and western congressional districts, and both houses of the legislature. Soundly beaten, Joseph Dixon retired temporarily from politics and concentrated his attention upon his western Montana business investments. Like Teddy Roosevelt, Dixon and the Montana Bull Moosers would soon return to the ranks of the Republican party. Thomas Walsh, meanwhile, went triumphantly off to

Washington, beginning a twenty-year Senate career which would prove to be one of the most distinguished in modern American history. He quickly developed a close relationship with President Woodrow Wilson and earned a reputation for honesty and efficient care of his constituents.

The 1912 campaign bears great significance in Montana's history. It not only launched Walsh's Senate career; equally important, it revealed the rising power of Treasure State progressives. For the first time since Heinze's fall, Montanans were organizing against the Company. This election, furthermore, witnessed the first large-scale use of direct legislation in Montana. The voters considered and passed four initiative proposals in 1912, thus writing into law a direct primary system, a campaign expenditures and corrupt practices act, a presidential preference primary, and a measure clarifying the popular election of senators. In a referendum vote they also rejected a law passed by the 1911 Legislature which had given the governor more liberal powers to call out the state militia in dealing with disturbances. Organized labor, joined by many other progressives, opposed this law, arguing that the Company had pushed it through in order to use the militia to crush strikes. In striking down the militia law through a referendum vote, the progressives believed they had handed Amalgamated a significant defeat.

These sweeping direct legislation victories of 1912 owed much to a progressive organization formed the year before, the People's Power League, which grew out of a June 1911 meeting held at Deer Lodge. The delegates who gathered there included many of Montana's leading reformers: lawyers like Walsh and Judge E. K. Cheadle of Lewistown, journalists like Miles Romney and W. K. Harber, labor leaders such as Montana Federation of Labor President M. M. Donoghue and Henry Drennan of the United Mine Workers. In forming the People's Power League, they elected Romney their president and Max McCusker of Livingston, a Northern Pacific machinist, their secretary-treasurer. The sole purpose of the new organization, they announced, was to secure "beneficial legislation through the initiative and referendum."

After its 1912 victories the People's Power League continued to press for reform. It found support from the Direct Legislation League, another progressive body which took shape in late March 1913. Made up heavily of Bull Moose Republicans, the Direct Legislation League worked especially hard to raise taxes on mining and other corporations. These two bodies shared many of the same aims, of course, and some of the same members. Leaders of the People's Power League, like Romney and Bozeman attorney Walter Hartman, also worked through the Direct Legislation League. Cleverly, the militant progressives pushed two measures that they hoped would serve to form an alliance between farmers and workers against corporate power. For the workers, they sponsored an initiative providing for a badly needed workmen's compensation system to care for the many victims of industrial accidents. For the farmers, they pushed an initiative which would enable the state to invest moneys from its common school fund in farm mortgage loans.

The progressives failed in their attempt to create a farmer-labor alliance. In the 1914 election labor helped the rural areas pass an initiative providing for the farm loans. But the Amalgamated and its allies were able to cut down farm votes for workmen's compensation by forming a group called the Montana Advancement Association, which sent speakers into the rural areas warning of the dangers of such a system. The 1914 initiative providing for workmen's compensation thus failed to pass. In the 1915 Legislature a Workmen's Compensation Law did pass, but it was less sweeping than the one envisaged by the reformers and more in tune with corporate wishes.

Losing on some fronts, the progressives gained on others. After the 1912 campaign Montana reformers won two triumphs that they had sought for years—the vote for women, and prohibition of alcoholic beverages. In the November 1914 election the voters of Montana approved a constitutional amendment granting woman suffrage. This victory capped a thirty-year struggle for feminine equality. Back in territorial days, Montana women had enjoyed a limited suffrage. As property owners, they could vote on special tax levies. They also had the right to vote for school district trustees and county school superintendents. Women's political rights first came up for serious discussion at the 1889 Constitutional Convention when P. W. McAdow and other delegates tried, without success, to guarantee women the vote in the state constitution.

During the 1890s Montana women made several attempts to secure a constitutional amendment for woman suffrage. Especially encouraged by the Populist party's endorsement of this measure, leaders such as Dr. Mary Moore Atwater of Marysville and Sarepta Sanders and Ella Knowles of Helena constantly hammered away at the legislature. After a long string of defeats, however, the woman suffrage movement lost its momentum. A handful of determined suffragettes, like physician Dr. Maria Dean and Mrs. Thomas Walsh of Helena, fought on but made no headway.

By 1905 the woman suffrage movement in Montana seemed dead. The rising winds of progressivism, however, breathed new life into the women's cause and gave it a more militant tone. Whereas women had previously demanded the vote on the simple grounds of equality, they now began to argue that the world needed women's superior social and moral qualities. As one of them said, "Now, it is woman, only woman . . . who can rescue poor, indiscreet and misguided man and lift him to the height above the seething, rotten condition into which he has gotten himself." Aided by progressive organizations and by feminist groups in neighboring states, the women's cause in Montana also benefited from the homestead movement. Most of the homesteaders, male and female, supported feminine equality in the belief that it would serve to cleanse society of its evils.

Leadership of the feminist cause in Montana now passed to Jeannette Rankin, an attractive, willful, and capable organizer. Young Miss Rankin, the product of a prominent Missoula family, had already gained prominence in national feminist circles and had worked on the campaign which in 1910 won the vote for women in the state of Washington. During the 1911 Legislature the women won a round when Representative D. J. Donohue of Glendive introduced a bill providing for a woman suffrage amendment to the Montana Constitution. The house of representatives granted Jeannette Rankin the privilege of appearing to discuss the bill, while Mary Long Alderson and Drs. Maria Dean and Mary Moore Atwater were honored with seats on the speaker's platform. Although the suffrage bill failed in 1911, the vote upon it showed mounting support, especially from the homestead counties.

During the 1912 campaign Miss Rankin and her friends succeeded in getting the major parties to put woman suffrage planks in their platforms. They also organized the Montana Equal Suffrage Association to lobby politicians on the issue. The women's crusade now gained momentum rapidly. In its 1913 session the Montana Legislature passed a suffrage amendment bill, which the voters would consider in 1914. Other groups hurriedly joined the Montana Equal Suffrage Association in the campaign to rally public opinion. Wellington D. Rankin, Jeannette's brother and fellow progressive, headed up a Montana chapter of the Men's League for Woman's Suffrage; and further help came from the Montana Federation of Women's Clubs and from the Women's Christian Temperance Union. In their campaign for the vote, the Montana feminists did have their differences. The W.C.T.U., for instance, wanted to link the suffrage movement with prohibition and to rally the support of immigrant groups. Miss Rankin and the Montana Equal Suffrage Association, on the contrary, wished to avoid the prohibition issue and distrusted the foreigners. In fact Miss Rankin even argued that women voters would and should help keep the immigrants from gaining political power.

In the election of November 3, 1914, the woman suffrage amendment narrowly passed by a vote of 41,302 to 37,588. The women gained their best support from the new homestead counties and found the toughest going in the older mining and agricultural areas. Savoring their victory, the suffragettes met at Helena in January 1915 and organized the Montana Good Government Association, forerunner of the Montana League of Women Voters, to continue their quest for political power. They demonstrated their political clout in the 1916 election when, for the first time, they had the power of the ballot box. Three women, Emma Ingalls, Maggie Smith Hathaway, and Gwen Burla, won seats in the Montana Legislature; and May Trumper was elected superintendent of public instruction. Most significantly, Jeannette Rankin secured a lasting place in American history by gaining election to one of Montana's two seats in Congress. She thus became the first woman ever to sit in Congress. When Miss Rankin arrived in Washington to assume her duties early in 1917, the nation watched intently to see whether a woman could indeed handle the responsibilities of high office. Events proved that she could.

The feminists had other goals in mind beyond merely gaining the vote. Like many other progressives, most of them viewed the saloon and the traffic in alcohol as great social evils and wanted to remove them through prohibition laws. The prohibition movement, like the women's rights movement, began far back in the nineteenth century, but it surged rapidly ahead during the progressive period. The prohibition campaign received much of its local support from the fast multiplying homestead communities, where strait-laced farm wives were determined to stamp out the saloon. Local chapters of the Women's Christian Temperance Union spread rapidly throughout Montana during 1896–1910; and so, especially after 1905, did the highly effective Anti-Saloon League. When Idaho and Washington adopted statewide prohibition, the Montana prohibitionists gained a powerful arguing point, warning that exiled saloon elements from those states were retreating to Montana.

During the legislative session of 1915, the "dry" forces, led by Joseph Pope, a Billings clergyman and head of the Anti-Saloon League campaign, pressured the lawmakers by showering them with petitions demanding a referendum on the prohibition issue. The Roman Catholics now joined the offensive too, and Bishops John P. Carroll and Mathias C. Lenihan of the Helena and Great Falls dioceses endorsed the referendum. Predictably, the prohibitionists got their referendum. And when the people voted upon it in November 1916, they approved the prohibition of alcoholic beverages by an overwhelming margin, 102,776 to 73,890. Montana officially went "dry" at the end of 1918, and in 1920 prohibition became national law through the Eighteenth Amendment to the United States Constitution.

The prohibitionists breathed a sigh of relief, concluding that their victory was securely won. They were wrong, of course, for prohibition failed all across the country, nowhere more spectacularly than in Montana. Soon hundreds of illegal "whiskey roads" would reach across the Canadian border, and rural folks would grow accustomed to the roar of "rumrunners" hauling their cargoes of booze along country roads. By the twenties prohibition was an obvious failure in the hard-drinking Treasure State. Liquor flowed openly, especially in working class towns like Butte and Havre. When the "great experiment" of prohibition ended in 1933, most Montanans seemed relieved.

In supporting naive reforms like prohibition, the progressives, in Montana and throughout the country, demonstrated a highly optimistic and moralistic outlook. If only the people had a free opportunity to vote, if only the necessary laws could be passed, then evil would surely be eradicated and progress would be guaranteed. As usual, Miles Romney of Hamilton summed up their attitudes well. Through that "invincible force, enlightened public opinion," he wrote, the "people will control. The railroad corporations, the beef trust, the timber trust and every other predatory adjunct of capitalism that seeks special privileges and to unjustly tax the public will be brought up with a short turn and caused to obey laws." Always optimistic, the progressives were basically enlightened conservatives: with only a few changes, they argued, the system would again work nicely, and all would be well. Many of them would later become disillusioned when they found that their reforms did not work so perfectly as they had imagined. Prohibition would fail; direct democracy would not automatically get rid of political bosses; workmen's compensation would sometimes lead to scandal; the Public Service Commission would not always regulate industries in the public interest. And the Company would still be there, still awesomely powerful, when the progressives were dead and gone. Despite their failures, though, the progressives had a major impact upon the political development of Montana.

THE RADICALS

There were, of course, thousands of conservative Montanans during the Progressive Era. They generally opposed reform and favored the status quo. Represented by men like Republican Senator Thomas Carter and Democratic Governor Sam Stewart, the conservatives had no particular quarrel with the Company and no particular use for the progressive reformers. Interestingly, Montana in the early twentieth century also produced a powerful radical movement on the far left. To these people, the heirs of the 1890s Populists, piecemeal progressive reform was not enough: the capitalist system itself had to be altered fundamentally or replaced. The radicals reached the peak of their strength in Montana on the eve of World War I.

Of the organizations on the far left, the most famous and feared was the Industrial Workers of the World, commonly known as the I.W.W. or the "Wobblies." Founded in 1905, the I.W.W. was a radical labor organization which advocated working class solidarity, conflict with the capitalist system, and the gathering of all workers, skilled and unskilled, in one large industrial union. The Wobblies opposed capitalism itself and favored replacing industrial management with "syndicates" made up of workers. Butte labor leaders played a significanct role in organizing the nationwide I.W.W., and the union had a sizable following in Montana's mining towns and lumber camps. Although it never came near gaining a majority of local workers as members, the I.W.W. kept the labor pot boiling and stirred up considerable unrest between management and the working force.

A large and powerful Socialist party also flourished in Montana during these years. Like the Wobblies, the Socialists relied upon the laboring class for support and drew most of their strength from the industrial counties of Silver Bow, Deer Lodge, and Cascade. The Socialist party surfaced here in 1902, when one of its members, George Sproule, ran for Congress and received 3,000 votes. Over the next few years Socialist strength mounted rapidly. By 1908 Socialists held positions in the governments of working class towns like Red Lodge and Livingston; and in 1911 they joined forces with the I.W.W. to elect a Socialist city government in Butte with Unitarian minister Lewis Duncan at its head. The Socialists reached the peak of their strength in 1912–14. Lewis Duncan polled over 12,500 votes running for governor in 1912 and received only slightly fewer in a 1914 congressional race.

As radical discontent spread through the laboring class, it also appeared in the rural areas. The farmer-radicals voiced their anger, as they had during the Populist period, at receiving unfairly low prices for their products while being gouged by railroads and other corporations. In 1914 local branches of the American Society of Equity began to appear in the Treasure State. The society concentrated upon forming marketing and purchasing cooperatives, but it also supported equity insurance programs, fought for lower rail rates, and—so significant in Montana—demanded a more equitable system of taxation. The reappearance of rural radicalism sent shudders of fear through the ranks of Montana conservatives, for the homestead invasion was bringing new voting strength to northern and eastern Montana. What might happen if the labor radicals and the farmer radicals should join forces? Despite their differences, such an alliance was a real possibility. As historian Theodore Saloutos put it: "Common hatreds, not a feeling of common interests, threatened to bring the two together; the farmers hated the mining interests because of tax-dodging and their stranglehold on state politics, and labor hated them because of their labor policies."

By late 1916 an organization far more powerful and radical than the Society of Equity began to take root in eastern Montana. This was the fiery Nonpartisan League. Founded in North Dakota, the Nonpartisan League advocated a sweeping program of state-owned banks, grain elevators, packing plants, marketing facilities, and insurance systems. It was outspoken in its opposition to railroads and large corporate interests. More so than the Montana Society of Equity, the "N.P.L." favored direct political action: it aimed, not to form a Populist-style third party, but to use the direct primary to seize control of either of the established parties. By such guerrilla action, it could nominate its friends in either the Democratic or the Republican columns, or both.

As drought and depression hit the Northern Plains after 1917, the Nonpartisan League spread rapidly beyond the borders of North Dakota. Thousands of hard-pressed dirt farmers in northern and eastern Montana joined its ranks. In Montana the league lashed out at the Anaconda Company, arguing that, by avoiding its fair share of the tax burden, it was placing great strains upon agriculture to pay the costs of government. As in North Dakota, the Montana N.P.L. attempted to gather in laboring class members. William F. Dunne of the Butte Electricians' Union supported the league, spoke before its meetings, and later voiced many of its policies through his radical newspaper, the Butte *Bulletin.* Wherever the Nonpartisan League appeared, it roused feverish debate between friends and foes. Progressive reformers, although suspicious of the league's radicalism, often welcomed its political support. Conservatives, however, hated and feared the "wild men from the prairies" and attacked them as Socialists, anarchists, and Bolsheviks. Like the Wobblies in western Montana, the Nonpartisan Leaguers were on the rise as America entered the Great War.

THE IMPACT OF WORLD WAR I

When war erupted in Europe during the summer of 1914, the United States and its faraway province of Montana quickly felt the impact. At first, the fighting between Germany and Austria-Hungary on the one side and France, England, and Russia on the other disrupted the trade of neutral America. Soon, however, the combatants, especially England and the "Allies," had to turn to the United States for foodstuffs and manufactured items. Throughout 1915–16 trade with the Allies fueled a major boom in the American economy. Skyrocketing farm prices intensified the great plow-up of eastern Montana, and escalating demands for copper and zinc caused the western mining towns to flourish. Butte reached the peak of its production and population during these years.

Finally, after nearly three years of nervous neutrality, the United States entered the Great War in the spring of 1917. The decision to go to war, though supported by a majority of American citizens, caused great dissension. Nowhere did the debate between patriots and critics of the war flare hotter than in Montana and the Northwest. Of course, most Montanans, like most Americans in general, supported the war enthusiastically. They believed, with President Wilson, that the war would lead to lasting peace and would "make the world safe for democracy." Montana demonstrated its support of the war by surpassing all other states in enlistment rates and draft quotas for the armed forces. Twelve thousand five hundred young Montana males volunteered for service. And due apparently to confused population estimates, the Selective Service drafted nearly twenty-eight thousand more. So nearly forty thousand men—almost 10 percent of the population—went to war, a rate of contribution that no other state even approached.

While the majority of Montanans waved the red, white, and blue, large minorities openly opposed our involvement in the war. In the farming regions many of the immigrant homesteaders turned instinctively against the war effort. The large German population naturally disliked making war on the Fatherland, and thousands of the state's Scandinavian farmers brought neutral, antiwar sentiments with them across the Atlantic. Furthermore, the large Irish population of Butte and western Montana detested our alliance with Britain, which at this very time was using military force once again to beat down an independence movement in Ireland. The most vehement foes of the war, though, were the radicals on the left, who viewed the whole thing as a capitalist conspiracy, "a rich man's war and a poor man's fight." Many spokesmen for the I.W.W. and the Socialist party condemned the war, and so did some of the Nonpartisan Leaguers.

With both patriotism and antiwar sentiment rising to fever pitch, suppression and violence were probably inevitable. In Montana, as elsewhere, German-Americans and suspected opponents of war were hounded and sometimes openly terrorized. German immigrants, most of them perfectly loyal, often had to demonstrate their Americanism by kneeling to kiss the flag or by buying Liberty Bonds under threats of punishment. Many towns and cities established Liberty Committees to police local nonconformists. Billings had a "Third Degree Committee" to look after "troublemakers," and in Glendive, a local mob nearly lynched a German Mennonite minister simply because of his pacifist views. Naturally, bullies frequently took advantage of patriotic feelings to push people around; and extreme conservatives sometimes whipped up public opinion in order to beat down the antiwar radicals. Will Campbell, for example, the wild-eyed editor of the Helena *Independent*, kept up a running attack on the radicals and a constant search for German agents. The *Independent* of October 18, 1917, asked: "Are the Germans about to bomb the capital of Montana? Have they spies in the mountain fastnesses equipped with wireless stations and aeroplanes? Do our enemies fly around our high mountains where formerly only the shadow of the eagle swept?"

The often hysterical drive to crush critics of war immediately became entangled in the most violent wave of strikes in Montana history. Many of the strikers were antiwar radicals, after all, and patriotic Montanans argued that the strikes hindered the war effort by cutting down desperately needed production. Amidst the shouting and bitterness many people failed to note that the workers had legitimate grievances. Even though the war brought full employment, runaway inflation was wiping out wage gains. Working conditions, furthermore, were miserable in most of the lumber camps and many of the mines.

The trouble in western Montana began with a wildcat strike at the Eureka Lumber Company in mid-April of 1917. Within less than a week, Governor Stewart had a company of national guardsmen on the scene to protect property. The strike collapsed in a short time, and by the end of the month work had resumed. Unfortunately, the end of the strike at Eureka did not end the horrible conditions in the lumber camps. Working long hours at low pay in incredibly remote locations, the lumbermen, many of them uneducated transients, lived in company bunkhouses, ate in company commissaries, and bought at company stores. They slept, often two to a bunk, on straw ticks, and almost everyone suffered from lice and bedbugs. Eating and cooking areas swarmed with insects, and kitchens often sat next to outhouses, stables, and pigpens.

Just before the Eureka strike, the Industrial Workers of the World had called a general strike to shut down the entire lumber industry of the Northwest. By June 28 Montana's two largest lumber mills were closed. An easy end of the strike seemed impossible: the radical I.W.W. opposed negotiation, and Anaconda and the other employers refused to bargain with any union. In the meantime most of the state's press favored the operators and pointed alarmedly at the I.W.W.'s antiwar position. Some even charged that German money and saboteurs stood behind the strike.

Finally, the federal government moved in. During late August–early September, government agents unleashed a series of raids on I.W.W. headquarters and meeting halls throughout the West, and over one hundred Wobblies eventually ended up in prison on such charges as sedition and obstructing the draft. As a result of this federal crackdown, the Northwest lumber strike ended on September 7 in a union defeat. Despite the I.W.W. defeat, though, the men did make a few gains. Anxious to avoid further work stoppages, the Montana Lumber Manufacturers Association, led by Kenneth Ross of the Anaconda lumber division, agreed to make some desperately needed improvements in working conditions.

As peace returned to the lumber camps, bitterness continued to erupt in the Montana mining industry. For more than a dozen years prior to 1917, the long-powerful Butte Miners' Union and its sister organizations had seen their strength deteriorate. In contrast to the old days under Marcus Daly, the Amalgamated Copper Company under John Ryan and Cornelius Kelley handled its workers with little sensitivity. As conditions worsened, the men became increasingly alienated from their employers. At the same time the Butte-Anaconda labor force was becoming more and more internally divided. Thousands of Finnish, Slavic, and Italian workers, many of them illiterate, poured into Butte after 1900, and the older, established Irish and English families often failed to accept them. So Butte, traditionally peaceful, began to seethe with unrest. Discontented workers seemed more and more interested in the extremist goals of the radical I.W.W., which stepped up organizational drives in Butte. Frightened by the radicals, the Company hired spies to infiltrate the unions and, at least according to rumor, it "influenced" union leaders to do its will.

Challenged by the I.W.W. on the left, infiltrated by the Company on the right, the Butte Miners' Union began to break under the strain. The union became bitterly divided into two factions: a conservative wing peaceful toward the Company and toward the established Western Federation of Miners leadership, and a radical wing more friendly toward the I.W.W. In December 1912 the union revealed just how weak it had become by its willingness to accept the new "rustling card" system that Amalgamated-Anaconda now put into effect. Under this heavy-handed procedure, a worker had to obtain a "rustling card" from the Company before gaining work on the Hill. By refusing to grant the cards to trouble-makers or radicals, the Company, in effect, ignored the union and favored whichever workers it chose. Not surprisingly, B.M.U. members increasingly lost faith in their leaders.

The mounting labor frustration exploded violently in June 1914. June 13 was Miners' Union Day at Butte, the most festive holiday of the year. When the traditional parade began this time, though, the "radical" or reform wing of the B.M.U. boycotted and then attacked it with Wobbly support. The rebels roughed up some of the union heads and then proceeded to sack the union hall, throwing the organization's records out the window into the street. Rioting persisted all day and into the night, as angry union men looked for their "copper-collared" leaders. For the next several days the pot continued to boil. The reform wing of the Butte Miners' Union gathered together and formed a new organization called the Butte Mine Workers' Union, under the presidency of a miner with the fine name of Muckie McDonald. Although the new union insisted that it had no I.W.W. affiliation, many of its members obviously sympathized with the Wobbly program.

The trouble at Butte climaxed on June 23, 1914. When the regular Butte Miners' Union held its meeting that night, an unruly crowd gathered outside. Shooting broke out, and two men were killed. After the B.M.U. leaders and the Butte police had fled the scene, a group of men—who may

Herding cattle in eastern Montana (Courtesy of Special Collections, Montana State University, Bozeman)

Sheep grazing in western Montana (Courtesy of Special Collections, Montana State University, Bozeman)

James J. Hill (Courtesy of Montana Historical Society, Helena)

Railroad construction in the late 1880s. Photograph, Great Northern Railroad (Courtesy of Montana Historical Society, Helena)

Convertors, Montana Ore Purchasing Company Smelter, Butte (Courtesy of Montana Historical Society, Helena)

utte. Photograph by R. E. Calkins Co. (Courtesy of Montana Historical Society, Helena)

iners' drilling contest, Columbia Gardens, outside Butte (Courtesy of Montana Historical Society, Helena)

Marcus Daly (Courtesy of the Anaconda Company)

Senator W. A. Clark (Courtesy of Montana Historical Society, Helena)

F. Augustus Heinze. Photograph from "Fight of the Copper Kings" by L. P. Connolly, *McClure's Magazine*, May 1907 (Courtesy of Montana Historical Society, Helena)

Ella L. Knowles, ca. 1894 (Courtesy of Montana Historical Society, Helena)

Eva Iddings by her Chouteau County homestead shack, 1910 (Courtesy of Special Collections, Montana State University, Bozeman)

dvertisement for the Chicago, Milwaukee nd St. Paul Railway (Courtesy of Montana istorical Society, Helena)

A locator's promotion (Courtesy of Special Collections, Montana State University, Bozeman)

Water wagon for threshing machine, near Scobey (Courtesy of Special Collections, Montana State University, Bozeman)

Digging a well, Pleasant Valley, ca. 1910 (Courtesy of Special Collections, Montana State University, Bozeman)

afts Holdup Saloon, Red Lodge, 1900. Left to right: Jim Virtue, later owner of the bar; George Taft, owner; uniden-
fied; Mina Minar; Charlie Aiken (Courtesy of Montana Historical Society, Helena)

seph M. Dixon (Courtesy of Montana Historical
ociety, Helena)

Jeannette Rankin (Courtesy of Montana Historical
Society, Helena)

Al Smith's presidential campaign tour, Billings, September 24, 1928. Left to right: Senator B. K. Wheeler; Al Smith; Governor John Erickson; Senator T. J. Walsh; unidentified (Courtesy of Montana Historical Society, Helena)

President Roosevelt and party at the East Hill Observation Point during his second visit to Fort Peck Dam, October 3, 1937. Left to right: Congressman James O'Connor; Secret Service man; James Roosevelt; President Roosevelt; Governor Roy E. Ayers; Senator James E. Murray; Major Clark Kittrell, District Engineer. Photograph by U.S. Army Corps of Engineers, District of Omaha (Courtesy of Montana Historical Society, Helena)

or may not have been I.W.W.'s or members of the new union—set off twenty-five different dynamite blasts and destroyed the famous old Miners' Union Hall. For weeks afterward the great mining city trembled on the brink of anarchy. Finally, on September 1, Governor Stewart declared martial law and sent in the National Guard. The result was a total defeat for organized labor. While the troops occupied Butte, Muckie McDonald and some other leaders of the new union were tried and imprisoned. Socialist Mayor Lewis Duncan and Sheriff Tim Driscoll, following summary grand jury investigation, were removed from office. And on September 9 Anaconda announced that it would no longer recognize either union. In other words, the once powerful Butte miners now found themselves impotent under the hated "open shop" system. The Company had had its way, and the mining labor movement lay broken and helpless.

When America entered the Great War in 1917, therefore, the labor situation was dormant but still tense. It erupted again in early summer as a result of the terrible disaster at the Speculator Mine, a property of the North Butte Mining Company. On the night of June 8, a carbide lamp accidentally ignited some frayed electrical insulation in the Granite Mountain shaft of the Speculator. The fire spread rapidly as the updraft fanned the flames. Gases, especially carbon monoxide, quickly permeated the tunnels, and some men died before they knew what was happening. Despite heroic rescue efforts 164 men lost their lives. The horrible tragedy at the Speculator Mine caused unionism to re-emerge.

On June 11 a wildcat strike hit the Elm Orlu Mine. Two days later a spontaneous gathering of laborers produced yet another organization, the Metal Mine Workers' Union, with Tom Campbell as president and Joe Shannon, a known Wobbly, as vice president. From the beginning the Metal Mine Workers' Union disclaimed any affiliation with the Industrial Workers of the World, but many of its members either belonged to or sympathized with the I.W.W. Launching an all-out membership drive, the M.M.W.U. demanded recognition by the mine owners, an end to the despised rustling card system, and better wages and working conditions. They pledged, furthermore, to avoid the violence of three years before. Nonetheless, Anaconda and the lesser mine owners refused to bargain with the new union. They branded the unionists as being the same old trouble makers of 1914; and by pointing to the antiwar views of some Wobbly leaders, they labeled the M.M.W.U. men as unpatriotic. So another major strike began. As various smaller craft unions on the Hill joined in, roughly fifteen thousand men had abandoned their posts by the end of June. The "richest hill on earth," one of the nation's key sources of copper, shut down operations. The Company and its allies brought in over two hundred detectives as spies and "goon squads," and violence once again threatened.

Onto this inflammable stage came Frank Little, "the toughest, most courageous and impulsive leader the IWW ever had." Little, a half-breed Indian, arrived in Butte on July 18 and immediately tried to draw the M.M.W.U. directly into the ranks of the I.W.W. He also delivered biting speeches against United States involvement in the war. These antiwar speeches bitterly angered Montana patriots and made Little an object of intense hatred. On the night of August 1, six masked vigilantes entered the Wobbly's boarding house, beat him up, dragged him behind their car to the outskirts of town, and hanged him from a railway trestle. The note left on Little's corpse bore the old vigilante insignia, 3-7-77. To this day, the murderers of Frank Little remain unknown. They may have been company agents, rival union men, or simply superpatriotic vigilantes. Aside from the Helena *Independent*—which brushed aside the murder by remarking, "Good work: Let them continue to hang every I.W.W. in the state"—most of the press disapproved the murder, if not the departure of Mr. Little. The Butte working class gave Frank Little an impressive good-by. Three thousand people marched in his funeral column, while many thousands more watched in solemn silence.

The murder of Little raised wartime emotions to a frenzy. Fearful of civil war and a permanent shutdown of the mines, the federal government sent troops into Butte on August 11. Already, the strike had begun to lose momentum. Now, with the Army occupying their town and with public opinion turning increasingly against them, the M.M.W.U. strikers marched despondently back to work. By early autumn the Butte mines were working at roughly 90 percent capacity once again. As in 1914, unionism collapsed, the victim of internal labor divisions, antiradical public opinion, and company manipulation.

Little's remarks and spectacular murder further enflamed the hectic search for traitors and subversives around the state. The man who found himself in the center of this storm, and who eventually became the most powerful politician in all the state's history, was Burton K. Wheeler, the United States District Attorney for Montana. A native of Massachusetts and the son of Quaker parents, "B. K." Wheeler first came to Butte in 1905, a tall, gangling young lawyer with a quick wit and an engaging personality. He moved up quickly and, while serving in the 1911 Legislature, struck up a key friendship with Thomas Walsh by supporting him for the Senate. Once in Washington, Walsh rewarded Wheeler by arranging his appointment as District Attorney for Montana, the chief guardian of federal laws in the state. The outbreak of war placed Wheeler in the hot seat, for superpatriots and conservatives demanded that he prosecute radical antiwar groups like the I.W.W. and the Nonpartisan League on the grounds that they were obstructing the war effort. Wheeler, however, was tough. As an advanced progressive, he sympathized with some of the radicals' beliefs, and he refused to be stampeded into prosecuting people on flimsy or false evidence. Thus Wheeler himself became the target of the superpatriots and Red hunters.

The demand that Wheeler either prosecute the antiwar critics or resign came from many quarters, but especially from the Montana Council of Defense. Governor Stewart first created this body at the request of the Wilson Administration, which asked each state and county to establish such councils, all to be coordinated under a Council of National Defense, in order to aid in furthering the war effort. Like other state councils, the Montana Council of Defense spread war propaganda and promoted the sale of bonds; but also like many other state councils, it got completely carried away in the search for traitors, "slackers," draft dodgers, and other nonconformists.

Aided by most of the Montana press and by various local and statewide groups, the Montana Council of Defense constantly hounded Wheeler and Attorney General Sam Ford, demanding more prosecutions. The superpatriots found another archvillain in the person of flamboyant Judge George M. Bourquin of the Butte district court. Like Wheeler and Ford, the handsome, strong-willed, and domineering Judge Bourquin kept a cool head in wartime and refused to convict people simply because of their unpopular opinions. He once dismissed his critics by saying, "This court may be wrong, but not in doubt." More than any other incident, it was the famous Ves Hall Case which raised storms of rage against the judge. Ves Hall, a rancher in remote Rosebud County, got himself into trouble merely by uttering remarks critical of American involvement in the war. When the Hall Case came before Bourquin's court early in 1918, the judge quite correctly directed a verdict of innocent, since Hall had broken no law. For this, the advocates of total loyalty never forgave him.

Faced by federal prosecutors and judges who would not do their bidding, the Montana Council of Defense and its allies pressured the governor to convene the state legislature in special session. Meeting in February 1918, the legislature immediately set to work beating down the antiwar crowd. It considered, but failed to pass, resolutions demanding that the federal government remove both Wheeler and Bourquin from office. It did manage to impeach and force the removal from office of Judge Charles L. Crum of Montana's Fifteenth Judicial District, simply because Crum had criticized the war and had testified on behalf of Ves Hall. The lawmakers went on to pass a Criminal Syndicalism Act, aimed at outlawing the I.W.W., and to expand the powers of the Montana Council of Defense so that it could act, in effect, as a fully constituted arm of state government. Incredible as it may seem today, the frightened legislators even passed a gun registration law.

Most significantly of all, the legislature enacted the amazing Montana Sedition Law.

In effect, the Montana Sedition Law seemed to make it illegal to criticize the federal government, the armed forces, or even the *state* government in wartime. The law stated in part:

> . . . any person or persons who shall utter, print, write or publish any disloyal, profane, violent, scurrilous, contemptuous, slurring or abusive language about the form of government of the United States, or the constitution of the United States, or the soldiers or sailors of the United States, or the flag of the United States, or the uniform of the army or navy . . . or shall utter, print, write or publish any language calculated to incite or inflame resistance to any duly constituted Federal or State authority in connection with the prosecution of the War . . . shall be guilty of the crime of sedition.

Through the efforts of Senators Walsh and Henry Myers, this Montana law became the model for the notorious federal Sedition Law of May 1918, a law which was widely used to stifle criticism of the war and which many authorities consider the most sweeping violation of civil liberties in modern American history.

Before, and even after the war ended in November 1918, the campaign against dissenters continued. The Montana Council of Defense even banned use of the German language in the state. The council, the Montana Loyalty League, and other outfits pressed especially hard against the Wobblies and the Nonpartisan League. In Montana and elsewhere the I.W.W. and other radical labor groups rapidly lost their influence. The federal government aided the mine owners and labor conservatives in crushing the left wing laborites: between September 1914 and April 1920, national guardsmen and federal troops occupied Butte six different times. During the strike of April 1920, Company-paid guards shot into a group of picketers at the Neversweat Mine, killing one and wounding fifteen others.

By the early twenties the Wobblies were beaten and scattered, and mining unionism seemed little more than a corpse. The Nonpartisan League suffered much the same treatment. Its organizers and speakers were frequently harassed and refused the right of free speech. At Miles City, league organizer Mickey McGlynn was dragged into the Elks Club basement and beaten severely. When Attorney General Ford and local authorities pressed charges against the perpetrators of this crime, a local justice of the peace dismissed them all. The Nonpartisan League held on for several more years; but by the early twenties its influence, like that of the Wobblies, was fast melting away.

Thus, under storm clouds of wartime hysteria, the radicals, and the more outspoken progressives, too, were driven from the field. The Company and the far right seemed to rule supreme. Those who had hoped for a liberal farmer-labor alliance saw their dreams dashed and their two favorite politicians—Burton K. Wheeler and Jeannette Rankin—driven from office in 1918. Of course Wheeler, the darling of the workers and small farmers, held a federally appointive office. But spokesmen for the Company and other conservative elements put pressure upon Senator Walsh, who was up for re-election in 1918, to secure Wheeler's removal. Torn between conscience and desire for re-election, Walsh buckled and got Wheeler to resign as District Attorney. Wheeler thus stuck to his principles and lost his job, while Walsh bent with the wind and kept his. As for Miss Rankin, a lifelong pacifist and progressive, she created a major sensation and lost much support by voting against war in 1917. Openly backed by the Butte workers and the Nonpartisan League, she ran for the Senate as an independent in 1918 and went down to defeat. As World War I came to an end, therefore, its main casualties in Montana seemed to be the radical and progressive reformers, who appeared to be beaten beyond recovery.

CHAPTER XII

Drought, Depression, and War: 1919–46

DURING and immediately after World War I, a severe drought and an international decline of farm prices combined to produce a serious depression in Montana and the Northern Plains region. The events of these years mark a great turning point in Montana's history, the end of the homestead boom and of the entire frontier process, the beginning of a twenty-year period of drought, wind, and poverty. Slowly, almost imperceptibly, the experience of these years changed the whole course of the state's development. The frontier boom cycle turned into a bust; the flood of immigration reversed itself and became an exodus to greener pastures elsewhere; and the dreams of the boosters soured into bitter memories. The Montanan, once the classic frontier optimist, became more and more the cautious cynic, hardened to adversity and suspicious of change. Montana was entering its modern era.

THE POSTWAR DEPRESSION

The agricultural depression actually began during the war, and then intensified at its conclusion. Once again, as in the collapse of the open range cattle industry, the region's roller coaster, boom-and-bust economic cycle plummeted downward. It seemed again as though the forces of nature and of man conspired against the Treasure State. Nature struck first. Cycles of drought, as the old-timers well knew, are a natural part of the Great Plains climate. Most of the homesteaders, however, did not know this. They had come during a time of unusually ample rainfall, and to them this exception seemed the general rule. The drought cycle began, stealthily, in 1917, the first year of American participation in the Great War. At first only certain areas, mainly the "High Line" counties north of the Missouri River, felt its withering force. Then in 1918 the drought moved southward, encompassing the eastern two-thirds of the state.

In 1919, perhaps the most calamitous year Montana ever saw, the drought became generalized, spreading even into the normally well watered valleys of the western mountains. The dry cycle brought other problems in its wake. Great forest fires swept the western woodlands, and hordes of gophers and swarms of locusts plagued the beleaguered farmers. In their desperation, Montana farmers imported over one hundred thousand turkeys to eat the grasshoppers, but it was no use. Although the turkeys thrived, so did the locusts. Roast turkey soon became a cheap staple in dozens of small town restaurants. High winds set in during 1920, whipping away great clouds of highly pulverized top soil into the hideous dust storms that became so familiar again a decade later. The homesteader now paid dearly for his wasteful methods of cultivation. Deep plowing conserved soil moisture, but it also led to wind erosion, and to disaster.

As if the natural calamity were not enough, economic dislocations following World War I brought even more severe complications. The prices of wheat and other commodities had, as we have seen, been inflated by high wartime demands and by federal price controls. Farm prices stayed up, momentarily, after the war ended. But by 1920, as Europe recovered from the ravages of war, it began once more to supply most of its own food needs. Farm prices thus entered a period of international decline, and to make matters worse the federal government abruptly removed its price controls. As a result, farm prices fell off sharply. Wheat, which sold for $2.40 per bushel in August 1920, dropped to $1.25 per bushel in October. Farmers faced both light harvests and low prices. Accustomed to yields of 25 bushels to the acre, Montana farmers averaged a pitiful 2.4 bushels per acre in 1919. Now in 1920, they were staggered not only by another bad crop year, but also by wheat prices skidding toward one dollar to the bushel.

Montana's mining and lumber towns also felt the squeeze, for the end of swollen wartime demands for raw materials meant local shutdowns and unemployment. All of this added up, naturally, to a regionwide disaster. Although the country as a whole suffered a sharp recession after the war, the national economy had generally recovered by 1922. In this agriculturally dependent region, however, the depression hit harder and lasted longer. The worst was over by 1922, but the crisis did not really pass until the return of adequate rainfall in the mid-1920s.

Meanwhile the people suffered. The summer of 1919 saw the worst of it. In Hill County of northern Montana, three thousand people faced the coming winter without adequate means of support. Wagons and jalopies rolled out of Big Sandy, with mattresses and belongings tied alongside and occasionally a grimly humorous sign such as "Goodby Old Dry!" Who could help them? The Red Cross had little to offer and neither did the state government. Governor Sam Stewart called a special session of the legislature during the midsummer, but the state obviously lacked the tax base to offer much assistance to its distressed citizens. The legislators enacted a law authorizing the county commissioners to issue road construction bonds, hoping that such projects might employ the destitute farmers. But the bonds found few buyers, and the homesteaders found few jobs. Uncle Sam offered very little assistance. The Wilson Administration extended over two million dollars' worth of seed loans to local farmers during 1918–20, but such scant relief barely scratched the surface.

So the Montanan faced it on his own, and grim statistics tell his story. During the period 1919–25 roughly two million acres passed out of production; and eleven thousand farms, about 20 percent of the state's total, were vacated. Twenty thousand mortgages were foreclosed, and one of every two Montana farmers lost his land. The average acre-value of farm lands fell by 50 percent. During the flush times prior to 1918, Montana had become heavily overstocked with banks, many of them reckless in their lending policies. Now these overextended banks fell like dominoes. Between 1920 and 1926, 214 of Montana's commercial banks—over one-half of the state's total—failed, carrying thousands of family savings accounts down with them. Montana had the highest bankruptcy rate in the United States.

The haunting face of depression appeared everywhere: roads and gullies blown full of dust and sprouting weeds and thistles, homestead shacks now abandoned and forlorn, quiet main streets with boarded up store fronts. The most ominous sign of all was the great exodus of the state's rural population. Sixty thousand people left Montana during the twenties, many of them seeking new horizons on the Pacific Coast. Montana was the only state of the forty-eight to lose population during the "prosperous" 1920s. As rural Montanans moved on, the state began increasingly to assume a different population profile. Before the war Montana had been a typical frontier state, a state of the young and ambitious. Now, as so many younger families fled, it came more and more to be a state of the very young and the very old, with disproportionately few young and middle-aged adults. Such it has remained.

Who was to blame? Like so many rural Americans of the twenties and thirties, Montanans in their distress lashed out at the boosters who had misled them, especially the bankers and the railroad promoters. When Joseph Kinsey Howard, the eloquent journalist from Great Falls, singled out Jim Hill as the arch-villain in his widely read *Montana: High, Wide, and Handsome,* many agreed with him. Montana children of the time sang this ditty:

> Twixt Hill and Hell, there's just
> one letter;

Were Hill in Hell, we'd feel
                much better.

Howard also sounded a common sentiment when he accused the federal
government of bungling. Montanans remembered, after all, that the government had encouraged them, through price supports and patriotic ser-
mons, to plow up their marginal lands in wartime. After the war the Wilson
Administration had dropped the supports with what seemed a cruel haste.
They remembered, too, that on a per capita basis, Montana had sent more
men to the war than any other state. As a result, Montana lost more men,
per capita, than any other state. Howard's most angry, and popular, indict-
ment focused upon the Federal Reserve Board and particularly upon the
district bank in Minneapolis. According to Howard's accusations, which
were not entirely accurate, the Federal Reserve restricted credit to Montana banks at exactly the time when it should have extended it, thus making
a bad situation much worse.

In the final analysis, there was blame enough to share. The bitterness of
those years becomes much easier to understand when we realize how
serious the postwar crisis really was. In truth, the collapse of the Montana
homestead movement after 1918 marked the end of the frontier itself. The
closing of the frontier ended a cycle of spectacular economic growth and
began an era of economic stagnation and population loss. As prosperity
vanished, so did optimism. Indeed, Montana lost more in the postwar
depression than merely its marginal farmers. To a considerable extent, it
also lost its self-confidence and its faith in the future.

THE DIXON ADMINISTRATION

Interestingly, the hard times produced considerable political discontent
and breathed new life into the progressive and radical groups that had been
staggered during the War. The Nonpartisan League, for instance, which
had been placed on the defensive by wartime patriots, now appealed once
again to thousands of small farmers who suddenly found themselves the victims of a cruel economic system. Both the progressive and radical forces in
Montana regrouped themselves for one last campaign against the Company. The gubernatorial election campaign of 1920, perhaps the most bruis-
ing encounter in the state's history, thus became a showdown between the
reformers and the Anaconda.

The hottest real issue in this campaign involved the taxation of mines. Almost ever since the 1889 Constitutional Convention, liberal forces had
tried—and failed—to increase the levy on metal mines. Now their arguments took on new urgency, for the depression was drying up the income
from the property tax. In 1919 the mine tax question suddenly burst into

the open when Louis Levine, a young economics professor at Montana State University in Missoula, published a small book entitled *The Taxation of Mines in Montana*. Levine's book was hardly radical. Rather, it simply revealed what well informed Montanans already knew, that mining taxes were inequitably low. Levine became a *cause célèbre*, though, partly because he was a Russian Jew at a time when when "subversives" and "Bolsheviks" were being hunted down throughout the country, and partly because the Company and its friends pressured the university to dismiss him. In a flagrant and highly publicized abuse of academic freedom, Levine lost his job. Although the university later reinstated him, the tormented professor soon moved on to a distinguished career elsewhere. Levine's little book, followed by his dismissal, drew statewide attention to the tax situation.

In August 1920 progressive candidates won the gubernatorial nominations of both political parties. Both nominees were long-time foes of the Company, and both advocated an increase in the mines tax. Joseph M. Dixon, the veteran reformer, won the Republican nomination; and controversial Burton K. Wheeler, backed by the Nonpartisan League, gained the Democratic nod. It turned into a hard fought, sometimes vicious campaign. The Anaconda identified Wheeler as its main enemy and thus mutely accepted Dixon. An emotional and effective campaigner, B. K. Wheeler attacked the Company, its newspapers and political empire, from one end of the state to the other. The Anaconda papers and other conservative spokesmen, in turn, roasted Wheeler. Nicknaming him "Bolshevik Burt," they accused him of being a socialist and even reported that Wheeler and the Nonpartisan League advocated free love. Public opinion turned heatedly against the outspoken Democrat. Denouncing the Nonpartisan League "takeover" of their party, thousands of conservative Democrats deserted Wheeler. He could not even gain access to speaking facilities in Miles City.

Joseph Dixon meanwhile billed himself as a moderate alternative to Wheeler, neither a radical nor a Company man. As a result, Dixon won a great victory, and Wheeler became one of the worst defeated political candidates in Montana's history. Ironically, Dixon's victory launched him into a sea of troubles, while Wheeler's defeat soon turned to triumph. Only two years after his landslide burial, Wheeler ran for the United States Senate in 1922. This time he struck a more moderate pose and kept his distance from the sagging Nonpartisan League. As a consequence, he gained the support of a reunited Democratic Party and won an easy election to the Senate, where he would hold forth for the next quarter-century.

The newly elected governor, Joseph Dixon, was an earnest, capable, and honest man, who well understood the state and its problems. He may well have been the best governor Montana ever had. But Dixon faced terrible problems. On the one hand he had the misfortune to govern during a severe depression. Inevitably, this meant that he would take the blame for the bad times, the declining tax revenues, and the mounting state debt. On the other hand Dixon faced unfriendly legislatures. Although his fellow Republicans controlled both the House and the senate, they were mostly conservatives and generally friendly toward the Company. These conservative Republicans, remembering the Bull Moose rebellion of 1912, had no love for the progressive Republican who sat in the governor's chair.

Undaunted, Dixon pressed forward with a general reform program. True to his campaign promises, the governor aimed at tax reform. He presented the legislatures of 1921 and 1923 with a blueprint for a modern and equitable tax system, including a tax commission and new levies on mines, oil and gasoline, motor vehicles, and inheritances. Under a blitz of Company lobbying, the lawmakers refused to follow the governor's lead. Only the oil and inheritance measures passed, the latter just in time to nail the estate of the late William A. Clark. Both in 1921 and again in 1923, the key tax commission and mines tax bills went down to defeat. Dixon coldly pointed out the glaring fact that, although Montana's metal mines produced over $20 million in 1922, they paid only $13,559 in state taxes. Not surprisingly, the Company press chose not to circulate this information. Instead, it lambasted the governor for his "reckless" extravagance.

Although one frustration followed another, still Dixon managed some gains. Most significantly, he employed Nils P. Haugen, former director of the Wisconsin Tax Commission, to initiate new methods of assessing railroads and utilities, thus increasing their taxable value. This marked a major progressive victory. So did the enactment of an old age pension law by the 1923 Legislature, a feat which made Montana, along with Nevada, the first states to provide such support for their elderly citizens. Courageously, Dixon fired the iron-handed and controversial warden of the state penitentiary, Frank Conley. Responding to this entirely proper act, the Helena *Independent* accused the governor of coddling "slackers, seditionists, highwaymen, rapists, porch climbers, and jail breakers."

The issue of mine taxation, so symbolic of Anaconda's naked power, remained unresolved as Dixon's term expired. In good progressive fashion, Dixon decided that, since the legislature refused to act, he would take his case directly to the people. He prepared the famous Initiative 28 for submission to the voters in the 1924 election. If passed, this initiative would levy a graduated tax of up to 1 percent of gross production upon any mine that produced over $100,000 gross per year. This meant war. The Company and its newspapers, which had reluctantly accepted Dixon in 1920, now tore into him as he stood for re-election in 1924. Charging the governor with such serious "extravagances" as buying expensive silver dishes for the governor's mansion, the Anaconda press predicted more shutdowns and deeper depression if he were re-elected.

Dixon never really had a chance. His Democratic opponent John E. Erickson, backed by the Anaconda, beat him soundly by running on a low-keyed platform of thrift and retrenchment. As the people removed Dixon from office, though, they also passed his Initiative 28, which would raise the Company's taxes dramatically over the years to follow. Clearly Joseph Dixon fell victim to the Company's attack. But, as passage of Initiative 28 reveals, other factors also contributed to his loss, especially the fact that he was, after all, a depression governor who got blamed for the bad times. Dixon never regained political power in Montana. After failing in a 1928 Senate race against Wheeler, he served as assistant secretary of the Department of the Interior under President Herbert Hoover and died in 1934.

Dixon's 1924 defeat marked the end of a political era in Montana. He was the most powerful of the Montana progressives, and his failure at the hands of the Company signaled the end of the age of reform. In the years since then, many Montanans have seen in Dixon's fall the failure of liberalism itself. The progressive impulse was spent, while the awesome might of the Company remained. Actually, the forces of liberalism did not die with Joseph Dixon. They merely went into momentary eclipse. As for now, though, in the aftermath of 1924, the conservatives—and the Anaconda—ruled supreme.

PROSPERITY AND POLITICAL CALM

During the years immediately following Dixon's defeat, Montana entered a brief period of renewed prosperity. The rain cycle returned during the middle and late twenties, and with it came good crops once again. At the same time the great nationwide boom of 1922–29 finally began to improve the state's dormant economy, as local industries responded to rising nationwide demands for metals, lumber, and oil. Momentarily at least, the bad times seemed to be over. This short interlude of prosperity brought with it a period of political calm that contrasted sharply with the heated atmosphere of the Dixon years. In fact it was during this time, the later twenties and early thirties, that a political pattern began to appear which has persisted to the present day: a pattern of conservative government at the state level, curiously balanced by liberal representation in Washington, D.C.

Conservatism clearly prevailed in Helena during this period, as it did in most states. From 1925 until 1931, the Republicans controlled the state legislature with lopsided majorities. These Republicans steadily stressed the need for economy, not innovation, in state government and demanded reductions of the large state debt that had accumulated during the depressed years of the Dixon Administration. Governor John E. ("Honest John") Erickson was a Democrat, but he was also a conservative and got along well with the Republicans. Erickson, a tall and strikingly handsome son of Norwegian immigrants, won three gubernatorial elections and served from 1925 until 1933. An instinctive conservative and party regular, he had no desire to fight the Company. Having beaten Dixon in 1924 on a platform of "economy and efficiency through retrenchment and clean business methods," Erickson ran a low-keyed operation. He was proud of his administration's reductions of the state debt and its efficiency in cutting down and managing the bureaucracy. As long as the prosperity lasted, so did Erickson's popularity. Ironically, though, after having defeated a depression governor, Erickson was about to become a depression governor himself, and to suffer the same loss of esteem as Dixon had earlier.

While conservatives ruled at home, Montana gained widespread fame during the 1920s for its liberal representation in the United States Senate. Both of Montana's senators—Thomas J. Walsh, in office from 1913 until 1933, and Burton K. Wheeler, 1923–47—were progressive Democrats. And both became favorites of the national liberal community because of their investigations into the corruption of President Warren G. Harding's administration. Actually, these two men, so often compared and grouped together, were quite unalike, either in personality or in political profile.

Senator Walsh, a cold and aloof man, was a moderate progressive and an unexciting campaigner. He made his reputation, both in Montana and in the Senate, as a truly great legal mind and as an honest and dignified public servant. Walsh gained nationwide fame during 1923–24 when he directed the brilliant investigation that uncovered the Teapot Dome Scandal, involving the improper leasing of naval oil reserves in Wyoming and California. As a result of Walsh's work and the efforts of others, Harding's Interior Secretary, Albert B. Fall, became the first cabinet member in United States history to serve a prison term. After Teapot Dome, Walsh rose to the highest ranks of political prestige and power. He served as chairman of the Democratic national conventions of 1924 and 1932, and in 1928 he made an unsuccessful bid for the Democratic presidential nomination. By 1925 Walsh was clearly the most powerful political figure in the state.

While serving his first Senate term, Walsh's younger colleague, Burton K. Wheeler, also joined in exposing the wrongdoings of the Harding cabinet. Wheeler led in the Senate investigation that eventually forced Attorney General Harry Daugherty to resign from office. This effort, which prompted eastern newspapers to speak of the "Montana mudgunners" or "Montana scandalmongers," also made Wheeler a leading force among American liberals. In 1924 he ran unsuccessfully for the vice presidency on the Progressive party ticket which put up Robert La Follette for president. Unlike Walsh, Wheeler was an advanced progressive who leaned toward Populist-style radicalism. He loved political infighting and was a natural campaigner. Joseph Kinsey Howard once recalled a typical Wheeler performance on the stage:

> He was a solid man on the platform, nearly six feet tall with broad shoulders and a big head; he wore comfortably rumpled suits with ill-fitting coat collars. He would bring his knees together, weave almost to the floor, and thrust his hands out beseechingly—or gesture with fingers spread just above the footlights, as if he were playing on a concealed piano keyboard. He was never a good speaker, but he was entertaining—a good campaigner. His effective use of pauses, seeming to grope for phrases and then repeating them, lent his words an air of sincerity.

Wheeler, much younger than Walsh, at this time looked forward to a long and distinguished career.

This "political schizophrenia," by which Montana presented a liberal face nationally and a conservative face locally, has provoked some interesting explanations over the years. For instance, some conservatives have argued that Montanans are merely realistic: they keep the thrifty conservatives at home while sending the spendthrift liberals off to fetch them federal monies. Liberals have replied that the real explanation lies in the simple fact that local conservative interest groups focus their main attention upon state, not national, offices. Neither theory seems entirely convincing. Whatever the real reasons for this peculiar political posture, one fact appears obvious: it reveals a delicate balance of competing liberal and conservative forces.

The conservative community in Montana, which held the upper hand during this period, had powerful forces behind it. Clearly, the Anaconda Copper Mining Company—with its highly efficient political network, its chain of newspapers, and its corporate partner, the Montana Power Company—was the most powerful conservative force in the state (on the formation of Montana Power, see discussion in chap. XIII). As seen in the case of Governor Dixon, "the Company" did not hesitate to lash out at its enemies. Its newspapers were a potent weapon, and its lobbying team in Helena wielded legendary strength. Back in those days, the Company ran twenty-four-hour-a-day "watering holes" for the free use of legislators. It also maintained a free bill drafting service to assist the lawmakers and an efficient information bureau that served as the key source of information for many of them. A Company lobbyist boasted once to John Gunther: "Give me a case of Scotch, a case of gin, one blonde, and one brunette, and I can take any liberal." But the Company was not immune to change. Even by 1930, as we shall see, younger executives were beginning to soften its political approach and subdue its methods.

Many Montanans, and many outside observers as well, simply felt that the Company ran the state as its own private bailiwick. Of course, this was never literally true. For one thing, other groups, too, contributed their support to conservatism. Among corporate interests, five major railroads did business in Montana, including the Northern Pacific with its huge landholdings. Coal, oil, lumber, and smaller metal mining firms also made their influence felt, as did bankers, merchants, and chambers of commerce. Then there were the cattlemen and wool-growers. Highly organized through the Montana Stockgrowers Association and the Montana Wool Growers Association, they leaned heavily toward conservatism and toward the Republican party; and their strength in the legislature was often even greater than that of the Company. Naturally, the conservatives also drew considerable support from the broad middle and upper middle classes who, in Montana as elsewhere, worried about big government, excessive spending and maintaining the status quo.

So much for the conservatives, but who were the liberals, the groups who kept sending men like Walsh and Wheeler to Washington? Despite its image as a conservative, corporate-dominated state, Montana actually contained powerful liberal organizations. As in other states of the Northwest, the leading liberal elements in the Treasure State were labor unions and small farmers, both of whom inclined increasingly toward the Democratic party. Organized labor, it is true, had been beaten down during World War I; but, as we shall note, its strength would reappear during the turbulent 1930s.

During the 1920s the smaller farm operators were in an angry mood due to the trials of depression. In fact some of them, around the northeastern Montana community of Plentywood, even organized an active Communist movement and published their own newspaper, the *Producers News*, edited by Charles E. "Red Flag" Taylor. Few, however, moved this far to the left. Instead, as the Nonpartisan League faded in the early twenties, more and more small farmers drifted into the ranks of the National Farmers Union. Although the liberal Farmers Union had first entered the state back in 1912, it really took deep root only after organizational drives of the later 1920s. Montana became, and has remained, one of the six states where the Farmers Union is the leading agricultural organization. The Farmers Union was, and still is, the true heir of Populist-style liberalism, and it has long been a bulwark of liberal causes in Montana.

Thus Montana became and would remain a delicately balanced state, a state where Democrats and Republicans, liberals and conservatives, usually competed on fairly even terms. This close balance tended to make the state a political weathervane. In only one presidential election since 1900, the Kennedy-Nixon contest of 1960, did Montana fail to support the winning candidate. The period following Joseph Dixon's defeat was a time of conservative rule, but a new cycle of drought and depression was about to lift liberal Democrats into power.

THE GREAT DEPRESSION

The brief honeymoon of late 1920s prosperity abruptly vanished during 1929–30, as a new ordeal of drought and depression began. This time the droughts would last longer than before, intermittently for nearly a decade. And this time, more so than in 1919–22, a terrible nationwide and worldwide depression would vastly complicate Montana's own local problems. The drought began sporadically in 1929, intensified in 1930, and reached truly disastrous proportions in 1931. By midsummer of that terrible year, twenty-eight of Montana's fifty-six counties had filed for aid from the Red Cross. Most of these counties lay in the arc of dry farming and stockgrowing lands reaching from the "High Line" north of the Missouri River, southeastward along the Dakota border. The years 1932 and 1933 brought increases in rainfall to many localities, but again in 1934, 1936, and 1937 there were more searing droughts and frightening, dust-laden winds.

Along with the drought came a steep drop in food prices, as the worldwide depression led to declining food purchases and mounting crop surpluses. An amount of wheat worth $100 in 1920 brought only $19.23 in 1932, when the going price stood at 32 cents per bushel. Stockmen joined farmers in hardship as the drought withered forage and hay crops, and as meat and wool prices collapsed. Beef cattle sold for $9.10 per hundredweight in 1929, only $3.34 in 1934. Sheep brought $8.14 per hundredweight in 1929, only $3.12 in 1934.

Once again hunger, poverty, and desperation stalked the countryside. Daniels County, in the state's northeastern corner, typified the crisis. Back in the good years of the later 1920s, the county seat, Scobey, had once advertised itself as the world's largest wheat shipping point. By the spring of 1933, after four years of sub par rainfall, thirty-five hundred of the county's five thousand people needed relief assistance. After touring the eastern reaches of the state in August 1931, Governor John Erickson could only bury his head in his hands, lamenting, as an associate later recalled, that if only someone could find a solution to the problem, he would gladly embrace it. The people, he wrote, were "in rather a desperate condition. The grain crops and feed crops are practical failures." In some areas the only green vegetation he saw sprouted forlornly where last winter's snow fences had trapped some traces of moisture.

Montana did not lie in the heart of the "Dust Bowl" of the "dirty thirties," but like other states of the Great Plains it fully experienced the ravages of drought, dust, and depopulation. Many left the land, as they had ten years before. The number of Montana farms fell from 47,495 in 1930 to 41,823 in 1940. Like the "Okies" described by John Steinbeck or the "Dokies" from the neighboring Dakotas, Montanans joined the general exodus of poor folks toward the West Coast. Those who stayed, many of them at least, would eventually prosper during the wet and profitable years of World War II. But for now, most of them felt the squeeze. The aggregate value of Montana farms, including both land and buildings, totaled $527,610,002 in 1930. Even despite the farm relief programs of the New Deal, it fell to $350,178,461 by 1940. The average Montana farm, valued at $11,109 in 1930, was worth only $8,373 in 1940. Slowly, inexorably, the rural depression squeezed the life blood out of the parched Great Plains.

To a much greater extent than in the depression of 1918–22, Montana's industries and cities now suffered along with the farmers and ranchers. Like most states of the Mountain West, Montana lacked heavy industry. Its industries were extractive, dealing in raw materials, and so they were slow to feel the full impact of the "Great Crash" of 1929. By 1931, however, the Treasure State reeled under the full brunt of the Great Depression. As the nationwide construction business fell off, so eventually did the lumber industry of Montana and the Pacific Northwest. As such major copper consumers as the brass companies and the electrical utilities cut back production, so too did the western producers.

At this time Montana relied much more heavily upon copper mining than it does today. The oil, coal, and lumber industries, so important in the 1970s, were much smaller operations then. Throughout the 1920s, as we shall see, the Anaconda Copper Mining Company had expanded into a worldwide enterprise. In the process, it became heavily indebted. So when the Great Depression hit, it flattened the highly competitive copper industry, especially the overextended Anaconda. As markets contracted, copper prices steadily fell, from 18 cents per pound in 1929, to 8 cents per pound in 1931, to 5 cents per pound in 1933. Anaconda stock, which sold as high as 175 on the New York Exchange in 1929, dropped to an incredible low of 3 in 1932. This meant that at its lowest point the stock was worth 6 cents on the dollar of book value. Cheap African and South American copper flooded the market, and the American copper industry cut back production to one-fourth of its 1929 peak level.

Naturally, these trends spelled disaster for Montana's mining towns. The Company steadily cut back its Butte production: from over 300,000 wet tons of ore monthly in early 1929, to 30,000 per month early in 1933. In Butte and in the smelting and refining towns of Anaconda, Great Falls, and East Helena, machinery ground to a halt, and armies of unemployed men filled the streets. At Butte-Anaconda in particular, poverty was grim and undisguised. A 1934 Department of Commerce survey of Butte revealed that 64 percent of the city's homes needed repair, 32 percent had inadequate space for the inhabitants, nearly 20 percent had no indoor toilets, and almost 30 percent had neither bath nor shower. A Consumers' Council survey of the same year reckoned that, for every well fed child in Butte, five lacked sufficient nourishment.

Montana had seen hard times before, as in the Panic of 1893 or the post–World War I depression, but it had never known anything like this. Tens of thousands of Montanans were in desperate need of relief by the early thirties, but to whom could they turn? President Herbert Hoover argued that private charities and the state and local governments—but not the federal government—should meet the emergency. Private charity, though, had little to give. As part of its nationwide drought relief program, the American Red Cross dispensed food, clothing, medicines, fuel, and feed throughout eastern and northern Montana during 1930–32. But the Red Cross simply lacked adequate resources. Its average food grant was a pathetic ten cents per person per day.

The state government offered little more promise. Like the governor himself, most legislators were conservatives with little inclination to indebt the state in order to support the poor. In fact they seemed to have little choice. Montana relied upon the property tax, and the depression increasingly devalued property, drying up the wellsprings of state revenue. Borrowing offered little hope either. The Montana constitution required a special election in order to exceed a $100,000 indebtedness. So Erickson, like most governors of his time, saw inaction as the only alternative. When the state legislature met early in 1931, he advised the lawmakers to slash appropriations and to avoid new commitments. They were happy to oblige. The lawmakers did pass a state income tax law, but its importance lay in the more distant future. Aside from authorizing a $6 million debenture to finance road construction work, the legislature steered away from new obligations. As the politicians well knew, Montana did not have the financial means to solve its problems.

Thus, from 1929 through 1932, the state and the nation sank deeper and deeper into depression. As things got worse, the demand for federal assistance to the needy mounted apace. President Hoover generally resisted these demands; and this resistance, more than any other factor, led to his defeat at the hands of Democrat Franklin D. Roosevelt in the election of 1932. The inauguration of President Roosevelt early in 1933 began the New Deal, the greatest reform movement—and the most revolutionary period in federal-state relations—that the United States has ever seen.

THE NEW DEAL

The New Deal reform movement began in March 1933 and continued until it lost momentum in 1938–39. Historians still argue about its motives and about its success or failure in ending the depression. Roosevelt's basic purpose, though, was simple enough: he sought to use the spending and regulatory powers of the federal government to combat the deadening impact of the depression. This meant a sudden funneling of government funds into every state in the Union. More significantly, the New Deal sparked enormous changes in federal-state relationships. The New Deal began a massive increase in the power of the federal government. At the same time it also prompted the state governments to expand their operations. By the close of the 1930s, both the federal and state bureaucracies had ballooned in size and assumed large new roles in the lives of the people.

The Roosevelt Administration poured a great deal of money into Montana during the 1930s. From 1933 through 1939, the federal government spent $381,582,693 in the state and loaned another $141,835,952. On a per capita basis this meant that Montana received $710 per person and another $264 per person in loans, ranking the state second in the nation in New Deal investments. This high per capita expenditure resulted largely from the fact that Montana, with so few people, contained huge tracts of public lands and many miles of federally funded highways.

How were these New Deal dollars spent? Much of the money went directly to farmers. In 1933 the ambitious Agricultural Adjustment Administration (A.A.A.) began operations, with Montanans prominently involved in its organization. Montana State College professor M. L. Wilson played a key role in planning the A.A.A.; and a local farm editor, Chester Davis, directed the agency for a time. The A.A.A. attempted to raise farm prices through a variety of means aimed at reducing the huge crop surpluses that glutted the market. Most notably, the A.A.A. made direct cash benefit payments to farmers who agreed to restrict crop acreages.

The Agricultural Adjustment Administration program had a tremendous, revolutionary impact upon the great wheat producing state of Montana. For the first time in history, its farmers received massive federal aid. In turn they became increasingly reliant upon Uncle Sam. Between 1933 and 1937, the A.A.A. made nearly 140,000 contract agreements with Montana farmers and channeled from $4.5 million to nearly $10 million annually into the state's prostrate economy. What did this mean to the Treasure State? For many a farm family it meant a new change of clothes, an automobile, or a movie for the first time in years. To dozens of small farm towns, it meant busy main streets and ringing cash registers for the first time since 1929 or 1930. By 1938, as the rains again began to fall, local farmers enjoyed a 98 percent increase in cash income over what they had received in 1932.

Rural Montana received other New Deal benefits, too. The Farm Credit Administration extended low interest loans to farmers and ranchers, thus allowing them to refinance on reasonable terms and to avoid the calamity of mortgage foreclosures. F.C.A. loans totaled nearly $78 million in Montana by mid-1938. Ranchers obtained a major windfall with the 1934 Taylor Grazing Act, which allowed organized groups of stockmen to lease federal lands cooperatively for grazing purposes (see p. 244, below). The federal government thus offered the ranchers reliable pasturage at low cost, without the obligation of purchasing the land. Another New Deal agency which meant much to rural Montana was the Rural Electrification Administration. Beginning in 1935–36, this agency extended loans to farmers' cooperatives and other organizations, enabling them to build rural electrical distribution systems. As a result the number of electrified farms in Montana jumped from 2,768 in 1935 to 6,000 in 1939; and this was only the beginning. A new way of life was coming to the farm.

The Civilian Conservation Corps, among the most popular of all New Deal programs, appeared on the scene in 1933. This agency aimed to employ young men and teach them job skills by putting them to work in conservation camps on forest and range lands. The Forest Service and the Army directed operations. Beyond dispute the C.C.C. did much for Montana. Throughout the thirties it maintained an average of thirty to forty camps on Montana lands. The C.C.C. boys fought insects and blights such as the terrible Blister Rust fungus, built mountain roads, lookout stations, and reclamation dams, combated forest fires, and planted trees in the woodlands and grasses on the prairies. They left behind many enduring monuments, like the renovated Lewis and Clark Caverns on the Jefferson River or the Squaw Creek Ranger Station in the beautiful West Gallatin Canyon.

Many other New Deal efforts, too numerous to mention, had their impact upon the Treasure State. The Silver Purchase Act of 1934, for example, instituted a government buying program which raised the price of silver and stimulated a renewed mining of the metal in Montana. The Home Owners Loan Corporation refinanced home loans and thereby saved families from losing their homes to mortgage foreclosures. During this period the busy Reconstruction Finance Corporation made over 160 major loans to Montana banks and financial institutions, saving many of them from failure. Of all the many New Deal programs, though, none aroused more praise or protest than the efforts to provide relief for the poor.

Immediately in 1933 the Roosevelt Administration set out to provide work for the unemployed. As a first step, the Federal Emergency Relief

Administration offered federal matching funds to the states in order that they, in turn, might give relief to the needy. The F.E.R.A. was soon supplemented by the Public Works Administration, a federal operation created to build large scale projects and to provide jobs for skilled and semi-skilled workers. Neither of these agencies worked out very well: the F.E.R.A. became ensnarled in red tape, and the P.W.A. moved too slowly, employing too few men. So in 1935 the New Deal came up with its final answer to the relief problem, the Works Progress Administration, a strictly federal agency which offered work to all employable men who could find no jobs.

These agencies brought vital relief to hard-pressed Montana. Incredible as it seems, there were times when roughly one-fourth of the population was reliant upon some form of relief. The Works Progress Administration directly benefited more Montanans than any of its counterparts. As late as mid-1939, the W.P.A. directly employed over fourteen thousand local workers, thus supporting perhaps forty thousand or more people. Some W.P.A. projects involved "made work" or "boondoggling," but most were of real value. W.P.A. workers in Montana built and improved thousands of miles of streets, highways, and county roads, constructed nearly two hundred public buildings and schools, built aqueducts, sewers, and reservoirs, and even erected over ten thousand rural privies! As in other states, the Montana W.P.A. also offered special programs, such as the National Youth Administration for young people, a Writers' Program for authors, and sewing rooms for housewives.

The greatest of all New Deal work projects in Montana, in fact one of the largest in the entire country, was construction of the enormous, earth-filled Fort Peck Dam on the Missouri River. This huge project resulted from the demands of downstream states for flood control and was placed under the jurisdiction of the Public Works Administration and the Army Engineers. It employed many men. At the peak of construction in 1936, over 10,500 workers labored along the barren banks of the Mighty Missouri. They lived in raunchy little makeshift cities, like New Deal, Square Deal, Delano Heights, and Wheeler. For diversion, they hit the "hot spots," such as Ruby Smith's place, whose owner had started out on the Klondike. Here, one could buy a nickel beer; and, for the price of another beer, he could enjoy the company of a "taxi dancer." The bustling red light district, "Happy Hollow," had a large clientele.

By the time of its completion, Fort Peck stood as the greatest earthen dam in the world: 242 feet above the river bed, over 9,000 feet across, backing up nearly 20 million acre-feet of water. It was and is, quite simply, the greatest single alteration man has ever made on the Montana landscape. During the thirties, before the shanty towns were deserted and returned to nature, Fort Peck was more than just a big dam. It symbolized the entire New Deal effort: jobs for the unemployed, over $110 million pumped into the local economy, and a harnessing of the forces of nature. To friend and foe alike, Fort Peck Dam became the epitome of the New Deal in Montana.

By 1939, the year of the dam's completion, the New Deal had ground to a halt as the nation became increasingly preoccupied with the impending war in Europe. Obviously, this greatest of American reform movements had a lasting impact upon the Treasure State. Not only did the New Deal offer temporary relief to thousands, but it also left behind thousands of lasting improvements—dams, roads, schoolhouses, city halls, reservoirs, and forest trails. The New Deal began an enduring program of federal support to agriculture; and, as will be seen, it sparked a massive resurgence of the labor movement. It offered Social Security to the elderly and insurance to the unemployed. In Montana, as in all states, the New Deal began a "new federalism," a new federal-state relationship. It tremendously expanded the role of the federal government, so that the average Montanan came to look increasingly to Washington, not Helena, for the solution of his or her problems. By 1940 Uncle Sam wielded as great an influence in Montana as did the Company, the stockmen, or any other force.

Significantly, the New Deal also stimulated a great expansion of state governmental activity, the most dramatic expansion, in fact, that Helena has ever seen. At Roosevelt's urging, for instance, the Eighteenth Amendment was repealed in 1933, ending the era of prohibition. Like other states of the Northwest, Montana responded to the legalization of alcoholic beverages by placing their sale under a system of state monopoly. The 1933 Legislature created a Montana Liquor Control Board, which was empowered to supervise the distribution and sale of liquors and wines through a system of state owned stores. Naturally, this state liquor system immediately became a major source of revenue. It also became one of Montana's largest bureaucracies, a fount of political patronage, and an occasional source of scandal.

The unfolding New Deal prompted the Montana Legislature to create a number of new boards and agencies in order to obtain federal matching funds and to coordinate state with federal activities. These included a Water Conservation Board, a Grazing Commission, a State Planning Board, and a Highway Patrol and Patrol Board. Most important of all, in this regard, was the New Deal's Social Security Act of 1935. This highly complex law provided for much more than federal old age pensions: it also offered federal grants to the states for the purposes of unemployment insurance and care for the crippled, the blind, and dependent mothers and children. Like most states, Montana moved quickly to secure these federal benefits; and in doing so, it laid the foundation of its modern welfare system. The busy 1937 Legislature created two very important new agencies: a modernized Department of Public Welfare and an Unemployment Compensation Commission. Obviously, therefore, the New Deal not only expanded federal authority; it also triggered a similar boom in state activities.

THE POLITICS OF THE NEW DEAL ERA

Predictably, the New Deal spending programs, as well as Franklin D. Roosevelt personally, enjoyed enormous popularity in depressed Montana. Roosevelt visited the state in 1932, 1934, and 1937; each time he received a hearty welcome. Sioux and Assiniboine Indians even made him a chief in 1934. Borrowing a well known New Deal symbol, they gave him the name "Fearless Blue Eagle." In each of his four presidential campaigns, Roosevelt carried Montana by wide margins. F.D.R.'s popularity and power naturally gave Montana's Democratic party an enormous boost. From 1933 until 1941 the Democrats overwhelmingly dominated state government. Never, before or since, has one political party so completely held sway over the Treasure State.

Early in the game, Montana political leaders allied themselves to Roosevelt. Senator Burton K. Wheeler was one of the first nationally prominent figures to endorse F.D.R. for the presidency. At the Democratic National Convention of 1932, Montanans played major roles in the triumphant Roosevelt cause. Senator T. J. Walsh, an F.D.R. man, served as permanent chairman of the gathering; and the state's national committeeman, J. Bruce Kremer, chaired the all-important rules committee. When Roosevelt swept Montana in the 1932 election, he carried many local Democrats into office on his coattails. These included Governor John Erickson for a third term, and two new congressmen named Roy Ayers and Joseph Monaghan.

In part to reward Montana for its support, President Roosevelt chose prestigious Thomas J. Walsh to be his attorney general. The Walsh appointment drew widespread praise. Tragically, however, the seventy-three-year-old Montanan did not live to assume office. Enroute to the inauguration in early March of 1933, he suffered a massive heart attack and died. With his passing, Montana lost perhaps the most distinguished citizen it had ever known. Aside from depriving his adopted state of a powerful voice in Washington, Walsh's death also raised serious political complications. Governor John Erickson now had to choose a Senate successor. Besieged on all sides by Democrats who wanted the job, Erickson finally made a decision which was immediately and inevitably denounced as a "deal." On March 13, 1933, Erickson resigned as governor and was replaced by the Democratic lieutenant governor, Frank H. Cooney, who then appointed Erickson to fill the Walsh seat in the Senate. Erickson's "self-appointment" provoked howls of anger throughout Montana. The Sidney *Herald*, for instance, viewed him as a poor successor of the distinguished Walsh, "whose shoes he can no more fill in these trying times than could a child." More significantly, the Erickson-Cooney "deal" turned the normal Montana political pattern upsidedown: it placed a conservative in the Senate and a liberal in the governor's chair.

Like the other governors of his day, Frank Cooney faced enormous problems and hectic conditions. The inpouring of New Deal dollars, the demands for state matching funds, and the rapidly expanding state bureaucracy all aroused political appetites and tempers; and the governor stood in the eye of the storm. An Irish Catholic Democrat and a successful Butte and Missoula businessman, Cooney leaned toward an independent, progressive position, but he had never held statewide office before 1933 and no one knew what to expect of him. He set out at once to assert himself as a real, not a caretaker, governor; and when he did, powerful interest groups quickly rallied against him.

Cooney struggled mightily, and with some success, to bring the expanding bureaucracy under control and to get maximum New Deal benefits for the state. He placed the state liquor system on a solid footing and fought successfully to channel federal funds into the water conservation program which was his pride and joy. He fought tooth and nail with Company employees and friends whom Erickson had appointed to direct the state relief operation, and with federal support he got some of them removed. Naturally, he made enemies. When Cooney called the legislature into special session to raise matching funds for relief during the winter of 1933–34, his conservative enemies filed impeachment charges against him. The charges were mostly trivial, but the governor only narrowly escaped impeachment. Until he died of heart failure late in 1935, the scrappy little man continued to govern and to demonstrate his independence. President pro tem of the state senate W. Elmer Holt of Miles City then served as acting governor until a newly elected governor could be seated in 1937. With Cooney's passing and Holt's arrival, the governorship passed back to customary conservative hands.

Montana's governor during the later New Deal years was Roy E. Ayers, a Fergus County rancher who had been a Democratic congressman from 1933 until 1937. During his term, 1937–41, Ayers became deeply embroiled in controversies which reflected the expanding state bureaucracy. The key issue arose from the 1937 Legislature's passing of House Bill 65, the so-called "Hitler Bill," which gave the governor sweeping powers over the hiring and firing of state employees. Republicans, and many Democrats as well, accused Ayers of using these new powers to build a large political machine within the state bureaucracy. By the end of his administration,

Ayers had lost many of his earlier political supporters and faced an uphill battle for re-election.

While the New Deal created headaches for administrators, it also opened up great opportunities for the Democrats. In the elections of 1934 and 1936, almost all Democratic candidates won easily. They gained control of both houses of the legislature and held that control until 1941. Both Montana seats in the United States Senate were put to the vote in 1934. Running as a Roosevelt ally, Senator Burton K. Wheeler faced the Republican opposition of conservative Judge George M. Bourquin, who denounced the New Deal and attacked the Fort Peck project as a useless "duck pond." Wheeler destroyed Bourquin by a better than two-to-one margin and carried every county in the state.

The senate seat vacated by Thomas Walsh was also contested in 1934—for a short, two-year term. In the hard-fought Democratic primary, wealthy Butte attorney James E. Murray took the nomination away from Senator John Erickson, whose appointment to the seat had aroused such bitter controversy the year before. Murray easily went on to win the general election, thus beginning a highly successful political career and the longest Senate tenure in Montana's history, from 1935 until 1961. Little known outside Butte before 1934, the liberal Senator Murray soon became a favorite both of President Roosevelt and of the progressive farmer-labor groups in Montana. By the late 1930s this "Millionaire Moses" had become one of the most powerful New Dealers in the Senate.

The Democrats scored even greater gains in the Roosevelt landslide of 1936. This time, they won a full six-year term for Murray, the governorship for Roy Ayers, control of the legislature, and, incredibly, every elective administrative office. Both congressional seats went to freshman Democrats, Jerry J. O'Connell in the western district and James F. O'Conner in the east. The Republicans, and conservatives in general, seemed securely buried. Immediately after the 1936 landslide, however, the great New Deal–Democratic majority began to break up. Both in Montana and in the nation at large, the Democratic party split increasingly into liberal and conservative factions, pro- and anti-Roosevelt in their viewpoints. In Montana this breakup ushered in a period of fierce partisanship and crumbling party lines. By the close of the New Deal era, party loyalty—never one of Montana's more abundant resources—was shattered; and the forces of conservatism were once again on the rise.

Open warfare erupted within the Democratic party in 1937, when powerful Senator B. K. Wheeler broke relations with the President over Roosevelt's controversial attempt to "pack" the Supreme Court with friendly judges. Wheeler, who was fast drifting away from his earlier progressivism, effectively led the Senate forces that defeated the Court bill and thus began his famous feud with the President. When F.D.R. visited Fort Peck in October 1937, he snubbed Wheeler and did not even invite him to the occasion. More to the point, the President began to deprive the Montana senator of political patronage and to distribute it instead to other Democratic leaders.

Joined by many Republicans, the more conservative Democrats applauded Wheeler's defiance of the President. But the liberal Democrats of Montana, the farmer-labor groups who had always before supported Wheeler, now began to turn against him. Senator Murray openly feuded with his colleague. And freshman Representative Jerry O'Connell, an outspoken young radical, reported that the President had encouraged him to "go out there and fight like hell to defeat Senator Wheeler's machine so he wouldn't be back in 1940." The fiery O'Connell announced that he would challenge Wheeler for the senate nomination in 1940.

In opposition to Wheeler, to Governor Ayers, and to the conservative interests in the state, the left wing of the Democratic party rose up in open rebellion. Representatives of the American Federation of Labor and the Congress of Industrial Organizations, the Farmers Union, and the unemployed joined hands in 1938 to create the Montana Council for Progressive Political Action. The council was outspokenly liberal and outspokenly opposed to the Company and its allies. A year after its founding, the council supported publication of a reform-minded newspaper, the *People's Voice*, which would carry the liberal banner in Montana for the next three decades. Clearly, here in embryonic form was a potentially ultraliberal farmer-labor party like similar bodies in Minnesota and North Dakota. Once again, as on the eve of World War I, there was thunder on the left in Montana.

Alarmed by these developments, the more conservative Democrats reached out toward alliance with the Republicans. Cleverly, Wheeler and his political allies helped engineer the defeat of Jerry O'Connell when the young Democratic congressman came up for re-election in 1938. Blacked out by the Company press and undercut by the Wheeler Democrats, the firebrand O'Connell lost to an obscure Republican named Jacob Thorkelson, who soon gained nationwide attention for his anti-Semitic views in and out of Congress.

The chaotic campaign of 1940 demonstrated clearly how liberal-conservative factionalism had broken up the New Deal majority. Angrily, the Montana Council for Progressive Political Action, which consisted mainly of liberal Democrats, set out to defeat the more conservative Democrats, especially Senator B. K. Wheeler and Governor Roy Ayers. They succeeded in their drive against Ayers, who lost the election to Republican Sam C. Ford. But they failed to unseat Wheeler in the primary; the tough old warhorse gathered in thousands of Republican votes to win a landslide re-election for a fourth senate term. Aside from electing Ford to the governor's chair, the Republican also made other substantial gains in 1940. They regained control of the state senate and re-elected the antiwar crusader Jeannette Rankin to the House of Representatives.

In the election of 1940, therefore, the Democratic party lost its near monopoly hold over Montana politics, and the era of the New Deal came to a close. Once again, things returned to normal, and the political parties of the Treasure State competed on fairly even terms. The burning issues raised by the New Deal, however, centering on the proper role of government, and spending and taxation—carried into the 1940s and beyond. The New Deal had restored the power of the liberal community in Montana, and it closed in 1938–40 with an incredible scrambling of party lines. Liberal and conservative Democrats parted company, and, by joining hands with the conservative Democrats, the Republicans were able to regain power. This confused political situation would make the next half-dozen years one of the most peculiar times in the history of the state.

WORLD WAR II: A TIME OF CHANGE

Between 1941 and 1945, the Second World War brought enormous social and economic changes to every part of the United States. The war caused massive movements of population, unprecedented prosperity for farmers and ranchers, and the appearance of new industries in most western states. In one way or another all of these trends had a profound impact upon Montana. In Montana as elsewhere, the war years saw a great agricultural boom, resulting both from high wartime demands and prices and from ample rainfall. In 1941 the state enjoyed its best crop year since 1927. The yields of 1942 were the best since World War I, and 1943 was the best year yet seen. Crop values that year surpassed $188 million, and cash income from livestock and livestock products totaled over $134 million. With somewhat lesser yields, these trends continued through 1944–45. Farmers and ranchers prospered; property valuations soared; and operators stepped up their investments in both land and machinery. Between 1940 and 1948 the net cash income of Montana ranchers increased by 188 percent. At long last, prosperity returned to the agricultural regions of Montana. There were fewer farms and ranches now, but those remaining were rapidly growing in size, shifting toward mechanization, and increasing in value and income.

The war also had a strong impact upon Montana industries. Lumber production mounted, as small operators filtered into western Montana from the Pacific Northwest. Soaring demands for minerals quickly intensified the mining of copper and other metals in Butte, revived the coal mining industry in Red Lodge, and shot crude oil production up to roughly eight and one-half million barrels annually by 1944–45. Compared to many other western states, though, Montana's wartime growth seems less than impressive. No great new manufacturing industries came here which could compare with the Geneva Steel Works in Utah or the shipyards, airplane factories, or aluminum mills of Washington. Rather, these heavy, war-born industries tended to cluster around the few urban centers of the region, leaving such rural states as Montana, the Dakotas, and Wyoming without competitive employment. Defense spending did, however, touch Montana directly in 1942, when a large Army Air Corps base was located near Great Falls. This complex installation, today's Malmstrom Air Force Base, remains one of America's major military centers and a vital economic force in Cascade County.

The war caused the most massive, rapid, and hectic population movements in all American history, and these mass migrations touched the Treasure State in contrary ways. Thriving mining and lumbering industries and the high demand for farm labor combined to lure thousands of restless Americans into the state. At the same time, though, the armed services and high paying defense industries, especially those on the Pacific Coast, drew tens of thousands of young Montanans away. Just as in the First World War, military enlistments and the draft took disproportionately high numbers of Montana youths. Roughly forty thousand were in uniform by 1942, about the same number as had served in the earlier war. And as before, many of these would never return.

The booming war industries of the Pacific Northwest and California drew away even more Montanans than did the military. As John Gunther noted at the time, why should men work for $7.75 per day in the dangerous underground mines of Butte when they could make $14.00 per shift rolling aluminum at Spokane or riveting B-17 bombers at Seattle? Population estimates showed the results. From a 1940 total of 559,456, Montana's population fell, according to estimates based on the issuance of wartime ration cards, to about 470,000 in 1943. Of course, this population decline later reversed itself when the veterans came home and new job opportunities opened up after the war's end. But surely no other period, not even the gold, copper, or homestead boom eras, ever witnessed such drastic population shifts in Montana as did World War II. One is still reminded of this fact by the thousands of Montanans who recall their arrival here in wartime, or by the tens of thousands who wistfully attend "Montana Day" picnics in Los Angeles, San Francisco, Seattle, and Spokane.

The war years were a curious and confusing time in Montana's political history. As in most other states, the forces of New Deal liberalism lost ground here to a reviving conservatism. In Montana this trend was complicated by the incredible scrambling of party lines that resulted from the 1940 election. State government, in effect, came to be dominated during the war by an informal alliance of moderately conservative Republicans, who were led by Governor Sam C. "Model T" Ford, and conservative Democrats led by Senator Burton K. Wheeler. Despite their differing party labels, Wheeler and Ford were old political friends. Both had broken into politics years ago as outspoken liberals, and both had drifted to the right as the years passed by. In Joseph Kinsey Howard's view, both seemed to be "tired radicals" by the 1940s.

This precarious bipartisan alliance between Governor Ford, Senator Wheeler, and their powerful and wealthy Republican ally Wellington Rankin was open and effective. Two well known Democratic friends of Wheeler, J. Burke Clements and Barclay Craighead, presided respectively over the Montana Industrial Accident Board and the Montana Unemployment Compensation Commission under Republican Governor Ford. But, despite charges of a Wheeler-Ford-Rankin "axis" or "triumvirate," this arrangement never really amounted to a genuine political "machine." It was, rather, an alliance of convenience; and critics from both the right and the left attacked it. Republican National Committeeman Dan Whetstone, a conservative and intelligent newspaper publisher from Cut Bank, hotly criticized Ford for passing out political jobs to Wheeler Democrats. And the liberal Democrats, led by Senator Murray and the ultraliberal Montana Council for Progressive Political Action, thundered at both Ford and Wheeler from the left.

Through the end of the war, neither conservative Republicans nor liberal Democrats were able to break up the Ford-Wheeler-Rankin alliance. The most formidable challenge came in the gubernatorial election campaign of 1944, when liberal Democrat Leif Erickson ran against Ford in a heated, free-swinging contest. The hottest issue of 1944 involved the proposal for a Missouri Valley Authority, sponsored by Senator Murray and the Roosevelt Administration. Patterned after the Tennessee Valley Authority, the Missouri Valley Authority looked toward a massive federal development of the Missouri Basin based upon a series of dams built to provide public power, reclamation, and flood control. Erickson and the liberal Democrats pushed the M.V.A., while Ford and the conservatives opposed it. In the end Ford won re-election, and the controversial M.V.A. bill later died in congressional committee.

Like Ford, Wheeler also faced mounting opposition from the left. Following his landslide re-election in 1940, the shrewd old senator seemed unbeatable. He rose to new heights of worldwide fame as an isolationist critic of Roosevelt's foreign policy, claiming that the President was steering the country toward involvement in another war. Early in 1941, while speaking against F.D.R.'s Lend-Lease Bill, Wheeler made his oft-quoted remark denouncing Lend-Lease as "the New Deal's triple-A foreign policy; it will plow under every fourth American boy." Deeply angered, Roosevelt publicly replied: "That is really the rottenest thing that has been said in public life in my generation."

Until our entry into the war late in 1941, Wheeler's popularity and political power remained impressive. Representatives O'Connor and Rankin, as well as Governor Ford, were his friends and allies. But the bombs which fell on Pearl Harbor undercut Senator Wheeler's position, for the old isolationists now found themselves in an untenable situation. The liberal farmer-labor groups, who had always backed Wheeler until his break with Roosevelt, increasingly turned against him as he moved to the right. When Wheeler ran for renomination to a fifth senate term in the 1946 primary, he confounded most observers, including himself, by losing to his liberal opponent Leif Erickson, the same man who had lost to Ford in 1944. Generally speaking, two factors caused Wheeler's defeat. His outspoken isolationism cost him the votes of many veterans and their families; and his drift to the right turned the liberals, especially the labor unions, against him.

The 1946 defeat of B. K. Wheeler truly marked the end of a political era in Montana. Wheeler was the last of those old-style progressives who had cut their political teeth on battling the Anaconda. By 1946 both the Company and Wheeler had changed. The young progressive had become an elderly conservative. It is both interesting and illuminating that Wheeler entered Montana politics nicknamed "Bolshevik Burt," and that a quarter-century later he exited under attack as "America's Number One Fascist." Neither label was accurate, but, taken together, they signaled his passage from the left to the right side of the political spectrum. With his departure, a certain element of vigor and controversy disappeared from Montana's political life. For, as his biographer Richard Ruetten has noted, no man, before or since, ever wielded such political power in Montana as did Burton K. Wheeler.

CHAPTER XIII

The Modern Montana Economy: 1920–75

O VER the past half century Montana's fragile economy has become increasingly stable and diversified, in other words more healthy. When measured by national standards, though, the state's economic growth seems much less impressive. Montana, like other states of the agricultural West, languished in depression throughout most of the 1920s and 1930s. Then the Second World War ushered in a period of unprecedented prosperity, enduring into the early 1950s. Since that time, the economy has expanded, but only in uneven cycles of growth and decline. Although the hard times of the terrible 1930s have never returned, the economy of Montana, in comparison to that of most other states, has grown at a snail's pace. The basic historical explanation of this sluggish growth rate is simple enough: those two traditional mainstays of the Montana economy, agriculture and metal mining, have sharply declined in employment since the 1920s. Meanwhile, such new growth areas as lumber, petroleum, tourism, and government employment have risen only slowly to fill the gap left by the erosion of these two static industries. Montana still relies heavily upon unpredictable extractive industries, and it still lacks major manufacturing. For these reasons it continues to lag behind most other states in employment and prosperity. Let us first turn our attention to agriculture and mining, those age-old Montana livelihoods, and then turn to the major growth industries of recent years.

TRENDS IN AGRICULTURE

Following the collapse of Northern Plains agriculture during the depression of 1918–22, Montana's farmers and ranchers faced a dismal future. Low farm prices and recurring droughts drove many of them from the land and punished those who stayed throughout the twenties and the "dirty thirties." The long road back to agricultural prosperity would demand major readjustments. It would require moving toward bigger land units, mechanizing operations, experimenting with new scientific methods, and inevitably it would require aid from the federal government. Most dramatically, the road back to prosperity would force the abandonment of thousands of small homesteads: in the future, fewer and fewer operators would work larger and larger farms and ranches.

The hard times of the twenties and thirties prompted both farmers and stockmen to experiment with and to adapt new techniques. Beginning in the 1920s, those local farmers who could afford it began to mechanize their operations in a big way. Small, internally geared gasoline tractors appeared in large numbers by the mid-1920s, and by 1930 nineteen thousand of them were at work on fourteen thousand Montana farms. Trucks came into common use at roughly this same time, as did the mobile, tractor-drawn grain combines. These complex and expensive machines, and others like them, revolutionized farming and vastly increased the acreage that one man could work efficiently.

Increasingly, Montana farmers diversified their operations, combining wheat production with the raising of other crops like barley or irrigated hay and sugar beets. Many grain growers converted to the so-called "combination farms," which joined crop farming with the raising of livestock. Summer fallowing, or alternate year cropping, came into more and more general use as a method of building up moisture and fertility in the soil. In order to combat the wind and soil erosion that resulted from intensive cultivation and summer fallowing, farm experts of the 1920s advocated a clod mulch, developed by such implements as rod weeders and duckfoot cultivators. By the 1930s this system was being supplanted by a "trashy fallow," prepared with the Noble Blade and other implements. From Canadian experiments, local farmers adapted such effective techniques as strip cropping and contouring fields in order to cope with wind erosion. During the "Dust Bowl" years of the windblown 1930s, many of them planted long rows of trees, or "shelterbelts," to blunt the knifing, highly destructive winds. They found that new drought-resistant types of wheat, such as the Ceres, Yogo, Winalta, and Cheyenne varieties, made dry land farming much safer than it once had been.

Interestingly, Montanans of those years pioneered in many types of agrarian reform. Some of the above mentioned innovations were sponsored by the Montana Extension Service and the Agricultural Experiment Station at Montana State College in Bozeman. M. L. Wilson of the Extension Service, an intelligent and likable agricultural economist, gathered together a unique and fascinating group of young scientists, economists, and county extension agents. By using such imaginative techniques as "farm success" studies and the "Fairway Farms" project, which set up experimental farms around the state, Wilson and his associates generated ideas that gained nationwide prominence. In Teton County, meanwhile, Robert Clarkson, Otto Wagnild, and their neighbors worked out a land classification–tax assessment program that contributed greatly to unified county planning across the state and region. And in Phillips County a group of grass roots planners developed the famous "Malta Plan," America's first "resettlement program" of retiring submarginal farm lands and relocating the impoverished families who had been working them.

Throughout the dry and depressed years between the two world wars, ranchers faced the same basic problems as did the farmers. They too staggered under the burden of low commodity prices and found that they must adapt more efficient and scientific methods. During the 1920s the rising nationwide demand for younger beef led Great Plains ranchers to move increasingly onto a "calf crop basis" and to market their animals at the age of only two years. More and more Montana ranchers sold their stock to midwestern feedlots for finishing instead of keeping it, as before, on range pastures until maturity. At the same time the breakup of the great central beef markets in Chicago led to the establishment of local auction markets throughout the midwestern and far western regions. Montana's first permanent livestock auction market appeared at Billings in 1924. By mid-century ten such markets operated in the state, and over half of the Montana cattle sold each year passed through the local markets. Since the 1950s many area ranchers, especially the larger operators, have turned to contract sales, through which they deal directly with meat processors.

Although Montana ranchers learned early in the game that they must put up hay for winter feeding, their most persistent problems still centered upon the range—how to control and manage it. The homestead movement had severely damaged much of the best range land, and it had broken up ownership patterns and driven up land prices. Ranchers throughout the West concluded from their experience that leasing range land, from either public or private owners, usually made more sense than buying it at high costs. In this field as in so many others, Montanans, compelled by hardship, pioneered new techniques.

In 1928 a group of southeastern Montana ranchers, cooperating with the federal and state governments and the railroads, created America's first "cooperative grazing district." Forming the Mizpah–Pumpkin Creek Grazing Association, these stockmen joined together in taking a lease on over one hundred thousand acres of Rosebud and Custer county range land, which was owned by both public and private interests. Carefully controlling the number of animals allowed on the range, the grazers soon restored it to full productivity. Clearly, the Mizpah–Pumpkin Creek Project was a stunning success: it proved the feasibility of leasing public lands to stockmen who organized grazing districts. In 1933 the Montana Legislature provided for the general formation of grazing districts. And in 1934 the United States Congress passed the Taylor Grazing Act which, based on this Montana precedent, began the entire modern practice of leasing federally owned range lands to stockmen.

The Great Depression and the droughts of the 1930s proved, if nothing else, that agriculture could never hope to solve the problems of overproduction and low farm prices without federal aid. Beginning in 1933 with President Roosevelt's New Deal program, farmers and ranchers began to receive massive federal assistance for the first time in American history. As noted earlier, the Agricultural Adjustment Act of 1933 and later legislation paid farmers to withdraw land from production. These laws were based on the complex "domestic allotment" plan, which had been pushed for years by M. L. Wilson and other agricultural reformers, and they poured millions of dollars into depressed Montana.

Under the New Deal, Montana agriculture also received many other forms of federal assistance. Beginning in 1938, the federal government placed in effect a system of "price support" payments in order to maintain fair ("parity") prices for wheat and other commodities. Various federal agencies refinanced farm loans, subsidized the building of electrical lines into rural areas, eradicated such pests as groundhogs and gophers, bought up surplus livestock in order to provide meat for the unemployed, and helped to restore the range. With federal assistance, roughly 1,500,000 Montana acres were reseeded with nutritious crested wheat-grass by 1941. Federal monies also helped the State Water Conservation Board build dozens of dams and storage reservoirs across the length and breadth of Montana. Later, after World War II, the Bureau of Reclamation and other agencies would develop such major projects as Canyon Ferry and Yellowtail dams, which would provide further aid to agriculture. By 1940, whether they liked it or not, farmers and ranchers of the Treasure State had come to rely heavily indeed upon their Uncle Sam.

Although the New Deal programs provided invaluable support, real prosperity returned to the farm only with the high food prices and abundant rainfall that came during the Second World War, 1941–45. On the one hand, the war pulled away many badly needed farm workers, and it hurt the labor-intensive sheep industry badly. Generally speaking, though, it brought vastly increased profits to those who had held on through the Depression. High food prices and generous federal price supports kept Montana's farm prosperity going for several years after the war's end. Booming new food markets on the West Coast, especially in California, gave the agricultural economy of Montana a further boost. By 1946 California led all other states in consumption of Montana beef. Finally, in the early fifties, the great wartime and postwar boom began to level off.

Over the past quarter century, rising and falling prices and alternating wet and dry cycles have combined to make Montana agriculture, as always, an unpredictable livelihood. Amidst the bountiful years of 1950, 1951, 1958, and 1966 came the poor ones of 1954, 1959, and 1961. Never, though, have things fallen apart as they did during the 1930s. Federal aid, in such forms as price supports, food purchase programs, and soil conservation payments, has served to stabilize the business. More importantly, so have the ever increasing mechanization and scientific management of Treasure State farms and ranches.

Many modern-day visitors are surprised at the extent to which agriculture is diversified in Montana. They find that some local stockgrowers specialize in sheep or hogs rather than cattle. Dairy farms dot the floors of the high mountain valleys; cherry orchards beautify the shores of Flathead Lake; irrigated crops of sugar beets, corn, and hay ripen along the river bottoms. And barley, of both the malting and feed varieties, is a major cash crop, worth nearly ninety-four million dollars in cash receipts during 1973 and accounting for almost 9 percent of Montana's total farm income.

The striking trend of Montana's agricultural economy since World War II, however, is not diversification. Quite the contrary, it is concentration upon the production of two major commodities—wheat and beef. Combined, these two products total roughly three-fourths of most years' farm marketings. With few exceptions, those Montana operations not specializing either in wheat or in cattle are isolated, small, or in decline. Beaten down by nationwide and worldwide competition, the local production and processing of fruit and vegetables has eroded badly and nearly vanished altogether from many areas, like the Gallatin Valley, where it used to thrive. Sugar beets, although still an important Montana commodity, have given way in many areas to hay crops or corn. Most of the state's old beet-sugar refineries, like its old breweries, are now closed. And the state's once mighty sheep industry, oppressed by declining markets for lamb and wool, by predators, and by rising labor costs, contributed less than 3 percent to total farm income in 1973. By the mid-1970s fewer than nine hundred thousand sheep grazed on Montana pastures, compared to four million during the 1930s. While some signs of diversification seem promising —such as the production of seed potatoes, honey, and especially hogs —wheat and beef rule supreme in Montana agriculture.

Montana's expansive, modern wheat and barley farms are truly "factories in the field," which bear little resemblance to the homesteads of sixty years ago. Riding in air-conditioned cabs atop huge and highly expensive four-wheel-drive tractors and self-propelled combines, today's farmers can work incredibly large tracts of land with few or no hired hands to help them. Synthetic fertilizers, highly effective pesticides, and new varieties of drought- and rust-resistant grain have all added greatly to the quality, quantity, and dependability of production. As always, Montana's high-protein spring and winter wheat fares very well in national and international markets. In more recent years it has moved increasingly toward markets in Asia, especially in Japan. By the seventies well over one-half of the state's wheat crop flowed into the export trade, and a new barge port at Lewiston, Idaho, promised to ease the passage of grain to seaports on the north Pacific Coast.

Similarly, Montana's cattle ranches are far more sophisticated and specialized outfits than most people suspect. Some ranchers specialize in production of breeding stock, but most produce calves and finished animals for market. There are cow-calf and cow-calf-yearling ranchers who sell their animals at ages under two years, other ranchers who market more mature steers and heifers, and still others who buy young stock and graze it for varying periods before sale. Of course, many operators combine some or all of these functions. Traditionally, most Montana cattle have been shipped for finishing to out-of-state feedlots, especially those in the Midwest. Since the 1950s, though, in-state feedlots have increased in size and number. Marketings of Montana-fed cattle rose from 100,000 head in 1962 to 247,000 head in 1972. But, since that 1972 total represents only 1 percent of the national marketings of fed cattle, the Montana feedlot business obviously has a long way to go.

During the past few years Montana agriculture has witnessed some spectacularly abrupt changes—widespread droughts in 1972–74, followed by abundant rains in 1975, sky-high grain and cattle prices beginning in 1972–73, followed by declining prices and a terrible cost-squeeze upon grain-fed cattle. Even allowing for the effects of inflation, agriculture has generally prospered during the 1970s. Total cash receipts from the marketing of Montana farm commodities climbed from $603,154,000 in 1970 to $823,816,000 in 1972 to $1,074,079,000 in 1973. In 1974 and especially in the bountiful year of 1975, wheat farmers prospered while many cattlemen stood severe losses due to the rising price of feed and the sagging price of fattened beef. Montana agriculture today faces a number of serious problems, such as unstable prices, the uncertainties of the livestock industry, and the spreading appearance of the dangerous "saline seep," which is salinating and ruining thousands of acres of agricultural land. But there are many bright signs on the horizon, too: unprecedented prosperity for wheat farmers, booming export markets in Japan and elsewhere, and new access to water transportation on the Snake and Columbia rivers, among others.

Agriculture is today, as it has been since the early years of this century, Montana's "number one industry." Beyond dispute, agriculture lies at the heart of the state's economy, providing not only its largest cash income, but also the marketing base for dozens of towns and cities. Yet, in Montana as elsewhere, mechanization and concentration have robbed agriculture of both population and social influence. Gone are the tens of thousands of farm workers who once sacked wheat, pitched hay, or dug sugar beets. Gone are most of the small "family farms" that were the dream of Jim Hill. Between 1920 and 1974, as the size of an average agricultural unit climbed from 608 acres to 2,510 acres, the total number of farms and ranches decreased amazingly from 57,677 to only 26,400. In 1920, 82,000 Montanans found employment in agriculture. By 1970, this total had dropped to a mere 36,100.

These cold, heartless figures tell us much about what has happened to Montana over the past half century. While agriculture has stabilized and generally prospered, paradoxically, it has also lost population and strength relative to other livelihoods. Agriculture is less the style-setter and pace-setter of Montana than it used to be. As families leave the farm, the small towns that grew up to serve them inevitably lose population, too. Following a trend that began about 1920, rural Montana anxiously watches its people, especially its young people, move away to the cities. That beautiful dream of sixty years ago—of building a rural commonwealth based on the small family farm—is forever lost, a victim of "progress."

THE DECLINING ROLE OF METAL MINING

Much like agriculture, metal mining has fallen sharply in employment and influence since 1920. Sixty years ago, the mining of copper, the Anaconda Copper Mining Company, and the city of Butte dominated the economic, social, and political life of the state. The Anaconda, having crushed and absorbed most of its competition, controlled the "Richest Hill on Earth" and relied upon Butte's underground mines as its main source of copper. Anaconda, of course, had interests reaching well beyond Butte. It also had smelters, refineries, and reduction works at Anaconda, East Helena, and Great Falls, hundreds of thousands of acres of western Montana timberland, lumber mills at Bonner, a powerful chain of newspapers, and many other investments. And not to be forgotten, the "Company" also had a robust "Siamese twin," the Montana Power Company.

The Montana Power Company took shape in 1912 when John D. Ryan, president of the Amalgamated Copper Company (Anaconda after 1915), merged several small hydroelectric plants, most of them located along the Great Falls of the Missouri, into one large firm. Ryan, a capable and hard-boiled man, wanted to sell power both to his giant Anaconda and to the Milwaukee Railroad, of which he was a director. Although the energetic Ryan served as president of both Anaconda and Montana Power until his death in 1933, the utility was never really an Anaconda subsidiary. Ownership of Montana Power passed in 1928 to an eastern holding company, American Power and Light, and in 1950 to individual stockholders throughout the country. Despite this loose corporate connection, Montanans often referred to Anaconda–Montana Power as simply "the Company"—and with good reason. For twenty years the two firms were joined at the head, like Siamese twins, under the presidency of John Ryan. And for many years thereafter, they shared the same legal, political, and publicity staffs. Combined, the two corporations formed a political team of awesome strength.

During its heyday, from 1900 until the 1940s, the Anaconda Company wielded such enormous power in the state that Montana gained the unenviable reputation of being little more than a corporate asset. In the mid-1940s, for instance, John Gunther wrote these famous words in his *Inside U.S.A.:* "Anaconda, a company aptly named, certainly has a constrictorlike grip on much that goes on, and Montana is the nearest to a 'colony' of any American state, Delaware alone possibly excepted. . . ." In truth, however, for all its naked power and all its heavy-handed manipulation of state politics, Anaconda never literally ran Montana. It shared and contested power with other interest groups, and, like any other corporation, it changed with the changing times.

Beginning in the 1920s, Anaconda's role in Montana subtly started to change, and eventually to recede. Under the ambitious direction of John Ryan and his close associate Cornelius Kelley, Anaconda, like so many American corporations of the twenties, launched a major program of expansion. In 1922 the Company bought control of the Connecticut-based American Brass Company, the world's greatest producer of brass. Brass, of course, is a copper alloy; and this purchase made Anaconda, which was already the leading copper producer, into the world's leading copper fabricator as well. The all-important acquisition of American Brass allowed Anaconda to stabilize copper sales and production. In 1929–30 the firm created another fabricating subsidiary, the Anaconda Wire and Cable Company, with plants at Great Falls and other locations outside the state.

The Company's move into brass obviously increased its appetite for copper. Since Butte's complex underground mines involved high labor and operating costs, Ryan and "Con" Kelley began a search for new, cheaper sources of the red metal. These were the years when the mining industry was turning heavily toward the open pit removal of low grade ores with enormous earth-moving equipment, a much cheaper method than working high grade deposits through underground tunnels. In 1923 Anaconda negotiated the purchase of the world's greatest copper ore bodies, the holdings of the Guggenheim family in the towering Andes Mountains of Chile. For these mines, especially the fabulously rich open pit at Chuquicamata,

Anaconda paid seventy-seven million dollars, the largest cash transfer that Wall Street had ever seen. Chuquicamata and its sister mines in Chile soon became Anaconda's prime sources of copper. They came to produce two-thirds of its primary copper and three-fourths of its earnings. The Anaconda expanded in other areas, too. It bought up the remaining Montana properties of the late W. A. Clark in 1928 and completed its acquisition of the valuable Green Cananea Copper Company of northern Mexico in 1929.

Anaconda's spectacular expansion had a profound impact upon the state of its birth, for now Montana was only one province in a far-flung corporate empire. Oftentimes, when storm clouds would gather on the political horizon in Montana, rumors would circulate that the Company might shut down its high cost Butte operation altogether and turn exclusively to its more profitable Latin American mines. Fears of a total Anaconda pullout lifted dramatically in 1947, however, when Con Kelley announced his "Greater Butte Project," a multi-million dollar program aimed at extracting low grade ores by a method of underground blasting called "block-caving." In the words of *Forbes* Magazine, the project turned out to be a "costly bust"; and within a few years it gave way to the open pit mining of copper, a development that had earlier seemed impossible since it meant blasting away large parts of the city itself.

Open pit mining has literally transformed the city of Butte. As the huge Berkeley Pit relentlessly deepens and widens, it eats constantly away at the old uptown area of the city. Residents and businessmen flee, meanwhile, toward the "Flats," south of town. Steadily, over the past two decades, the expensive underground mines have closed down, and the colorful old hardrock miners are fast becoming extinct. Open pit mining, which is highly automated, requires far fewer employees than does underground mining. Thus Butte, once the economic and political hub of the state, has seen its population and political power base crumble steadily away. Gradually, almost imperceptibly, the Company's shadow over Montana grew smaller and smaller. Anaconda's one wholly new commitment to the state after World War II was its aluminum operation, based locally at Columbia Falls and Great Falls, which opened in 1955.

Not surprisingly, as Anaconda diversified and expanded into a global corporation, and as the old lieutenants of Marcus Daly passed from the scene, the firm began to inch away from the iron-fisted political methods of the past. Even as early as the 1930s, younger executives like W. H. Hoover and the talented lobbyist and public relations man Al Wilkinson started pushing the Company toward a more restrained approach. Following the retirement of Cornelius Kelley, who reportedly clung to the old ways until the end, changes came rapidly. Anaconda sold its newspapers, at long last, in 1959. Equally important, the Company drifted farther and farther away from its once intimate cooperation with the Montana Power Company. By the late 1960s Anaconda bore little resemblance to the fiery dragon of yesteryear. It acted instead like most other extractive corporations in most other western states—lobbying quietly for its interests in Helena, advertising to win public favor, and stewing about tough new pollution standards. Anaconda had entered the twentieth century.

The seventies have been cruel to the Anaconda Company. In 1971 the firm suffered a staggering blow when the leftist government of Chile seized and nationalized its invaluable mines there, without compensation. As a result of this debacle, Anaconda declared a net loss of $357.3 million for 1971. Suddenly, as one observer put it, the corporation had passed "From Riches to Rags" and was now fighting for its very life. A tough-minded banker, John B. M. Place, took over the presidency of the wounded Anaconda and began slashing overhead in a desperate attempt to bring the Company within its reduced means.

Loss of its Chilean properties forced Anaconda to rely more heavily upon domestic mines in Montana, Arizona, Nevada, and elsewhere. At the same time, however, the firm's critical need to cut expenses led to dramatic shutdowns of some costly old operations in Montana. The zinc operation, based at Great Falls and Anaconda, received the axe; and, in a move of great importance, Anaconda gave up its lumber operation entirely. In mid-1972 Place engineered the sale of Anaconda's lumber division, including 670,500 acres of Montana forest land, to Champion International for a price of $117 million. The most sweeping cuts began in the mid-1970s. In December 1974 Anaconda announced the termination of roughly seven hundred to a thousand Butte area jobs. Soon afterward, in February 1975, the even more devastating word arrived that fifteen hundred more layoffs would follow. These shattering job losses, amounting to nearly one-third of Anaconda's Montana payroll, resulted mainly from the phasing out of the last of the underground mines, as well as the old ore concentrator and foundry at Anaconda and the recently begun Continental-East open pit mine at Butte.

All of this, naturally, holds much significance for Montana's present and future. Absorption of Anaconda by another corporation looms as a possibility, and so does the threat of further cutbacks. The long-term trends of Anaconda withdrawal, erosion of metal mining employment, and the loss of population and political power from Butte all seem likely to continue into the future.

Undeniably, the losses in mining employment cause severe problems for Butte and for the state at large. The Montana economy today, though, is much healthier than in days of old, when it relied so heavily upon one unstable industry. And, of course, the political climate is much more free and open today than in those incredible times when one large company controlled much of the press and dominated affairs of state in Helena.

LABOR

Union labor and metal mining grew up together in Montana, and for many years the well organized Butte-Anaconda miners and smeltermen formed the hard core of union power in the state. By 1912 a local writer could describe Butte, with a semblance of truth, as "the strongest union town on earth." A two-member chimney-sweeps' union enjoyed recognition at Butte, and unions there once threatened to boycott the cemetery unless the lone gravedigger won his demands. As seen previously, the turmoil surrounding World War I broke the power of the Butte Miners' Union. From 1914 until 1934, the open shop prevailed at Butte and the unions stagnated, as they did throughout much of the country during those years.

In Montana and throughout the nation, the Roosevelt New Deal of the 1930s sparked a massive resurgence of union strength. Such New Deal laws as the National Labor Relations Act directly encouraged and supported unionization. Suddenly, in response to government encouragement as well as to local stirrings, Butte labor sprang back to life once again. During the summer of 1933, the Montana State Federation of Labor, led by its fiery president, Jimmy Graham, kicked off a high geared organizational drive. The International Union of Mine, Mill and Smelter Workers, successor to the old Western Federation of Miners, spearheaded a mighty effort to revitalize the nearly dormant Butte Miners' Union. In a July 9 rally at the Fox Theatre in Butte, organizers signed up twenty-three hundred miners. By July 20 they had forty-five hundred new members.

The main challenge facing the "Mine, Mill" organization, its Butte Miners' Union local, and the related smelting and crafts unions was to gain recognition and to win a favorable contract from the Anaconda Copper Mining Company. Negotiations between the Company and the unions dragged on until May 8, 1934, and then broke up, leading to the most important strike in Montana's history. Over sixty-five hundred Mine, Mill and crafts unionists walked off the job. Once again tension polarized the mining city as company guards and labor organizers, some of them radicals, lined up against one another. Although many predicted violence, both sides worked to avoid it. The great strike of 1934 continued for four months, then finally ended on September 17 in a major union victory. Anaconda granted the striking unions a wage increase, a forty-hour work week, and, most important of all, full recognition. After twenty years of impotence, Butte labor had regained the "closed shop."

After the 1934 strike, the older, established American Federation of Labor locals in Montana steadily expanded their membership and political power. New unions, like the United Cannery Workers and the International Sheep Shearers, sprang up to join them. The most important and powerful of all Montana unions, of course, was the Butte Miners' Union affiliate of the Mine, Mill and Smelter Workers. During 1937–38, Mine, Mill joined nine other nationwide unions to form the militant Congress of Industrial Organizations. Throughout the 1930s and into the 1940s, unions affiliated with both the American Federation of Labor and the Congress of Industrial Organizations rose to new heights of economic and political power in Montana.

The Montana miners and smeltermen, though, fell upon hard times after World War II. Cutbacks in underground mining cost them many jobs, and their union became embroiled in controversy. After determining that Communists had gained considerable influence among the leadership of the Mine, Mill and Smelter Workers Union, the C.I.O. expelled that organization from its ranks in 1950. The C.I.O. then gave jurisdiction over the metal miners, smeltermen, and refinery workers to one of its largest unions, the United Steelworkers of America. In Montana, however, the mineworkers refused to part with their old union. The vast majority of them were obviously not Communists, and they cared less about such charges than about loyalty to the union of their fathers. For years the C.I.O. and the Steelworkers hammered away at the Mine, Mill locals in Butte, Anaconda, East Helena, and Great Falls. Finally, through a 1967 merger agreement, the Steelworkers in effect absorbed and took over the local affiliates of the once-mighty Mine, Mill Union.

Over the past thirty years, as the mining unions steadily declined in membership, a series of strikes periodically shut down the Montana mining industry, hitting Butte-Anaconda and indeed the entire state with severe jolts. A major strike began in April 1946, calling out seven thousand men in four Montana cities. Violence erupted at Butte when bands of men, women, and children sacked the homes of nonunion "scab" workers. Strikes followed in a rhythmic pattern thereafter, in 1954, 1959–60, and 1962. Finally, the last major copper strike—in fact, the longest and costliest strike in the state's history—took place in 1967–68. The Steelworkers stayed out for eight and one-half months, and in wages alone Montanans lost thirty-four million dollars.

As the mine, smelter, and refinery workers' unions eroded in membership and influence after World War II, other unions have quietly grown up to take their place. For many years two powerful union groups, the Railroad Brotherhoods and the United Mine Workers, have wielded formidable strength in certain areas of the state. Although drastic cuts in railroad employment have thinned the ranks of the Rail Brotherhoods, they still figure largely in the politics of such railroad towns as Deer Lodge, Havre, Livingston, and Laurel. Declining demand for coal robbed the United Mine Workers of many members after the war, but the union held on in the Treasure State. Indeed, one of the Montana U.M.W. officers, Tony Boyle, rose to the national presidency of the union—and to controversy in the headlines. Now, the resurgence of coal mining is creating once again a large work force of unionized shovel operators, carriers, and laborers in this industry.

During the three decades since the end of World War II, Montana unions have markedly increased their membership and influence. Older, established organizations like the Retail Clerks have been joined by fast risers, such as the Teamsters; the State, County and Municipal Employees; and the teachers' groups. Today, the Montana A.F.L-C.I.O., headquartered at Helena, has some 32,600 members, roughly 60 percent of the unionized employees in the state. Carpenters are the largest group by trade, and the biggest locals are the Operating Engineers at Helena; the Lumber, Production and Industrial Workers at Kalispell; and the Pulp, Sulphite and Paper Millworkers at Missoula. Organized labor wields impressive political power at both the local and state levels in Montana. Led by the A.F.L.-C.I.O., the unions are undoubtedly the key liberal force in state politics and the most potent supporter of the Democratic Party.

LUMBER, OIL, AND COAL

Three "extractive" industries—lumber, oil, and coal—have expanded over the past twenty-five years to take up the slack left by eroding employment in agriculture, metal mining, and railroading. Each of these resource industries holds real growth potential for the future. On the other hand, though, each of them is fluctuating and unsteady, wavering with the slightest shifts in the national and world economy. And each of them, in its own way, poses a threat to the fragile air, water, and land environment of the state.

Of course, the lumber industry is as old as Montana itself. Frontier lumbermen, serving mainly the scattered mining camps, cut timber wherever they found or needed it. Big-time lumbering came with the railroad and industrial mining booms of the 1880s. The Missoula-based firm of Eddy, Hammond and Company handled lucrative contracts for the Northern Pacific. In partnership with the railroad and with Marcus Daly, this powerful firm later formed the Montana Improvement Company to supply local rail and mining demands. As seen earlier, the Montana Improvement Company and its partners soon found themselves in difficult straits as a result of timber cutting on public lands. During the 1890s the Great Northern

Railroad completed its construction program, and Jim Hill's lowered freight rates allowed Montana lumber to penetrate markets in the Midwest and the East.

In order to satisfy its voracious appetite for construction timber and fuel, the Anaconda Copper Mining Company eventually went directly into the lumber business itself. By 1910 the firm had acquired over one million acres of timberland. With its operations centered at the company town of Bonner, east of Missoula, Anaconda was the largest wood producer in Montana. The state's lumber industry assumed its classic posture during the first four decades of this century. Production was irregular and small by national standards, usually totaling only 250 million to 400 million board feet per year, roughly 1 percent of the national output. A few large concerns, mainly Anaconda at Bonner, the Great Northern's Somers Lumber Company near Kalispell, and the J. Neils Company at Libby, cut most of the timber logged in Montana, supplemented by a scattering of smaller outfits. Until the close of World War II, the industry showed little growth. In 1939 lumber and wood products employed only 2,676 workers.

Until comparatively recent times, lumbering in Montana and elsewhere was a frightfully wasteful business. Today's hikers find reminders of this fact every time they come upon the abandoned burners, collapsing buildings, and ravaged hillsides where a "cut-out and get-out" logging camp once stood. Montanans, like most other westerners, were slow to grasp the need for forest conservation. Many of them howled in anger when President Theodore Roosevelt withdrew huge tracts of federal timberlands and placed them in National Forest Reserves during 1901–9. More than any other event, the terrible forest fire of August 1910 convinced local folks of the environmental dangers facing them. This calamitous blaze, whipped by seventy-mile-per-hour winds, devastated the Idaho-Montana border country, killed eighty firefighters, destroyed much of Wallace, Idaho, and several small towns in Montana, and consumed three million acres of timberland. Smoke from the fire reddened the sun at Denver and Kansas City. As the years went by, the local majority came to realize that the National Forests are really an invaluable resource, where timber can be harvested as a renewable crop, watersheds can be protected, forest fires curbed, and where man and beast can find a sanctuary. The federal government now owns nearly 12,000,000 of Montana's 17,300,000 acres of forest land.

Montana's lumber industry grew dramatically during and especially after World War II. The increased nationwide demand for wood during the great postwar building boom could not be fully supplied by the prime timber stands of the West Coast and Great Lakes. Montana's great forests of fir, spruce, and lodgepole and ponderosa pine, hitherto of generally marginal value, now attracted more and more loggers. By 1948 there were 434 mills, most of them small, working in the state. Employment in the wood products industry shot upward, to 5,374 in 1950 and to 7,150 in 1955. The boom decreased during the later 1950s, and many of the smaller operators closed down. By this time, however, newer and more momentous trends were emerging. Big-time investors began to appear from the outside, and with them came a truly diversified wood products industry.

In 1957 the Hoerner Boxes and Waldorf Paper Products companies opened a large pulp mill west of Missoula. This operation steadily enlarged over the next several years, and in 1966 the owners merged into the Hoerner-Waldorf Company of Montana. Hoerner-Waldorf's pulp and paper enterprise brought hundreds of new jobs to the Missoula area and helped make that city *the* Montana boom town of the 1960s. The firm also helped stabilize operations for the dozens of mills that regularly supply it with wood chips and fuel. Unfortunately, the plant also contributed heavily to an air pollution problem that gained nationwide attention for Missoula and aroused many of its citizens to demonstrations of anger. Local women formed an organization known as G. A. S. P.—Gals Against Smog Pollution. By the seventies a major effort was under way to clean up the smog problem at Missoula.

During the sixties and seventies the wood products industry, based mainly at Missoula and Libby and in the Flathead Valley, continued to expand and diversify. The manufacturing of particle board and formaldehyde began at Missoula; and veneer mills, new and larger plywood plants, and other finished or semifinished products operations began to appear at various locations. Christmas tree growers did well in the Flathead Valley, and pole producers increased their cutting and processing in those many areas of Montana that grow lodgepole pine.

The diversified lumber and wood products industry is now Montana's leading manufacturing enterprise, employing roughly eight thousand to ten thousand workers by the seventies. As always, lumbering is surrounded by controversy; in recent years, environmentalists have severely criticized the Forest Service for its clear cutting and land exchange policies. And as always, the local lumber industry depends heavily upon federal resource policy and responds quickly to national building trends. Recession and construction slumps have recently delivered two successive blows to the industry, the first in 1969–71, and the second hitting with severe force in 1974–75. Wood products mean much to western Montana, but the instability and environmental hazards of the business can cause serious problems.

Oil production began in Montana during the second and third decades of this century, when the rising use of the automobile sent petroleum explorers scurrying around the world in search of new deposits. The first significant oil field in the state was opened in 1915 at Elk Basin, along the

Wyoming border in Carbon County. Others followed in 1919, at Devil's Basin near Roundup and at Cat Creek on the lower Musselshell River. In 1922 Gordon Campbell, the developer of Devil's Basin and the key figure in Montana's fast-rising oil industry, made a highly important find on the Miller Ranch. This strike, north of Shelby, opened the rich Kevin-Sunburst Field, one of the greatest in Montana's history.

Throughout the 1920s, Montana's first oil boom centered in the state's north-central region, and the Kevin-Sunburst Field held the limelight. Welcome oil money flowed into the nearby towns of Cut Bank and Shelby. In a burst of unrestrained optimism, a group of Shelby promoters tried to put their town on the map in 1923 by staging there a world's heavyweight championship fight between Jack Dempsey and Tommy Gibbons. They lost their shirts in the biggest flop in world boxing history when fewer than eight thousand people paid to attend.

Drilling activities in this region steadily expanded. In 1927 the Pondera Field opened near Conrad, and in 1931–32 the highly important Cut Bank Field began to produce. Independents like R. C. Tarrent and Tip O'Neil first developed the Cut Bank deposits, and soon larger companies like Texaco and Montana Power moved in to process its high quality crude oil and natural gas. By 1936 the Cut Bank Field ranked number one in Montana. Although a number of small refineries sprang up to work Montana oil, the Great Depression of the 1930s dampened prospecting and production and blighted the boom of 1922–32.

Measured by national standards, Montana's oil production, like its lumber production, remained small-time until the postwar era. Most of the state's oil continued to flow from the north-central fields and from the revived Elk Basin operations. Then, as postwar prosperity shot up demands for petroleum, exploration and refining activities mounted apace in the Treasure State. Large firms like Union Oil, Standard Oil, and the Farmers Union Central Exchange made heavy investments in Montana; and in the late forties Continental Oil and Carter Oil built elaborate new refineries at Billings. The most important breakthrough came in 1951, when major oil discoveries in the Williston Basin launched Montana's second boom.

The Williston Basin is a huge and deep oil field lying beneath western North Dakota, southern Saskatchewan, and easternmost Montana. Following initial strikes in North Dakota and Dawson County, Montana, a frenzied race for oil leases set in across eastern Montana. One field came in after another throughout the early and middle fifties—at Cabin Creek, East Poplar, and at scattered vicinities such as Glendive, Sidney, Wibaux, and Baker. Montana oil production doubled as a result of the Williston Basin boom, and Billings emerged as the center of the state's petroleum industry. More large oil companies moved into Billings, and refineries hurriedy expanded their operations. In 1954 the $20,500,000 Yellowstone Pipeline was completed from Billings to Spokane. Billings boomed in population throughout the 1950s and took on the appearance of an Oklahoma-Texas-style oil town. By 1970 its refineries handled over 85 percent of all oil processed in the state.

As oil rose to major importance in Montana, so too did natural gas. Following initial 1915 discoveries in the Baker-Glendive area, the Montana-Dakota Utilities Company began marketing natural gas to industrial and residential customers in far eastern Montana. Kevin-Sunburst, Cut Bank, and other of the old north-central fields yielded gas as well as oil. Starting in the 1920s and 1930s, pipelines carried the gas to west-central Montana towns, and Montana Power went into the business in a big way. By the fifties Montana was producing over twenty billion cubic feet of natural gas per year, and many homes and businesses had come to rely on this cheap and efficient fuel for heating and power. Both Montana Power and Montana-Dakota Utilities made increasingly large investments in the product, and Montana Power imported sizable quantities from Canada and Wyoming to serve its local customers.

The late fifties and sixties saw a leveling trend in the Montana oil and gas business. Employment actually declined, and the future of the industry seemed doubtful. The year 1967, however, brought new hopes for both the oil and the gas developers. In Blaine County the Tiger Ridge natural gas field opened during that year and proved to be the greatest discovery in nearly forty years. At almost the same time Denver oilman Sam Gary brought in the mammoth Bell Creek oil field in Powder River County near Broadus. The shallow Bell Creek Field, which now ranks eighty-fourth among United States deposits in proven reserves, sent tremors of excitement through the Montana oil industry and offered hopes of a great new boom.

The 1970s, though, failed to produce a major oil boom. Instead, the Montana oil industry followed its traditional pattern: relatively few workers, but a high value of production. Only about three thousand employees found work in the oil and gas business during 1974; but the total value of Montana oil production amounted to nearly $203,000,000, and natural gas output totaled $17,604,000. Although the energy crisis of the mid-seventies is sharply driving up the prices of oil and gas, uncertainties about government regulation and market trends have restrained growth in Montana. At the present time Bell Creek, which contains nearly 25 percent of Montana's known reserves, dominates the oil picture; but production continues at impressive levels in the Williston Basin and the old north-central fields. Natural gas exploration and drilling is expanding rapidly across northern and central Montana, especially in Hill, Blaine, Phillips, and Pondera counties. With Canada putting the squeeze on gas imports to Montana, the Montana Power Company is rapidly developing many new wells in the Bear Paw Mountains. Clearly, the global energy crisis will step up oil and gas production and pipeline construction in Montana, but these activities will bring only relatively slight increases in employment.

Of course, Montana's premier energy resource is not oil but coal. Montana leads all other states in coal reserves. According to recent estimates of the United States Geological Survey, the Treasure State has roughly 108 billion tons of minable coal, far more than its closest contenders, Illinois (66 billion tons) and Wyoming (51 billion tons). Most of this minable coal lies in shallow, easily strip-mined seams in southeastern and east-central Montana. Generally speaking, the coal is sub-bituminous and lignite, which is low in heating quality but also low in polluting sulfur content. The question of how, when, where, and by whom this coal will be mined lies like a great, ominous question mark across the face of Montana today. A glimpse into the past offers some insights; for, contrary to what some people think, coal mining in Montana is nothing new.

Small coal mines were opened in western Montana during the 1860s mining rushes, but significant development came only with the coal-fired, steam-powered railroads of the 1880s and 1890s. The Northern Pacific played a major role in developing Montana's first important mines, those in the vicinity of Bozeman Pass. Here, along the Yellowstone-Gallatin divide, several bustling little towns sprang up to mine the rich seams of bituminous coal, among them Chestnut, Timberline, Cokedale, and the Anaconda's company town of Storrs. The Bozeman area coal towns, and those nearby on the upper Yellowstone, such as Electric and Aldridge, crested in the 1890s and then faded into ghost towns after World War I. By then the centers of production had moved elsewhere.

Cascade County took over the lead in Montana coal output when the Great Northern Railroad and the Anaconda Company began developing a number of deposits near Great Falls. The Great Northern relied especially upon the coal towns of Stockett and Sand Coulee, and the Anaconda concentrated upon the mines at Belt, later shifting its emphasis also to Sand Coulee. Following its 1906–9 expansion through Montana, the Milwaukee Railroad spurred development of the coal rich Bull Mountains north of Billings. Roundup and Klein became important mining towns in this area, and production here remained important until past mid-century.

The Northern Pacific, meanwhile, shifted its operations base from the Bozeman area to the much richer coal veins around Red Lodge. The Northwestern Improvement Company, a Northern Pacific subsidiary, led in the development of these mines; and by the early twentieth century, the Red Lodge district dominated Montana coal production. Boasting nearly five thousand inhabitants by 1910, Red Lodge was one of the most fascinating cities in the state, with a polyglot population of Welshmen, Slavs, Scandinavians, Germans, and Irish. The high-employment underground mines of the Red Lodge–Bearcreek vicinity continued to produce for years, but high labor costs and strikes after World War I convinced the Northwestern Improvement Company to shift from underground to open pit mining. Surface mining of lower grade coal could by now be done with large shovels, and with only a fraction of the work force needed for underground mining. So in 1924 the Northern Pacific–Northwestern Improvement Company, through a contract with the Minnesota-based Foley Brothers, began strip-mining coal at Colstrip, south of Forsyth. By the mid-1930s 40 percent of the coal produced in Montana came from the Colstrip pits.

In Montana, as in the nation at large, the coal industry fell upon hard times during the twenties and thirties. Demand for coal fell sharply as railroads increasingly converted to diesel, and as more and more homes and businesses turned to fuel oil, natural gas, or electricity for heat and power. Production at all of Montana's underground mines—Red Lodge, Roundup, and Cascade County—sagged lower and lower. World War II momentarily rekindled the demand for coal, and once again some of the underground mines came back to life. Montana's worst coal mining disaster occurred at this time, in 1943, when seventy miners lost their lives at the Smith Mine near Red Lodge. After the war, though, the coal industry stagnated once again. By the sixties Montana was producing under five hundred thousand tons per year; and by 1968 fewer than one hundred employees worked at coal mining in the state.

As Montana's coal industry faded into insignificance, knowledgeable people knew that someday it would rise again. Montana holds 13 percent of the nation's coal reserves, and it was only a matter of time until the more desirable fuels became more scarce and expensive. When that happened, these easily stripped coal seams of southeastern Montana would once again attract developers. The recovery of Montana's coal industry began visibly in 1968. Through its subsidiary Western Energy Company, Montana Power had earlier secured a long-term lease arrangement at Colstrip from the Northern Pacific. Now Montana Power began stripping coal there and carrying it to a new steam generating plant at Billings. At the same time, the Peabody Coal Company started shipping coal from the Colstrip area by large "unit trains" to Minnesota for use by electric utilities.

Suddenly, in October of 1971, Montanans realized the full impact that a corporate coal boom might have upon them when the Bureau of Reclamation, in cooperation with a number of energy and mineral companies, released the so-called North Central Power Study. The study, anticipating the energy crisis that soon followed, called for construction of forty-two new coal-powered generating plants, each of them to produce a whopping ten thousand megawatts annually. Twenty-one of the proposed plants were designated for eastern Montana, with the others to be located nearby in the Dakotas and Wyoming. An eventual 2.6 million acre-feet of water from the Yellowstone River system, it was estimated, might be needed each year to cool the gargantuan coal plants. Although the study did not become working policy, it did call the state's attention to the rush for coal leases that was already under way, and it fueled the environmentalist crusade that had been mounting for several years. Fearful of the scarred landscape, damaged river systems, air pollution, and social dislocations that such massive development might bring, many Montanans reacted with alarm. The legislature started passing tough environmental protection laws in 1971, and environmentalist groups like the Northern Plains Resource Council launched anti–strip-mining campaigns.

While the controversy mounted, so did the mining of coal. Tonnage mined increased from 6,983,168 in 1971 to 8,224,118 in 1972 to 10,639,379 in 1973 to 14,000,000 in 1974. In partnership with Pacific Northwest utilities, Montana Power stepped up its Colstrip mining and built two 350-megawatt generating plants there, with more scheduled to follow. Westmoreland Resources, a creature of various other energy-related corporations, began operations at Sarpy Creek. Peabody Coal, a subsidiary of Kennecott Copper, opened its Big Sky Mine near Colstrip in 1969; and in 1972 the Decker Coal Company started mass coal shipments to Chicago and later to Detroit utilities. According to some estimates, Montana coal production could climb by 342 percent over the next decade.

By the mid-1970s, amidst public deliberations over whether or not Montana Power would be allowed to construct Colstrip units 3 and 4, coal was easily the hottest issue in Montana. Would the Northern Plains become, as one panel of experts put it, a "National Sacrifice Area"—an unreclaimed maze of worked-out coal seams, diverted waterways, and twentieth century ghost towns? On what terms would coal be extracted from the Crow and Northern Cheyenne reservations? How would scarce water be divided between mining and agricultural interests? Since so much of the land and its subsurface coal belongs to a federal government obviously "friendly" to the energy companies, how much of a voice would the state itself even have in these matters? The environmental issue seemed to draw Montanans together as few issues ever have. But an attitude of fatalism prevails in many quarters, an attitude typified by the words a coal executive recently spoke to an obstinate Bull Mountains rancher: "You can be as hard-boiled about this as you want. But we'll get you in the end."

THE BROADER VIEW

Beyond the obvious cases of lumber, oil, and coal, few other growth industries have arisen in Montana during recent times. One obvious growth area is tourism, which now ranks third, behind agriculture and mining, among the major income producers in the Treasure State. Tourism of a sort dates from Montana's earliest days, but we can chart the formal beginnings of tourism as a business from the later nineteenth century. The creation of Yellowstone National Park (1872) and Glacier National Park (1910) insured a lasting flow of sightseers, visitors, and sportsmen to the state. So did the preservation of national forests and pristine environments like the Bob Marshall Wilderness.

Naturally, the railroads played a key role in developing Montana's early tourist industry. The Northern Pacific heavily promoted Yellowstone Park and based its entry point at the city of Livingston. The Milwaukee Road developed a Yellowstone tourist route through the West Gallatin Canyon; and, of course, the Great Northern had a large interest in Glacier. During the later years of the last century, a number of elaborate resorts and spas appeared in the state, some of them advertising the benefits of local hot springs and mineral waters. The most elaborate of these was the Broadwater Hotel and Natatorium, erected by transportation magnate C.A. Broadwater west of Helena in 1889. Dude ranchers developed another type of tourism, mainly during the early years of this century. By 1930 over one hundred such outfits welcomed outdoor enthusiasts to Montana. The heaviest concentration of dude ranches dotted the mountain bastions north of Yellowstone Park. Rail-based tourism brought valuable dollars into the state: the average annual income from tourism 1900–10 totaled roughly five hundred thousand dollars.

Beginning with the second decade of this century, the automobile abruptly worked a revolution in American tourism. As roads improved and as middle class families acquired dependable cars, roadside "motels," camping spots, and restaurants began to challenge the old downtown hotels and railroad resorts. In 1914 Yellowstone Park authorities bowed to the inevitable and allowed cars to enter that silent wonderland via West Yellowstone. The Depression and war years blighted the industry, but the great postwar prosperity brought an enormous boost to western tourism. By automobile, airplane, train, and camper, the affluent tourists came in ever increasing numbers. They came mainly for outdoor recreation—hunting and fishing, hiking and sightseeing, skiing and snowmobiling. Along the state's main highways, cities and towns sprouted new motels, restaurants, and gas stations to serve them.

According to reliable estimates, out-of-state tourists spent $72 million in

Montana during 1964. Out-of-staters spent roughly $190 million in 1974, an impressive 166 percent increase over the previous decade. Yet, although tourism had become a mainstay of the economy, Montana continued to lag behind other states, such as Colorado, in its lack of large, multipurpose resorts. In 1970, however, the Chrysler Realty Corporation, in partnership with other investors and with famed newsman Chet Huntley, announced that it would construct a multi-million-dollar resort complex, Big Sky of Montana, on the West Fork of the Gallatin River. This announcement seemed to signal the beginning of a new, corporate form of tourism for Montana. But Big Sky has taken shape more slowly than expected; and the gas price squeeze and recession of the mid-1970s are casting some uncertainty over the future of western tourism in general. Beyond dispute, tourism figures largely in the current economic picture, but its low wage scales, seasonal fluctuations, and direct reliance on national prosperity make it a less than steady support for statewide prosperity.

Turning our focus to a broader view of the Montana economy, we see that the state closely reflects many national trends. As in the nation as a whole, most employment growth since World War II has not come from the "primary" or basic production industries, but rather from "derivative" industries—those that provide services, such as retail trade, government, banking and finance, construction, and communication. Total Montana employment grew from 228,500 in 1950 to 265,700 in 1970. The main reason for this sluggish growth rate was that, during those twenty years of national prosperity, Montana lost roughly 16,700 jobs in agriculture, 3,600 jobs in mining, and 7,400 jobs in railroading. Employment in the service industries, meanwhile, jumped ahead sharply. During that same twenty-year period, employment in state and local government rose from 20,000 to over 40,000, in wholesale and retail trade from 36,700 to 48,100, in services and finance from 23,400 to 41,800. There are today far more Montanans employed in state and local government, including education, than in farming and ranching combined. More Montanans work for Uncle Sam (12,800 in 1974) than at all kinds of mining (7,400 in 1974). In Montana and throughout the country, white collar workers are replacing blue collar workers, and more and more women are joining the work force.

From a historical perspective, there are two ways to view Montana's recent economic development, one tending toward optimism and one toward pessimism. If we compare the state's slow but steady growth of 1945–75 to the hard times of 1918–38, the progress seems obvious. Agriculture, though less populous than before the war, has stabilized considerably and is less vulnerable to drought and price fluctuations. And Montana relies much less heavily upon the unpredictable metal mining industry than in days of old. Although each of the state's major primary growth industries—lumber, oil, coal, and tourism—is somewhat unstable, they combine to give the state a much broader and more solid economic base than it had before.

Not to be forgotten, the federal government has also played a major hand in stabilizing the modern Montana economy. Large federal agencies like the Forest Service, the Defense Department, and the Bureaus of Reclamation and of Indian Affairs keep sizable and relatively stable work forces in the state. In addition to farm subsidies and Social Security payments, major federal construction projects, such as the mammoth Interstate Highway program, Hungry Horse and Canyon Ferry dams in the forties and fifties, Yellowtail and Libby dams and the I.C.B.M. missile installations of the sixties and seventies, have all poured massive transfusions of federal money into the local economy. Defense spending is important too. Although Montana suffered badly when Uncle Sam closed the Glasgow Air Force Base in 1968–69 and then terminated the Anti-Ballistic Missile program in 1972, the Great Falls area still relies heavily upon Malmstrom Air Force Base as a source of employment and income. In terms of per capita federal aid, Montana, small in population but large in federally owned acreage, ranks ninth among the fifty states. The state always receives considerably more in federal expenditures than it pays in federal taxes. Without these dollars from Washington, Montana would suffer severely.

So, if we view Montana today against the background of its depressed past, we may find many encouraging signs. But if we measure Montana's slow growth against the rapid growth of the country as a whole, we see a much different, more depressing picture. Two reasonably accurate gauges of prosperity are per capita income and rises or falls in the population. Per capita income—the income of Montana's average citizen—stood at an impressive level in 1950, 8 percent higher than the nationwide average. Strikingly, by 1970 Montana's per capita income had fallen to roughly 12 percent *below* the national average. Population trends show the same pattern. During the 1950s the nation as a whole grew by 18.5 percent. Montana's growth rate of 14.2 percent approximated the national average. In the 1960s, though, while the United States increased by 13.3 percent, Montana lagged far behind with a mere 2.8 percent rate of growth. In other words, during the prosperous 1960s, Montana's natural birth increase in population barely compensated for its net out-migration of population. Between 1960 and 1970, according to estimates, fifty-eight thousand more residents left the state than entered it.

These important statistics tell us much about the present and past condition of the state. The decline of per capita income and the exodus of Montana's young people mainly reflect a lack of economic opportunity and of high-paying white collar jobs. This lack, in turn arises from the simple fact that faraway Montana, with its high transportation costs and absence of urban centers, has not attracted the large manufacturing industries that have brought jobs and prosperity to neighboring states like Washington, Utah, or Minnesota. Montana remains today what it always has been—a supplier of raw wealth, not a processor of that wealth. With considerable merit, many Montanans today argue that their state should not encourage large employers, not even "clean" industries, to enter its borders. Such growth, they say, will inevitably destroy the state's charm and beauty. They may well be right. But without such development, Montana will no doubt continue to fall farther behind the economic standards of the nation and will continue to lose its most valuable resource of all, its youth. Indeed Montana today faces, in magnified form, the dilemma that confronts the entire world: the urgent need for economic improvement, as opposed to the threat that such "development" poses to a fragile environment.

CHAPTER XIV

A Social and Cultural Profile

MONTANA is a more complex and cosmopolitan place than most people assume. Outside observers, for instance, often depict it as an extension of the upper Midwest, mainly rural and Protestant in background and population. This is misleading. In addition to midwestern farmers, a fascinating diversity of peoples came to Montana. In many parts of the state, their descendants still cling to the old ways. And we must remember that urban centers, in the peculiar form of mining camps, came to Montana long before most of the wide open areas began to attract a rural population. Despite the problems that face so few people living in such a large and forbidding area, Montanans have always displayed a genuine commitment to education and to cultural achievement. The state developed over the years a comprehensive educational system and a far-flung network of public universities and colleges. It also evolved a vigorous journalistic tradition which, after being blighted for years by Anaconda's ownership of most of the major daily newspapers, is now surfacing once again. Most impressively of all, Montanans, so few in number, have made surprisingly large contributions to American art and literature.

THE PEOPLE

The census of 1870, Montana's first, revealed that the new territory contained fewer than twenty-one thousand people. By 1970 Montanans numbered roughly seven hundred thousand. This one-hundred-year increase came unevenly, as rises and declines of economic opportunity caused population movements to ebb and flow. Thus the boom decade of the 1880s produced a whopping 265 percent population increase, and the homestead invasion of 1909–18 brought tens of thousands of people to northern and eastern Montana. The depressed 1920s, though, witnessed a population decline of 2.1 percent; and, except for the 14.2 percent jump during the prosperous 1950s, Montana's growth rate has been sluggish ever since. The sixties produced an increase of only 2.9 percent, as thousands of younger citizens continued to abandon the state in search of economic opportunity.

Montana's slow growth rate has caused it to slip steadily downward on the ladder of state ranking. In 1920 it stood thirty-ninth among the states in population, but by 1970 it had fallen to the lowly position of number forty-four. With its large area—Montana is the fourth largest state—and its sparsity of population, Montana's population density is unbelievably low. The 1970 Census found that, in the nation at large, there were 57.5 persons for each square mile. Montana had only 4.8 people per square mile. Such figures are somewhat misleading, however, for the Treasure State has joined in the nationwide trend toward urbanization. The 1960 Census recorded a highly significant fact: for the first time, more Montanans lived in cities than in rural areas. Ever since the collapse of homesteading fifty-five years ago, the rural areas have sadly watched their population melt steadily away. Between 1960 and 1970 forty of the state's fifty-six counties lost population. Well over half of Montana's people now live in seven counties: Yellowstone, Cascade, Missoula, Silver Bow, Flathead, Lewis and Clark, and Gallatin. Consequently, many of those Montanans who remain in the country experience a degree of isolation that most other Americans can hardly imagine.

From the very beginning Montana attracted a wide variety of peoples. The fur trade brought in a scattering of Frenchmen and Scots, and the placer gold camps housed people from all corners of the earth. Especially prominent were the Irish, English, Germans, and Scandinavians. There were a few blacks, and many Chinese following the gold frontier. As usual, the mining frontier also brought with it a sprinkling of Jewish merchants. Typical of these was Julius Basinski, who prospered as a businessman at Radersburg and Bozeman, and later at Miles City.

The rise of industrial mining added greatly to the population mix. Marcus Daly imported thousands of his fellow Irishmen to Butte; and many "Cousin Jacks" from Cornwall, experienced and capable hardrock miners, came too. The Irish and the Cousin Jacks rose to dominate Butte society. They had their religious differences and sometimes had terrible fights, but they usually got along. The two groups even helped one another celebrate their respective holidays, St. Patrick's Day and St. George's Day. Butte in its prime was one of America's most colorful "melting pots."

By 1910 slightly over one-fourth of Montana's population was foreign born. Canada, Ireland, Germany, and Scotland still supplied the largest numbers of immigrants. But by then, more and more newcomers were arriving from central and southern Europe. The railroads and the Butte

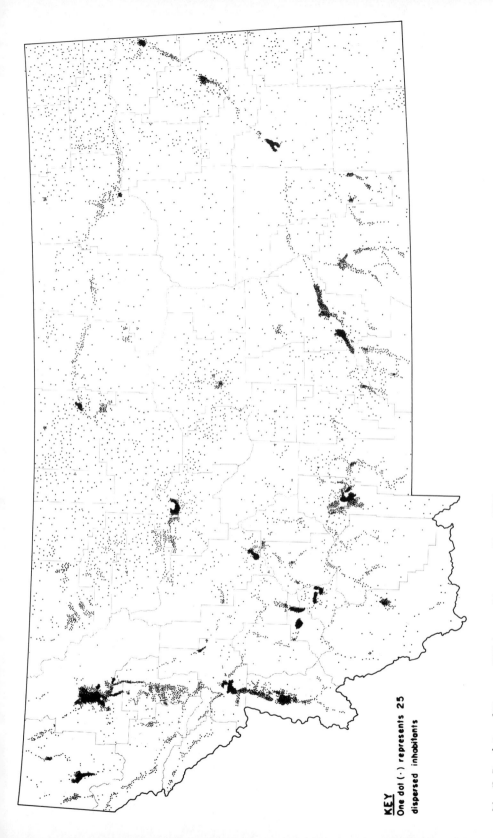

KEY
One dot (·) represents 25
dispersed inhabitants

Map 7. Population of Montana, 1970 (source, *Montana in Maps: 1974*)

mines employed a smattering of Greeks, Bulgarians, Rumanians, Serbs, Croatians, Poles, Czechs, and large numbers of Finns and Italians. For years the state's largest Italian community was the Butte suburb of Meaderville, one of the liveliest gambling centers in the West. Most of the Butte Italians worked as hardrock miners; but some, like Dominic Bertoglio and Vincent Truzzolino, went successfully into business.

The inpouring flood of immigrant peoples changed the complexions of other communities than just Butte. Large numbers of Irish, Welshmen, Slavic peoples, Italians, and Finns came to Red Lodge, Roundup, and other coal towns. They came also to man the smelters and refineries of Great Falls, East Helena, and Anaconda. The Norwegians, Swedes, Danes, and Finns gravitated heavily toward lumbering communities such as Bonner-Milltown and Libby. After 1910 the homestead invasion carried thousands of Scandinavian farmers, and many German farmers too, across the northern High Line and into east-central Montana. These Scandinavian and German farm families have left their imprint upon the state in many ways—in towns named Lothair and Opheim, in the liberal politics of the Farmers Union, in the prevalence of the Lutheran religion.

Interestingly, some of the immigrants came in community groups. A cluster of Dutch settlements grew up in the Gallatin Valley, and Frenchtown near Missoula was long famed for its handsome women. Belgians settled communally near Valier, German-Russians in the Yellowstone Valley, and Danes at Dagmar. Strong religious bonds held these communities tightly together. The state lost one such group during World War I when the Montana Council of Defense foolishly banned the use of the German language, driving hundreds of German Mennonite families into Canada. The last of the communal groups to arrive were the Hutterites, German-speaking Anabaptists who live in closed colonies. Ever since the Reformation, the Hutterites have wandered about Europe in search of peace and seclusion. Late in the last century they began migrating to America. They came first to South Dakota, then during World War I moved to Canada. Between 1943 and 1947 discriminatory legislation in Canada sent some of them into Montana looking for new colony sites. They eventually founded twenty-two communes in the Treasure State, with a total population of approximately two thousand.

In Montana as in the country as a whole, large-scale immigration ended about fifty years ago. The immigrants' children have intermarried and mostly abandoned the traditional ways, so that few of the old world customs now remain. Yet in many parts of Montana, one sees clearly the mark of the immigrants. The delicious Cornish meat pies called "pasties" are still a Butte delicacy, and Scandinavian families still loyally savor their lutefisk and lefse. St. George's Day is seldom observed any more, but St. Patrick's

Day is still a raucous occasion at Butte, Helena, and Great Falls. Until very recently, Slavic groups in Montana continued to celebrate a pre-Lenten festival called "Mesopust," including among other things, the trial of "Slarko Veljacic," a dummy who symbolized last year's misfortunes. Slarko was always found guilty, stabbed, and burned at the stake. The long famous Welsh, Cornish, and German singing groups have persisted into modern times; and so have such fraternal groups as the Ancient Order of Hibernia, the Sons of Hermann, Sons of Norway, and the Narodjini Dom and Trobjnica lodges.

National origins, of course, had much to do with religious preferences. Three denominations, the Roman Catholic, Methodist, and Episcopal, were especially active on the Montana gold frontier. Already at work among the Indians, Catholic priests began saying mass at Virginia City in 1863; and in that same year Father Urban Grassi built the first church for white men at Hell Gate. Methodist missionaries first arrived in the gold camps during 1864, but truly effective organization came later in the 1870s with the work of F. A. Riggin and W. W. Van Orsdel. For many years the Reverend Van Orsdel, affectionately known as "Brother Van," was the best known Protestant missionary on the Montana frontier. Bishop Daniel S. Tuttle launched the Episcopal Church in Montana when he came to Virginia City in 1867. By 1880, when Leigh R. Brewer was consecrated as Bishop of Montana, the Episcopalians had built up an impressive organization throughout the territory.

Other denominations were slower in getting started. Following preliminary work by Reverend Sheldon Jackson, the Presbyterians effectively entered Montana in 1872, when a small group of Princeton men founded seven churches in sixteen days. Thereafter, the Presbyterian clergymen canvassed the entire territory. Baptist, Lutheran, and Congregationalist groups began to appear during the 1880s. The Lutherans, heavily German and Scandinavian, came mostly during the post-1900 homestead rush and moved heavily into northern and far eastern Montana. The Congregationalists, fewer in number and heavily German, concentrated especially in the Yellowstone Valley, and many of them fled in the post-1918 depression.

Roman Catholicism has always been Montana's dominant religion. In 1906 a major census of religions by the federal government found that about 74 percent of all regular communicants in the state were Catholics—exactly twice the national Catholic percentage. The heavy concentration of Irish in western Montana largely explains that fact. In that same year the largest Protestant groups were the Methodist, Presbyterian, Episcopal, and Lutheran churches. During the decade following 1906 homesteading swelled the Lutheran ranks, until by 1916 Lutheranism ranked as Montana's second largest faith, a position it still holds today. By the early 1970s homogenizing population trends had worked some changes. The Catholics remained in first place, but now with only 41 percent of church adherents. The Methodists continued to rank third, but the Episcopal Church had slipped dramatically from fourth place to eighth. Replacing it as number four among Montana denominations was the fast rising Mormon Church, especially strong in the southwest. Various Baptist groups have grown markedly in recent years, as have a number of small, fundamentalist sects.

In contrast to Montana's slowly growing white population, its Indian populace has expanded dramatically. Only 11,343 Indians lived in Montana at the turn of the century. By 1970, however, Montana Indians numbered 27,130, an increase of 139 percent in seventy years, due in large part to improved health care and living conditions. Most of the Indians live on or near one of Montana's seven reservations. While the reservations vary greatly in size, wealth, land-ownership patterns, and population, they share one enormous fact of life—an overwhelming dependence upon the federal government.

As noted earlier, the all-important Dawes Act of 1887 attempted to guarantee the assimilation of the Indians into white society by allotting reservation lands to individual Indians. Allotment, the reformers wrongly assumed, would make the reservation Indians into happy, self-sufficient farmers. The extent to which the allotment process was carried varied from reservation to reservation. The tiny Rocky Boy's Reservation, created long after the others in 1916, was never allotted; and the land remains completely in tribal hands. On the other six reserves, allotment produced complex patterns of land ownership. At three reservations—Blackfeet, Crow, and Fort Belknap—more than half of the land belongs to individual Indians. Roughly 45 percent of the large Flathead (Salish-Kutenai) Reservation consists of tribal lands, but individual Indians own little of the remaining 55 percent. Most of it belongs to whites, who bought up the allotted lands years ago. The extent of actual tribal ownership varies widely, from 100 percent at Rocky Boy's, to about 60 percent on the Northern Cheyenne, to twenty-five percent or less on the Blackfeet, Crow, Fort Belknap, and Fort Peck reservations. Except for Rocky Boy's, the Montana reservations are thus checkerboards of lands owned by the tribes, by individual Indians, by whites, and by the state and federal governments.

In 1924 Congress passed the Snyder Act, conferring citizenship upon all Indians. While Indians are thus not literally wards of the federal government any longer, they are still dependent upon Uncle Sam in special ways. The federal government acts as trustee for their lands and other resources and for various of their funds. Since trust lands and some other kinds of Indian property are exempt from state taxation, the federal government supplies some services on the reservations that would otherwise be supplied by the state. Clearly, citizenship did nothing directly to improve the Indians' lot. During the 1920s, while Indian Bureau agents were still trying to turn them into farmers and herdsmen, the native Americans suffered dreadfully from poverty, malnutrition, and such diseases as tuberculosis and trachoma. Slowly, the "Great White Father" began to realize that the Dawes Act philosophy of forcing the Indians into the white man's mold could never work.

Ironically, the Great Depression of the 1930s actually led to improvements on the reservations. Various New Deal agencies provided relief, employment at comparatively high wages, improved health care, and new roads and public buildings. More importantly, the New Deal also brought to fruition a basic reorientation of government policy with passage in 1934 of the Indian Reorganization (Wheeler-Howard) Act, which was guided through the Senate by Montana Senator B. K. Wheeler. The Wheeler-Howard Act ended the allotment of lands to individual Indians and encouraged them to preserve their native cultures and to develop tribal self-government. It authorized each tribe to organize as a federal corporation, to adopt a constitution, and to create a tribal council to govern itself. Except for the Crows and the Fort Peck tribes, all of the Montana Indians quickly incorporated under the Wheeler-Howard Act, formed constitutions, and turned the management of their affairs over to elected tribal councils. The Fort Peck people continued under an earlier constitution; the Crows use a slightly different procedure. They deliberate all important matters in a general council, which is composed of all adult members of the tribe, and delegate administration and lesser subjects to special executive committees.

World War II changed the lives of many Indians. Some men and women served in the armed forces, and others took jobs in war plants. Those who returned after the war showed a new interest in self-government and demanded better education, an improved standard of living, and a tighter administration of reservation affairs. In 1946 Congress established the Indian Claims Commission to investigate charges that the federal government had taken Indian lands either in violation of treaty rights or with inadequate compensation. Later, during the 1960s and early 1970s, the Crows, Northern Cheyennes, and Salish-Kutenais won major settlements through the commission.

Generally speaking, though, Washington showed little sympathy for native Americans during the postwar period. Tiring once again of the "Indian Problem," Congress drifted back toward Dawes Act thinking—quick assimilation into white society. Two important measures of 1953 reflected this attitude. The states were allowed, on the one hand, to assume civil and criminal jurisdiction over the reservations. More significantly, Congress approved the controversial policy of "termination," which meant a total cutoff of federal supervision over the tribes. In line with this philosophy, the Bureau of Indian Affairs launched a "relocation" program during the 1950s, aimed at removing Indians from the reservations and placing them in areas of greater employment opportunity. Luckily for Montana's tribes, these disastrous programs affected them less than many Indians elsewhere.

Since the early 1960s the termination policy has been abandoned in all but name. Replacing it, especially through the Great Society programs of the Johnson Administration, have been renewed efforts to improve life on the reservations. Conditions on the state's seven reservations today are varied. Generally, population growth has surpassed the capacities of the reservations to support their people. Predictably, the result is high unemployment, heavy welfare loads, and other social problems. In most cases even those Indians employed at farming and ranching need supplemental wages. The problem is that the reservations are located in isolated rural areas where there are few employment opportunities, especially for those with limited job skills.

The Salish-Kutenai Reservation is Montana's most prosperous, mainly because of its favored location. Only about half of the enrolled Salish-Kutenai people even live on the reserve. Much of the land was allotted and passed into white hands; however, most of the land remaining under Indian control is tribal land that produces valuable stands of timber. The tribe profits from timber and Christmas tree sales, from valuable grazing leases, from annual payments by Montana Power for rental rights on Kerr Dam, and from employment opportunities in the lumber industry. Recreational possibilities are endless in the Flathead Valley, and the tribes own a resort at Blue Bay on Flathead Lake. The Salish-Kutenais have their problems, but they are generally better off than their neighbors.

The story elsewhere is generally one of poverty and substandard living conditions. Traditionally, agriculture has offered the main nonfederal source of income. Roughly half of the Blackfeet families, for instance, receive some income from agriculture. The Blackfeet also rely upon logging, oil and gas leases, and the sale of Indian crafts at Browning and St. Mary. The Crows lease most of their farming and ranching lands. Coal mining, though, seems likely to determine their future, as it does for the Northern Cheyennes. At Rocky Boy's, Fort Belknap, and Fort Peck, the outlook seems least promising of all; for, in terms of agriculture, the land there cannot begin to support the population. Over the past decade the tribes have increasingly tried to improve conditions by attracting industry. The Crow, Blackfoot, and Fort Peck Indians have all established industrial parks, so far with only limited success. The Blackfeet now manufacture pencils and ship doors; a New York–based plastics concern offers some employment on the

Northern Cheyenne Reservation at Ashland; and there are several small industries on the Fort Peck Reservation.

THE SCHOOLS

Significantly, despite the large foreign-born element in its historical population base, Montana has long boasted a literacy rate far above the national average. In 1900 only 6.6 percent of Montana's population was illiterate, compared to 11.3 percent of the nation as a whole. By 1960 the state's illiteracy rate had fallen to a miniscule 1.0 percent, still less than half the national percentage of 2.4. This good showing is due, in large part, to the absence of either urban or rural poverty on a massive scale. It is also due to Montana's long-term commitment to public education.

Public schools appeared in Montana soon after the territory's creation in 1864. Like most frontiersmen, Montanans looked upon common schools as vital agencies of civilization. In his 1865 address to the first territorial legislature, Governor Sidney Edgerton asked the lawmakers to establish a public school system in words that typified American ideals. In "a free government like ours," Edgerton argued, "where public measures are submitted to the judgment of the people, it is of the highest importance that the people should be so educated as to understand the hearing of public measures. A self-ruling people must be an educated people, or prejudice and passion will assume power, and anarchy will soon usurp the authority of government."

The legislature responded to Edgerton's appeal with a law authorizing county commissioners to establish local school boards and school districts and to impose a one mill property tax to support public education. Under this law Montana's first public school opened at Virginia City in March 1866. A second began classes at Bozeman during the following winter. It proved hard, though, to keep schools going in the unstable mining camps, and early progress was disappointingly slow. By 1870 Montana reported only fifteen schools, employing twenty-seven teachers to handle approximately seven hundred students.

Using the California code as a model, the 1872 Legislature passed a new school law that became the basis of Montana's modern educational system. The 1872 law provided increased financial support, clarified the powers of county superintendents and the duties of teachers, and placed sweeping powers in the hands of a territorial superintendent of public instruction. It also required that "education of children of African descent shall be provided for in separate schools." Wisely, Governor Potts appointed Cornelius Hedges to be superintendent of public instruction. With bachelor's and master's degress from Yale and a law degree from Harvard, Hedges held impressive credentials for the job, and his capable performance in office earned him the title "Father of Education in Montana." During Hedges' three consecutive terms, which began in 1872 (he served a fourth in 1883–85), the number of schools increased dramatically, the school term expanded from three to five months, and mandatory teachers' institutes improved the quality of instruction. The first high schools in the territory also appeared during Hedges' tenure, at Helena in 1876, Deer Lodge and Bozeman in 1878, and Butte in 1879. By 1880 Montana had a firmly established public school system.

As the years went by, the legislature further revamped the school laws. In 1881 it set up a textbook commission to select uniform texts for all the schools. The state continued to use such a commission, in one form or another, until 1943. In 1883 the lawmakers enacted Montana's first compulsory school attendance law and, in the same measure, repealed that section of the 1872 law requiring separate schools for blacks. Statehood brought further changes. The new state received its due when, in passing the Enabling Act of 1889, Congress set aside Sections 16 and 36 in each Montana township as public school lands for the purpose of supporting education. Montana's 1889 Constitution made the office of superintendent of public instruction elective and placed control over education in the hands of a State Board of Education, composed of the governor, the superintendent of public instruction, the attorney general, and eight citizen members appointed by the governor.

The problems confronting the state board changed little over the years— how to secure adequate funding, how to upgrade teacher certification requirements, how best to determine teaching and disciplinary methods. Naturally, curriculum content posed a major concern. The 1872 law provided for the usual fundamentals: reading, writing, spelling, arithmetic, geography, English, American history, bookkeeping, health, physical training, and morals. Most of the changes made in this basic curriculum over the years have aimed at turning it in a more "practical" direction. In 1911 the legislature authorized training in industrial and vocational skills; and in 1917 Congress passed the Smith-Hughes Act to provide federal aid for such programs. These programs, of course, aim less at real education than at job training. They have been joined by a variety of others that emphasize patriotism, consumerism, or coping with such social problems as race prejudice, drugs, and alcohol.

By doubling the number of Montana school children, the great homestead boom of 1909–18 placed enormous strains upon the state's educational system. Numerous little school districts resulted from the effort to bring scattered farm children within reasonable traveling distance of a schoolhouse. Then, when the bottom fell out of agriculture, hundreds of

Results of drought, ca. 1935 (Courtesy of Montana Historical Society, Helena)

Results of soil drifting, Two Triangles Farm, Coalridge. Fence is covered over and soil has drifted onto thistles caught in fence. Photograph by H. B. Syverud, "East Coalridge Community Scrapbook," Vol. 1 (Courtesy of Montana Historical Society, Helena)

Cornelius F. Kelley, "Mr. Copper." Photograph by the Anaconda Company (Courtesy of Fordham News Service, Fordham University)

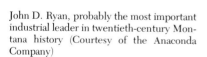

John D. Ryan, probably the most important industrial leader in twentieth-century Montana history (Courtesy of the Anaconda Company)

Berkeley Pit, Butte. Photograph by Garry Wunderwald (Courtesy of Travel Promotion Unit, State Department of Highways, Helena)

Downtown Billings, viewed from the Rimrocks (Courtesy of Billings Chamber of Commerce)

Charles M. Russell (Courtesy of Montana Historical
Society, Helena)

A. B. Guthrie, Jr. (Courtesy of Montana Historical Society, Helena)

Capitol Building, Helena. Photograph by Garry Wunderwald (Courtesy of Travel Promotion Unit, State Department of Highways, Helena)

Main Hall, University of Montana, Missoula (Courtesy of Montana Historical Society)

Montana State University, Bozeman (Courtesy of Montana State University)

Senator Mike Mansfield (Courtesy of Montana Historical Society, Helena)

Governor Sam C. Ford (Courtesy of Montana Historical Society, Helena)

Senator Lee Metcalf (Courtesy of Montana Historical Society, Helena)

these rural districts lost their tax bases. As roads improved and reliable buses became available, rural people came to realize that consolidation of school districts was the only real answer to their problems. In 1929 there were still roughly 2,500 one-room and two-room schools in Montana. By 1950 only 1,321 of these remained; and by 1970 the state had cut back to 574 elementary districts and 166 high school districts. And yet the trend continues, as more and more rural schools face the certain prospect of closure.

Closely related to the number of school districts is the problem of school finance. Prior to 1927, school districts had to depend mainly upon the property taxes they could raise on their own. This simple arrangement caused great variations between school districts, both in tax burden and in quality of education. Attempting to improve schooling in the small, poorer districts, the 1927 Legislature created a Common School Equalization Fund, supplied with revenues from the inheritance, oil, and metals taxes. The State Board of Education was empowered to distribute the funds. In 1949 the legislature revised its aid to education system by enacting the landmark School Foundation Program Law, which is the basis of all modern state policy. The 1949 law sought to guarantee every Montana youngster a basically sound education by channeling state funds into those districts where local and county tax dollars were not adequate to meet minimal needs and standards. By passing this law, the State of Montana committed itself to underwriting the education of all its needy children.

In addition to the public schools, a scattering of parochial schools, most of them operated by the Roman Catholic Church, also serve to educate Montana youth. Of Montana's total 192,084 elementary and secondary students in 1969–70, roughly 17,300 attended parochial schools. Of these, 10,734 were in Catholic schools. The remainder attended schools supported by the Lutheran, Hutterite, Seventh Day Adventist, Mennonite, and Christian Reformed churches. In more recent years mounting inflation and the cost squeeze have forced many parochial grade schools and high schools to close their doors. Especially distressing to the Catholics were the recent closures of their high schools in both Helena and Great Falls, the seats of the Dioceses of Western and Eastern Montana.

HIGHER EDUCATION

In Montana, as in most states, the first colleges were privately, not publicly, endowed. Citizens of Deer Lodge first took the initiative by founding the Montana Collegiate Institute in 1878. After faltering along for a few years with tiny enrollments, the institute passed into the control of the Presbyterian Church, which renamed it the College of Montana. Aided by W. A. Clark, the college brought in graduates from the Columbia University School of Mines and established courses in mining engineering and metallurgy. Some of its young faculty later went on to distinguished careers, among them the renowned humanist and literary critic Irving Babbitt. But the College of Montana never really prospered. It lost enrollment through the 1890s, closed and reopened, and then finally shut down permanently in 1916.

The Methodists started an institution of their own in 1890, when they opened Montana University in the Prickly Pear Valley north of Helena. As this name quickly became a problem when the state created a public university system, the Presbyterian institution was renamed Montana Wesleyan University and later Montana Wesleyan College. In 1898 the institution was moved into Helena. Montana Wesleyan merged in 1923 with the College of Montana under the new name of Intermountain Union College. After the Helena earthquake of 1935 damaged its campus, Intermountain Union College merged, in turn, with the Billings Polytechnic Institute, which had been founded back in 1908. This new institution, located in Billings, named itself Rocky Mountain College, and such it remains today.

Montana has two Roman Catholic colleges. In 1909 Bishop John P. Carroll opened Mount St. Charles College as a boys' school supported by the Diocese of Western Montana at Helena. The campus was renamed Carroll College in 1932 in order to honor its founder. In that same depression year the Diocese of Eastern Montana opened the Great Falls Junior College as a girls' school. The institution received four-year accreditation in 1939 and changed its name to the College of Great Falls. Both these Catholic colleges eventually became co-educational, Great Falls in 1937 and Carroll in 1946. And both continue in operation today, the College of Great Falls at a handsome new campus opened in 1960.

Montana was delayed several years in creating a state-supported system of higher education because of the intense jockeying between various cities over which would become the capital. Finally, after this contest had narrowed into a battle between Helena and Anaconda, the 1893 Legislature tackled the education question. Unfortunately, the lawmakers decided, in the tradition of frontier logrolling politics, to create a multi-unit system which would gratify several ambitious cities and keep hard feelings to a minimum. They chose to locate a university in Missoula, an agricultural college in Bozeman, a school of mines at Butte, and a normal college at Dillon. In thus opting for an expensive, multi-unit university system, the legislators turned down a lucrative and sensible offer from Paris Gibson, the founder of Great Falls. Gibson offered the state a grant of land and a sizable cash endowment if it would locate a single-unit state university in his city. Impressed less by Gibson's logic than by the demands of other cities

and the argument that a decentralized system would bring higher education within easy travel of any family, the legislature turned him down.

Following this irreversible decision, four separate campuses slowly took
shape. Since few Montana students had access to high school education
until early in this century, the campuses at first devoted much of their
energy and resources to "preparatory departments" which, in effect, prepared the students for college level course work. High schools soon sprang
up to serve most areas, though, and the university units, especially those at
Missoula and Bozeman, then began rapidly developing new courses and
degree programs. Predictably, the state campuses increasingly competed
with one another, lobbying the legislature for funds and beating the brush
for students. With good reason, a Montana educator would later describe
the university system's first two decades as "years of guerrilla warfare."

Competition between the university units was obviously wasteful and expensive, as critics like Gibson had foreseen, and it led to a strong movement for "consolidation" of the four units into one central campus. Real
consolidation, which meant closing down campuses, proved then, as it
would later, to be politically impossible. So, as an alternate solution, the
1913 Legislature attempted to coordinate the four units, cut down duplication, and lower expenses by welding them into a single university system
composed of four integrated parts. The legislature increased the super-
visory powers of the State Board of Education and authorized it to employ a
chancellor to oversee the entire university system.

In the meantime the homestead movement brought thousands of new
families to northern and eastern Montana, areas far removed from the four
campuses, which all lay in the state's southwestern corner. Those who
favored consolidation now faced even stronger opposition from these newly
settled regions, which of course wanted new colleges built to serve them.
In the end the consolidationists lost, and the expansionists won. The voters
turned down a 1914 initiative measure providing for consolidation, and the
lawmakers turned instead in the opposite direction by authorizing two new
campuses: Northern Montana College at Havre and Eastern Montana Normal College (now Eastern Montana College) at Billings. These two new
colleges would not open their doors until the later 1920s, after the bottom
had already dropped out of homesteading. Hardpressed Montana taxpayers
now found themselves with six, rather than four, campuses to support.

The failure of consolidation meant mounting demands for state revenue,
which came mainly from the general fund raised by the statewide property
tax. Beginning with voter approval of two initiative measures in 1920, the
state turned to special mill levies for help in carrying the higher education
tax load. Again in 1930 the electorate renewed the one and one-half mill

levy of ten years before, and in 1940 they increased it to three and one-half mills. In Montana as elsewhere, the end of World War II placed enormous strains on the university system as thousands of veterans knocked on college doors with federal funding under the G.I. Bill. The 1947 Legislature responded by referring two referenda to the people, one raising the university levy to six mills and the other providing for a five-million-dollar building bond issue. Both were approved in the 1948 election. This all-important six mill levy of 1948 was renewed in 1958 and again in 1968.

Adoption of the chancellorship system in 1913 did little to satisfy critics of the far-flung university system. In fact the first two chancellors, Edward C. Elliott and M. A. Brannon, both found themselves surrounded by political controversy. Legislators, hard hit by pleas for tax relief during the Great Depression, aimed their knives at the chancellor and the university system. During the 1933 session the lawmakers turned back bills to close the Havre and Billings campuses and chose instead to make wholesale cuts throughout the system. They forced Chancellor Brannon to resign by refusing to appropriate any funds to pay him. The systemwide budget cuts of 1933 dealt a near lethal blow to the Montana system of higher education. Reporting to the State Board of Education in 1935, President Alfred Atkinson of Montana State College at Bozeman commented plaintively "that we have lost 25 faculty members since 1933 because they went to more remunerative positions. The aggregate of their beginning salaries in their new positions was an increase of 47.2 per cent."

The university system remained underfunded and without a chancellor for years to come. As part of his general effort to rationalize the operations of state government, Governor Sam Ford succeeded in convincing the 1943 Legislature to reinstitute the chancellorship. The State Board of Education then appointed University of Montana President Ernest O. Melby as chancellor, and Melby accepted with the stipulation that he be allowed to remain in Missoula. Of course, this arrangement led inevitably to trouble, for supporters of the other five units immediately accused Melby of bias. Chancellor Melby and the Board of Education launched yet another campaign to tighten control over the six units. Melby wished to convert the Dillon campus into a vocational school and to turn the Havre and Billings units into junior colleges. Predictably, the legislature turned him down flat.

Since Melby's day Montana has re-examined its university system time and time again, but major changes did not come until adoption of the 1972 Constitution. Having proven itself ineffective, the chancellor's position was abandoned after 1950. In 1959 the legislature designated the Board of Education, when acting on university system matters, as the Board of Regents and created the position of executive secretary to handle its business. Following a steady increase through the 1950s, student enrollment in the university system mushroomed during the prosperous 1960s. And the campuses, especially those at Missoula and Bozeman, expanded with the addition of new buildings and new faculty. The university system came increasingly to be a major arm of state government investment and employment.

The state made significant new commitments to higher education during these growth years. With federal assistance Montana established vocational-technical education centers in Billings, Butte, Great Falls, Helena, and Missoula in 1969. In a highly important decision of 1971, the legislature provided partial state funding for Montana's three community colleges, in Glendive, Miles City, and Kalispell. The lawmakers placed these hitherto locally run colleges under the authority of the Board of Regents. In order to provide its students with specialized training that its own university system could not afford, Montana joined in two cooperative, interstate programs. Through the Western Interstate Commission for Higher Education (WICHE), which evolved in 1950–51, students from Montana and twelve other states can enroll in out-of-state universities for specialized training in such areas as medicine, dentistry, and veterinary medicine. And through the WAMI (Washington, Alaska, Montana, Idaho) program, set up by the University of Washington Medical School in 1970, twenty Montana students each year begin their medical education at Montana State University and finish it at the University of Washington.

The great boom of the sixties only compounded the problems of duplication and lack of coordination in the university system. Montanans tried once more to rationalize and reorder the system in their new Constitution of 1972. The new constitution provided for separating control of higher education from that of public education in general. It placed higher education under a distinct Board of Regents, who "shall have full power, responsibility, and authority to supervise, coordinate, manage and control the Montana university system." In order to facilitate their control and coordination of the universities, the regents were directed to employ a commissioner of higher education. Presently, the office of the commissioner, so reminiscent of the old chancellor arrangement, is rapidly expanding its staff and functions.

By the mid-1970s the university system consisted, in effect, of nine units; and once again Montana tried desperately to consolidate its expensive network of campuses. At the request of Governor Thomas L. Judge, the 1973 Legislature created a thirty-member Commission on Post-secondary Education, armed with a three-hundred-thousand-dollar appropriation to support "a detailed and thorough study of postsecondary education in the state." This expensive assessment ended up accomplishing very little. Although its staff favored closing the Dillon campus and converting Montana

Tech in Butte into a community college, the commission decided against both recommendations and chose to leave things pretty much as they were. Only time will tell what effects the commission's 127 recommendations may have or what may be the impact of the newly strengthened Board of Regents. History indicates, though, that basic changes in the state's multiunit system are highly unlikely.

THE MEDIA

Newspapers appeared early on the Montana frontier. Local editors were always community boosters and were usually outspokenly partisan in their political views. From the appearance of the territory's first newspaper, the *Montana Post* of Virginia City in 1864, until well into this century, Montana supported an interesting, vigorous, and highly personal brand of journalism. Some of the best known early editors, like Thomas Dimsdale of the *Montana Post* or R. E. Fisk of the Helena *Herald,* were better known for their prejudices than for their talent. But others, like R. N. Sutherlin of the *Rocky Mountain Husbandman* of White Sulpher Springs and W. K. Harber of the Fort Benton *River Press,* were men of real intelligence, honesty, and candor. Some of their editorials still make good reading today.

The War of the Copper Kings had a critical impact upon Montana journalism. Each of the great copper magnates, Clark, Daly, and Heinze, used the press to further his own interests; and the result of this partisan warfare was Anaconda control over most of the state's major daily newspapers. After being attacked by W. A. Clark's paper, the Butte *Miner,* Marcus Daly brought in a very capable journalist named John H. Durston to create a paper of his own. A Yale graduate and holder of a Ph.D. in philology from the University of Heidelberg, Durston made Daly's Anaconda *Standard* into the state's best newspaper. By the early 1900s the *Standard* appeared regularly on the newsstands of fourteen cities outside Montana, including New York, Chicago, and all major cities on the West Coast.

Not to be outdone by his elders, young F. A. Heinze founded a newspaper too, the *Reveille* of Butte. Heinze's venomous editor, P. A. O'Farrell, specialized in broadsiding Standard Oil and the Amalgamated Copper Company. "The Standard Oil Trust," he proclaimed, "Will Ride Into Montana Much As Charles the Fifth Rode Into Antwerp." By 1900 the Butte press had become little more than a pawn of the warring copper kings. As veteran journalist Martin Hutchens later recalled, "The newspapers spouted mud in a manner to cause the Yellowstone geysers to look like toy fountains." Stung by Heinze's attacks and beaten in the 1900 campaign, Standard Oil–Amalgamated Copper ominously began buying up daily newspapers in order to bend statewide public opinion in its direction.

By 1929 Anaconda owned eight daily newspapers: the Anaconda *Stan-*

dard, the *Daily Post* and *Montana Standard* of Butte, the Daily Missoulian and *Sentinel* of Missoula, the Billings *Gazette,* the Helena *Independent Record,* and the Livingston *Enterprise.* These Company papers commanded roughly 55–60 percent of the daily press circulation in the state. Furthermore, through its many statewide business connections and through its ties with Montana Power, the Company could also influence weekly papers and such independent dailies as the Great Falls *Tribune.* Although Company officials denied, over the years, that they controlled editorial or news policies, such denials were hardly convincing. As John M. Schiltz once remarked, the sameness of Company papers defied coincidence. Al Himsl, a veteran Montana journalist and one-time employee of the Company-owned Billings *Gazette,* stated categorically that "the individual papers enjoyed little autonomy. They were told what to do from the top." According to Himsl, Anaconda strongmen Cornelius Kelley and Dan Kelly always kept a close eye on the press. After Con Kelley's passing in the mid-fifties, Himsl contended, the Company editors remained in this rut out of habit.

Anaconda press policy did, however, change over the years. Until the later 1920s Company editors continued the old-time practice of free-swinging attacks upon their enemies, such as B. K. Wheeler in 1920 and Joseph Dixon in 1924. During the 1928 gubernatorial campaign, for instance, the Anaconda *Standard* described anti-Company candidate Wellington Rankin as having "all the dignity of a baboon, all the self-restraint and poise of a tomcat, all the calm deliberation and judicial decision of a jackass, all the finer emotions and sentiments of a yellow dog, all the nobility and character of a snake."

Perhaps Anaconda found such attacks to be self-defeating, for by the early thirties its press policy had turned completely around. Instead of attacking its foes, the Company press now simply ignored them, "blacking out" controversial candidates and issues. On their editorial pages, Company papers largely avoided state affairs and dwelt instead upon problems far from home—a tactic men in the trade called "Afghanistaning." Anaconda's papers became, in the words of Richard T. Ruetten, "monuments of indifference." The modern Montanan can only wince at the thought of what effect this press policy must have had upon the working of democracy in the state. In its March 1957 issue, *Quill,* the monthly magazine of the journalism honorary society Sigma Delta Chi, ranked the states on the basis of news coverage of their legislatures. Montana stood forty-seventh among the forty-eight states.

After years of mounting criticism for its "captive press" policy, Anaconda finally announced in June 1959 that it was selling its entire press operation to Lee Newspapers, a midwestern chain. Almost immediately, the Lee management introduced sweeping changes that brightened up the drab old Anaconda papers and brought them out of the green eyeshade era. It upgraded personnel policies and mechanical facilities, expanded and improved its news staffs, established a state bureau in Helena, and supplemented its Associated Press coverage with the New York *Times* News Service. In order to improve the work of reporters and editors, Lee encouraged them to attend conventions and conferences, including the American Press Institute seminars at Columbia University. At long last all Montanans had access to objective and professional news reporting.

Viewed in broader perspective, the end of Anaconda journalism was actually part of a larger nationwide trend toward fewer daily papers owned by fewer and larger firms. Lee Newspapers combined the Butte *Daily Post* with the *Montana Standard* in 1961, joined the Missoula *Sentinel* with an enlarged *Missoulian* in 1969, and sold the Livingston *Enterprise* to the Star Printing Company of Miles City in 1970. More significantly, the Warden family of Great Falls announced in 1965 the sale of its paper, the Great Falls *Tribune*, to the Minneapolis Star and Tribune Company. This word came as something of a shock to Montanans, for the *Tribune* had for many years been their only large, independently owned daily. Indeed, of Montana's twelve daily newspapers, not one is now home-owned. The Bozeman *Chronicle*, Kalispell *Inter Lake*, and Havre *News* belong to the Scripps chain; and the Miles City *Star* and Livingston *Enterprise* are parts of a Denver-based network.

While depending upon the daily papers and upon television and radio for broader news coverage, rural and small-town Montanans rely upon their sixty-eight weekly and two semiweekly newspapers for local information. Most of the small town editors have usually confined their focus to local horizons, but some of them addressed larger issues in the best tradition of American journalism. In more recent years, a list of such able country editors would include Dan Whetstone of Cut Bank, Miles Romney of Hamilton, Tom Stout of Lewistown, Hal Stearns of Harlowton, and Mel Ruder of Columbia Falls. Ruder won a Pulitzer Prize in 1965 for his coverage of the terrible 1964 floods in the *Hungry Horse News*.

Like all other Americans, Montanans have become increasingly reliant upon the electronic media since the 1920s. The Great Falls *Tribune* launched Montana's first licensed radio station, KDYS, in 1922, broadcasting to only fifteen receiving sets in the entire city. After eighteen months of service, which included remote coverage of the Dempsey-Gibbons fight at Shelby, KDYS quit the business. Montana's first permanent station was KFBB, which F. A. Buttrey began at Havre late in 1922 and moved to Great Falls in 1929. All of Montana's larger cities supported radio stations by the 1930s, and Ed Craney of Butte united a number of them into his XL

Radio Network. By mid-1972 fifty-four radio stations operated in the Treasure State.

Like the radio boom of thirty years earlier, the television craze came to rural areas such as Montana in the early 1950s. Ed Craney, the state's leading radio entrepreneur, set up its first television station in 1953, KXLF-TV at Butte. Other cities followed suit until, by the mid-1970s, twelve different TV stations were operating in the state. Cable TV service brought a wide variety of program offerings to local viewers, mainly Spokane stations to the state's western region and Salt Lake City channels to the east. During the past few years, the Montana Television Network has vastly improved the quality and variety of state news coverage offered through its affiliated TV stations. More than any other single influence, radio-television has broadened the horizons of Montana's people, drawing them ever closer into the mainstream of American life.

MONTANA AND THE ARTS

Considering its small population, Montana has made some striking contributions to the visual arts and to literature. The word "art" in this state seems almost synonymous with the name of Charles M. Russell, that self-taught painter, illustrator, sculptor, and writer whose statue fittingly represents Montana in the National Statuary Hall of the Capitol in Washington, D.C. A St. Louis native, Charlie Russell first came to Montana as a sixteen-year-old cowboy in 1880. To the great amusement of his fellow cowhands, Russell's natural compulsion to art kept him constantly busy painting, drawing, and modeling clay. His first published work appeared in *Harper's Weekly* in 1888, and during the 1890s his creations increased rapidly in quality and quantity. Charlie took a wife, Nancy Cooper, and she forced him both to toe the mark and to think commercially. He hit his prime during 1905–20. Following his first one-man show in New York in 1911, he staged a steady parade of showings in cities that included London and Rome, Chicago, Minneapolis, and Los Angeles. The Prince of Wales bought one of his paintings to hang in Buckingham Palace, and in 1925 the great Corcoran Gallery of Art in Washington, D.C., celebrated the cowboy artist in a special Russell exhibition.

Charlie Russell's art works provide us with a panorama of the passing frontier. In part, Russell's great power as an artist stems from his genius with colors, his incredible mastery of detail, his uncanny ability to capture the Northern Plains environment and people. But equally important is his romantic reaction against "progress," his melancholy attachment to the untrammeled Old West which he saw fading into history. Russell stirs in us a love for the land itself and for its native inhabitants. He lived among the Blackfeet for a time during 1888, and he always identified strongly with them. "Those Indians have been living in heaven for a thousand years," he once told Teddy Blue Abbott, "and we took it away from 'em for forty dollars a month." Probably no other character of Montana's past can inspire the affection that this humble and sentimental cowboy artist received from later generations.

Although overshadowed by Russell, three other Montana artists also deserve special note. Edgar S. Paxson, an upstate New Yorker, came to Montana in 1877 and worked for a time as a freighter, Indian fighter, and scout. He settled briefly in Deer Lodge and supported himself by painting signs, buildings, and theater scenery. Eventually, Paxson was able to devote full time to painting, first at a studio in Butte and later at another in Missoula. By the time of his death in 1919, he had completed over twenty-five hundred paintings, six of them now in the state capitol, and eight others in the Missoula County Courthouse. Paxson was a painstaking perfectionist: he spent twenty years preparing his famous mural "Custer's Last Stand." Like Russell, he was a romantic, but his works deal less with cowboys than with trappers, Indians, and larger historic events.

Danish-born Olaf Carl Seltzer, like his close friend Charlie Russell, lived at Great Falls. Seltzer worked as a machinist for the Great Northern until the early 1920s, when he was finally able to rely upon his artistic talents for a living. His earlier paintings touched many themes, but later on the West captured his full attention. Seltzer worked beautifully with oils, water colors, and pen and ink, and his wildlife studies are popular masterpieces. Less famous but equally significant was German-born Winold Reiss, who first came west in 1919–20. Fascinated by the Blackfeet and by their history of buffalo hunting and intertribal warfare, Reiss produced many striking studies of Indian life, which gained wide recognition when the Great Northern began reproducing them on its calendars. Reiss opened an art school at St. Mary Lake during the 1930s, where several prominent artists, including the Indians Victor Pepion and Albert Racine, studied.

During more recent years a striking number of professional and amateur Montana artists have risen to national prominence. Among the best of these are Elizabeth Lochrie, who specializes in interpreting Indians, wood-carver John Clarke, sculptor and taxidermist Bob Scriver, and the versatile Branson Stevenson. Stevenson, who is best known for his pottery and etchings, is one of Montana's truly outstanding artists. His work has been shown at New York's Metropolitan Museum, the Library of Congress, Pittsburgh's Carnegie Institute, the Denver Museum, and in the State Department's International Traveling Craft Exhibit. Local artists find many outlets for their creativity. In addition to such nationally famous art centers as the C. M. Russell Museum in Great Falls and the Montana Historical Society Museum in Helena, many other cities take great pride in their collections and exhibits. Founded in 1948, the Montana Institute of the Arts offers all sorts of support to all sorts of artists. And the Archie Bray Foundation, established in Helena in 1951, has done much to further local interest in pottery.

Most of Montana's contemporary artists, like their predecessors, employ a realistic style to depict the land, the wildlife, the natives, and the dramatic events from Montana's colorful past. One sees this clearly in the work of such popular Montana painters as Shorty Shope, J. K. Ralston, and Ace Powell. In large part we can ascribe the prevalence of realism to the influence of Russell and to the fascination of Montanans with their history. But surely the key factor here is the land itself, its overwhelming beauty and grandeur. Billings water-colorist James Haughey put it nicely: "In Montana the country . . . almost dictates working in the direction of realism rather than abstraction, but if I were back in New York and living in that environment I'm inclined to think that I might become an abstract painter. Out here the relationship of man to the country, the land to the sky, suggests a more realistic way of working than would life in a metropolitan area."

Montana's writers have shown the same fondness for realistic studies of the land, the wildlife, and the history of this area as have its painters. Among the best of Montana's early writers were James Willard Schultz and Frank Bird Linderman. Schultz came to the state in 1877 and lived among the Blackfeet until the death of his Indian wife in 1903. During most of those years, he ranched in the Two Medicine River country and supplemented his income by guiding hunting parties and writing stories for popular magazines. After 1903 Schultz devoted his full time to writing, mainly juvenile stories about Indians and the frontier. At his best and most serious he wrote realistically and affectionately of the Indians he knew so well. Schultz eventually produced thirty-seven books. Among these, the best nonjuvenile works are *My Life as an Indian* (1907) and *Friends of My Life as an Indian* (1923).

Like Schultz, Frank Bird Linderman knew and loved the Indians, and he wrote about them with greater skill and precision. Linderman came to Montana in 1880 and pursued an active life as a woodsman, assayer, merchant, newspaperman, state legislator, and insurance salesman. His fascination with the Indians and their culture dominated his life. Linderman played a key role in creating the Rocky Boy's Reservation, and he devoted his later years to accurate portrayals of Indian life and legend. Among the best of his works are *Indian Why Stories* (1915) and *How It Came About Stories* (1921). Also noteworthy are *American* (1930), the life of Crow Chief Plenty Coups; *Red Mother* (1932), a biography of the Crow woman Pretty Shield; and two novels of the fur trade era, *Lige Mounts: Free Trapper* (1922) and *Beyond Law* (1933).

Since the days of Schultz and Linderman, a surprising number of professional writers have made Montana their home. Authors of fiction pursue
various themes. Margaret Scherf of Kalispell, for instance, has produced
over twenty mystery novels since 1940. Here as elsewhere, though, the
western motif prevails. The first Montanan to take up western fiction in a
big way was former school teacher Bertha Muzzey. Writing under the
name B. M. Bower, she produced more than five dozen novels of the West
between 1904 and 1952, the most famous being *Chip of the Flying U*
(1904). Great Falls, the home town of Dan Cushman, Norman A. Fox, and
Robert J. McCaig, has long been a center of western writing. Of this group,
Cushman is easily the most significant. His humorous study of impoverished Indians, *Stay Away, Joe* (1953), is, according to Vine Deloria, Jr.,
"the favorite of Indian people." Fox, like B. M. Bower, produced vast
quantities of western pulp fiction. The total circulation of his books runs
into the millions, and Hollywood turned three of them into movies.

Among Montana's more recent writers, the most notable are Joseph Kinsey Howard, Dorothy M. Johnson, and A. B. Guthrie, Jr. Howard grew up
in Great Falls, and at a young age he became a highly successful journalist.
During his tragically brief career, he produced a number of influential articles and several books of nonfiction. His most significant work was *Montana: High, Wide, and Handsome* (1943), an impressionistic history of the
state. When this book first appeared, many reviewers regarded it as one of
the nation's best regional studies. It has continued to sell well over the past
thirty years and has probably affected people's thinking about Montana
more than any other work. Howard's treatment of history was heavily
romantic and melodramatic: the good land where the "sky is so big," cruelly
misused and despoiled by wave after wave of mindless or evil exploiters.
Modern historians have rejected many of Howard's simplistic conclusions,
but readers will always return to his beautifully written pages.

Dorothy Johnson grew up in Great Falls and Whitefish and attended the
University of Montana, where she studied creative writing under a great
teacher, H. G. Merriam. During the thirties and forties she worked as an
editor, mostly in New York City, and wrote successfully on nonwestern
themes. After the war, though, she turned to western fiction, and in 1950
she returned to Whitefish and worked for her home-town newspaper. Her
western stories found quick success. The first collection, *Indian Country*
(1953), helped win her an appointment to teach creative writing at the University of Montana School of Journalism; and a second collection, *The
Hanging Tree*, appeared in 1957. Hollywood based a major movie upon the
title story of this volume, appropriately starring Montana actor Gary
Cooper. Later, two more of Miss Johnson's stories, "The Man Who Shot
Liberty Valance" and "A Man Called Horse," also became successful

motion pictures. As many popular magazines have folded up over the past fifteen years, Miss Johnson has devoted more of her attention to writing books for juveniles.

A. B. Guthrie, Jr., a native of Choteau, Montana, is not only the state's foremost author but is in fact one of the finest novelists ever to emerge from or write about the American West. Like Dorothy Johnson, Guthrie studied with H. G. Merriam at Missoula. He worked twenty-seven years as a journalist in Kentucky; and in the late 1930s he began trying his hand at fiction. His first book, *Trouble at Noon Dance* (1943), was undistinguished. Guthrie himself later called it "trash." The great turnaround in his career came in the mid-1940s, when a Nieman Fellowship won him a year's study at Harvard. Here, Guthrie worked under the distinguished Theodore Morrison and developed many valuable associations.

The main body of Guthrie's work consists of five novels, which collectively view regional history from the early frontier to recent times. First in the series was his masterpiece, *The Big Sky* (1947), a study of the mountain men which is one of the finest historical novels in all American literature. *The Way West* (1949) recounted life on the Oregon Trail and won a Pulitzer Prize in 1950. *These Thousand Hills* (1956) dealt with the Montana cattlemen's frontier; and *Arfive* (1970) and *The Last Valley* (1975) rounded out the sequence by depicting life in a small Montana town. In addition to his historical novels, Guthrie's other books include *The Big It* (1960), a collection of short stories; *The Blue Hen's Chick* (1965), an autobiography; and *Wild Pitch* (1973), a mystery.

In 1953 Guthrie moved back to Montana, the place of his birth and the setting of his best literary works. Recently, in writings and public appearances, he has become an outspoken leader of the conservation movement in Montana, arguing eloquently against a mindless form of "development" that threatens to destroy the environment. This role is altogether appropriate, for a major theme of his historical novels is the encroachment of "civilization" and its destruction of the natural habitat. Even Guthrie's mountain men, unthinking agents of "progress," worked unwittingly to destroy the very wilderness they treasured. Perhaps, like Boone Caudill in *The Big Sky*, modern man is drawn by his own lust to destroy that which he most cherishes.

CHAPTER XV

The Recent Political Scene: 1945–75

SINCE the close of World War II, Montana's political culture has changed in many ways, some dramatic and some subtle. These changes, naturally, arise from deeper-lying shifts in the state's basic economic-social order. On both the right and the left ends of the political scale, the trend has been away from polarity and toward diversity and modernization. To the right of center, the once awesome power of Anaconda has declined, while the roles of other corporations and conservative interest groups have increased. At the same time, the old left wing coalition of small farmers and metal miners has given way to a more broadly based and less strident medley of liberal groupings. Montana's political record of the past three decades clearly reflects these changes. Today, a broad range of conservative and liberal forces compete for political power in Montana, and they compete on fairly even terms. If this modern situation is less colorful than the wide open confrontations of the past, when all political storms seemed to swirl around the hurricane's eye of Company domination, it is also much healthier and more openly democratic. Interestingly, amidst all these changes, one long-term characteristic has remained relatively unchanged. Montana still presents a liberal image in national politics while acting and voting more conservatively at home.

THE CHANGING POLITICAL PROFILE

Like every other state, indeed like every other political community, Montana has a distinctive "political culture" all its own. This political culture arises naturally from the needs, demands, desires, and prejudices of the people and interest groups residing within its borders. Although the state is small in population, its political culture is surprisingly complex. No one interest group, no one ideology, no one political party prevails here. In contrast to the old Democratic South or the Republican Midwest, Montana's two major parties have traditionally been quite evenly matched ever since the 1880s. And compared to such conservative neighbors as Wyoming, Idaho, or Nebraska, Montana has a strong liberal bent that usually balances equally strong conservative tendencies. All of this leads, of course, to close and hard fought political contests. Montana's political battles sometimes discourage us, but they seldom bore us.

The key political factor in Montana, as in all other open societies, is the match of strength between conservative and liberal forces, between those who resist change and those who demand it. Conservatives in Montana, naturally enough, are essentially like conservatives elsewhere throughout the land. They come mostly from the middle and upper classes, and they are basically opposed to big government, deficit spending, and social permissiveness and experimentation. In Montana and across the nation, they have generally opposed the growth of the welfare state system that began with the New Deal of the 1930s.

In terms of support, Montana conservatives have powerful groups behind them. Their greatest financial and organizational backing comes from big-time agriculture and from corporations. Throughout the modern history of Montana, ranchers and the larger grain farmers have usually thrown their support behind conservative—especially conservative Republican—causes and candidates. Tightly knit and determined groups like the Montana Stockgrowers Association, the Montana Wool Growers Association and the Montana Farm Bureau Federation are always active and alert, especially during election campaigns and legislative sessions. Although the erosion of rural population has eaten into their power base, these conservative organizations still wield great influence. A frustrated young legislator from Wolf Point named Ted Schwinden underscored that fact during the archconservative 1961 session of the assembly. Pointing to the capitol dome, Schwinden commented that, while it was made of copper, it should be shaped like a stetson!

Here as elsewhere, corporations provide the key financial muscle for conservative efforts. As we have seen, the old corporate giant of Montana, Anaconda, steadily retreated from its earlier political domination after World War II. The clearest signals of this retreat were the 1959 sale of the Company newspapers and the breakup of the firm's close union with the Montana Power Company. The split between the "Montana Twins," which had become obvious by the early 1960s, apparently arose from executive rivalries and from conflicting attitudes toward public power, especially power from Hungry Horse Dam. While the two firms continued to ally on specific issues, each increasingly went its own separate way. Anaconda, for instance, continued to work selectively within both political parties, as it always had. Montana Power, however, preferred the Republican party and most always backed conservative candidates. According to most observers, Montana Power is today the most politically influential corporation in the state.

Thus Anaconda stands no longer alone as the hub of corporate influence in Montana. In a landmark piece of political reporting that appeared in a series of Billings *Gazette* articles during August–September 1972, Daniel J. Foley set forth an impressive analysis of the new corporate power structure in Montana. The *Gazette* study focused upon the state's big four businesses—Anaconda, Montana Power, Burlington Northern, and the First Bank System—and it found "considerable evidence that it is these companies who run Montana. 'The company,' it seems, has been replaced by a 'corporate power structure.' " Foley's report found a high degree of corporate cooperation: "The four companies are linked in a vast web of economic concentration: they have interlocking directorates, they retain the same prominent law firms and they have common business interests."

Most significantly, the *Gazette* underscored a point of common knowledge—that these corporations have wielded and continue to wield great influence over certain areas of state government. Through lobbying, political contributions, and other methods of "persuasion," they have ordinarily gained favorable treatment from the legislature, the State Board of Equalization, the Supreme Court, the Public Service Commission, and from other branches of government. In cases decided by the Montana Supreme Court, the *Gazette* study found that Montana Power "has won 14 favorable decisions out of 15 cases since 1957. In the 15th case, the utility won a partial victory. In four of the favorable decisions, the high court reversed lower court rulings." These businesses, and others such as the lumber, coal, and oil firms, the airlines, truckers, and contractors, obviously wield great strength in Montana. But they wield that strength more subtly than in the past. The heavy-handed lobbying techniques of Montana's history are now generally abandoned, replaced by more genteel methods. By 1971, for instance, the notorious old "watering holes" that the companies used to maintain for legislators had been shut down.

When the Billings *Gazette* study concluded that corporations "run Montana," it clearly overstated the case. It is easy to forget that the liberal forces in Montana hold a strong countervailing power. Like the conservatives, Treasure State liberals come from all levels of society, especially from the laboring classes, the legal profession, and from the students and faculties of the campuses. Also like the conservatives, Montana liberals draw upon the support of powerful organizations. Union labor and smaller farmers, traditionally the bastions of local liberalism, are still vitally important today. In

Montana as in many other states, the A.F.L.-C.I.O. is the dominant liberal force and the key element within the Democratic party. The Farmers Union, on the other hand, has lost much of its membership with the declining number of small farms, and it faces growing competition from the militant National Farmers Organization. Nonetheless, the Farmers Union is still a potent, well organized power in local politics.

On the left, as on the right, the trend in recent years has been toward a dispersal of political power. Since the 1930s the rural electrical cooperatives, spawned by the Rural Electrification Administration, have been a progressive force of real significance, strong enough to protect themselves from attacks by the state's investor-owned utilities. Liberal environmentalist groups like the Sierra Club and the Northern Plains Resource Council emerged, especially in the 1970s and especially among young people, as a significant political factor. Probably the most important—and subtle—new base of progressive support lies among the white collar, middle class employees of the urban areas. Many of these people are unionized teachers and public employees, and they tend heavily toward a middle-of-the-road brand of Kennedy-style liberalism. Liberals and conservatives alike, therefore, are becoming more diversified and, generally speaking, more moderate in viewpoint.

What we have here, then, is an intricately balanced kaleidoscope of diverse interests, reaching from the far right to the far left, with an increasingly heavy concentration in the center. In fact, the political balance is so delicately poised that Montana has usually swung predictably, like a weathervane, with the shifting winds of national sentiment. The state almost always offers a close reflection of the national mood. America entered the postwar era in a conservative frame of mind, and so did Montana. The "Eisenhower Equilibrium" of the 1950s found its local manifestation in the complacent political styles of J. Hugo Aronson and Mike Mansfield. Nationally and locally, politics became heated again in the late sixties and the seventies, as voters reacted angrily and cynically to issues like Viet Nam, Watergate, and, on the local level, threats to the environment and scandals in government.

One of the most refreshing aspects of Montana politics is its open, breezy, grass roots–democratic atmosphere. The state's small and unpretentious population has ready access to political leaders and political power, and local folks like their politics low keyed and down to earth. Senator Mansfield, to many Montanans, is simply "Mike," and homespun ex-Governor Hugo Aronson won many votes because he appealed to people as the "Galloping Swede." New York *Times* writer Tom Wicker captured the flavor of Montana politics in describing a typical campaign gathering at Billings in 1966:

. . . there were the candidates up there on the truck bed, earnest and tongue tied, and there were the ladies serving potatoe salad under the trees and there were several hundred big, informal, sun-burned American men who were willing to eat chili burgers on a hot Sunday while listening to the speaking. The cry of the politician may be too much with us, but in places like Pioneer Park, where the process begins, it has the authentic ring of an authentic people that is all too seldom heard in Washington.

MONTANA IN WASHINGTON: THE LIBERAL TRADITION

Despite the many broadening changes in Montana's political order, the "political schizophrenia" that first appeared during the 1920s has persisted into the 1970s. Montanans still seem to prefer liberals in Washington and conservatives in Helena. One reason for this puzzling ambivalence is obviously the fact that the liberal vote is, and always has been, heavily centered in a few urban areas. It can more easily sway statewide elections, especially primary elections, than localized legislative contests, where the more conservative rural interests have usually held an edge. Another factor favoring liberals running for congressional office is the nationwide dominance of liberal Democrats, which means to local voters that the Democrats they send to Washington will join the ruling congressional majority. Then again, liberals who run for national office usually face less opposition from local corporations than liberals who run for state office, where they might cause these interest groups more direct problems.

Whatever the explanations, the fact of Montana's preference for liberal representation in Washington is beyond dispute. This is particularly obvious in the state's choice of United State Senators. Incredibly, since the popular election of senators began in 1913, Montana has sent only one Republican to the U.S. Senate. Following the 1946 primary defeat of B. K. Wheeler, the state momentarily broke its normal pattern by choosing an archconservative Republican, Zales Ecton of Gallatin County, to join veteran liberal Democrat James E. Murray in the Senate. Ecton's Senate career, though, would be brief and unspectacular.

James E. Murray, who served in the Senate longer than any other Montanan (1935–61), first went to Washington during the heyday of the New Deal. Although a man of great wealth, Murray was also a determined and outspoken liberal. He was a less than dynamic campaigner, but the loyal support of liberal farmer-labor groups carried him through a long string of re-election victories, some of them by hairline margins. In the Senate, Murray proved himself a capable parliamentarian, an unwavering friend of organized labor, and one of the leading liberal lawmakers of the Roosevelt-Truman years. The list of key reform measures that Murray championed is an imposing one: the United Nations, legislation protecting small businessmen during World War II, the Employment Act of 1946, and the unsuccessful efforts for national health insurance and a Missouri Valley Authority, among many others. By the later 1950s old age had impaired Senator Murray's effectiveness, but his political career and record ranks as one of the longest in Montana's history.

In 1953 Murray was joined in the Senate by a low-keyed liberal Democrat named Mike Mansfield. Perhaps the most distinguished of all political figures in the state's history, Mansfield looks back upon an amazing and unique rise to fame. He broke into politics in 1940–42 as a little known history professor from the University of Montana at Missoula. Winning election to the western district congressional seat in 1942, Mansfield launched a ten-year career in the House of Representatives. Neither his political philosophy nor his style ever really changed much over the years. A compromising New Deal Democrat, he built a solid reputation as a businesslike congressman who looked carefully after the needs and wants of his constituents. Mansfield gained national recognition for expertise in foreign affairs, concentrating especially upon the Far East. In home state politics, meanwhile, he carefully skirted the hot issues and factional fights that destroyed so many other ambitious young politicians.

Mansfield reached the crossroads of his political journey in 1952, when he challenged the re-election bid of conservative Republican Senator Zales Ecton. The campaign was close, hard fought, and sometimes vicious. The Democrat ran largely on his successful record of fetching federal appropriations for his state, a record capped by the dedication of mighty Hungry Horse Dam just before the election. Mansfield was wounded, however, by a clumsy smear campaign certain extremist groups launched against him. This incredible attack upon his character, drawing upon the methods being used by Senator Joseph McCarthy in national politics, attempted to brand Mansfield as being soft on communism. It failed to work, as he pulled through to a close victory.

Since that narrow escape from defeat, Mike Mansfield has coasted to easy Senate re-election three times and has risen to a position of seemingly invincible strength. He won election as Senate Majority Leader in 1961 and has now held that prestigious post longer than any other man in American history. As always, he remains the soft-spoken, pipe-puffing moderate, standing aloof from and above the fray. This shrewd nonpartisan stance frequently angers liberal Democrats, who would like to see their leader more often on the front lines, but it allows Mansfield to draw in thousands of Republican votes. Most Montanans seem to regard him almost as a monument, and certainly as an asset; for Mansfield's protection of the state's interests in Washington is legendary. He has become so much a part of the state's political landscape over the past thirty-five years that the names Mansfield and Montana seem nearly inseparable. The senator's 1976 announcement that he would retire early in 1977 came as a shock to many of his fellow citizens.

Following Senator Murray's 1961 retirement, Lee Metcalf became Mansfield's junior partner in the Senate. Metcalf, a big strong man who seems consciously to avoid publicity, differs in many ways from his more famous colleague. Like Murray and unlike Mansfield, he has always been outspoken in his liberal views. He draws few conservative or Republican votes and relies heavily upon farmer-labor support to stay in office. Metcalf's long political career testifies to the enduring strength of the liberal vote in Montana. He started his career as a legislator and then moved on to a term on the Montana Supreme Court. In 1953 he replaced Mansfield as Montana's western district congressman.

During his four terms in the House, 1953–61, Lee Metcalf became known—perhaps better in Washington than in Montana—as one of the most determined liberals and conservationists in government. He was a key organizer of the Democratic Study Group, the core of liberal House strength in those days, and he led many a fight in protection of federal forest and grazing lands. As a United States Senator since 1961, Metcalf has followed the same tack. He is recognized as the Senate's leading critic of the giant electrical utilities industry, and his book *Overcharge* raised considerable controversy about utility rates and how they are set. In contrast to Mansfield, who usually faces only weak opposition, Metcalf has had to run against tough conservative opponents in each of his three Senate races— Orvin Fjare in 1960, Tim Babcock in 1966, and Hank Hibbard in 1972. Each time, tight organization and dedicated liberal support pulled him through. Mellowing somewhat, as his liberal constituents have mellowed, Lee Metcalf is clearly the heir to James Murray as the leader of the liberal community in Montana.

A glance at the occupants of Montana's two congressional seats over the past thirty years reveals a more mixed liberal-conservative pattern. The First Congressional District, embracing the western, mountainous counties, used to be known as the "safest Democratic district in the West," mainly because the labor-Democratic bastion of Butte-Anaconda dominated it. But in the Second District, which covers east-central Montana, the prevalence of conservative stockmen and large-scale farmers and the relative absence of labor unions made for more conservative-Republican voting patterns.

Thus we find a long series of liberal Democrats representing the western district: Mike Mansfield (1943–53), Lee Metcalf (1953–61), and Arnold Olsen (1961–71). Similarly, conservative Republicans held a near monopoly over the eastern district seat. Wesley D'Ewart, a staunch conservative and a favorite of the stockgrowers, held sway from 1945 until 1955; and another archconservative, Orvin Fjare, occupied the seat briefly in 1955–57. Democrat LeRoy Anderson took over during 1957–61, in part because of the unpopularity of President Eisenhower's farm policy and because of delays in starting construction of Yellowtail Dam. The eastern district returned to typically conservative hands, however, with the arrival of James "Big Jim" Battin (1961–69).

Interestingly, since 1969 the old pattern of liberal representation in the western district and conservative representation in the east has disappeared. Following the resignation of Representative Battin in 1969, Forsyth veterinarian John Melcher, a progressive Democrat, captured the eastern district seat. Melcher's impressive hold over this normally Republican district, which he has demonstrated in three subsequent elections, reveals both his own voter appeal and the rising weight of the moderate middle class vote in the urban centers of Billings and Great Falls. Coinciding with Melcher's rise, liberal Democrat Arnold Olsen lost his ten-year grip on the western district to conservative Republican Richard Shoup in 1970. Olsen's defeat seemed to symbolize the decline of both Butte-Anaconda's dominance and of the old liberal farmer-labor coalition in western Montana. It also underscored the new importance of middle class votes in Missoula, Helena, Bozeman, and Kalispell. After two terms in Congress, Shoup lost to Max Baucus, a Kennedy-style liberal, in the post-Watergate Democratic sweep of 1974. Thus the mid-1970s found Montana completely liberal-Democratic in its congressional representation.

TRENDS IN STATE GOVERNMENT: THE CONSERVATIVE TRADITION

However one tries to explain the situation—rural muscle at election time, the watchful eye of local corporate interests, or the voters' determination to keep down the costs of state government—there is no disputing the fact that the same Montana voters who predictably send liberals to Washington usually choose more conservative candidates to rule at home. A brief glance at the key political issues and personalities since 1945 clearly reveals this peculiar voting pattern.

The major political issues of postwar Montana closely resemble those of other states, especially the neighboring states of the Intermountain West. As in all states, the key questions center on those gut issues of how tax dollars are raised and how they are spent. By the early 1930s Montana had come to rely upon the income tax and the statewide property tax as its main sources of revenue. By the 1940s conservatives were pressing hard for a sales tax in order to take the load off these two levies and to meet the ever-rising costs of government. Liberals, on the other hand, opposed the sales tax, arguing that it was "regressive" and that it would place the main tax burden on middle and lower income groups. Over the past thirty years, the sales tax issue has raised its head again and again. Each time, liberal-Democratic forces beat it down. Today, Montana belongs to the small minority of only five states that do not use the sales tax.

Naturally, the taxation issue interlocks with that great bundle of questions: what services do we expect from state government? These services determine the size of the budget and of the tax levy, and budgetary considerations, in turn, limit the breadth of state services. Ever since the great expansion of state government during the New Deal, liberal Democrats have generally pushed for, and conservative Republicans against, a larger and more active government. The many departments of state government, each with its own clientele, grew up side by side, competing with one another for available tax dollars. The multi-unit university system mushroomed into a huge bureaucracy as veterans from the war, followed by youngsters of the affluent 1950s and 1960s, streamed onto the campuses. Similarly, the Department of Highways boomed as both Montana and Uncle Sam committed millions to build and maintain broad, well graded highways and controlled-access interstate freeways.

A multitude of other departments also clamored, with varying degrees of success, for their shares of the tax dollar. Among these were the sadly neglected custodial institutions at Boulder, Warm Springs, and elsewhere, the Office of Superintendent of Public Instruction, the Public Service Commission, and the Departments of Justice and of Administration. Each governor's term and each legislative session has rocked with claims and counterclaims regarding the needs and shortcomings of these agencies. One effort has rhythmically followed another in Montana's unending struggle to contain its expanding bureaucracy, to coordinate its administration, and to eliminate waste and duplication.

Yet another cluster of perennial issues arose from the ever-more-complex relationships between the state and federal governments. During the four decades following the New Deal, a number of different arms of the federal government increased their sway over resource-rich states like Montana. They included the Departments of Agriculture; Interior; Health, Education and Welfare; and Transportation; and, more particularly, the Forest Service; the Federal Highway Administration; the Bureaus of Reclamation and Indian Affairs; the Army Corps of Engineers; the Interstate Commerce Commission; and more recently the Environmental Protection Agency. The state always seems to be locked in some angry quarrel with the federal government. A partial list of such fights would include the river-oriented controversies over a Missouri Valley Authority, Paradise Dam, and Yellowtail Dam, land-use questions like coal leases, clear cutting and grazing permits, funding cutbacks for farm price supports, highway construction and crop storage facilities, and the real or threatened shutdowns of such Montana facilities as Glasgow Air Force Base, Anti-Ballistic Missile sites near Conrad, Forest Service offices at Missoula, or the Veterans Administration hospital at Miles City.

Looking back over the past three decades, we see these issues emerging time and again in shifting political contexts. As the war ended in 1945, conservative Republicans enjoyed a firm control of state government. Two-term G.O.P. Governor Sam C. Ford (1941–49) sat in the governor's chair, and Republicans held comfortable majorities in both houses of the legislature. Ford, a capable administrator, was a veteran of the old progressive wing of the Republican Party. By the 1940s, though, he had drifted well to the right. As seen previously, Ford relied upon the support of Senator Wheeler and other conservative Democrats to maintain his political base. Pointing to this fact and to the power wielded by Ford's controversial ally Wellington Rankin, both angry Republicans to the right and angry Democrats to the left complained of a "Wheeler-Ford-Rankin triumvirate" that allegedly held the reins of government.

Debate during the Ford years centered on issues which, in one form or another, would persist for years afterward: the sales tax, funding help for public schools, how to manage the education, highway and liquor bureaucracies, and Senator Murray's bill in Congress proposing massive federal resource development through a Missouri Valley Authority. Ford and the wartime legislatures spent much energy trying to reorganize and pare down the bureaucracy that had mushroomed during the 1930s. Hired by a Governor's Committee on Reorganization and Economy, the management consulting firm of Griffenhagen & Associates produced, in fifty-nine large reports, a massive list of recommendations for change. Many of these recommendations would, over the long haul, be adopted.

The same problems that plagued Ford also beset his Democratic successor, John Bonner. A former attorney general and popular veteran of World War II, Bonner defeated Ford in a rough 1948 gubernatorial contest. Bonner charged Ford with neglecting or abusing the highway and liquor operations and with allowing the custodial institutions to deteriorate. In reply, Ford cried smear and called anyone voicing such charges "a dirty, rotten, contemptible rat . . . a deliberate and willful liar." Governor Bonner laid out a moderately liberal program, and the legislature generally cooperated with him. The most significant breakthrough of these years was the landmark School Foundation Program created by the 1949 Legislature, providing funds to equalize educational standards in all of Montana's many school districts. By 1951–52, however, Bonner and the Democrats were in trouble. Strong nationwide and statewide conservative trends aided the Republicans, and the Democrats were divided by factionalism and by accusations of personal misconduct against the governor.

In 1952 the nationwide triumph of Eisenhower Republicans was reflected by sweeping victories of conservative Republicans in Montana. The Treasure State's version of Eisenhower was popular Governor J. Hugo Aronson (1953–61). Nicknamed the "Galloping Swede," Aronson rose to fame as a humble immigrant who made it big as an oilman-rancher-businessman. The Swede's popularity stemmed from a jovial, down-to-earth manner and from his legendary physical strength, stories of which still abound in Montana. As chief executive, Aronson struck a subdued pose, somewhat as Eisenhower did in the White House, making little effort to change things or to crack the whip over lawmakers.

The Aronson years of the fifties were a time of conservatism and outward calm. The powerful liberal forces unleashed by the New Deal had mellowed by now, and consensus seemed to prevail. Two major controversies that did momentarily break the calm arose over the questions of oil leases on state lands and the use of gasoline taxes solely for highway construction. Both of these issues culminated in the 1956 election. By an overwhelming margin, the voters approved an "Anti-Diversion" amendment to the constitution which, in effect, provided the Department of Highways with its own exclusive source of revenue—the highway fuel and users' taxes.

At the same time the important oil lease question became the focus of a bitter gubernatorial fight between Aronson and his Democratic foe Arnold Olsen, the handsome attorney general who had captured liberal favor by his campaigns to lower utility rates and clean up illegal gambling. Olsen argued that the 12½ percent maximum royalty which the state received from oil wells located on its school lands was so low as to constitute a "steal." Aronson countered that Olsen's obstruction of leasing as attorney general had cost the state millions of dollars in lost revenue. In the end, Aronson narrowly defeated Olsen, and the conservatives won on the oil lease issue. Following the Aronson-Olsen fight of 1956, the political waters quickly calmed again. Conservatives ruled at the executive, legislative, and judicial levels of government. A momentous change did occur in 1957 when the legislature created the Legislative Council, a key fact-finding body that would provide the lawmakers with better intelligence and help free them from such heavy reliance upon lobbyists.

Montana's political pendulum swung even farther to the right in 1960 with the election of Donald Nutter to the governorship. An archconservative from Sidney, Nutter soundly defeated liberal Democrat Paul Cannon by running on a platform that called for a better business climate, reduced taxes, major cuts in government services and payroll, and, if necessary, a sales tax. Governor Nutter proved, as anticipated, to be an extreme rightist once in office, even refusing to proclaim United Nations Day in Montana. The 1961 Legislature, faced with a six-million-dollar deficit, followed Nutter's proposals and slashed expenditures for the custodial institutions, the university system, and other arms of government. With some measure of truth, many Montanans trace today's budget problems and erosion of state services back to the wholesale cuts of 1961.

Governor Nutter never had a chance to pursue his retrenchment program, for he died in a terrible January 1962 plane crash. Replacing him was Lieutenant Governor Tim Babcock, a wealthy trucker from Billings whose conservative leanings approached those of his predecessor. Babcock, who would later find himself caught up in the fund-raising scandals of Watergate, won election to a full term in 1964 and thus governed the state from 1962 until 1969. The state payroll grew rapidly during these prosperous years, and the conservative calm of the 1950s generally continued. Attempting to comply with the United States Supreme Court's "one man–one vote" ruling, the Montana legislature tried and failed to reapportion itself. So federal courts did the job in 1965. Reapportionment meant, of course, the loss of legislative seats for rural areas and gains for the growing cities. Overall, the conservatives lost and the liberals gained strength as a result of this momentous change.

Sixteen years of Republican rule finally came to an end in 1968 when Governor Babcock ran for re-election against Democrat Forrest Anderson, a former legislator, supreme court justice, and attorney general, and a seasoned veteran of Montana's political wars. Estimating that the state would need another fifty million dollars to fund mounting costs over the next biennium, Babcock campaigned for a 3 percent sales tax as the only solution. Anderson cagily responded by asserting that, through reorganizing government, cutting costs, and increasing existing taxes, the sales tax could be avoided. His slogan put it simply—some said too simply: "Pay More? What For!" Predictably, the sales tax issue allowed Anderson to defeat Babcock by a wide margin.

Although the Anderson Administration (1969–73) brought Democrats back to the helm, this did not mean a major shift to the left. Forrest Anderson was a moderate-to-conservative Democrat. On the stormiest issue of his term, the ballooning question of environmental protection, the governor generally sided with those who favored economic "development" against the environmentalists. He became embroiled in a marathon struggle with conservationist Fish and Game Director Frank Dunkle, threw his support behind the unsuccessful attempt by Anaconda to begin open pit mining of copper in the beautiful Lincoln area, and favored state construction of a controversial road to serve the Big Sky tourist development.

Government reorganization marked Anderson's major achievement. Following voter approval of an enabling constitutional amendment in 1970 and passage by the legislature of the Executive Reorganization Act in 1971, the

Anderson Administration began a major reshuffling of the bureaucracy, combining over one hundred state agencies into nineteen departments. Meanwhile, however, just as Babcock had forecast, the mounting demands and costs of government, intensified now by runaway inflation, outpaced the appropriations of the legislature. Funding failed to meet needs; and state agencies, especially the custodial institutions and the university system, found themselves in a crushing and destructive cost-price squeeze. The question "Pay More? What For!" seemed to be mutely answered.

THE WINDS OF CHANGE

From the close vantage of the mid-seventies it seems clear that, after a long period of relative quiet during the later fifties and the sixties, a period of rapid social, economic, and political change set in around 1970–71. As usual, history warns us that these changes were not so abrupt as they seem. The forces of change built up slowly during the preceding two decades until their mounting pressure, like an exploding earthquake, suddenly broke open the political landscape during and after the Anderson era. The subtle and slow building forces of change were many. As Montana's astute Commissioner of State Lands Ted Schwinden noted at a recent historical conference, the major forces were nationalizing trends, which worked to break down local peculiarities and to draw the state closer into the main current of American life.

No doubt the key long-term change was the slow and steady shift in the nature of the state's population. As farm population eroded, rural Montana gradually lost ground to the small but slowly expanding cities. Aided by reapportionment after 1965, the cities began to flex their muscles. Increasingly the cities, from traditionally Democratic Great Falls and Missoula to traditionally Republican Billings, became centers of moderate, middle class, consensus politics, closely divided between the two parties and receptive to arguments for change. Meanwhile the rural areas, having been hurt by change, tended to fear and resist it, moving in a more conservative direction. More and more, the growing urban middle class came to call the political tune.

Other trends, as noted earlier, blended with urbanization. As the Company's influence declined on the right, and the mining unions' influence declined on the left, the political center gradually expanded. Montanans, like other Americans, became less provincial and more cosmopolitan during the postwar decades. Travel, whether forced by the military or chosen for the purposes of business, employment, vacationing, or education, broadened their horizons. More importantly, so did the revolution in communications. The Lee Newspapers brought an open and vastly improved news coverage in the sixties. And radio-television, both in network and local programing, brought global, national, and state developments into closer focus.

By the later 1960s, interestingly, Montanans seemed to be changing their minds about their state and about themselves. Shocked, like most of their fellow countrymen, by the crises of America's great cities, they began to reassess what their state had to offer. Unlike previous generations, who tended to see the future for themselves and their children in leaving the state, the newer generations found appealing reasons for staying here. This attitude expressed itself in a new concern for preserving the environment, a renewed pride in the community, and a new interest in reforming and improving society and government. Never, at least not since the Progressive Era, had Montana seen such widespread popular participation in politics.

The new activism surfaced dramatically in the legislature. Beyond a doubt the lawmakers of the 1970s tended to be younger, better educated, more environmentally conscious, and more independent than their predecessors. They were less tied to party lines, harder to lobby, and more difficult for party leaders to discipline. Heralding these trends, the landmark legislature of 1971 began passing tough environmental laws and provided for executive reorganization. It also passed the first minimum wage law in Montana's history, prepared a referendum to allow the voters to decide directly upon the controversial sales tax issue, and made final preparations for an all-important constitutional convention.

No movement better captured the spirit of the times than did the drive for constitutional reform. The argument that the old 1889 Constitution was outdated and needed replacing reached back to the days of Governor Dixon and before. Significantly, however, the argument began to find a strong reception now, in the later 1960s. In the November 1970 election the voters approved Referendum No. 67, calling for a constitutional convention. Then in a special election of November 1971 they chose one hundred delegates to assemble for the purpose of drafting a new constitution. While choosing their "Con-Con" delegates, the people also gave their verdict on Referendum No. 68, for or against a sales tax. They rejected the Republican-sponsored sales tax by a better than two-to-one margin, and this issue caused an anti-Republican backlash that helps explain the election of an exceptionally liberal-minded group of delegates to the constitutional convention.

Assembled at Helena under the chairmanship of Leo Graybill, Jr., of Great Falls, the delegates did their work expeditiously. After fifty-four days they turned out a constitution twelve thousand words long (less than half the length of its 1889 predecessor), which many observers consider among the most advanced in the country. *Time* called it a "model document," and the federal government prepared a special film to portray it abroad as an example of grass roots democracy in action. Among the most significant innovations in the new constitution are: single-member legislative districts, annual (instead of biennial) legislative session,* statewide property tax assessment, and major efforts to strengthen the powers of the legislature. After a hard fought campaign that generally pitted urban interests in favor of the constitution against rural interests in opposition, the document passed by the slender margin of 116,415 in favor, and 113,883 opposed. The Farm Bureau spearheaded a conservative drive to strike down the new constitution in court, arguing that technically a majority of voters in the election had not approved the document. But the Montana Supreme Court narrowly upheld the vote, and the new constitution brought the state a modernized framework of government beginning in 1973.

The progressive tide carrying in the new constitution during 1971–72 continued to flow during the years that followed. In the 1972 general election, Lee Metcalf won a third Senate term against tough Republican opposition. And Thomas Judge, a moderately liberal Democrat, replaced Governor Anderson, who declined to run again because of ill health. Interestingly, both Judge's race against arch conservative rancher "Big Ed" Smith and the earlier fight over ratification of the constitution revealed a strikingly similar pattern. In both cases a moderately liberal urban vote confronted a strongly conservative rural vote—and in each instance, the liberals won. The liberal tide reached true flood proportions in the midterm elections of 1974, boosted no doubt by the nationwide anti-Republican reaction to Watergate. Montana Democrats took overwhelming control over both houses of the legislature. And with the victory of Max Baucus in the western district, liberal Democrats gained complete sway over the state's congressional delegation.

Most likely, the recent victories of the liberal Democrats will soon be countered by a conservative Republican comeback. That has been the pattern, after all, throughout Montana's political history. Regardless of their political beliefs, Montanans who survey their state's present situation can find grounds for either pessimism or optimism. On the dark side, one must consider the truly sad conditions at some of the custodial institutions, the spread of voter cynicism and apathy, and the ominously growing scandal in the state's Workmen's Compensation Commission. On the brighter side, though, we find an electorate that is better informed and more politically concerned, and a legislature that is probably more competent and closely attuned to the times, than ever before. Most reassuring of all, we find a pride in the statewide community that seems higher than at any time since the early years of this century.

* The voters rejected annual legislative sessions in a 1974 referendum vote.

Bibliographical Essays

While employing our own original research when possible, we have naturally relied heavily upon the work of others in preparing this book, for historical understanding is a communal enterprise. The following bibliographical essays, organized by chapter, indicate the sources that we have found most helpful on each topic. By necessity, they are selective and are not meant to include all of the historical writings upon every facet of Montana's history. Several general histories, which will appear again from time to time in the following pages, should be mentioned at the outset. Among the best books on Montana's frontier period are Merrill G. Burlingame, *The Montana Frontier* (Helena: State Publishing Co., 1942); James M. Hamilton, *History of Montana: From Wilderness to Statehood* (Portland: Binfords and Mort, 1957, 1970); Paul F. Sharp, *Whoop-Up Country* (3d ed.; Norman: University of Oklahoma Press, 1973); and Mark H. Brown, *The Plainsmen of the Yellowstone* (New York: G. P. Putnam's Sons, 1961).

General interpretive works include Joseph Kinsey Howard, *Montana: High, Wide, and Handsome* (New Haven, Conn.: Yale University Press, 1943); K. Ross Toole, *Montana: An Uncommon Land* (Norman: University of Oklahoma Press, 1959); Toole, *Twentieth-Century Montana: A State of Extremes* (Norman: University of Oklahoma Press, 1972); Michael P. Malone and Richard B. Roeder, eds., *The Montana Past: An Anthology* (Missoula: University of Montana Press, 1969); and Robert G. Athearn, *High Country Empire* (New York: McGraw-Hill, 1960). Subscription or "mug" histories are sometimes useful sources of information. We relied heavily upon the best and most recent of these, Merrill G. Burlingame and K. Ross Toole, eds., *A History of Montana* (3 vols.; New York: Lewis Historical Publishing Co., 1957). Earlier subscription histories include: Michael A. Leeson, *History of Montana: 1739–1885* (Chicago: Warner, Beers and Company, 1885); Joaquin Miller, *An Illustrated History of the State of Montana* (Chicago: Lewis Publishing Co., 1894); *Progressive Men of the State of Montana* (Chicago: A. W. Bowen and Co., c. 1900); Helen Fitzgerald Sanders, *A History of Montana* (3 vols.; Chicago and New

York: Lewis Publishing Co., 1913); Tom Stout, *Montana: Its Story and Biography* (3 vols.; Chicago and New York: American Historical Society, 1921); and Robert G. Raymer, *Montana: The Land and the People* (3 vols.; Chicago and New York: Lewis Publishing Co., 1930).

CHAPTER I. MONTANA IN PREHISTORY

On Montana's history and geography, see Robert L. Taylor, Milton J. Edie, and Charles F. Gritzner, *Montana in Maps: 1974* (Bozeman, Mont.: Big Sky Books, 1974); the Earth Sciences Department of Montana State University, which compiled this handsome work, is also preparing a historical atlas of Montana. Also valuable, although somewhat dated, are J. P. Rowe, *Geography and Natural Resources of Montana* (Missoula: University of Montana, 1933, 1941); Federal Writers' Project of the Work Projects Administration for the State of Montana, *Montana: A State Guide Book* (New York: Viking Press, 1939, 1949), and *The Montana Almanac* (Missoula: University of Montana Press, 1958, 1960), and its 1962–63 *Statistical Supplement* (Missoula: University of Montana Press, 1962). Eugene S. Perry discusses geological history in *Montana in the Geologic Past*, Montana Bureau of Mines and Geology, Bulletin 26 (Butte, 1962); see also Perry, "Montana before Man," in *A History of Montana*, ed. M. G. Burlingame and K. R. Toole (3 vols.; New York: Lewis Historical Publishing Co., 1957), 1:1–30.

Many histories and anthropological studies of the American Indians discuss their prehistory. Among the best are Harold E. Driver, *Indians of North America* (Chicago: University of Chicago Press, 1961, 1969); Alvin M. Josephy, Jr., *The Indian Heritage of America* (New York: Alfred A. Knopf, 1969); William Brandon, *The Last Americans* (New York: McGraw-Hill, 1974); Ruth M. Underhill, *Red Man's America* (Chicago: University of Chicago Press, 1953, 1971); William T. Hagan, *American Indians* (Chicago: University of Chicago Press, 1961); Clark Wissler, *Indians of the United States* (Garden City, N.Y.: Doubleday, 1940, 1966); and, for quick reference, D'Arcy McNickle, *The Indian Tribes of the United States* (London: Oxford University Press, 1962). Especially interesting for Indian prehistory is Peter Farb, *Man's Rise to Civilization as Shown by the Indians of North America . . .* (New York: Dutton, 1968).

Valuable, brief discussions of the Montana tribes can be found in Carling Malouf, "Montana's Aboriginal Inhabitants: The Indians," in *A History of Montana*, ed. M. G. Burlingame and K. R. Toole (3 vols.; New York: Lewis Historical Publishing Co., 1957), 1:31–53; and Malouf's similar discussion in *The Montana Almanac* (Missoula: University of Montana Press, 1957), pp. 99–112; and Merrill G. Burlingame, *The Montana Frontier* (Helena: State Publishing Co., 1942), chap. 2. Also of general Montana interest are John C. Ewers, *Indian Life on the Upper Missouri* (Norman: University of Oklahoma Press, 1968); Ella Clark, *Indian Legends from the Northern Rockies* (Norman: University of Oklahoma Press, 1966); and Edwin T. Denig, *Indian Tribes of the Upper Missouri* (Washington, D.C.: Bureau of American Ethnology, 1930).

Among the more useful histories of Montana Indians are, on the Salish, Olga W. Johnson, *Flathead and Kootenay* (Glendale, Calif.: A. H. Clark Co., 1969); Peter Ronan, *History of the Flathead Indians* (Minneapolis: Ross and Haines, 1890, 1965);

H. H. Turney-High, *The Flathead Indians of Montana* (Menasha, Wis.: American Anthropological Association, 1937); and John Fahey, *The Flathead Indians* (Norman: University of Oklahoma Press, 1974). On the Kutenai, see Olga W. Johnson's work, cited above, and Paul E. Baker, *The Forgotten Kutenai* (Boise: Mountain States Press, 1955); H. H. Turney-High, . . . *Ethnography of the Kutenai* (Menasha, Wis.: American Anthropological Association, 1941); and Franz Boas, *Kutenai Tales* (Washington, D.C.: Government Printing Office, 1918).

The Blackfeet are well treated in John C. Ewers' widely respected *The Blackfeet: Raiders on the Northwestern Plains* (Norman: University of Oklahoma Press, 1958); Ewers, *The Horse in Blackfoot Indian Culture* (Washington, D.C.: Government Printing Office, 1955); and Ewers, *Ethnological Report on the Blackfeet and Gros Ventre Tribes of Montana* (New York: Garland, 1974). See also George Bird Grinnell, *Blackfoot Lodge Tales* (New York: C. Scribner's Sons, 1892); Frank B. Linderman, *Blackfeet Indians* (St. Paul: Brown and Bigelow, 1935); Walter McClintock, *The Old North Trail* (Lincoln: University of Nebraska Press, 1968); and Clark Wissler, *Material Culture of the Blackfoot Indians* (New York: Trustees of the Anthropological Papers of the American Museum of Natural history, 1910).

For the Crow Indians, consult Robert H. Lowie, *The Crow Indians* (New York: Farrar and Rinehart, 1935); Lowie, *The Material Culture of the Crow Indians* (New York: Trustees of the Anthropological Papers of the American Museum of Natural History, 1922); Frank B. Linderman, *American: The Life Story of . . . Plenty-coups* . . . (New York: John Day Co., 1930); and Charles C. Bradley, Jr., *A History of the Crow Indians* (Lodge Grass, Mont.: Lodge Grass Schools, 1971). Edward E. Barry, Jr., discusses the Gros Ventres and Assiniboines in *The Fort Belknap Indian Reservation: The First One Hundred Years, 1855–1955* (Bozeman: Montana State University, 1974). See, too, Regina Flannery, *The Gros Ventres of Montana* (2 vols; Washington, D.C.: Catholic University of America Press, 1953–56); two works by Alfred L. Kroeber, published by the Trustees of the Anthropological Papers of the American Museum of Natural History: *Gros Ventre Myths and Tales* (New York, 1907); and . . . *Ethnology of the Gros Ventre* (New York, 1908); and David Rodnick, "The Fort Belknap Assiniboine of Montana . . ." (Ph.D. diss., University of Pennsylvania, 1936).

The Shoshonis are discussed by Virginia C. Trenholm, *The Shoshonis, Sentinels of the Rockies* (Norman: University of Oklahoma Press, 1964). For the Cheyennes, see Donald J. Berthrong, *The Southern Cheyennes* (Norman: University of Oklahoma Press, 1963); George B. Grinnell, *The Cheyenne Indians* (New Haven, Conn.: Yale University Press, 1923); Grinnell, *By Cheyenne Campfires* (New Haven, Conn.: Yale University Press, 1962); Peter J. Powell, *Sweet Medicine* (2 vols.; Norman: University of Oklahoma Press, 1969); and John Stands in Timber and Margot Liberty, *Cheyenne Memories* (New Haven, Conn.: Yale University Press, 1967). Thomas R. Wessel discusses the Chippewas, Crees, and Metis, in *A History of the Rocky Boy's Indian Reservation* (Bozeman: Montana State University, 1974); see also Carolissa Levi, *Chippewa Indians of Yesterday and Today* (New York: Pageant Press, 1956); and Verne Dusenberry, *The Montana Cree* (Stockholm: Almqvist and Wiksell).

CHAPTER II. EARLY EXPLORATIONS

Useful general studies of northern exploration are Bernard De Voto's masterful *The Course of Empire* (Boston: Houghton Mifflin, 1952); John B. Brebner, *The Explorers of North America: 1492–1806* (New York: Macmillan, 1933); Gordon Speck, *Northwest Explorations* (Portland: Binfords and Mort, 1954); and for the close connection between exploration and fur trading, Paul C. Phillips, *The Fur Trade* (2 vols.; Norman: University of Oklahoma Press, 1961). Stanley R. Davison provides a Montana perspective in "The Coming of the White Man," in *A History of Montana*, ed. M. G. Burlingame and K. R. Toole (3 vols.; New York: Lewis Historical Publishing Co., 1957), 1:55–70. William H. Goetzmann offers a superb history of western exploration during the forty years *after* Lewis and Clark in *Exploration and Empire* (New York: Alfred A. Knopf, 1966).

The historical literature on the expansion of the English and also the French and Spanish colonies is, of course, enormous. For recent, general studies of England's rivals in North America, see Charles Gibson, *Spain in America* (New York: Harper and Row, 1966); and W. J. Eccles, *France in America* (New York: Harper and Row, 1972). For the Hudson's Bay Company and other fur trading firms, see the bibliographic essay for Chapter III. On the Verendryes, consult Lawrence J. Burpee, ed., *Journals and Letters of Pierre Gaultier de Varennes De La Verendrye and His Sons*, Champlain Society Publication 16 (Toronto: Champlain Society, 1927; New York: Greenwood Press, 1968); Nellis M. Crouse, *La Verendrye: Fur Trader and Explorer* (Ithaca, N.Y.: Cornell University Press, 1956); and, especially illuminating upon the journey of 1742–43, John W. Smurr, "A New La Verendrye Theory," *Pacific Northwest Quarterly*, 43 (January 1952): 51–64. A. P. Nasatir discusses the white advance up the Missouri River, and includes pertinent documents, in *Before Lewis and Clark: Documents Illustrating the History of the Missouri, 1785–1804* (2 vols.; St. Louis: St. Louis Historical Documents Foundation, 1952).

On the Louisiana Purchase and its context, see among many writings, A. P. Whitaker, *The Mississippi Question, 1795–1803* (New York: D. Appleton, 1934); E. W. Lyon, *Louisiana in French Diplomacy, 1759–1804* (Norman: University of Oklahoma Press, 1934); W. E. Hemphill, "The Jeffersonian Background of the Louisiana Purchase," *Mississippi Valley Historical Review*, 22 (September 1935): 177–90; Oscar Handlin, "The Louisiana Purchase: Chance or Destiny," *Atlantic Monthly*, 195 (January 1955): 44–49; and John L. Allen, "Geographical Knowledge and American Images of the Louisiana Territory," *Western Historical Quarterly*, 2 (April 1971): 151—70.

There is an enormous body of historical literature concerning the Lewis and Clark Expedition. The Journals of that exploration are the most valuable source: see Reuben G. Thwaites, ed., *Original Journals of the Lewis and Clark Expedition, 1804–1806* (8 vols.; New York: Dodd, Mead, 1904–5). Easily the best abridgement of these is Bernard DeVoto's fine edition of *The Journals of Lewis and Clark* (Boston: Houghton Mifflin, 1953), with superb introduction and explanatory footnotes. Also of exceptional value are Ernest S. Osgood, ed., *The Field Notes of Captain William Clark* (New Haven, Conn.: Yale University Press, 1964); and Donald Jackson, ed., *Letters of the Lewis and Clark Expedition, with Related Documents,*

1783–1854 (Urbana: University of Illinois Press, 1962). John Bakeless' *Lewis and Clark: Partners in Discovery* (New York: W. Morrow, 1947) is popular; Richard Dillon's *Meriwether Lewis: A Biography* (New York: Coward-McCann, 1965) is good; see too Jerome O. Steffen, "William Clark: A Reappraisal," *Montana: The Magazine of Western History*, 25 (Spring 1975): 52–61; and Ingvard H. Eide's *American Oddyssey: The Journey of Lewis and Clark* (Chicago: Rand McNally, 1969) is a beautiful photohistory.

On more specialized topics are Charles G. Clarke, *The Men of the Lewis and Clark Expedition* (Glendale, Calif.: A. H. Clark Co., 1970); Paul C. Cutright, *Lewis and Clark: Pioneering Naturalists* (Urbana: University of Illinois Press, 1969); Drake W. Will, "Lewis and Clark: Westering Physicians," *Montana: The Magazine of Western History*, 21 (Autumn 1971): 2–17; M. O. Skarsten, *George Drouillard* (Glendale, Calif.: A. H. Clark Co., 1964); John L. Allen, *Passage through the Garden: Lewis and Clark and the Image of the American Northwest* (Urbana: University of Illinois Press, 1975); and Harold P. Howard, *Sacajawea* (Norman: University of Oklahoma Press, 1971). Three studies that provide especially good perspectives are Ernest S. Osgood, "Clark on the Yellowstone, 1806," *Montana: The Magazine of Western History*, 18 (Summer 1968): 8–29; John L. Allen, "Lewis and Clark on the Upper Missouri: Decision at the Marias," ibid., 21 (Summer 1971): 2–17; and Donald Jackson, "The Public Image of Lewis and Clark," *Pacific Northwest Quarterly*, 57 (January 1966): 1–7.

Chapter III. Era of the Fur Trade

Two standard, general histories of the fur trade are Paul C. Phillips, *The Fur Trade* (2 vols.; Norman: University of Oklahoma Press, 1961); and Hiram M. Chittenden, *The American Fur Trade of the Far West* (3 vols.; New York: Francis P. Harper, 1902). Bernard DeVoto's *Across the Wide Missouri* is less structured, but insightful and well written; and William H. Goetzmann's *Exploration and Empire* (New York: Alfred A. Knopf, 1966) places the fur trade in the general context of western exploration. For a Montana focus, see Paul C. Phillips, "The Fur Trade in Montana," in *A History of Montana*, ed. M. G. Burlingame and K. R. Toole (3 vols.; New York: Lewis Historical Publishing Co., 1957), 1:71–98; James M. Hamilton, *History of Montana: From Wilderness to Statehood* (Portland: Binfords and Mort, 1957, 1970), chap. 2; and Merrill G. Burlingame, *The Montana Frontier* (Helena: State Publishing Co., 1942), chap. 3. A valuable bibliography of original journals relating to the regional fur trade can be found in the *Contributions to the Historical Society of Montana*, 10 (Helena: Naegele Printing Co., 1940): 189–310.

On the British-Canadian fur trade, consult E. E. Rich, *The History of the Hudson's Bay Company, 1670–1870* (2 vols.; London: Hudson's Bay Record Society, 1958–62); and John S. Galbraith, *The Hudson's Bay Company as an Imperial Factor, 1821–1869* (Berkeley: University of California Press, 1957). For David Thompson, see Richard Glover, ed., *David Thompson's Narrative, 1784–1812* (Toronto: Champlain Society, 1962), which has a fine Introduction; also valuable are M. Catherine White, ed., *David Thompson's Journals Relating to Montana, 1808–1812* (Missoula: University of Montana Press, 1950); and White, "Saleesh

House," *Pacific Northwest Quarterly*, 33 (July 1942): 251–63. There are several editions of Ogden's "Snake Country Journals"; on that important brigade leader, see also Gloria G. Cline, *Peter Skene Ogden and the Hudson's Bay Company* (Norman: University of Oklahoma Press, 1974); and Edgar I. Stewart, "Peter Skene Ogden in Montana, 1825," *Montana Magazine of History*, 3 (Autumn 1953): 32–45. An insight into the later years of British activity is provided in Albert J. Partoll, "Fort Connah: A Frontier Trading Post, 1847–1871," *Pacific Northwest Quarterly*, 30 (October, 1939): 399–415.

Early American fur trade on the upper Missouri is discussed in Richard E. Oglesby, *Manuel Lisa and the Opening of the Missouri Fur Trade* (Norman: University of Oklahoma Press, 1963); Thomas James, *Three Years among the Indians and Mexicans* (St. Louis: Missouri Historical Society, 1916); Burton Harris, *John Colter: His Years in the Rockies* (New York: Scribner's, 1952); David C. Rowe, "Government Relations with the Fur Trappers of the Upper Missouri, 1820–1840," *North Dakota History*, 25 (Spring 1968): 481–505; and John E. Sunder, *Joshua Pilcher: Fur Trader and Indian Agent* (Norman: University of Oklahoma Press, 1968).

The literature on the Rocky Mountain Fur Company is enormous, but see especially LeRoy R. Hafen, ed., *The Mountain Men and the Fur Trade of the Far West* (10 vols.; Glendale, Calif.: A. H. Clark Co., 1965–72); Don Berry, *A Majority of Scoundrels* (New York: Harper and Brothers, 1961); Carl P. Russell, *Firearms, Traps, and Tools of the Mountain Men* (New York: Alfred A. Knopf, 1967); Lewis O. Saum, *The Fur Trader and the Indian* (Seattle: University of Washington Press, 1965); Dale L. Morgan, *Jedediah Smith and the Opening of the West* (Indianapolis: Bobbs-Merrill, 1953); and J. Cecil Alter, *James Bridger* (rev. ed.; Norman: University of Oklahoma Press, 1962).

A readable history of the American Fur Company, focusing upon Ramsay Crooks, is David Lavender, *The Fist in the Wilderness* (Garden City, N.Y.: Doubleday, 1964). On Astor, consult John U. Terrell, *Furs by Astor* (New York: Morrow, 1963); and Kenneth W. Porter, *John Jacob Astor, Business Man* (2 vols.; New York: Russell and Russell, 1931). Also relating to this firm, and the later period of the fur trade, are John E. Sunder, *The Fur Trade on the Upper Missouri, 1840–1865* (Norman: University of Oklahoma Press, 1965); and Elliott Coues, ed., *Forty Years a Fur Trader on the Upper Missouri: The Journal of Charles Larpenteur* (2 vols.; New York: F. P. Harper, 1898).

On the Jesuit missionaries, see William N. Bischoff, S.J., *The Jesuits in Old Oregon* (Caldwell, Ida.: Caxton Printers, 1945); Wilfred Schoenberg, S.J., *Jesuits in Montana: 1840–1960* (Portland: Oregon-Jesuit, 1960); Anne McDonnell, "The Catholic Indian Missions in Montana," in *A History of Montana*, ed. M. G. Burlingame and K. R. Toole (3 vols.; New York: Lewis Historical Publishing Co., 1957), 1:99–118; and Richard G. Forbis, "The Flathead Apostacy," *Montana Magazine of History*, 1 (October 1951): 35–40. Father DeSmet is the subject of H. M. Chittenden and A. T. Richardson, eds., *Life, Letters, and Travels of Father Pierre-Jean de Smet, S.J.* (4 vols.; New York: F. P. Harper, 1905); and John U. Terrell, *Black Robe: The Life of Pierre-Jean de Smet . . .* (Garden City, N.Y.: Doubleday, 1964). See also William L. Davis, S.J., "Peter John DeSmet," *Pacific Northwest Quarterly*, 32 (April 1941): 167–96; 33 (April 1942): 123–52; 35 (January 1944): 29–43, (April

1944): 121–42. The priests told their own story in Nicholas Point, S.J., *Wilderness Kingdom: Indian Life in the Rocky Mountains, 1840–1847* (New York: Holt, Rinehart and Winston, 1967); Lawrence B. Palladino, S.J., *Indian and White in the Northwest: A History of Catholicity in Montana, 1831–1891* (2d ed.; Lancaster, Pa.: Wickersham, 1922); and A. B. Partoll, ed., *Mengarini's Narrative of the Rockies . . . and St. Mary's Mission*, Sources in Northwest History, no. 25 (Missoula: University of Montana, 1938).

CHAPTER IV. THE MINING FRONTIER

Among the most valuable general works on western mining are William J. Trimble, *The Mining Advance into the Inland Empire* (Madison: University of Wisconsin Press, 1914); T. A. Rickard, *A History of American Mining* (New York and London: McGraw-Hill, 1932); William S. Greever, *The Bonanza West: The Story of the Western Mining Rushes, 1848–1900* (Norman: University of Oklahoma Press, 1963); Rodman W. Paul, *Mining Frontiers of the Far West, 1848–1880* (New York: Holt, Rinehart and Winston, 1963); and Otis E. Young, Jr., *Western Mining* (Norman: University of Oklahoma Press, 1970). Older, but still useful, are W. T. Mendenhall, *Gold and Silver Mining in Montana* (Boston: Collins Press, 1890); and James A. Macknight, *The Mines of Montana* (Helena: C. K. Wells, 1892).

Hubert Howe Bancroft's *History of Washington, Idaho, and Montana, 1845–1889* (San Francisco: History Company, 1890) is a mine of regional information. Good capsulized accounts are Merrill G. Burlingame, *The Montana Frontier* (Helena: State Publishing Co., 1942), chap. 4; and James M. Hamilton, *A History of Montana: From Wilderness to Statehood* (Portland: Binfords and Mort, 1957, 1970), chaps. 4, 6. Muriel S. Wolle's *Montana Pay Dirt* (Chicago: Sage Books, 1963) is a beautifully illustrated guidebook to ghost towns, containing a mass of scattered and undigested, but still valuable, facts. Larry Barsness' *Gold Camp: Alder Gulch and Virginia City, Montana* (New York: Hastings House, 1962) is good reading.

Among the best first-hand accounts of the gold frontier are Andrew F. Rolle, ed., *The Road to Virginia City: The Diary of James Knox Polk Miller* (Norman: University of Oklahoma Press, 1960); and L. Lyman Tyler, ed., *The Montana Gold Rush Diary of Kate Dunlap* (Denver: F. A. Rosenstock–Old West Publishing Co., 1969). See also the following reminiscences from various editions of the *Contributions to the Historical Society of Montana:* Henry Edgar, "Journal of Henry Edgar—1863," 3 (Helena: State Publishing Co., 1900): 124–42; Edgar, "Barney Hughes: An Appreciation," 7 (Helena: Montana Historical and Miscellaneous Library, 1910): 197–98; Peter Ronan, "Discovery of Alder Gulch," 3 (Helena: State Publishing Co., 1900): 143–52; James Fergus, "A Leaf from the Diary of James Fergus," 2 (Helena: State Publishing Co., 1896): 252–54; and David B. Weaver, "Early Days in Emigrant Gulch," 7 (Helena: Montana Historical and Miscellaneous Library, 1910), 73–96.

Otis E. Young, Jr., describes the prospector's craft in "The Prospectors: Some Considerations on their Craft," in John A. Carroll, ed., *Reflections of Western Historians* (Tucson: University of Arizona Press, 1969); and in "The Craft of the Prospector," *Montana: The Magazine of Western History*, 20 (Winter 1970): 28–39. Rodman W. Paul, in *California Gold: The Beginning of Mining in the Far West* (Lincoln:

University of Nebraska Press, Bison Books, 1965), discusses placer mining methods at length. On the boom psychology, see Grace Vance Erickson, "The Sun River Stampede," *The Montana Magazine of History*, 3 (January 1953): 73–78.

Two general assessments of western vigilanteism are Wayne Gard, *Frontier Justice* (Norman: University of Oklahoma Press, 1949); and W. Eugene Hollon, *Frontier Violence: Another Look* (New York: Oxford University Press, 1974). Vigilanteism in Montana is a subject in need of complete reassessment. The two most important first-hand accounts are Thomas J. Dimsdale's *The Vigilantes of Montana*, published serially in the *Montana Post* in 1865 and then as a book in 1866, and republished in numerous editions since then (e.g., Norman: University of Oklahoma Press, 1953); and Nathaniel P. Langford's *Vigilante Days and Ways*, first published in 1890 and republished several times, most recently by the University of Montana Press at Missoula in 1957. Both books are apologias, and most later histories of the state follow their uncritical approach.

For further insights into vigilanteism, see Helen Fitzgerald Sanders and William H. Bertche, Jr., eds., *X. Beidler, Vigilante* (Norman: University of Oklahoma Press, 1957), which is a self-congratulatory memoir; Hoffman Birney, *Vigilantes* (Philadelphia: Penn Publishing Co., 1929), which largely follows Dimsdale and Langford; and Hubert H. Bancroft, *Popular Tribunals* (San Francisco: History Company, 1887), which contains some information not found in other accounts. Also of interest are Rex C. Myers, "The Fateful Numbers 3–7–77: A Re-examination," *Montana: The Magazine of Western History*, 24 (Autumn 1974): 67–70; and Llewellyn L. Callaway, *Two True Tales of the Wild West* (Oakland: Maud Gonne Press, 1973). J. W. Smurr takes a critical look at Montana vigilanteism in "Afterthoughts on the Vigilantes," *Montana: The Magazine of Western History*, 8 (Spring 1958): 8–20; and John W. Caughey offers a more general criticism in "Their Majesties the Mob," *Pacific Historical Review*, 26 (August 1957): 217–34.

On western and regional transportation routes, consult Oscar O. Winther, *The Transportation Frontier: Trans-Mississippi West, 1865–1885* (New York: Holt, Rinehart and Winston, 1964); Winther, *Old Oregon Country: A History of Frontier Trade, Transportation, and Travel* (Bloomington: Indiana University Press, 1950); and W. Turrentine Jackson, *Wagon Roads West* (Berkeley: University of California Press, 1952). The Mullan Road is treated in Oscar O. Winther, "Early Commercial Importance of the Mullan Road," *Oregon Historical Quarterly*, 46 (March 1945): 22–35; Alton B. Oviatt, "Pacific Coast Competition for the Gold Camp Trade of Montana," *Pacific Northwest Quarterly*, 56 (October 1965): 168–76; Henry L. Talkington, "Mullan Road," *Washington Historical Quarterly*, 7 (October 1916): 301–6; and Alexander C. McGregor, "The Economic Impact of the Mullan Road on Walla Walla, 1860–1883," *Pacific Northwest Quarterly*, 65 (July 1974): 118–29.

William E. Lass, *A History of Steamboating on the Upper Missouri River* (Lincoln: University of Nebraska Press, 1962); and Hiram M. Chittenden, *History of Early Steamboat Navigation on the Missouri River* (2 vols.; New York: Francis P. Harper, 1903), are standard works; see also Alton B. Oviatt, "Steamboat Traffic on the Upper Missouri River, 1859–1869," *Pacific Northwest Quarterly*, 40 (April 1949): 93–105. An excellent study of the Whoop-Up Trail and its environs is Paul F.

Sharp, *Whoop-Up Country: The Canadian-American West, 1865–1885* (reprint ed.; Norman: University of Oklahoma Press, 1973).

The Northern Overland Route is discussed in Helen McCann White, ed., *Ho! For the Gold Fields: Northern Overland Wagon Trains of the 1860's* (St. Paul: Minnesota Historical Society, 1966); W. M. Underhill, "The Northern Overland Route to Montana," *Washington Historical Quarterly*, 23 (July 1932): 177–95; and W. Turrentine Jackson, "The Fisk Expeditions to the Montana Gold Fields," *Pacific Northwest Quarterly*, 33 (July 1942): 265–82. Lee Silliman discusses a minor route in "The Carroll Trail: Utopian Enterprise," *Montana: The Magazine of Western History*, 24 (April 1974): 2–17. On the Bozeman Road, see Merrill G. Burlingame, *John M. Bozeman: Montana Trailmaker* (Bozeman: Gallatin County Tribune, 1971); Burton S. Hill, "Bozeman and the Bozeman Trail," *Annals of Wyoming*, 36 (October 1964): 205–33; Grace R. Hebard and E. A. Brininstool, *The Bozeman Trail* (reprint ed.; Glendale, Calif.: Arthur H. Clark Co., 1960); and Dorothy M. Johnson, *The Bloody Bozeman* (New York: McGraw-Hill, 1971). Brigham D. and Betty M. Madsen, "The Diamond R Rolls Out," *Montana: The Magazine of Western History*, 21 (April 1971): 2–17, is useful on the Corinne Road.

Duane A. Smith discusses the mining frontier as an urban phenomenon in *Rocky Mountain Mining Camps: The Urban Frontier* (Bloomington: Indiana University Press, 1967); and "The Golden West," *Montana: The Magazine of Western History*, 14 (July 1964): 2–19. On anti-Negro discrimination, see J. W. Smurr, "Jim Crow out West," in *Historical Essays on Montana and the Northwest*, ed. J. W. Smurr and K. R. Toole (Helena: Western Press, 1957), pp. 149–203; and on the problems of the Chinese, Larry D. Quinn, " 'Chink Chink Chinaman': The Beginnings of Nativism in Montana," *Pacific Northwest Quarterly*, 58 (April 1967): 82–89. Larry Barsness treats the social problems and cultural life of the mining towns well in *Gold Camp*, cited above. See too Alice Cochran, "The Gold Dust Trail: Jack Langrishe's Mining Town Theaters," *Montana: The Magazine of Western History*, 20 (April 1970): 58–69; Harrison A. Trexler, *Flour and Wheat in the Montana Gold Camps* (Missoula: Dunston Printing and Stationary, 1918); W. W. Alderson, "Gold Camp Tubers," *The Montana Magazine of History*, 3 (October 1953): 46–49; and Dorothy M. Johnson, "Flour Famine in Alder Gulch, 1864," *Montana: The Magazine of Western History*, 7 (January 1957): 18–27.

CHAPTER V. MONTANA TERRITORY

For general discussions of the western territories, see Earl S. Pomeroy, *The Territories and the United States: 1861–1890* (2d ed.; Seattle: University of Washington Press, 1969); Jack E. Eblen, *The First and Second United States Empires* (Pittsburgh: University of Pittsburgh Press, 1968); Kenneth N. Owens, "Pattern and Structure in Western Territorial Politics," *Western Historical Quarterly*, 1 (October 1970): 373–92; and Owens, "Frontier Governors: A Study of the Territorial Executives in . . . Washington, Idaho, Montana, Wyoming, and Dakota Territories" (Ph.D. diss., University of Minnesota, 1959).

A solid study of Montana Territory is Clark C. Spence, *Territorial Politics and Government in Montana: 1864–1889* (Urbana: University of Illinois Press, 1975).

Also consult Spence, "The Territorial Officers of Montana," *Pacific Historical Review*, 30 (May 1961): 123–36; Robert E. Albright, "The Relations of Montana with the Federal Government: 1864–1889" (Ph.D. diss., Stanford University, 1933); Elinor E. Malic, "The Political Development of Montana, 1862–1889" (Master's thesis, University of California, Berkeley, 1923); and, for briefer accounts, James M. Hamilton, *History of Montana: From Wilderness to Statehood* (Portland: Binfords and Mort, 1957, 1970), chap. 7; and Merrill G. Burlingame, *The Montana Frontier* (Helena: State Publishing Co., 1942), chap. 7.

Montana's creation and naming are the subject of Wilbur E. Sanders, "Montana: Organization and Naming," *Contributions to the Historical Society of Montana*, 7 (Helena: Montana Historical and Miscellaneous Library, 1910): 15–60; Merle W. Wells, "Territorial Government in the Inland Empire: The Movement to Create Columbia Territory, 1864–69," *Pacific Northwest Quarterly*, 44 (April 1953): 80–87; and George R. Stewart, *Names on the Land* (2d ed.; Boston: Houghton Mifflin, 1958), pp. 306–10.

The early political situation and the role of Confederate sympathizers are variously assessed by Robert G. Athearn, "Civil War Days in Montana," *Pacific Historical Review*, 29 (February 1960): 19–33; James L. Thane, Jr., who de-emphasizes rebel influence, in "The Myth of Confederate Sentiment in Montana," *Montana: The Magazine of Western History*, 17 (April 1967): 14–19; and Stanley R. Davison and Dale Tash, who argue convincingly to the contrary, in "Confederate Backwash in Montana Territory," *Montana: The Magazine of Western History*, 17 (October 1967): 50–58. See too the provocative discussion by J. W. Smurr, "Jim Crow out West," in *Historical Essays on Montana and the Northwest*, ed. J. W. Smurr and K. R. Toole (Helena: Western Press, 1957), pp. 149–203.

James L. Thane, Jr., discusses early territorial politics and government in "Montana Territory: The Formative Years, 1862–1870" (Ph.D. diss., University of Iowa, 1972); "Thomas Francis Meagher: The Acting-One" (Master's thesis, University of Montana, 1967); "The Montana 'Indian War' of 1867," *Arizona and the West*, 8 (Summer 1968): 153–70; and "An Active Acting-Governor: Thomas Francis Meagher's Administration in Montana Territory," *Journal of the West*, 9 (October 1970): 537–51. See also W. Turrentine Jackson, "The Appointment and Removal of Sidney Edgerton, First Governor of Montana Territory," *Pacific Northwest Quarterly*, 34 (July 1934): 293–304; Jackson, "Montana Politics during the Meagher Regime, 1865–1867," *Pacific Historical Review*, 12 (June 1943), 139–56; Robert G. Athearn, *Thomas Francis Meagher: An Irish Revolutionary in America* (Boulder: University of Colorado Press, 1949); and Athearn, "Early Territorial Montana: A Problem in Colonial Administration," *Montana Magazine of History*, 1 (July 1951): 15–21.

Later and more general developments are discussed in Clark C. Spence, "Spoilsman in Montana: James M. Ashley," *Montana: The Magazine of Western History*, 18 (April 1968): 24–35; Spence, "Beggars to Washington: Montana's Territorial Delegates," ibid., 24 (Winter 1974): 2–13; Spence, "The Territorial Bench in Montana: 1864–1889," ibid., 13 (January 1963): 25–65; and Stanley R. Davison, "1871: Montana's Year of Political Fusion," ibid., 21 (Spring 1971): 44–55. Also valuable are John D. W. Guice, *The Rocky Mountain Bench: The Territorial Supreme Courts of*

Colorado, Montana, and Wyoming, 1861–1890 (New Haven, Conn.: Yale University Press, 1972); and John W. Hakola, "Samuel T. Hauser and the Economic Development of Montana: A Case Study in Nineteenth-Century Frontier Capitalism" (Ph.D. diss., Indiana University, 1961).

CHAPTER VI. INDIAN REMOVAL

By necessity this bibliography must be highly selective, and many of the tribal histories and general works cited for Chapter I are also relevant here. Among the best studies of post–Civil War Indian problems are Robert M. Utley, *Frontier Regulars: The United States Army and the Indian, 1866–1891* (New York: Macmillan, 1973); Robert G. Athearn, *William Tecumseh Sherman and the Settlement of the West* (Norman: University of Oklahoma Press, 1956); and Ralph K. Andrist, *The Long Death* (New York: Macmillan, 1964); Dee Brown's *Bury My Heart at Wounded Knee* (New York: Holt, Rinehart & Winston, 1971) focuses on the worst white atrocities. The two best discussions of Indian removal in Montana are James M. Hamilton's *History of Montana: From Wilderness to Statehood* (Portland: Binfords and Mort, 1957, 1970), chaps. 5, 9; and Merrill G. Burlingame's unparalleled *The Montana Frontier* (Helena: State Publishing Co., 1942), chaps. 2, 5, 8, 9–11, which is easily the best general discussion of dealings with the Montana tribes.

The Fort Laramie treaties are discussed in L. R. Hafen and F. M. Young, *Fort Laramie and the Pageant of the West* (Glendale, Calif.: Arthur H. Clark Co., 1938); and the Stevens treaties will be covered by Kent Richards in his forthcoming biography of General Stevens. Also of interest is A. Glen Humphreys, "The Crow Indian Treaties of 1868 . . . ," *Annals of Wyoming*, 42 (Spring 1971): 73–89. On the location of forts, consult H. L. McElroy, "Mercurial Military," *Montana Magazine of History*, 4 (Fall 1954): 9–23; and Robert G. Athearn, "General Sherman and the Montana Frontier," ibid., 3 (January 1953): 55–64. Robert J. Ege treats Major Baker sympathetically in *Strike Them Hard* (Bellevue, Neb.: Old Army Press, 1970); see too, Wesley C. Wilson, "The U.S. Army and the Piegans: The Baker Massacres on the Marias, 1870," *North Dakota History*, 32 (January 1965): 48–58. The Flathead removal is treated in Michael Harrison, "Chief Charlot's Battle with Bureaucracy," *Montana: The Magazine of Western History*, 10 (October 1960): 27–33; and Arthur L. Stone, "Charlot's Last March," in *Montana Margins: A State Anthology*, ed. J. K. Howard (New Haven, Conn.: Yale University Press, 1946), pp. 8–15.

The literature on the Sioux "problem" of 1866–77 is enormous, but see especially James C. Olson, *Red Cloud and the Sioux Problem* (Lincoln: University of Nebraska Press, 1956); George E. Hyde, *Red Cloud's Folk: A History of the Oglala Sioux* (Norman: University of Oklahoma Press, 1937); Robert A. Murray, *Military Posts in the Powder River Country of Wyoming, 1865–1894* (Lincoln: University of Nebraska Press, 1968); Dee Brown, *Fort Phil Kearny: An American Saga* (New York: G. P. Putnam's Sons, 1962); Dorothy M. Johnson, *The Bloody Bozeman* (New York: McGraw-Hill, 1971); Grace R. Hebard and E. A. Brininstool, *The Bozeman Trail* (2 vols.; Cleveland: Arthur H. Clark Co., 1922); Donald Jackson, *Custer's Gold: The United States Cavalry Expedition of 1874* (New Haven, Conn.: Yale University

Press, 1966); and, for a solid study in a regional setting, Mark H. Brown, *The Plainsmen of the Yellowstone* (New York: G. P. Putnam's Sons, 1961).

Among the limitless studies of the 1876 Sioux campaign, see especially James H. Bradley, *The March of the Montana Column*, ed. E. I. Stewart (Norman: University of Oklahoma Press, 1961); Martin F. Schmitt, ed., *General George Crook: His Autobiography* (Norman: University of Oklahoma Press, 1960); and C. C. Smith, "Crook and Crazy Horse," *Montana: The Magazine of Western History*, 16 (April 1966): 14–26. In sorting the enormous Custer bibliography, Edgar I. Stewart's *Custer's Luck* (Norman: University of Oklahoma Press, 1955) is still the best, most objective study of the battle; Robert J. Ege's *Curse Not His Curls* (Fort Collins, Colo.: Old Army Press, 1974) is the most recent of many defenses of the controversial colonel; and Jay Monaghan's *Custer: The Life of General George Armstrong Custer* (Boston: Little, Brown, 1959) is usually considered the best biography, although it is very admiring; Stephen E. Ambrose takes a new approach in *Crazy Horse and Custer* (Garden City, N.Y.: Doubleday, 1975). An interesting study of the Custer mystique is Robert M. Utley, *Custer and the Great Controversy: The Origin and Development of a Legend* (Los Angeles: Westernlore Press, 1962). Also of interest are John U. Terrell and George Walton, *Faint the Trumpet Sounds: The Life and Trial of Major Reno* (New York: D. McKay, 1966); and Harry H. Anderson, "Cheyennes at the Little Big Horn: A Study of Statistics," *North Dakota History*, 27 (Spring 1960): 81–94.

The successful Miles campaigns are discussed in Virginia M. Johnson, *The Unregimented General* (Boston: Houghton Mifflin, 1962); Nelson A. Miles, *Personal Recollections and Observations* (Chicago: Werner, 1896); Milo M. Quaife, ed., *"Yellowstone Kelly": Memoirs of Luther S. Kelly* (New Haven, Conn.: Yale University Press, 1926); and Don Rickey, Jr., "The Battle of Wolf Mountain," *Montana: The Magazine of Western History*, 13 (Spring 1963): 44–54. For an insight into Crook's and Terry's problems, see Robert G. Athearn, ed., "A Winter Campaign against the Sioux," *Mississippi Valley Historical Review*, 35 (September 1948): 272–84. For a glimpse into the postwar army life, consult Richard Upton, *Fort Custer on the Big Horn, 1877–1898* (Glendale, Calif.: Arthur H. Clark Co., 1973).

Among the many accounts of the fascinating Nez Perces, the best are Merrill D. Beal, *"I Will Fight No More Forever": Chief Joseph and the Nez Perce War* (Seattle: University of Washington Press, 1963); Alvin M. Josephy, Jr., *The Nez Perce Indians and the Opening of the Northwest* (New Haven, Conn.: Yale University Press, 1965); L. V. McWhorter, *"Hear Me My Chiefs!": Nez Perce History and Legend* (Caldwell, Ida.: Caxton, 1952); Francis Haines, *The Nez Perces: Tribesmen of the Columbia Plateau* (Norman: University of Oklahoma Press, 1955); and Mark H. Brown, *The Flight of the Nez Perce* (New York: Putnam, 1967). Mark Brown offers an interesting and controversial assessment of Chief Joseph in "The Joseph Myth," *Montana: The Magazine of Western History*, 22 (January 1972): 2–17. On the Bannocks, consult George F. Brimlow, *The Bannock War of 1878* (Caldwell, Ida.: Caxton, 1938).

Concerning the period after 1878, see especially Burlingame, *The Montana Frontier*, chap. 11; also, Gary Pennanen, "Sitting Bull: Indian without a Country," *Canadian Historical Review*, 51 (June 1970): 123–40; and Donald Smythe, S.J., "John J.

Pershing at Fort Assiniboine," *Montana: The Magazine of Western History*, 18 (January 1968): 18–23. On the extermination of the buffalo, see the bibliographical essay for chapter 7. Mari Sandoz treats the Northern Cheyenne retreat movingly in *Cheyenne Autumn* (New York: McGraw-Hill, 1953).

Indian difficulties on the reservations are the subject of Helen B. West, "Starvation Winter of the Blackfeet," *Montana: The Magazine of Western History*, 9 (January 1959): 2–19; Edward E. Barry, Jr., *The Fort Belknap Indian Reservation: The First One Hundred Years, 1855–1955* (Bozeman, Montana State University, 1974), chaps. 2–3; and Malcolm McFee, *Modern Blackfeet: Montanans on a Reservation* (New York: Holt, Rinehart and Winston, 1972), chaps. 3–4. On the Dawes Act and its background see Loring B. Priest, *Uncle Sam's Stepchildren: The Reformation of United States Indian Policy, 1865–1887* (New York: Octagon, 1942); Henry E. Fritz, *The Movement for Indian Assimilation, 1860–1890* (Philadelphia: University of Pennsylvania Press, 1963); and Wilcomb E. Washburn, *The Assault on Indian Tribalism: The General Allotment Law (Dawes Act) of 1887* (Philadelphia: J. B. Lippincott Co., 1975).

CHAPTER VII. STOCKMEN AND THE OPEN RANGE

Among the numerous general works on this subject, the best is still Ernest S. Osgood, *The Day of the Cattleman* (Minneapolis: University of Minnesota Press, 1929). Other sources of value include Louis Pelzer, *The Cattleman's Frontier* (Glendale, Calif.: Arthur H. Clark Co., 1936); Lewis Atherton, *The Cattle Kings* (Bloomington: Indiana University Press, 1961); C. W. Towne and E. N. Wentworth, *Cattle and Men* (Norman: University of Oklahoma Press, 1955); E. E. Dale, *The Range Cattle Industry . . . from 1865 to 1925* (2d ed.; Norman: University of Oklahoma Press, 1960); E. S. Osgood, "The Cattleman in the Agricultural History of the Northwest," *Agricultural History*, 3 (July 1929), 117–30; and Harold E. Briggs, "The Development and Decline of Open Range Ranching in the Northwest," *Mississippi Valley Historical Review*, 20 (March 1934): 521–36. Joseph Nimmo, Jr., *Report in Regard to the Range and Ranch Cattle Business in the United States* (Washington, D.C.: Government Printing Office, 1885), is an important contemporary account.

Robert S. Fletcher and Harold E. Briggs have provided us with the best accounts of the stockmen's frontier in Montana. See Fletcher's *Organization of the Range Cattle Business in Eastern Montana*, Montana Agricultural Experiment Station, Bulletin 265 (Bozeman, 1932); and "The End of the Open Range in Eastern Montana," *Mississippi Valley Historical Review*, 16 (September 1929): 188–211; and Briggs's *Frontiers of the Northwest: A History of the Upper Missouri Valley* (New York: D. Appleton-Century Company, 1940). Two volumes by Mark H. Brown and W. R. Felton, *The Frontier Years* (New York: Holt, Rinehart and Winston, 1955); and *Before Barbed Wire* (New York: Holt, Rinehart and Winston, 1956), contain useful commentaries, as well as generous selections of photographs by Miles City's L. A. Huffman. There are many relevant articles in *Montana: The Magazine of Western History*; vol. 11 (October 1961) is devoted to the cowboy and cattleman. Michael Kennedy edited selections from this magazine in *Cowboys and Cattlemen* (New York: Hastings House, 1964).

The best first-hand accounts of the Montana open range are Paul C. Phillips, ed., *Forty Years on the Frontier, as Seen in the Journals and Reminiscences of Granville Stuart* (2 vols.; Cleveland: Arthur H. Clark Co., 1925); John R. Barrows, *Ubet* (Caldwell, Ida.: Caxton Printers, 1934); E. C. Abbott and Helena H. Smith, *We Pointed Them North* (New York and Toronto: Farrar and Rinehart, 1939); Nannie Alderson and Helena H. Smith, *A Bride Goes West* (New York and Toronto: Farrar and Rinehart, 1942); Walt Coburn, *Pioneer Cattlemen in Montana: The Story of the Circle C Ranch* (Norman: University of Oklahoma Press, 1968); Isabelle Randall, *A Lady's Ranch Life in Montana* (London: W. H. Allen and Co., 1887); and Robert Vaughan, *Then and Now; or, Thirty-Six Years in the Rockies* (Minneapolis: Tribune Printing Company, 1900).

Among the many works on the buffalo and its demise, see especially Francis Haines, *The Buffalo* (New York: Crowell, 1970). Also important are James A. and C. Ivar Dolph, "The American Bison: His Annihilation and Preservation," *Montana: The Magazine of Western History*, 26 (Summer 1975): 2–13; and LeRoy Barnett, "The Ghastly Harvest: Montana's Buffalo Bone Trade," ibid., pp. 14–25. J. Orin Oliphant explores one source of Montana livestock in "The Cattle Trade from the Far Northwest to Montana," *Agricultural History*, 6 (April 1932): 69–83. For the economics of the open range, consult Gene M. Gressley, *Bankers and Cattlemen* (New York: Knopf, 1966); W. Turrentine Jackson, *The Enterprising Scot: Investors in the American West after 1873* (Edinburgh: Edinburgh University Press, 1968); and John Clay, *My Life on the Range* (New York: Antiquarian Press, 1924).

Studies of individual Montana ranchers and ranches include Lee M. Ford, "Bob Ford, Sun River Cowman," *Montana: The Magazine of Western History*, 9 (January 1959): 30–43; Donald H. Welsh, "Cosmopolitan Cattle King: Pierre Wibaux and the W Bar Ranch," ibid., 5 (April 1955): 1–15; D. MacMillan, "The Gilded Age and Montana's DHS Ranch," ibid., 20 (Spring 1970): 50–57; J. Evetts Haley, *The XIT Ranch of Texas* (2d ed.; Norman: University of Oklahoma Press, 1967); and W. M. Pearce, *The Matador Land and Cattle Company* (Norman: University of Oklahoma Press, 1964). Robert H. Fletcher studies the Montana Stockgrowers Association in *Free Grass to Fences: The Montana Cattle Range Story* (New York: University Publishers, 1960). On the cattlemen-vigilantes, see Oscar O. Mueller, "The Central Montana Vigilante Raids of 1884," *The Montana Magazine of History*, 1 (January 1951): 23–35. Two accounts of the tragic winter are Robert S. Fletcher, "That Hard Winter in Montana, 1886–1887," *Agricultural History*, 4 (October 1930): 123–30; and Ray H. Mattison, "The Hard Winter and the Range Cattle Business," *The Montana Magazine of History*, 1 (October 1951): 5–22.

Literature on the Montana sheep industry is very limited. Two general accounts that shed light on Montana are Harold E. Briggs, "The Early Development of Sheep Ranching in the Northwest," *Agricultural History*, 11 (July 1937): 161–80; and Edward N. Wentworth, *American Sheep Trails* (Ames: Iowa State College Press, 1948). Wentworth also presented an address, "History of the Montana Sheep Industry," to the Montana Wool Growers Association at Helena in 1940, which was reproduced in the *Montana Wool Growers News Letter*, vol. 14, nos. 4–10 (April–October 1940). On two important sheepmen, consult John F. Bishop, "Beginnings of the Montana Sheep Industry," *The Montana Magazine of History*, 1 (April 1951):

5–8; and Lee Rostad, "Charley Bair: King of Western Sheepmen," *Montana: The Magazine of Western History*, 20 (Autumn 1970): 50–61.

CHAPTER VIII: RAILROADS, SILVER, AND STATEHOOD

Among the most useful general studies of railroads are John F. Stover, *The Life and Decline of the American Railroad* (New York: Oxford University Press, 1970); Robert E. Riegel, *The Story of Western Railroads* (New York: Macmillan, 1926); and Julius Grodinsky, *Transcontinental Railway Strategy, 1869–1893* (Philadelphia: University of Pennsylvania Press, 1962). Brief sketches of rail building in Montana can be found in James M. Hamilton, *History of Montana: From Wilderness to Statehood* (Portland: Binfords and Mort, 1957, 1970), chap. 8; and in the various subscription histories, especially M. G. Burlingame and K. R. Toole, eds., *A History of Montana* (3 vols.; New York: Lewis Historical Publishing Co., 1957), vol. 2, chap. 19. Also valuable to the student of Montana are Rex C. Myers, "Montana: A State and Its Relationship with Railroads, 1864–1970" (Ph.D. diss., University of Montana, 1972); and Thomas T. Taber, "Short Lines of the Treasure State: The Histories of the Independently Operated Railroads of Montana" (April 1960), manuscript in Montana Historical Society Library, Helena.

Robert L. Peterson is currently completing his book-length history of the Northern Pacific. See his "The Completion of the Northern Pacific Railroad System in Montana: 1883–1893," in *The Montana Past: An Anthology*, ed. M. P. Malone and R. B. Roeder (Missoula: University of Montana Press, 1969), chap. 10. Also of interest are E. V. Smalley, *History of the Northern Pacific Railroad* (New York: G. P. Putnam's Sons, 1883); Theodore Schwinden, "The Northern Pacific Land Grants in Congress" (Master's thesis, University of Montana, 1950); and James B. Hedges, *Henry Villard and the Railways of the Northwest* (New York: Russell and Russell, 1930). See also two articles by Hedges: "Promotion of Immigration to the Pacific Northwest by the Railroads," *Mississippi Valley Historical Review*, 15 (September 1928), 183–203; and "The Colonizing Work of the Northern Pacific Railroad," ibid., 13 (December 1926): 311–42. Ross R. Cotroneo discusses the Northern Pacific land grant in "The History of the Northern Pacific Land Grant, 1900–1952" (Ph.D. diss., University of Idaho, 1967); and in "Western Land Marketings by the Northern Pacific Railway," *Pacific Historical Review*, 27 (August 1968): 299–320; see too, Thomas A. Clinch, "The Northern Pacific Railroad and Montana's Mineral Lands," *Pacific Historical Review*, 34 (August 1965): 323–35.

The best studies of the Utah and Northern are by Robert G. Athearn: "Railroad to a Far Off Country: The Utah and Northern," *Montana: The Magazine of Western History*, 18 (Autumn 1968): 2–23; and *Union Pacific Country* (Chicago and New York: Rand McNally, 1971), chap. 12. For the later railroads, consult Richard C. Overton, *Burlington Route* (New York: Knopf, 1965); and August Derleth, *The Milwaukee Road: Its First Hundred Years* (New York: Creative Age Press, 1948). R. W. and M. E. Hidy are presently completing their history of the Great Northern. Two admiring biographies are Stewart H. Holbrook, *James J. Hill: A Great Life in Brief* (New York: Random House, 1955); and J. G. Pyle, *The Life of James J. Hill* (2 vols.; New York: P. Smith, 1916–17). Also relevant are Howard Schonberger, "James J. Hill and the Orient," *Minnesota History*, 41 (Winter 1968): 178–90; and

John B. Rae, "The Great Northern's Land Grant," *Journal of Economic History*, 12 (Spring 1952): 140–45.

For industrial quartz mining, the general works listed in Chapter IV are also useful here. John W. Hakola, "Samuel T. Hauser and the Economic Development of Montana: A Case Study in Nineteenth-Century Frontier Capitalism" (Ph.D. diss., Indiana University, 1961), is highly informative on mining promotion and development. Uuno Mathias Sahinen, "Mining Districts of Montana" (Master's thesis, Montana School of Mines, 1935), is also useful. On the Helena area, consult Adolph Knopf, *Ore Deposits of the Helena Mining Region, Montana*, U.S. Geological Survey, Bulletin 527 (Washington, D.C.: Government Printing Office, 1913); and J. T. Pardee and F. C. Schrader, *Metalliferous Deposits of the Greater Helena Mining Region, Montana*, U.S. Geological Survey, Bulletin 842 (Washington, D.C.: Government Printing Office, 1933). The Marysville operations are treated in Charles W. Goodale, "The Drumlummon Mine, Marysville, Montana," *Transactions of the American Institute of Mining Engineers*, 49 (1915): 258–79; W. Turrentine Jackson, "The Irish Fox and the British Lion," *Montana: The Magazine of Western History*, 9 (April 1959): 28–42; and Clark C. Spence, "The Montana Company, Limited: A Case Study of Anglo-American Mining Investment," *Business History Review*, 33 (Summer 1959): 190–203.

On the Philipsburg area, see S. F. Emmons and E. C. Eckel, *Contributions to Economic Geology 1906*, U.S. Geological Survey, Bulletin 315 (Washington, D.C.: Government Printing Office, 1907); Donald L. Sorte, "The Hope Mining Company of Philipsburg" (Master's thesis, University of Montana, 1960). See also Dan Cushman, "Cordova Lode Comstock," *Montana: The Magazine of Western History*, 9 (October 1959): 12–21; and A. C. McMillan, "Granite's Glittering Glory," ibid., 14 (July 1964): 62–73. For some other mining districts, consult Walter Harvey Weed and Louis Valentine Pirsson, *Geology of the Castle Mountain Mining District*, U.S. Geological Survey, Bulletin 139 (Washington, D.C.: Government Printing Office, 1896); and Alexander N. Winchell, *Mining Districts of the Dillon Quadrangle, Montana and Adjacent Areas*, U.S. Geological Survey, Bulletin 574 (Washington, D.C.: Government Printing Office, 1914).

Foreign mining investment is the subject of Clark C. Spence, *British Investments and the American Mining Frontier: 1860–1901* (Ithaca, N.Y.: Cornell University Press, 1958); and Patrick Henry McLatchy, "A Collection of Data on Foreign Corporate Activity in the Territory of Montana, 1864–1889" (Master's thesis, University of Montana, 1961). On professionalization and promotion, see Clark C. Spence, *Mining Engineers and the American West: The Lace-Boot Brigade, 1849–1933* (New Haven, Conn.: Yale University Press, 1970); Lewis Atherton, "Structure and Balance in Western Mining History," *Huntington Library Quarterly*, 30 (November 1966): 55–84; and Atherton, "The Mining Promoter in the Trans-Mississippi West," *Western Historical Quarterly*, 1 (January 1970): 35–50. Statistics can be found in the ninth, tenth, and eleventh censuses and in the U.S. Geological Survey's annual *Mineral Resources of the United States*.

The best survey of the statehood movement and constitutional conventions of the 1880s is James M. Hamilton, *History of Montana: From Wilderness to Statehood* (Portland: Binfords and Mort, 1957, 1970), chap. 11. Margery H. Brown focuses mainly on the 1884 Constitutional Convention in "Metamorphosis and Revision," *Montana: The Magazine of Western History*, 20 (Autumn 1970): 3–17. John Welling Smurr offers provocative thoughts on the 1889 gathering in "The Montana Tax 'Conspiracy' of 1889," *Montana: The Magazine of Western History*, 5 (Spring 1955): 46–53, and (Summer 1955): 47–56; see also Smurr, "A Critical Study of the Montana Constitutional Convention of 1889" (Master's thesis, University of Montana, 1951); Brian E. Cockhill, "An Economic Analysis of Montana's Constitution" (Master's thesis, University of Montana, 1968); John D. Hicks, *The Constitutions of the Northwest States* (Lincoln: University of Nebraska Press, 1924); and *Proceedings and Debates of the Constitutional Convention* (Helena: State Publishing Co., 1921).

CHAPTER IX. COPPER AND POLITICS: 1880–1910

The rise of Montana's copper industry, and the accompanying political strife, has attracted considerable attention. A first-hand observer who wrote accurately and well, C. P. Connolly, first described these events in a gripping series of "muckraking" articles, collectively entitled "The Story of Montana," in *McClure's Magazine*, vols. 27–29 (August 1906–July 1907). Many years later, Connolly gathered together his account in *The Devil Learns to Vote* (New York: Covici Friede, 1938). Written in much the same vein is C. B. Glasscock's folksy *The War of the Copper Kings* (New York: Bobbs Merrill, 1935).

General histories of Montana that focus at length on copper developments are K. Ross Toole, *Montana: An Uncommon Land* (Norman: University of Oklahoma Press, 1959), chaps. 7–9; M. G. Burlingame and K. R. Toole eds., *A History of Montana* (3 vols.; New York: Lewis Historical Publishing Co., 1957), vol. 1, chap. 9; Joseph K. Howard, *Montana: High, Wide, and Handsome* (New Haven, Conn.: Yale University Press, 1943, 1959), chaps. 6–9; and Robert G. Raymer, *Montana: The Land and The People* (3 vols.; Chicago and New York: Lewis Historical Publishing Co., 1930), vol. 1, chap. 16. Also general in focus are K. Ross Toole, "A History of the Anaconda Copper Mining Company: A Study in the Relationships between a State and Its People and a Corporation, 1880–1950" (Ph.D. dissertation, University of California at Los Angeles, 1954); and Toole, "When Big Money Came to Butte," *Pacific Northwest Quarterly*, 44 (January 1953): 23–29.

On the rise of the Montana copper industry, see especially Robert G. Raymer, *A History of Copper Mining in Montana* (Chicago: American Historical Publishing Co., 1930); Isaac F. Marcosson, *Anaconda* (New York: Dodd, Mead, 1957), which, though uncritical, is the only corporate history of that firm; K. Ross Toole, "The Anaconda Copper Mining Company: A Price War and a Copper Corner," *Pacific Northwest Quarterly*, 41 (October 1950): 312–29. For an analysis extending into the 1930s, see the superb "Anaconda Copper," *Fortune*, December 1936, pp. 83–94ff.; and "Anaconda II," ibid., January 1937, pp. 71–77ff. The creation of the Amalgamated Copper Company is pungently described by an "insider," Thomas W. Lawson, in *The Crime of Amalgamated*, vol. 1 of *Frenzied Finance* (2 vols.; New York: Ridgway-Thayer, 1905).

The growth of labor unionism at Butte is discussed by Vernon H. Jensen, *Heritage of Conflict: Labor Relations in the Non-ferrous Metals Industry up to 1930* (Ithaca, N.Y.: Cornell University Press, 1954), chaps. 17–18, 23; and Richard E.

Lingenfelter, *The Hardrock Miners* (Berkeley, Los Angeles, and London: University of California Press, 1974), esp. pp. 182–95. An enjoyable look into Butte's origins and folklore is *Copper Camp*, compiled by the Writers' Program of the Montana Work Projects Administration (New York: Hastings House, 1943).

There is no book-length biography of either Daly or Clark, but see K. Ross Toole, "Marcus Daly: A Study of Business in Politics" (Master's thesis, University of Montana, 1948); William D. Mangam's critical little volumes, *The Clarks of Montana* (Washington: Service Printing Co., 1939), and *The Clarks: An American Phenomenon* (New York: Silver Bow Press, 1941); and, for a political slant, Forrest L. Foor, "The Senatorial Aspirations of William A. Clark" (Ph.D. diss., University of California at Berkeley, 1941). K. Ross Toole explores the political situation in "The Genesis of the Clark-Daly Feud," *The Montana Magazine of History*, 1 (April 1951): 21–33; and the lumber complications in Toole and Edward Butcher, "Timber Depredations on the Montana Public Domain, 1885–1918," *Journal of the West*, 7 (July 1968): 351–62.

The late Professor Thomas A. Clinch ably assessed Montana's Populist movement in *Urban Populism and Free Silver in Montana* (Missoula: University of Montana Press, 1970); and also in "Coxey's Army in Montana," *Montana: The Magazine of Western History*, 15 (Autumn 1965): 2–11. The Populist–Free Silver crusade is further discussed in Robert E. Williams, "The Silver Republican Movement in Montana" (Master's thesis, University of Montana, 1965); and James D. Harrington, "Free Silver, Montana's Political Dream of Economic Prosperity: 1864–1900" (Master's thesis, University of Montana, 1969).

On Fred Whiteside and his exposures, consult Dorothy M. Johnson, ed., "The Graft That Failed," *Montana: The Magazine of Western History*, 9 (Autumn 1959): 2–11; (Winter 1959): 40–50. A sympathetic study of Heinze is Sarah McNelis' *Copper King at War: The Biography of F. Augustus Heinze* (Missoula: University of Montana Press, 1968); also relevant is Daniel J. LaGrande, "Voice of a Copper King: A Study of the *Reveille*, 1903–1906" (Master's thesis, University of Montana, 1971). Jerre C. Murphy takes a caustic look at Amalgamated-Anaconda and its post-1903 political role in his facetiously entitled *The Comical History of Montana* (San Diego: E. L. Scofield, 1912). The two key figures in consolidating Butte copper under the control of Amalgamated-Anaconda are discussed in Sheryl Eliason, "John Dennis Ryan: Father of the Montana 'Twins,' " MS in authors' possession; and Thomas C. Satterthwaite, "Cornelius Francis Kelley: The Rise of an Industrial Statesman" (Master's thesis, Montana State University, 1971).

CHAPTER X. THE HOMESTEAD BOOM: 1900–18

By far the most important study of homesteading on the Northern Plains is Mary Wilma M. Hargreaves' authoritative *Dry Farming in the Northern Great Plains: 1900–1925* (Cambridge, Mass.: Harvard University Press, 1957), which focuses primarily upon dry farming and promotion. Two well written, briefer descriptions of Montana homesteading are Joseph K. Howard, *Montana: High, Wide, and Handsome* (New Haven, Conn.: Yale University Press, 1943, 1959), chaps. 16–18; and K. Ross Toole, *Twentieth-Century Montana: A State of Extremes* (Norman: University of Oklahoma Press, 1972), chaps. 2–3. Also valuable is Robert G. Dunbar, "Agriculture," in *A History of Montana*, ed. M. G. Burlingame and K. R. Toole (3 vols.; New York: Lewis Historical Publishing Co., 1957), vol. 1, chap. 12. For a general and regional perspective, consult Walter P. Webb, *The Great Plains* (2d ed.; Waltham, Mass.: Blaisdell, 1959); Carl F. Kraenzel, *The Great Plains in Transition* (Norman: University of Oklahoma Press, 1955); and Gilbert C. Fite, *The Farmers' Frontier: 1865–1900* (New York: Holt, Rinehart and Winston, 1966).

Early agriculture in Montana is discussed in M. L. Wilson, "The Evolution of Montana Agriculture in Its Early Period," *Proceedings of the Mississippi Valley Historical Association*, 9, pt. 3 (1917–18): 429–40; Merrill G. Burlingame, *The Montana Frontier* (Helena: State Publishing Co., 1942), chap. 15; James M. Hamilton, *History of Montana: From Wilderness to Statehood* (Portland: Binfords and Mort, 1957, 1970), chap. 8; J. Bruce Putnam, "The Evolution of a Frontier Town: Bozeman, Montana, and Its Search for Economic Stability, 1864–1877" (Master's thesis, Montana State University, 1973); and Frank Grant, "Robert N. Sutherlin: Prophet for the People" (Master's thesis, University of Montana, 1971). Stanley R. Davison describes the reclamationists as boosters in "Hopes and Fancies of the Early Reclamationists," in *Historical Essays on Montana and the Northwest*, ed. J. W. Smurr and K. R. Toole (Helena: Western Press, 1957), pp. 204–23; also valuable is John W. Hakola, "The Development of a Policy towards Irrigation in Montana to 1908" (Master's thesis, University of Montana, 1951).

Mary W. M. Hargreaves discusses dry farming, promotion, and land policy thoroughly in her work, cited above. On land policy, see Everett N. Dick, *The Lure of the Land: A Social History of the Public Lands* (Lincoln: University of Nebraska Press, 1970); and, more particularly, William S. Peters and Maxine C. Johnson, *Public Lands in Montana: Their History and Current Significance* (Missoula: University of Montana Press, 1959). On promotion consult Charles A. Dalich, "Dry Farming Promotion in Eastern Montana (1907–1916)" (Master's thesis, University of Montana, 1968); and James G. Handford, "Paris Gibson: Montana Yankee" (Master's thesis, University of Montana, 1952).

Two valuable studies of who the homesteaders were and the nature of their experience are M. L. Wilson, *Dry Farming in the North Central Montana "Triangle,"* Montana State College Extension Service, Bulletin 66 (Bozeman, 1923); and Marie Peterson McDonald, *After Barbed Wire* (Glendive, Mont.: Frontier Gateway Museum, 1963). The various county and local histories of Montana are, of course, indispensable to identifying the homesteaders and understanding their existence. See, among many others, Harold Joseph Stearns, *A History of the Upper Musselshell Valley of Montana (to 1920)* (Harlowton and Ryegate, Mont.: Times-Clarion Publishers, 1966); Janet S. Allison, *Trial and Triumph: 101 Years in North Central Montana* (Chinook: North Central Montana Cowbelles, 1968); and Albie Gordon et al., *Dawn in Golden Valley* (n.p., 1971).

For further insights into the homesteaders' experiences, consult Dan Whetstone, *Frontier Editor* (New York: Hastings House, 1956); Edward J. Bell, Jr., *Homesteading In Montana: Life in the Blue Mountain Country, 1911–1923* (Bozeman, Mont.: Big Sky Books, 1975); Paul T. DeVore, "Dry Farming Broke My Dad," *The Pacific Northwesterner*, 18 (Winter 1974): 1–11. See also John Talbot Graham, "The Last of the Homesteaders," *Montana: The Magazine of Western History*, 18 (April 1968):

62–75; and Marie Snedecor, "The Homesteaders: Their Dreams Held No Shadows," ibid., 19 (Spring 1969): 10–27. Richard B. Roeder examines the home-steaders' visions of building the model community in "Montana Progressivism: Sound and Fury and One Small Tax Reform," *Montana: The Magazine of Western History*, 20 (Autumn 1970): 18–26; and in "Montana in the Early Years of the Progressive Period" (Ph.D. diss., University of Pennsylvania, 1971).

The bulletins of the Montana Agricultural Experiment Station at Montana State University in Bozeman are extremely valuable sources of information on this and later farming eras. See, for example, F. B. Linfield and Alfred Atkinson, *Dry Farming in Montana*, Montana Agricultural Experiment Station, Bulletin 63 (1907); Atkinson and J. B. Nelson, *Dry Farming Investigations in Montana*, Bulletin 74 (1908); G. W. Morgan and A. S. Seamans, *Dry Farming in the Plains Area of Montana*, Bulletin 89 (1920); Marion Clawson et al., *Farm Adjustments in Montana . . .*, Bulletin 377 (1940); E. A. Starch, *Economic Changes in Montana's Wheat Area . . .*, Bulletin 295 (1935); and Carl F. Kraenzel, *Farm Population Mobility in Selected Montana Communities*, Bulletin 371 (1939).

Chapter XI. The Progressive Era and World War I

Literature dealing with Montana progressivism is very limited. The first effort to open the subject to investigation was Jules A. Karlin's essay, "Progressive Politics in Montana," in *A History of Montana*, ed. M. G. Burlingame and K. R. Toole (3 vols.; New York: Lewis Historical Publishing Co., 1957), 1:247–80. K. R. Toole touched briefly upon the period in *Montana: An Uncommon Land* (Norman: University of Oklahoma Press, 1959), chap. 10, arguing that progressivism had little impact here. Richard B. Roeder challenges this interpretation and discusses some of the early reforms in "Montana Progressivism: Sound and Fury and One Small Tax Reform," *Montana: The Magazine of Western History*, 20 (October 1970): 18–26. The fullest discussion of Montana progressivism is Roeder, "Montana in the Early Years of the Progressive Period" (Ph.D. diss., University of Pennsylvania, 1971).

Jules A. Karlin discusses Joseph Dixon's career in *Joseph M. Dixon of Montana*, Part 1: *Senator and Bull Moose Manager, 1867–1917*, and Part 2: *Governor versus the Anaconda, 1917–1934* (Missoula: University of Montana Publications in History, 1974); in "Congressman Joseph M. Dixon and the Miles City Land Office, 1903: A Study in Political Patronage," in *Historical Essays on Montana and the Northwest*, ed. J. W. Smurr and K. R. Toole (Helena: Western Press, 1957), pp. 231–49; and in "Young Joe Dixon in the Flathead Country," *Montana: The Magazine of Western History*, 27 (January 1967): 12–19. J. Leonard Bates is currently completing his biography of Thomas Walsh. See also his "Senator Walsh of Montana, 1918–1924: A Liberal under Pressure" (Ph.D. diss., University of North Carolina, 1952); *Tom Walsh in Dakota Territory* (Urbana: University of Illinois Press, 1966); "T. J. Walsh: Foundations of a Senatorial Career," *The Montana Magazine of History*, 1 (October 1951): 23–34; "Walsh of Montana in Dakota Territory: Political Beginnings, 1884–1890," *Pacific Northwest Quarterly*, 56 (July 1965): 114–24; and "Thomas J. Walsh: His Genius for Controversy," *Montana: The Magazine of Western History*, 29 (Autumn 1969): 2–15. Josephine O'Keane's *Thomas J. Walsh: A Senator from Montana* (Francestown, N.H.: M. Jones Co., 1955) contains some information but is uncritical; also of interest is Clarence L. Brammer, "Thomas J. Walsh" (Ph.D. diss., University of Missouri, 1972).

The best discussions of woman suffrage are Doris B. Ward, "The Winning of Woman Suffrage in Montana" (Master's thesis, Montana State University, 1974); and T. A. Larson, "Montana Women and the Battle for the Ballot," *Montana: The Magazine of Western History*, 23 (Winter 1973): 24–41. Also of interest is Ronald Schaffer, "The Montana Woman Suffrage Campaign," *Pacific Northwest Quarterly*, 55 (January 1964): 9–15. Jeannette Rankin still awaits a satisfactory biography, but see Hannah Josephson, *Jeannette Rankin: First Lady in Congress* (Indianapolis and New York: Bobbs-Merrill, 1974); John C. Board, "Jeannette Rankin: The Lady from Montana," *Montana: The Magazine of Western History*, 17 (July 1967): 2–17; Board, "The Lady from Montana: Jeannette Rankin" (Master's thesis, University of Wyoming, 1964); Ronald Schaffer, "Jeannette Rankin, Progressive-Isolationist" (Ph.D. diss., Princeton University, 1959); and Ted C. Harris, "Jeannette Rankin: Suffragist, First Woman Elected to Congress, and Pacifist" (Ph.D. diss., University of Georgia, 1972).

Labor developments are treated in the biennial reports of the Montana Department of Labor and Industry, 1913–20, and in Vernon H. Jensen, *Heritage of Conflict: Labor Relations in the Nonferrous Metals Industry Up to 1930* (Ithaca, N.Y.: Cornell University Press, 1950); Norma Smith, "The Rise and Fall of the Butte Miners Union, 1878–1914" (Master's thesis, Montana State University, 1961); and Paul F. Brissenden, "The Butte Miners and the Rustling Card," *American Economic Review*, 10 (December 1920): 755–75. Among the many studies of the I.W.W., see especially Melvyn Dubofsky, *We Shall Be All: A History of the Industrial Workers of the World* (Chicago: Quadrangle Books, 1969); Joseph R. Conlin, *Bread and Roses Too* (Westport, Conn.: Greenwood Publishing Co., 1969); and Patrick Renshaw, *The Wobblies* (Garden City, N.Y.: Doubleday, 1967). Two studies of the radicals and their suppression are H. C. Peterson and Gilbert C. Fite, *Opponents of War, 1917–18* (Madison: University of Wisconsin Press, 1957) (paperback ed.; Seattle: University of Washington Press, 1968); and William Preston, Jr., *Aliens and Dissenters: Federal Suppression of Radicals, 1903–1933* (Cambridge, Mass.: Harvard University Press, 1963).

Much has been written about the turbulence of World War I. On the Wobblies in the western woodlands, see George A. Venn, "The Wobblies and Montana's Garden City," *Montana: The Magazine of Western History*, 21 (October 1971): 18–30; and Benjamin G. Rader, "The Montana Lumber Strike of 1917," *Pacific Historical Review*, 36 (May 1967): 189–207. The Butte occupation of 1914 is discussed in Theodore Wiprud, "Butte: A Troubled Labor Paradise," *Montana: The Magazine of Western History*, 21 (October 1971): 31–38. Arnon Gutfeld focuses upon labor strife at Butte in "The Butte Labor Strikes and Company Retaliation during World War I" (Master's thesis, University of Montana, 1967); "The Speculator Disaster in 1917: Labor Resurgence at Butte, Montana," *Arizona and the West*, 11 (Spring 1969): 27–38; and "The Murder of Frank Little: Radical Labor Agitation in Butte, Montana, 1917," *Labor History*, 10 (Spring 1969): 177–92. Also concerning the Speculator episode, and mining conditions in general, consult two reports by Daniel Harrington, *Lessons from the Granite Mountain Shaft Fire, Butte* (Washington, D.C.:

Government Printing Office, 1922); and *Underground Ventilation at Butte* (Washington, D.C.: Government Printing Office, 1923). An interesting sidelight on I.W.W. folklore is S. Page Stegner, "Protest Songs from the Butte Mines," *Western Folklore*, 26 (April 1967): 157–67.

Wartime hysteria and Red-hunting in Montana are the subject of Arnon Gutfeld, "Years of Hysteria, Montana, 1917–1921" (Ph.D. diss., University of California at Los Angeles, 1971); Gutfeld, "The Ves Hall Case, Judge Bourquin, and the Sedition Act of 1918," *Pacific Historical Review*, 37 (May 1968): 163–78; Robert E. Evans, "Montana's Role in the Enactment of Legislation Designed to Suppress the Industrial Workers of the World" (Master's thesis, University of Montana, 1964); Guy Halverson and William E. Ames, "The Butte *Bulletin:* Beginnings of a Labor Daily," *Journalism Quarterly*, 46 (Summer 1969): 260–66; Kurt Wetzel, "The Defeat of Bill Dunne: An Episode in the Montana Red Scare," *Pacific Northwest Quarterly*, 64 (January 1973): 12–20; and K. Ross Toole, *Twentieth-Century Montana: A State of Extremes* (Norman: University of Oklahoma Press, 1972), chaps. 6–7.

On the Montana Council of Defense, see Nancy R. Fritz, "The Montana Council of Defense" (Master's thesis, University of Montana, 1966); and Charles S. Johnson, "The Montana Council of Defense," *Montana Journalism Review*, 16 (1973): 2–16. A gripping tale of wartime persecution is Rufus M. Franz, "It Happened in Montana," *Mennonite Life*, 7 (October 1952): 181–84. For the life of B. K. Wheeler, consult two theses by Richard T. Ruetten, "Burton K. Wheeler, 1905–1925: An Independent Liberal under Fire" (Master's thesis, University of Oregon, 1957); and "Burton K. Wheeler of Montana: A Progressive between the Wars" (Ph.D. diss., University of Oregon, 1961). For Wheeler's own views, see Burton K. Wheeler and Paul Healy, *Yankee from the West* (Garden City, N.Y.: Doubleday, 1962). Very little has been written on the farmer radicals, but for a beginning, turn to Theodore Saloutos, "The Montana Society of Equity," *Pacific Historical Review*, 14 (December 1945): 393–408; Robert L. Morlan, *Political Prairie Fire: The Nonpartisan League, 1915–1922* (Minneapolis: University of Minnesota Press, 1955); and Rosemarie Fishburn, "The Montana Farmer: An Ideological Analysis, 1915–1922" (Master's thesis, University of Montana, 1971).

CHAPTER XII. DROUGHT, DEPRESSION, AND WAR, 1919–46

On the postwar depression and its effects, see K. Ross Toole, *Twentieth-Century Montana: A State of Extremes* (Norman: University of Oklahoma Press, 1972), chap. 3; Joseph K. Howard, *Montana: High, Wide, and Handsome* (New Haven, Conn.: Yale University Press, 1943, 1959), chaps. 19–21; Robert G. Raymer, *Montana: The Land and the People* (3 vols.; Chicago and New York: Lewis Historical Publishing Co., 1930), 1:622–24; M. L. Wilson, *Dry Farming in the North Central Montana "Triangle,"* Montana State College Extension Service, Bulletin 66 (Bozeman, 1923), pp. 17–24; Donald Jerome Elliott, "Commercial Bank Failures in Montana, 1920–1926" (Master's thesis, University of Montana, 1967); and Jeffrey Lee Cunniff, "The Gilman State Bank: A Case Study of a Montana Bank Failure: 1910–1923" (Master's thesis, University of Montana, 1971).

The mine taxation issue and the 1920 campaign are described in Arnon Gutfeld,

"The Levine Affair: A Case Study in Academic Freedom," *Pacific Historical Review*, 39 (February 1970): 19–37; Louis Levine, *The Taxation of Mines in Montana* (New York: B. W. Huebsch, 1919); H. G. Merriam, *The University of Montana: A History* (Missoula: University of Montana Press, 1970), pp. 54–55; Burton K. Wheeler with Paul F. Healy, *Yankee from the West* (Garden City, N.Y.: Doubleday, 1962), pp. 165–84; and Mary Lou Koessler, "The 1920 Gubernatorial Election in Montana" (Master's thesis, University of Montana, 1971). On a subject related to the Levine case, see Sheila MacDonald Stearns, "The Arthur Fisher Case" (Master's thesis, University of Montana, 1969). For Dixon's gubernatorial term, consult Jules A. Karlin, *Joseph M. Dixon of Montana, Part 2: Governor versus the Anaconda, 1917–1934* (Missoula: University of Montana Publications in History, 1974); Toole, *Twentieth-Century Montana*, chap. 10; and Shirley DeForth, "The Montana Press and Governor Joseph M. Dixon, 1920–1922" (Master's thesis, University of Montana, 1959).

Political trends of the later twenties and early thirties remain generally unexplored by historians. Election trends can be followed in Ellis L. Waldron, *Montana Politics since 1864: An Atlas of Elections* (Missoula: University of Montana Press, 1958), pp. 211–38; the political profile of those years, as compared with more recent times, can be found in Michael P. Malone, "Montana as a Corporate Baliwick: An Image in History," soon to be published by the William Andrews Clark Memorial Library at the University of California at Los Angeles. For general works on Senators Walsh and Wheeler, refer to the essay for Chapter XI. Relevant to the 1920s in particular are J. Leonard Bates, *The Origins of Teapot Dome* (Urbana: University of Illinois Press, 1963); T. J. Walsh, "The True Story of Teapot Dome," *The Forum*, 72 (July 1924): 1–12; Burl Noggle, *Teapot Dome* (New York: W. W. Norton, 1962); Paul A. Carter, "The Other Catholic Candidate: The 1928 Presidential Bid of Thomas J. Walsh," *Pacific Northwest Quarterly*, 55 (January 1964): 1–18; and Richard T. Ruetten, "Senator Burton K. Wheeler and Insurgency in the 1920's," in *The American West: A Reorientation*, ed. Gene M. Gressley (Laramie: University of Wyoming Press, 1968), pp. 111–31.

The local impacts of the Great Depression and the New Deal must be gleaned from scattered sources. A memoir of the drought is Charles Vindex, "That Dwell in Dust," *Antioch Review*, 11 (Fall 1951): 363–75. Richard D. Seibert deals mainly with federal spending statistics in "New Deal Expenditures in Montana: 1933–1939" (Master's thesis, Utah State University, 1970). To place Montana in regional and national perspective, consult Leonard Arrington, "The New Deal in the West: A Preliminary Statistical Inquiry," *Pacific Historical Review*, 38 (August 1969): 311–16; James T. Patterson, "The New Deal in the West," ibid., pp. 317–27; and Patterson, *The New Deal and the States: Federalism in Transition* (Princeton, N.J.: Princeton University Press, 1969).

The relief situation is depicted in Carl F. Kraenzel, *The Relief Problem in Montana*, Montana Agricultural Experiment Station, Bulletin 343 (Bozeman, 1937). Roy E. Huffman notes Montana's key role in agricultural planning in "Montana's Contribution to New Deal Farm Policy," *Agricultural History*, 33 (October 1959): 164–67. On the liquor issue, see Larry D. Quinn, *Politicians in Business: A History of the Liquor Control System in Montana* (Missoula: University of Montana Press,

1970). The important Fort Peck project is the subject of "10,000 Montana Relief Workers Make Whoopee on Saturday Night," *Life*, November 23, 1936, pp. 9–17; James Rorty, "Fort Peck: An American Siberia," *Nation*, September 11, 1935, pp. 300–1; and John T. Ryan, "Chapters on the Fort Peck Development" (Master's thesis, University of Montana, 1961).

The political side of the New Deal is discussed in Michael P. Malone, "The Montana New Dealers," in *The New Deal*, vol. 2: *The State and Local Levels*, ed. John Braeman, Robert H. Bremmer, and David Brody (2 vols.; Columbus: Ohio State University Press, 1975), pp. 240–68; and Malone, "Montana Politics and the New Deal," *Montana: The Magazine of Western History*, 21 (Winter 1971): 2–11. Among the many descriptions of Senator B. K. Wheeler's activities during these years, the best include Richard T. Ruetten, "Showdown in Montana, 1938: Burton Wheeler's Role in the Defeat of Jerry O'Connell," *Pacific Northwest Quarterly*, 54 (January 1963): 19–29; Richard L. Neuberger, "Wheeler of Montana," *Harper's Magazine*, May 1940, pp. 609–18; and Catherine C. Doherty, "The Court Plan, B. K. Wheeler and the Montana Press" (Master's thesis, University of Montana, 1954). Among many assessments of why Wheeler lost in 1946, the fullest is Joseph P. Kelly, "A Study of the Defeat of Senator Burton K. Wheeler in the 1946 Democratic Primary Election" (Master's thesis, University of Montana, 1959). For a good description of Senator James Murray during this period, see Forrest Davis, "Millionaire Moses," *Saturday Evening Post*, December 8, 1945, pp. 9–10ff.

Historians have not yet examined the crucial effects of World War II upon Montana. John Gunther offers a sketchy profile of the state at war's end in his *Inside U.S.A.* (New York and London: Harper and Brothers, 1947), chap. 11. Montana's most prolific writer of this time was Joseph Kinsey Howard, who wrote from a strongly liberal perspective. Howard discussed the current Montana scene in *Montana: High, Wide, and Handsome*, chap. 27; the Missouri Valley Authority issue in "Golden River," *Harper's Magazine*, May 1945, pp. 511–23; and the political trends of the forties in "The Decline and Fall of Burton K. Wheeler," *Harper's Magazine*, March 1947, pp. 226–36; "The Montana Twins in Trouble," *Harper's Magazine*, September 1944, pp. 334–42; and "Jim Murray's Chances," *Nation*, October 9, 1948, pp. 397–99.

CHAPTER XIII. THE MODERN MONTANA ECONOMY: 1920–75

Easily the most valuable reference work on this subject is the six-volume *Montana Economic Study*, issued in 1970 by the Bureau of Business and Economic Research at the University of Montana. The *Montana Business Quarterly* publishes constantly up-to-date assessments of the economy: see especially, Maxine C. Johnson, Paul E. Polzin, and Maurice C. Taylor, "Economic Report to the Governor," *Montana Business Quarterly*, 13 (Winter 1975): 7–26. The U.S. Census reports, of course, provide massive amounts of data; we have relied especially upon the 1970 Census, the 1969 Census of Agriculture, and the 1972 Census of Manufactures. Among the various collections of data by the state government, the most useful include Montana Department of Planning and Economic Development, *Montana Data Book* (Helena, 1970); Montana Department of Intergovernmental Relations, Economic Development Division, *Montana Overlook* (Helena, 1974); and Montana

Department of Agriculture and United States Department of Agriculture, Statistical Reporting Service, *Montana Agricultural Statistics*, Vol. 15: *County Statistics, 1972 and 1973* (Bozeman: Color World of Montana, 1974).

Merrill G. Burlingame interprets modern economic trends in "Montana in the Twentieth Century," James M. Hamilton, *History of Montana: From Wilderness to Statehood* (2d ed.; Portland: Binfords and Mort, 1970), pp. 615–41. There are a number of still useful chapters on the economy in M. G. Burlingame and K. R. Toole, eds., *A History of Montana* (3 vols.; New York: Lewis Historical Publishing Co., 1957), especially those on agriculture, metal mining, forest and stream, and oil and gas.

Two books by John T. Schlebecker place Montana agriculture in national perspective: *Whereby We Thrive: A History of American Farming, 1607–1972* (Ames: Iowa State University Press, 1975); and *Cattle Raising on the Plains: 1900–1961* (Lincoln: University of Nebraska Press, 1963). The bulletins of the Montana Agricultural Experiment Station at Montana State University in Bozeman cover all facets of agricultural development. See, for instance, R. R. Renne, *Montana Farm Foreclosures*, Bulletin 368 (February 1939); Layton S. Thompson, *Montana Cooperative Grazing Districts in Action*, Bulletin 481 (December 1951); and Willard H. Godrey, Jr., and Gail L. Cramer, *Costs and Returns of Producing Sugar Beets and Other Irrigated Crops in Montana*, Bulletin 635 (September 1969). The U.S. Department of Agriculture and the Montana Department of Agriculture issue a steady flow of reports on current developments. On M. L. Wilson and his associates, see William D. Rowley, *M. L. Wilson and the Campaign for the Domestic Allotment* (Lincoln: University of Nebraska Press, 1970); Ronald Lee Kenny, "The Fairway Farms: An Experiment in a New Agricultural Age" (Master's thesis, Montana State University, 1969); and the forthcoming biography of Wilson by Harry McDean. Ralph E. Ward, "Wheat in Montana: Determined Adaptation," *Montana: The Magazine of Western History*, 25 (Autumn 1975): 16–37, is interesting. For a current perspective, consult Malcolm D. Bale and Roland R. Renne, "World Trade and Montana Agriculture," *Montana Business Quarterly*, 12 (Winter 1974): 17–22; and Great Falls *Tribune*, Progress Edition, February 16, 1975.

For the Anaconda Company and its changing role since 1920, see the works by Marcosson, Toole, and the editors of *Fortune* Magazine cited in Chapter IX. A starting point on Montana Power is offered in Douglas F. Leighton, "The Corporate History of the Montana Power Company, 1882–1913" (Master's thesis, University of Montana, 1951). Michael P. Malone discusses Anaconda's transition in a political context in "Montana as a Corporate Bailiwick: An Image in History," to be published soon by the William Andrews Clark Memorial Library at UCLA. Recent developments are the subject of "Anaconda's 500-Year Plan," *Forbes* Magazine, December 15, 1968, pp. 22–32; "From Riches to Rags," ibid., January 15, 1972, pp. 24–25; "A Neat Job," ibid., December 1, 1972, pp. 40, 42; and "An Ex-Banker Treats Copper's Sickest Giant," *Business Week*, February 19, 1972, pp. 52–55. On a related theme, see Donald Macmillan, "A History of the Struggle to Abate Air Pollution from Copper Smelters of the Far West, 1885–1933" (Ph.D. diss., University of Montana, 1973).

Montana's labor history desperately needs examination. The annual yearbooks of the state A.F.L.-C.I.O. provide basic information. Vernon H. Jensen surveys the Mine, Mill and Smelter Workers in *Heritage of Conflict: Labor Relations in the Non-ferrous Metals Industry up to 1930* (Ithaca, N.Y.: Cornell University, 1950); and in *Nonferrous Metals Industry Unionism: 1932–1954* (Ithaca, N.Y.: Cornell University Press, 1954). On the 1934 strike, see Charles E. Sebold, "No Troops—No Violence," *Christian Century*, October 17, 1934, pp. 1310–11; and Ward Kinney [Joseph K. Howard], "Montana Challenges the Tyranny of Copper," *Nation*, July 25, 1934, pp. 86–87, 98–99.

Delores Morrow discusses the rise of the lumber industry in "Our Sawdust Roots: A History of the Forest Products Industry in Montana" (n.d.), MS in Montana Historical Society Library, Helena. Also instructive are Edward B. Butcher, "An Analysis of Timber Depredations in Montana to 1900" (Master's thesis, University of Montana, 1967); K. Ross Toole and Edward Butcher, "Timber Depredations on the Montana Public Domain, 1885–1918," *Journal of the West*, 7 (July 1968): 351–62; and John J. Little, "The 1910 Forest Fires in Montana and Idaho: Their Impact on Federal and State Legislation" (Master's thesis, University of Montana, 1968). The entire Spring 1972 edition of the *Montana Business Quarterly* is devoted to Maxine C. Johnson's discussion of "Wood Products in Montana." The reader may keep abreast of oil and natural gas developments by perusing the *Montana Oil Journal* and Al Raymond's weekly columns in the Sunday Great Falls *Tribune*. A dated but still valuable discussion is Don Duoma, "The History of Oil and Gas in Montana," in *A History of Montana*, ed. M. G. Burlingame and K. R. Toole (3 vols.; New York: Lewis Historical Publishing Co., 1957), 2: 31–52.

For the history of coal mining in Montana, see Robert A. Chadwick, "Coal: Montana's Prosaic Treasure," *Montana: The Magazine of Western History*, 23 (Autumn 1973): 18–31; Rita McDonald and Merrill G. Burlingame, "Montana's First Commercial Coal Mine," *Pacific Northwest Quarterly*, 47 (July 1956): 23–28; William B. Evans and Robert L. Peterson, "Decision at Colstrip: The Northern Pacific Railway's Open Pit Mining Operation," *Pacific Northwest Quarterly*, 61 (July 1970): 129–36; and William B. Evans, "Public Response to Strip Mining in Montana, 1920's to 1973," *Montana Business Quarterly*, 11 (Summer 1973): 16–20. The current coal situation is explored in Helena H. Smith, "The Wringing of the West," *Washington Post*, February 16, 1975, Outlook Section, pp. B1, B4; Alvin M. Josephy, Jr., "Plundered West: Coal Is the Prize," ibid., August 26, 1973, pp. C1, C4; James Conaway, "The Last of the West: Hell, Strip It!," *Atlantic*, September 1973, pp. 91–103; and Louis D. Hayes, "Who Will Control Montana's Coal?," *Montana Business Quarterly*, 13 (Spring 1975): 26–32. For statistics and impact assessments, consult Montana Energy Advisory Council, *Coal Development Information Packet* (Helena, 1974); and Institute for Social Sciences Research, University of Montana, *A Comparative Case Study of the Impact of Coal Development on the Way of Life of People in the Coal Areas of Eastern Montana and Northeastern Wyoming: Final Report* (Missoula, 1974).

Montana tourism is a badly neglected topic. A brief sketch can be found in Rita McDonald, "Commerce and Industry," in *A History of Montana*, ed. M. G. Burlingame and K. R. Toole (3 vols.; New York: Lewis Historical Publishing Co., 1957), 1: 396–98. More recent developments are surveyed in Robert F. Wallace and

Daniel R. Blake, *Montana Travel Study* (Missoula: University of Montana, Bureau of Business and Economic Research, 1966). R. R. Renne and his associates at Montana State University are currently preparing a thorough study of tourism. Michael P. Malone studies the environment of the Big Sky development in "The Gallatin Canyon and the Tides of History," *Montana: The Magazine of Western History,* 23 (Summer 1973): 2–17; and Robert T. Smith assesses the resort in "The Big Sky Development: A Lesson for the Future," *American West,* 12 (September 1975): 46–47, 62–63. Statistical indexes of modern economic trends can be found throughout the six volumes of the *Montana Economic Study* and the article by Maxine C. Johnson, et al., "Economic Report to the Governor," cited above.

Chapter XVI. A Social and Cultural Profile

All population discussions, of course, are based upon the massive reports of the U.S. Bureau of the Census. A still useful examination of Montana's ethnic heritage is H. G. Merriam, "Ethnic Settlement of Montana," *Pacific Historical Review,* 12 (June 1943): 157–68. Among the more valuable discussions in *Montana: The Magazine of Western History* are: Leona Lampi, "Red Lodge," 11 (Summer 1961): 20–31; Andrew F. Rolle, "The Italian Moves Westward," 16 (January 1966): 13–24; and Robert E. Levinson, "Julius Basinski: Jewish Merchant in Montana," 22 (Winter 1972): 60–68.

On specific ethnic groups, see Carl Wittke, *The Irish in America* (New York: Russell and Russell, 1956, 1970); Arthur C. Todd, *The Cornish Miner in America* (Glendale, Calif.: Arthur H. Clark, 1967); A. L. Rowse, *The Cousin Jacks* (New York: Scribner, 1969); John Rowe, *The Hard-Rock Men: Cornish Immigrants and the North American Mining Frontier* (New York: Barnes and Noble, 1974); and Henry S. Lucas, *Netherlanders in America: Dutch Immigration to the United States and Canada, 1789–1950* (Ann Arbor: University of Michigan Press, 1955). Of more general interest are Louis Adamic, *A Nation of Nations* (New York: Harper and Brothers, 1944); and Conrad and Irene B. Taeuber, *People of the United States in the Twentieth Century* (Washington, D.C.: Government Printing Office, 1971).

Montana's religious profile can be drawn from U.S., Bureau of the Census, *Religious Bodies: 1936,* vol. 1, *Summary and Detailed Tables* (Washington, D.C.: Government Printing Office, 1941); E. S. Gaustad, *Historical Atlas of Religions in America* (New York: Harper and Row, 1962); and Douglas W. Johnson et al., *Churches and Church Membership in the United States: An Enumeration by Region, State and County* (Washington, D.C.: Glennary Research Center, 1974). Of interest on a relatively unexplored topic is Hans D. Radtke, *The Hutterites in Montana: An Economic Description,* Montana Agricultural Experiment Station, Bulletin 641 (Bozeman, 1971); see, too, John Andrew Hostetler, *Hutterite Society* (Baltimore: Johns Hopkins University Press, 1974); and Hans J. Peterson, "Hilldale: A Montana Hutterite Colony," *Rocky Mountain Social Science Journal,* 7 (April 1970): 1–7.

Among the best general works on the Indian is Alvin M. Josephy, Jr., *The Indian Heritage of America* (New York: Alfred A. Knopf, 1969). Verne Dusenberry published several valuable essays in *Montana: The Magazine of Western History:* "The Rocky Boy Indians," 4 (Winter 1954): 1–15; "The Northern Cheyenne," 5 (Winter

1955): 23–40; and "Waiting for a Day That Never Comes," 8 (April 1958): 26–39. On specific Montana reservations, see the essay for Chapter 1, and especially Malcolm McFee, *Modern Blackfeet: Montanans on a Reservation* (New York: Holt, Rinehart and Winston, 1972); Edward E. Barry, Jr., *The Fort Belknap Indian Reservation: The First One Hundred Years, 1855–1955* (Bozeman: Montana State University, 1974); Barry, "From Buffalo to Beef: Assimilation on Fort Belknap Reservation," *Montana: The Magazine of Western History*, 26 (Winter 1976): 38–51; Thomas R. Wessel, *A History of the Rocky Boy's Indian Reservation* (Bozeman: Montana State University, 1974); and Charles C. Bradley, Jr., *A History of the Crow Indians* (Lodge Grass, Mont.: Lodge Grass Schools, 1971).

General studies of the Montana public school system are: James M. Hamilton, *History of Montana: From Wilderness to Statehood* (Portland: Binfords and Mort, 1957, 1970), chap. 10; M. G. Burlingame and K. R. Toole, eds., *A History of Montana* (3 vols.; New York: Lewis Historical Publishing Co., 1957), vol. 2, chap. 31; Emmet J. Riley, *Development of the Montana State Educational Organization: 1864–1930* (Washington, D.C.: Catholic University of America, 1931); C. R. Anderson, *Know Your Schools: Public Education in Montana* (Helena: State Publishing Co., 1972); and Dale R. Tash, "The Development of the Montana Common School System: 1864–1884" (Ed.D. thesis, Montana State University, 1968).

On higher education, see the works by Burlingame and Toole and by C. R. Anderson cited above. Also consult: M. A. Brannon, "The Montana System of Administering Higher Education," *School and Society*, 35 (February 1932); 269–77; H. G. Merriam, *The University of Montana: A History* (Missoula: University of Montana Press, 1970); Merrill G. Burlingame, *A History of Montana State University* (Bozeman: Montana State University Office of Information, 1968); Edward Byron Chenette, "The Montana State Board of Education: A Study of Higher Education in Conflict, 1884–1959" (Ed.D. diss., University of Montana, 1972); and Montana Commission on Post-secondary Education, *Review of Prior Studies of Post-secondary Education in Montana* (Helena, 1973). *Montana Fourth Estate*, the monthly trade journal of the Montana Press Association, and the *Montana Journalism Review*, the annual journal of the University of Montana School of Journalism, contain much information on the press. The quotes from Himsl are drawn from Steve L. Smith, "Profile of a Wire Editor," *Montana Journalism Review*, 17 (1974): 47–52. Five useful studies are: Richard T. Ruetten, "Anaconda Journalism: The End of an Era," *Journalism Quarterly*, 37 (Winter 1960): 3–12, 104; John M. Schiltz, "Montana's Captive Press," *Montana Opinion*, 1 (June 1956): 1–11; Francis E. Walsh, "News Dissemination in the State Capital" (Master's thesis, University of Montana, 1972); William Edward Larson, "News Management in The Company Press" (Master's thesis, University of Montana, 1971); and Ruth James Towe, "The Lee Newspapers of Montana: The First Three Years, 1959–1962" (Master's thesis, University of Montana, 1969).

Paul A. Rossi and David C. Hunt, *The Art of the Old West* (New York: Alfred A. Knopf, 1971), is informative on the Russell and Seltzer holdings of the Gilcrease Institute in Tulsa, Oklahoma. Literature on Russell is very extensive. See, for instance: Ramon F. Adams and Homer E. Britzman, *Charles M. Russell, the Cowboy Artist: A Biography* (Pasadena, Calif.: Trail's End Publishing Co., 1948); Harold

McCracken, *The Charles M. Russell Book: The Life and Work of the Cowboy Artist* (Garden City, N.Y.: Doubleday, 1957); John Willard, *The CMR Book* (Seattle: Salisbury Press, Superior Publishing Co., 1970); and Frederic G. Renner, *Charles M. Russell: Paintings, Drawings, and Sculpture in the Amon G. Carter Collection* (2d ed.; New York: Harry N. Abrams, 1974). Two useful briefer accounts are John C. Ewers, *Artists of the Old West* (Garden City, N.Y.: Doubleday, 1973), chap. 13; and F. G. Renner, "Rangeland Rembrandt: The Incomparable Charles Marion Russell," *Montana: The Magazine of Western History*, 7 (October 1957): 15–28. *Montana: The Magazine of Western History* devoted an entire issue of volume 8 (October 1958) to Russell. Two other articles of note in that magazine are: J. Frank Dobie, "The Conservatism of Charles M. Russell," 2 (April 1952): 27–31; and Lee Silliman, "CMR: The Cowboy on Canvas," 21 (January 1971): 40–49.

Notable articles in *Montana: The Magazine of Western History* on other local artists include: K. Ross Toole, "E. S. Paxson: Neglected Artist of the West," 4 (Spring 1954): 26–29; Franz R. Stenzel, "E. S. Paxson: Montana Artist," 13 (September 1963): 50–76; Michael Kennedy, "O. C. Seltzer: Meticulous Master of Western Art," 10 (July 1960): 2–21; and John C. Ewers, "Winold Reiss: His Portraits and Proteges," 21 (July 1971): 44–55. J. M. Moynahan has two books on Powell: *The Ace Powell Book* (Kalispell: Ace Powell Art Galleries, 1974); and *Ace Powell's Montana* (n.p., 1974). On Scriver's works, see Montana Historical Society, *Scriver* (Helena, 1972); and Bob Scriver, *An Honest Try* (Kansas City, Mo.: Lowell Press, 1975). Dale A. Burk, *New Interpretations* (n.p.: Western Life Publications, 1969) provides information on several Montana artists.

Still worthwhile are H. G. Merriam, "Montana Writing," in *A History of Montana*, ed. M. G. Burlingame and K. R. Toole (3 vols.; New York: Lewis Historical Publishing Co., 1957), 2: 265–90; and Rufus Coleman, "Creative Writing in the Northwest: Whence? Why? Whither?," in *Historical Essays in Montana and the Northwest*, ed. J. W. Smurr and K. R. Toole (Helena: Western Press, 1957), pp. 250–94. On Schultz, see Jessie Donaldson Schultz, "Adventuresome, Amazing Apikani," *Montana: The Magazine of Western History*, 10 (October 1960): 2–18; on Linderman, see H. G. Merriam, "Sign-Talker with Straight Tongue," ibid., 12 (July 1962): 2–20; on B. M. Bower, see Stanley R. Davison, "Chip of the Flying U: The Author Was a Lady," ibid., 23 (April 1973): 2–15; and on Howard, see Norman A. Fox, "Joseph Kinsey Howard: Writer," ibid., 2 (April 1952): 41–44. For Johnson and Guthrie, consult two 1969 University of Montana Master's theses: Stephen L. Smith, "The Years and the Wind and the Rain: The Biography of Dorothy M. Johnson"; and Charles E. Hood, Jr., "Hard Work and Tough Dreaming: A Biography of A. B. Guthrie, Jr."

Chapter XV. The Recent Political Scene: 1945–75

Montana's political history since 1940 remains largely unwritten. The most valuable studies of the contemporary scene are Thomas Payne, "Montana: Politics under the Copper Dome," in *Politics in the American West*, ed. Frank H. Jonas (Salt Lake City: University of Utah Press, 1969), pp. 202–30; and Neil R. Peirce's astute look at Montana in *The Mountain States of America* (New York: W. W. Norton, 1972), pp. 90–119. See, too, Ellis Waldron, "Montana," in *Rocky Mountain Urban Politics*, ed. JeDon Emenhiser (Logan: Utah State University Press, 1971), pp. 73–99.

Ellis Waldron offers ready access to pre-1958 election data and maps in *Montana Politics since 1864: An Atlas of Elections* (Missoula: University of Montana Press, 1958). For post-1958 data, one must turn to the secretary of state's compilations. The most valuable commentaries on postwar political trends are found in the series of state-by-state election analyses carried in the *Western Political Quarterly* from 1949 until 1971. These assessments can be found in the spring or summer issues of the odd-numbered years' volumes following biennial elections. The elections of 1948 and 1952 are examined by Jules A. Karlin, all elections from 1954 through 1968 by Thomas Payne, and the election of 1970 by Brad E. Hainsworth. A dated but still somewhat useful bibliography is Thomas Payne, "Bibliography on Montana Politics," *Western Political Quarterly*, 11 (December 1958): 65–72.

In order to place Montana in national perspective, see the Peirce article, cited above. Also sample these general works by political scientists: Ira Sharkansky, *The Maligned States* (New York: McGraw-Hill, 1972); Herbert Jacob and Kenneth N. Vines, eds., *Politics in the American States: A Comparative Analysis* (2d ed.; Boston: Little, Brown, 1971); and Thomas R. Dye, *Politics in States and Communities* (2d ed.; Englewood Cliffs, N.J.: Prentice-Hall, 1973).

Little is available on the various interest groups involved in Montana politics. On the corporate role, consult Daniel J. Foley's important series in the Billings *Gazette*, August 20, August 27, September 3, and September 10, 1972. More limited comments in the same vein can be found in *The People's Voice* (Helena), October 4, 1957, and May 29, 1959. Michael P. Malone assesses the changing corporate role in "Montana as a Corporate Bailiwick: An Image in History," soon to be published by the William Andrews Clark Memorial Library at U.C.L.A. The political views and concerns of the stockmen may be gleaned from Robert H. Fletcher, *Free Grass to Fences: The Montana Cattle Range Story* (New York: University Publishers, 1960). For the political views of the Farmers Union, see John A. Crampton, *The National Farmers Union: Ideology of a Pressure Group* (Lincoln: University of Nebraska Press, 1965); Gladys T. Edwards, *This Is the Farmers Union* (Denver: National Farmers Union, 1951); and Mildred K. Stoltz, *This Is Yours* (Minneapolis: Lund Press, 1956). On a related topic, consult Frank J. Busch, "History of Montana Rural Electric Cooperatives, 1936–1971" (Ph.D. diss., University of Montana, 1975).

None of Montana's postwar congressional figures has yet received extensive biographical treatment. Timothy J. Carman's "Senator Zales Ecton: A Product of Reaction" (Master's thesis, Montana State University, 1971) focuses upon Ecton's election campaign of 1946. An interesting characterization of Murray in his prime is Forrest Davis, "Millionaire Moses," *Saturday Evening Post*, December 8, 1945, pp. 9–10, 103–4, 106. See also Joseph K. Howard, "Jim Murray's Chances," *Nation*, October 9, 1948, pp. 397–99; George L. Bousliman, "The 1954 Campaign of Senator James E. Murray" (Master's thesis, University of Montana, 1964); and Thomas H. Nilsen, "Senator James E. Murray and Reconversion (1943–1945)" (Master's thesis, University of Montana, 1973). Of course the popular press is filled with material on Mansfield. The one attempt to view his entire career is Michael P. Malone and Pierce C. Mullen, "Mansfield of Montana," ms in authors' possession. An interesting depiction of Metcalf is Robert Sherrill, "The Invisible Senator," *Nation,* May 10, 1971, pp. 584–89.

Historians have barely touched the surface of state level politics in Montana since World War II. Focusing upon the elections of 1952 and 1954 is William D. Miller's "Montana and the Specter of McCarthyism: 1952–1954" (Master's thesis, Montana State University, 1969). J. Hugo Aronson and L. O. Brockmann, *The Galloping Swede* (Missoula: Mountain Press, 1970), is an entertaining autobiography, but is nearly devoid of political content. Politics of the 1960s are the subject of Judith B. Rollins, "Governor Donald G. Nutter and the Montana Daily Press" (Master's thesis, University of Montana, 1963); and Jerry R. Holloron, "The Montana Daily Press and the 1964 Gubernatorial Campaign" (Master's thesis, University of Montana, 1965). On the movement for governmental reform which culminated in the 1972 Constitution, see Richard B. Roeder, "Energy in the Executive," *Montana Law Review,* 33 (Winter 1972): 1–13. An admiring look at the constitutional convention is "Fresh Chance Gulch," *Time,* April 10, 1972, p. 18.

Index

Abbott, Teddy Blue, 117, 127, 284
Absaroka Indians. *See* Crow Indians
"Accustomed range," 120, 123-24
Adolph, Chief, 92
Agricultural Adjustment Act, 229, 244
Agricultural Experiment Station, Montana, 182, 184, 242
Agriculture: in nineteenth century, 179-80; homestead boom, 181-94; becomes major industry, 186; impact of World War I upon, 191, 194; impact of Great Depression upon, 226-27; New Deal programs for, 229-30; impact of World War II upon, 237; since 1920, 241-47; relative decline of, 247
Agriculture, U.S. Department of, 296
Agriculture, Labor and Industry, Montana Bureau of, 183
Alder Gulch, 51, 54, 60, 67
Alderson, Nannie, 127, 128
Aldridge coal field, 258
Alexander, Chief, 88
Alice Mine, 143, 153, 159
Alien Land Law (1887), 149
Allen, J. F., 140
Almost-a-Dog, 107
Alta Mine, 144
Amalgamated Copper Company: founding of, 158-59; triumph over Heinze and consolidation of Butte Hill, 170-77; liquidation of, 176; mentioned, 167, 168, 169, 196, 198, 200, 201, 202, 209, 210, 247, 280
American Brass Co., 248
American Farm Bureau Federation, 289, 302
American Federation of Labor, 236, 252, 253, 291
American Fork, 50

American Fur Co., 36; monopolization of Upper Missouri fur trade, 42-47
American Power and Light Co., 248
Anaconda: founding of, 155; loses capital to Helena, 161, 162
Anaconda Company, 158. *See* Anaconda Copper Mining Co.
Anaconda Copper Mining Co.: antecedents of, 154, 157; incorporation of, 158; passes under control of Amalgamated Copper Co., 158-59; described as of 1915, 172; divorce from Amalgamated Copper, 176; anti-radical and anti-labor campaigns during World War I, 209-10; battles against reformers, 219-22; political power of, 224-25; impact of Great Depression upon, 227-28; diminishing role of, 247-51; lumber operations, 254; newspaper policies of, 280-82; decline of political domination, 289-90; mentioned, 167, 168, 169, 172, 176, 177, 207, 214, 215, 223, 236, 240, 299, 300
Anaconda Mine, 154, 172
Anaconda Mining Co., 158
Anaconda Reduction Works, 157
Anaconda *Standard*, 160, 165, 169, 280, 282; quoted, 281
Anaconda Wire and Cable Co., 248
Ancient Order of Hibernia, 268
Anderson, Forrest, 299, 302
Anderson, LeRoy, 295
Anderson, Reece, 50
Anti-Ballistic Missile program, 263, 297
Anti-Diversion amendment, 298
Anti-Saloon League, 204
Anti-Trust party, 198
Apex Law, 171